D1195125

Contemporary English in the Elementary School

second edition

Contemporary English in the Elementary School

Iris M. Tiedt
University of Santa Clara

Sidney W. Tiedt
San Jose State University

PRENTICE-HALL, INC., ENGLEWOOD CLIFFS, NEW JERSEY

Library of Congress Cataloging in Publication Data

Tiedt, Iris M

Contemporary English in the elementary school.

Includes bibliographies.

1. English language—Study and teaching (Elementary)
I. Tiedt, Sidney W., joint author. II. Title.
LB1576.T55 1975 372.6 74–12139
ISBN 0–13–169961–X

Printed in the United States of America

10 9 8 7 6 5 4 3 2 1

Prentice-Hall International, Inc., *London*
Prentice-Hall of Australia, Pty. Ltd., *Sydney*
Prentice-Hall of Canada, Ltd., *Toronto*
Prentice-Hall of India Private Limited, *New Delhi*
Prentice-Hall of Japan, Inc., *Tokyo*

contents

to the reader...

"Thurber did not write the way a surgeon operates, he wrote the way a child skips rope, the way a mouse waltzes. . . ." Those of you who have read the whimsical writing of James Thurber can appreciate this comment made by another imaginative lover of language, E. B. White, author of *Charlotte's Web*.

It is this feeling for language, delight in words, enthusiasm for literature that we have tried to project throughout *Contemporary English in the Elementary School,* for we are concerned with projecting this love of language to elementary school children everywhere, and it is through you that we hope to achieve our purpose.

Thus began the introduction to the first edition of *Contemporary English* which was published in 1967. As we prepare this revised edition, we find that the goal expressed here continues to deserve primary emphasis. We have, therefore, endeavored to strengthen this aspect of our presentation in each chapter.

There have, on the other hand, been significant changes in education and in the teaching of English that must be recognized. Such important concerns as individualization of instruction, affective education, and the child's acquisition of language represent new aspects of English education that did not appear in the earlier edition.

The reader will note, too, a strong emphasis on language, the foundation of language arts studies. Chapter Three, for example, focuses on the language of the young child and the implications of studies in this area for the teaching of reading and the other language skills. Special needs of ethnic groups permeate all chapters rather than being segregated in a separate chapter. Represented also are such current concerns as sex role stereotyping in children's books, studies of dialectology and their implications, as well as teaching that develops positive self-concepts.

Since this text first appeared with its perceptive combination of theory and practice, ideas that aid the teacher's effectiveness, there has been renewed interest and acceptance of such approaches. *Contemporary English* continues, however, to stand out as a comprehensive coverage of the field that still delights teachers with its supply of creative teaching strategies—designed for the language arts course, designed for teachers working in classrooms.

As authors, we are excited about what we have to offer elementary English educators. Dr. Iris Tiedt, Director of the Graduate Reading Program at the University of Santa Clara, is also Editor of *Elementary English,* an official publication of the National Council of Teachers of English. Dr. Sidney Tiedt, Professor of Elementary Education at San Jose State University, works with pre-service teacher education and is an educational consultant and writer.

imt
swt

Contemporary English in the Elementary School

teaching english

chapter 1

The goal of education is not to increase knowledge but to create possibilities for a child to invent and discover, to create men who are capable of doing new things.

Jean Piaget

By almost any criteria used the study of English is the most important subject included in the elementary school curriculum. Elementary schools from their humblest beginnings were basically language schools. In our early colonial days the schools developed primarily as reading and writing schools which utilized the famous Hornbook and the Blueback Spellers as texts.

Not only historically has English been prominent, however, for it continues in importance in spite of the rise of newer curricular areas such as science and mathematics. More classroom time is spent on English than on any other single subject. In California the importance of English is codified in state law which reads: "Instruction is required [in the areas of English] for a minimum of 50% of each week in grades 1 to 6." [1]

There is good reason for this emphasis on language study, for it is

[1] California Education Code; California Administration Code, Title 5. Education 7604 a,b,c.

ability to use a language which has lifted man above all other animals. As Charlton Laird phrased it, man is a "*languagized* animal." In spite of our numerous problems of communication, language remains an amazing achievement the origin of which will probably never be known. It is impossible for us to imagine a world without language. Consider for a moment how our lives would differ if there were no human language. The fish is the last to know the sea, it is said, and this analogy may be extended to include students and their language, for although we use our language daily, we don't really know much about it.

Another factor making the study of English increasingly important to us is the tremendous growth of communication in the modern world. Communication has increased in many ways—in terms of time spent communicating, expense, volume, and economic significance. We live in a verbal world, one in which language plays an essential role.

The Role of the Teacher

The crucial component in the educational enterprise is the teacher. We can talk about what we shall teach, why we teach it, and how, but the teacher plays the paramount role in the pedagogical encounter with the student.

Because teachers are of such importance it behooves us to discuss their education, their attitudes toward English, and to suggest ways the prospective elementary school teacher can prepare for teaching. The chief needs of the elementary school English teacher are (1) improved training and (2) a contemporary attitude toward English.

TRAINING IN ENGLISH

"Theory without practice is like a cloud without rain," states an old Japanese saying. The teacher needs well-balanced training in both content and strategy of teaching, for the modern teacher must be able to teach those who are not always willing to learn. We must take time to develop a style of teaching as well as to discover what is going on in the field of English. For this reason, we must consider teaching as an art, a craft, and an applied science.

The well-prepared elementary school teacher needs at least a minor in English, which should include work in modern grammar, children's literature, history of the English language, poetry, advanced composition, and a course in English teaching methods. We do not see any conflict between those who stress content in English and those who stress methods, for clearly both are necessary for effective teaching.

The following journals are worth knowing as you continue to gain knowledge in the field of the English language arts and teaching in general.

Elementary English. Urbana, Ill.: National Council of Teachers of English. A comprehensive, up-to-date journal for the elementary language arts teacher; focuses on teaching.

Elementary Teacher's Ideas and Materials Workshop. West Nyack, N.Y.: Parker Publishing Co. This monthly journal is a practical approach to teaching in all subject areas.

Learning. Palo Alto, Calif.: Education Today Co. A journal that gives ideas for creative teaching.

Teacher. Greenwich, Conn.: Macmillan Professional Magazines. A general journal in the elementary education field.

The Instructor. Dansville, N.Y.: Instructor Publishing Co. One of the major idea magazines in the field of elementary education.

NEW ATTITUDES TOWARD ENGLISH

In almost all cases teacher attitudes toward English require modification. This is particularly true of attitudes toward language and specifically toward usage. Most people tend to be conservative toward their language, and teachers might be said to be "museums of virtue" when it comes to language. Linguists, however, have pointed out the constant change in language, noting that this change represents normal growth, not necessarily to be considered deterioration. We shall explore this aspect of language more thoroughly in Chapter 2.

Teachers also need to be more critical, more aware of the fundamental issues in English. Like an editor, they select methods, materials, and content, which should enliven the life and the professional role of the teacher, for English cannot continue to be taught in the same conventional way which teacher has passed to teacher throughout the decades. We must strive to teach with a flair and feeling for the language. English must be taught, not as a fossil subject, but as a dynamic, ever-changing force. Teachers of English have the most fascinating content to work with of all the curriculum in the elementary school. There is no reason, therefore, why English should not be the most interesting and vital subject.

As teachers, we need constantly to be looking for new ideas to add stimulus to the classroom. Here are a number of idea books to explore:

George, Mary Yanaga. *Language Art: An Ideabook.* San Francisco: Chandler Publishing Co., 1970.

Laliberte, Norman, and Kehl, Richey. *100 Ways to Have Fun with an Alligator and 100 Other Involving Art Projects.* New York: Art Education, 1969.

Northam, Saralie. *Child.* Portland, Oregon.: Northwest Regional Educational Laboratory, 1970.

Smith, James A. *Adventures in Communication: Language Arts Methods.* Boston: Allyn and Bacon, 1972.

Tiedt, Sidney, and Tiedt, Iris. *Elementary Teacher's Complete Ideas Handbook.* Englewood Cliffs, N.J.: Prentice-Hall, Inc., 1965.

YOUR PERSONAL GROWTH

It is one thing to help you assess your knowledge and ability, but it is quite another to assist you in remedying any weakness and to guide you in your personal growth as a potential English teacher. The writing of this book represents our major effort at helping you become excellent teachers; however, we would like to suggest another avenue which you can begin exploring now and which you will continue to investigate as you continue to grow.

One of the most important aspects of your development as a teacher is your growth toward being a self-actualizing person. This growth is not accomplished overnight, of course, but it is worth working toward. The following selected titles represent books that will help you grow as a person.

Harris, Thomas. *I'm O.K., You're O.K.* New York: Harper and Row, 1967.

Jourard, Sidney. *The Transparent Self.* New York: Van Nostrand Reinhold Co., 1971.

Lederman, Janet. *Anger and the Rocking Chair.* New York: McGraw Hill Book Co., 1969.

Rogers, Carl. *Person to Person.* New York: Pocket Books, 1971.

Shostrom, Everett. *Man the Manipulator.* Nashville, Tenn.: Abingdon Press, 1967.

Organizing for Learning

Toward what goals shall we teach? We would like to suggest the following general aims for the elementary school English program:

1 To understand the English language and how it works.
2 To communicate fluently and clearly in written and oral forms.
3 To decode and encode English easily.
4 To know and appreciate our literary heritage of prose and poetry.

WHAT IS ENGLISH?

The elementary school English program, as it presently exists, defies definition. Graham Wilson approaches the problem of clarifying the structure of English with some doubts, as he says:

> . . . Certainly something special is called for to see a concept of over-all structure in English as a discipline in schools and colleges today. To begin with: the structure of what? There is *language*, which may include grammar, philology, anthropology, semantics, and general semantics, psychology, and English as a foreign language: *literature*, which may be English, American, world, and when the time comes, interplanetary; *composition*, which may include grammar (again), rhetoric, semantics (again), and logic. Language artists speak of reading, writing, speaking, listening. This is quite a mixture. . . .[2]

Although the job is imposing, it is not impossible, and it is necessary. Let us in the succeeding pages describe some of the attempts to define and unify the English curriculum.

How will we organize the language arts curriculum as we focus on teaching English? This is an important decision because the organization reflects our perception of English and how the language arts are related. We need to consider alternatives for the English curriculum and to select that approach which best fits our philosophies of education as well as our knowledge about English. What we really believe will be clearly demonstrated by what we do in the classroom.

Separate subject approach The separate subject approach is currently prevalent in the elementary schools. The so-called "language arts" designation exists in name only, for there has been little attempt to unify the study, and each subject continues to be taught separately. The use of the term "language arts" in elementary school curriculum may, therefore, be a dangerous deception.

We commonly teach reading, language, or English (which may include grammar, usage, punctuation), spelling, and handwriting. Many teachers teach creative writing as a separate subject. Note that literature as a subject is not taught in the elementary school. Usually each class has its own specified time in the class schedule, and there are often curriculum guides developed for each subject. There may also be guides for listening and oral language although these areas are seldom designated as separate subjects. Not only is each subject listed taught as a discrete subject but each has its own texts and workbooks. Reading probably receives the larger portion of class time.

Communications The communications approach to defining English attempts to focus attention as much on the processes of English as on the content. This approach dichotomizes communication into sending and receiving. Sending encompasses speaking and writing whereas receiving includes listening and reading as illustrated in the following diagram.

[2] Graham Wilson, "The Structure of English," in *The Structure of Knowledge and the Curriculum*, G. W. Ford and L. Pugno, eds. (Chicago: Rand McNally, 1964), pp. 71–72.

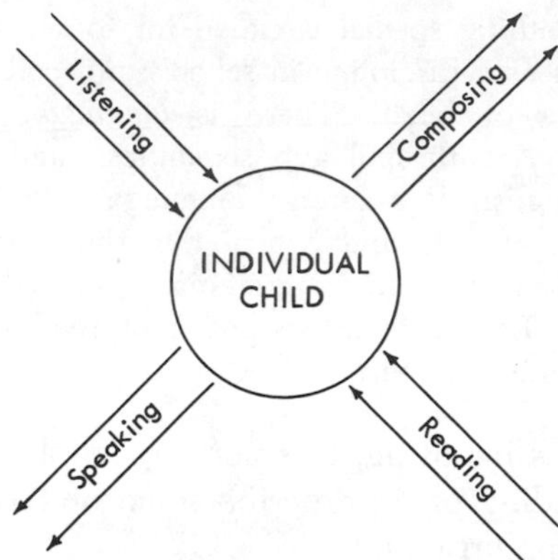

Actually the communications approach divides English into a quartet—speaking, writing, listening, and reading—the skills or processes involved in communication. To a greater extent than the previous model this definition relates to the elementary school program.

A language-centered program Our own inclination is to find unity and structure for English through a language-centered English program. As it now exists, English in the elementary school is highly diverse and lacks unity. This model, focused on the English language as the key component in any English program, not only centers on the language content but also brings to bear on this content the four processes of reading, writing, speaking, and listening. The diagram, "Dimensions of the English Language," illustrates graphically the diverse elements to be united in a language-focused English program which includes phonics, spelling, reading, writing, speaking, listening, and literature as well as many other concepts related to the study of the English language and the skills involved in using language. The philosophy behind this program is that, as Priscilla Tyler of the University of Illinois states: "The teaching of English is primarily the study of language."

Trends in English Teaching

What trends can be noted in English instruction at the elementary school level? In what direction is English moving? What efforts are being made to upgrade the teaching of English? In selecting the more important trends to be included here, several criteria were used. So many changes have been taking place in education that it is difficult, perhaps impossible, to assess all the many movements in one field. The intent, therefore, of this section is to examine some of the newer, more significant, and more promising directions in the field of English as they relate to the elemen-

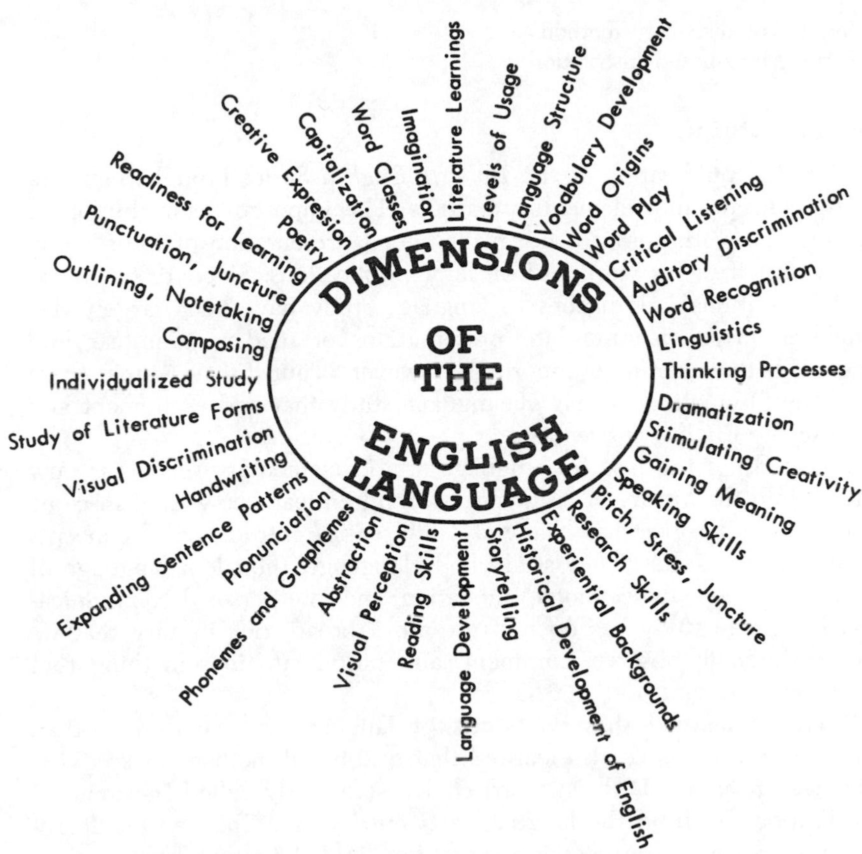

tary school. To be included, a trend must have some geographic spread and must have appeared in the literature. These ideas are not just newly created by fertile brains but represent movements that have made substantial contributions to the field of elementary education. The following trends are discussed in this overview:

Study of language
Early childhood education
Affective education
Individualization of instruction
Varied media
Differentiated staffing
Creativity and English
Studies of varied dialects and languages
Rethinking reading
Sex stereotyping

Inquiry or discovery method
Performance-based instruction

STUDY OF LANGUAGE

In 1966, the publication of the *Roberts English Series* brought new linguistic concepts into elementary schools. The important contribution of this author's work does not lie in the actual presentation of information but in the effect his work had on later publications. Since 1966, for example, traditional approaches to language study have been largely discarded in favor of up-to-date presentations of modern grammar and usage. What is even more important, however, is our discovery that there are many fascinating aspects of language study that add excitement and value to the English curriculum.

The study of the English language arts in elementary schools is now delving into the history of language, as children learn how English came into being and how it has changed. Children are introduced to concepts taken from semantics. They study body language, the silent language of different cultures, dialectology, intonation, and interpersonal communication. Language study has opened up into a broad, rich inquiry that invites children to observe, comment, and participate in something that is alive and growing.

We have learned that the study of language is much more than grammar, and we have also learned that traditional methods of studying language are passé. Drill on word choices (formerly called "grammar") has disappeared from the language-arts curriculum. Children are learning through using the language. They are guided toward awareness of variations in usage—not in terms of "correct" or "incorrect" English, but in terms of dialect differences. They are invited to explore the rich vocabulary of English as they search out synonyms or reach out to "big words."

This perception of English can exist only if teachers are excited and informed about their language. For this reason we have focused on language in several chapters. You will find, too, that this conception of the English language arts program permeates the book in its entirety from the introduction to the last page because that's where it's at as far as we're concerned. We don't want to be held responsible for sending out any *lol's,* male or female, who go around "correcting" children's speech, when there are so many exciting things to be done.

EARLY CHILDHOOD EDUCATION

One of the most current developments is interest in the education of the young child, as preschool programs multiply. The study of the young child's acquisition of language plays an important part in developing such programs as we gain insight into how a child learns to speak the language of his or her community. We find that children learn language eagerly and enthusiastically with little instruction. The young learners demand input from those around them—parents, other children, and other adults. They design their own individual means of learning, which proves to be highly successful.

The adult role in language development comes into question as we rethink our tendency to structure the teaching/learning situation. Studies show that the child does not need "correction" as we have been inclined to offer it. Rather, the child needs more language input, expansion of what is already known. Children need informants as they study this complex and fascinating body of material through an exciting inquiry approach to learning. It is essential that we adults learn to help, not hinder, the child's learning.

The important consideration is how to provide a rich language environment in our classrooms as children continue to learn language. We need to provide varied ways that children can use language through speaking, listening, writing, and reading. This is such a vital new concern for English education that we have explored the young child's language in one full chapter. It is important that teachers gain new understandings of this aspect of language learnings.

AFFECTIVE EDUCATION

Affective education deals with education related to the emotions and feelings. We have typically been concerned with the cognitive development of our students, their growth in reading skills, in language skills, or in spelling skills. We are only now learning the importance of the emotional development of each child.

Many writers such as Carl Rogers, Richard Jones, Herbert Greenberg, and William Glasser are suggesting specific ways that the classroom teacher can teach affectively. In a recent study of goals for education in the state of California, Assemblyman John Vasconcellos found that along with the traditional goals related to the three Rs, parent and school people listed the goal of developing self-esteem as an important function of the school. Today, therefore, we are greatly concerned about developing positive self-images or self-concepts through classroom activities planned toward these ends.

These goals lie in the *affective domain.* As John Dewey stated long ago, the whole child comes to school. The child comes to school with his or her thoughts and feelings, with both heart and head. The field of English education lends itself particularly well to developing understanding of self-identity, human relations, and interpersonal communication through literature, writing, and discussion.

Another significant emphasis in the affective domain has been termed *values clarification.* This effort is directed toward helping children consider their personal values and the relationship of these values to behavior. Sidney Simons and others have developed a number of strategies and procedures to use with students in elementary classrooms. Many of these activities involve speaking and writing and serve to add a new dimension to teaching these aspects of the English language arts curriculum.

The following books are worth exploring if you want to know more about affective approaches to teaching:

Glasser, William. *Schools Without Failure.* New York: Harper and Row, 1969.

Greenberg, Herbert M. *Teaching With Feeling.* Indianapolis, Ind.: Pegasus, 1969.

Jones, Richard M. *Fantasy and Feeling in Education.* New York: New York University Press, 1968.

Lewis, Howard R., and Streitfeld, Harold S. *Growth Games.* New York: Bantam Books, 1971.

O'Banion, Terry, and O'Connell, April. *The Shared Journey—An Introduction to Encounter.* Englewood Cliffs, N.J.: Prentice-Hall, 1970.

Reichert, Richard. *Self-awareness Through Group Dynamics.* Dayton, Ohio: George A. Pflaum, 1970.

Simon, Sidney; Howe, Leland, and Kirschenbaum, Howard. *Values Clarification.* New York: Hart Publishing Co., 1972.

INDIVIDUALISM OF INSTRUCTION

An important trend that has come to the fore since the first edition of this book appeared in 1967 is the development of individualized instruction. The concept of individualization has been around for some time, but it is only recently that the idea has really been implemented to any great extent in elementary classrooms.

One of the reasons for this increased interest in individualized programs is that teachers now have some methods as well as materials that seem to work. The Learning Center, for example, is a workable idea that is an essential element of individualized instruction. Teachers frequently developed a Library Corner or a place where students could write, but these areas were usually called Interest Centers and were clearly not part of the mainstream curriculum that was being developed. Now in many classrooms you will see a Writing Center, Spelling Center, Word Center, or Publication Center—all integral components of the English language arts curriculum in which all children are involved.

Another teaching device that has worked well with individualized programs is the Contract. A teacher can determine through diagnostic techniques just what an individual student needs. The teacher then prescribes a lesson or series of lessons at a Learning Center for this student. The contract aids the teacher in giving individual work to youngsters according to their needs.

The trend toward individualization is part of a larger major trend in our society and in education toward greater concern for the individual and toward humanization of instruction. As a result, we try to provide for choices among alternatives, experience in decision making, and for interaction among students at interpersonal levels. There are many individual learning styles. It is hoped that individualized instruction will permit the utilization of alternative ways of learning as children develop to their fullest potentials. Throughout the chapters in this book you will see references to activities that are appropriate for Learning Centers or other individualized approaches.

Following is a short list of references, which you can explore for additional information on individualized instruction.

Dell, Helen. *Individualizing Instruction Materials and Classroom Procedures.* Chicago: Science Research Associates, 1972.

Esbensen, Thorwald. *Working With Individualized Instruction.* Belmont, Calif.: Fearon Publishers, 1968.

Howes, Virgil M. *Individualization of Instruction.* New York: The Macmillan Co., 1970.

Howes, Virgil M. *Individualizing Instruction in Reading and Social Studies.* New York: The Macmillan Co., 1970.

Kaplan, Sandra; Kaplan, Jo ann; Madsen, Sheila; and Taylor, Bette. *Change for Children.* Pacific Palisades, Calif.: Goodyear Publishing Co., 1973.

Noar, Gertrude. *Individualized Instruction: Every Child a Winner.* New York: John Wiley and Sons, 1972.

Wilson, S. R., and Tosti, D. T. *Learning Is Getting Easier.* San Rafael, Calif.: Individual Learning Systems, 1972.

VARIED MEDIA

More and more elementary teachers are using exciting new media to add interest and effectiveness to the English curriculum. One of the most useful of the new devices on the market is the small cassette tape recorder. Students are using these tapes to listen to stories, to dictate stories, and to record their original plays or dramatizations. These recorders are flexible, easy to use, and fit in well with individualized approaches presented in Learning Centers. There are many other forms of media at the disposal of the creative teacher as listed here:

Computers can grade papers, keep records, translate languages, and they can program learning.

Tape recorders are all-purpose machines which will record lessons for presentation, assist with oral pattern practice, replay a speech, permit evaluation of oral language, teach listening.

Videotape machines will capture a school performance so that it can be reviewed or replay a television program at a more convenient time.

Television permits large group instruction (even across the country) and makes full use of an expert who can speak to many students at one time; it helps the teacher teach subjects by presenting information visually and orally to supplement text presentations.

Records of books, stories, and poetry add to the study and enjoyment of literature; specially prepared records aid the study of dialectology and vocabulary development.

Transparencies used with overhead projectors assist the presentation of information about language, poetry, any subject; transparencies of student themes can quickly be made for purposes of group evaluation; overlays permit the supplying of answers to a test or a word game or aid in showing students how to expand a basic sentence pattern.

Programmed instruction can be in booklet form or a machine which will "wash the dirty dishes" for the English teacher by teaching spelling, usage, punctuation, and vocabulary. It helps individualize instruction.

Tele-lectures bring any person in the United States into your classroom at a prearranged time; students can question the expert.

Duplicating facilities have been improved to permit the preparation of a ditto master and a transparency at the same time.

A Listening Center combines listening with reading as children use earphones to hear a story while they follow the book in their hand.

Films can present a book, information about authors, background information for literature, or motivation for poetry writing experiences. New loop films can be operated by any child and can be viewed individually or projected on a screen for group viewing.

Filmstrips and slides can be animated and used to present any concepts about language, poetry, literature. Used in combination with records or tape they present possibilities for use by individuals or groups.

If you include books in the category of media, one of the most interesting trends is that of the paperback edition. Paper editions have been used for many years on the college level, and for several years they have pre-empted the high school literature anthology. Now we find the paperback book moving into the elementary school as teachers, administrators, and parents recognize the advantages of these inexpensive editions of good literature. Children are encouraged to purchase books for personal libraries through the establishment of bookstores in the school itself.

DIFFERENTIATED STAFFING

The use of teacher aides, lay readers, or paraprofessionals represents a trend toward utilizing a type of semiskilled person with perhaps junior college education who is able to handle some of the more routine matters of the instructional program. The following are tasks which can be performed by the paraprofessional:

grading tests
reading student writing
preparing duplicated material
working with reading groups
telling or reading stories
giving individual help during writing
operating varied media

School districts are utilizing paraprofessionals to assist in the education of the disadvantaged child. Here they are employed to help youngsters with language deficiencies by talking to and with them or listening as children work with oral pattern practice. The aide facilitates work with smaller groups than would be possible with a teacher working alone. In his book *Careers for the Poor,* David Reissman advocates hiring persons from the disadvantaged community as aides, which not only provides a job that is needed but also helps develop good public relations for the educational program in the community which may show some resistance.

The addition of a semiskilled person in the classroom to work with a trained teacher may change the role of the teacher. The classroom teacher must develop administrative abilities to coordinate the learning experiences and must learn to delegate part of the classroom work to another person. He or she becomes a type of internist who diagnoses educational ills and prescribes a remedy or refers the patient to a specialist. We can see this role of the teacher extending so that specialized functions are developed requiring different levels of ability—paraprofessional, assistant teacher, classroom teacher, supervising teacher.

CREATIVITY AND ENGLISH

Research in the field of creativity has had an important influence on the English curriculum and methods of instruction, specifically in composition. Teachers have found that, like children's art, children's writing represents a fresh view of the world, and there has continued to be much interest in motivating "creative writing" which has proved pleasurable and successful.

Torrance, a leading researcher in creativity, points out that:

> Everyone possesses to some degree the ability involved in being creative, that these abilities can be increased or decreased by the way children are treated, and that it is a legitimate function of the home and the school to provide the experiences and guidance which will free them to develop and function fully.[3]

Writers in the field of creativity, for example, Torrance, Taylor, and Guilford, have been influential in changing attitudes toward evaluation of student writing. They have tended to liberate the teacher from concentration on detailed marking of all procedural mistakes made by the student in favor of appreciating the ideas expressed. This approach leads to stress of positive reinforcement rather than the negative carping which has been characteristic of so much of our grading of student effort.

In the 1967 edition to this text we presented creativity as a trend and devoted a full chapter to its discussion. Scholars are still writing and researching this aspect of learning today, so that creativity is still very much on the scene in English. Teachers continue to be excited about ideas for teaching creative writing and for stimulating creative thinking. These topics are developed in two chapters which offer many specific suggestions for working with children in classrooms.

STUDIES OF VARIED DIALECTS AND LANGUAGES

The study of the special needs of children who speak varied dialects and different languages has contributed important understanding and changed perceptions of the needs of the children involved. Early writings concerning children who spoke varied dialects labelled the dialects as "substandard" in contrast to "standard English." Gradually the term *substandard* was replaced by *nonstandard,* which was less evaluative. Today the trend is to avoid labelling the language of a person and to accept the child's language, whatever it is, as an essential part of the child's being, very much related to the child's self.

Earlier scholars thought, too, that so-called "disadvantaged" children had little or no language with which to work. Today we are recognizing that children do have language if we just listen. Their language may not fit our expectation of what the nebulous "standard English" is, but it is a language that is serviceable in the child's community. Frequently, as the child who speaks another dialect is exposed to textbooks written in

[3] E. Paul Torrance, *Guiding Creative Talent.* Englewood Cliffs, N.J.: Prentice-Hall, 1962.

standard English, he or she will skillfully translate standard English into that dialect. We are learning to understand that these translations are not errors; the child has an obvious control of meaning, which is being translated into the native dialect.

Attitudes toward different dialects and languages in the classroom are gradually changing as educators truly understand that we all speak a dialect of English. Both regional and social dialects are fascinating to observe in our classrooms, as is the process of linguistic change that is constantly in operation. The concepts of "right" and "wrong" are gradually being eliminated from language lessons as informed teachers talk about differences in usage and pronunciation and how people themselves change language over a period of time. We also discuss the importance of language in communicating and the need to be aware of varied dialects—the dialect presented in schoolbooks and the dialects we speak at home or with our friends.

This topic is developed more fully in the chapters on language; we discuss the language of young children and oral language development throughout the elementary school years.

RETHINKING READING

Reading has always been a major concern for teachers in the elementary school. Today, however, there are two new directions in the teaching of reading that are influencing development in this area of the curriculum.

The first is the rethinking of reading that is coming from the field of psycholinguistics. The study of the child's acquisition of language has provided fresh input into our perception of the learning of any language skills, including reading. If children learn enthusiastically and efficiently to speak a complex language without formal instruction, can reading be learned in this manner, too? Psycholinguists also are exploring the reading process and revealing the important function of the brain in reading. The brain needs concepts, words as labels for things, ideas to work with before reading can take place. Clearly, the child needs a strong development of oral language *before* reading and *concurrently* with learning to read. We discuss this aspect of reading more fully in Chapter 3.

A second development in the field of reading is stressing reading instruction at junior and senior high school levels. Many teacher training programs are requiring prospective high school teachers to take at least one course in the teaching of reading. All teachers are considered teachers of reading whether the subject matter is mathematics or history. This emphasis on reading will strengthen remedial reading efforts, but it will also reinforce developmental reading programs that will benefit all students.

SEX STEREOTYPING

"Every teacher knows that what we read, both on the printed line and between the lines, affects what and how we think," states the Committee on the Role and Image of Women of the National Council of Teachers of English.[4] The concern of this committee and many others today is that women be portrayed fairly and that every effort be made to eliminate the stereotyped images of women that have appeared in books for children.

Studies of reading textbooks as well as children's tradebooks show that Mother is usually depicted as a passive, rather dull person, who operates from the family kitchen. The "apron syndrome" includes not only human mothers but also animal mothers such as Sylvester's mother in *Sylvester and the Magic Pebble.*

Girls, too, follow Mother's lead and are commonly shown helping in the kitchen. They serve as spectators for the boys' more exciting adventures or play house with their dolls and other little girls. The assumption is clear that girls are clean, nonassertive, stay close to home, and never have interesting things to do or think about. No wonder boys don't want to read stories about girls—except for somebody like Pippi Longstocking, a girl who does things any boy or girl would love to emulate.

The broad concerns that are involved in eliminating sterotyping include socialization of young children through books and other means. There is a real need for new models for girls in the form of biographies about women who have achieved in our society and books about alternative career choices for women. There is a need, too, for conscious efforts on the part of teachers to change attitudes and practices in the classroom. This topic is explored in more detail on page 375.

INQUIRY OR DISCOVERY METHOD

One of the most exciting ideas to come on the English horizon is the inquiry, or discovery method. Briefly, the inquiry method is an approach which encourages student generation of theories or generalizations from data which they collect or which are presented to them. The steps of the approach involve:

1 Observation of data
2 Discovery of elements
3 Generalization.

[4] From "Guidelines for Publications," a free brochure from the National Council of Teachers of English, 1111 Kenyon Rd., Urbana, Ill. 61801.

4 Testing of generalization
5 Possible modification of the generalization

This process is similar to John Dewey's five steps to problem solving.

An example of the inductive method in English might teach children about haiku poetry in this manner. The students are first presented with a duplicated sheet of examples of haiku. After studying these examples, students observe the characterstics of this poetry form, for example:

Each poem contains three lines.
The lines do not rhyme.
Each poem refers to nature.
The lines follow the same pattern.

These and any other observations are written on the board for future reference as students perhaps explore other examples to check their generalizations. They can be led to discover the specific syllabic pattern also.

The deductive method, a more commonly used teaching strategy, would teach students about this poetry form through a presentation by the teacher. The students would be told rather than guided to "discover." The advantages of the inquiry method are the following:

1 The student is involved in learning through questioning, researching.
2 It develops the questioning attitude and the ability to probe, to investigate, to ask intelligent questions.
3 Emphasis is on the process of acquiring knowledge rather than on storage of knowledge.
4 Focus remains on thinking rather than on rote memorization.
5 Students have a chance to develop their own potency; they develop confidence in their ability.
6 The student finds that there is still much to discover and much to create.
7 Intuitive thinking abilities are developed and encouraged.

PERFORMANCE-BASED INSTRUCTION

An increasing emphasis is being placed on accountability of teachers at all levels. Today, therefore, we see teacher education programs based on performance criteria that clearly spell out goals and objectives. Primary teachers are being held accountable for the achievement of children in their classrooms particularly in the area of reading. All teachers are rethinking courses taught in order to specify objectives and the means of evaluation.

This emphasis has resulted in considerable controversy, especially among those who teach the English language arts. English teachers argue that the things we teach can't be measured. How can you measure the affective aspects of teaching—the love of literature, creative writing of poetry, development of individual writing styles? If teachers are judged on these criteria, then they will teach only those things that are clearly measurable such as spelling, usage, or grammar.

Whatever the viewpoint, however, we must reckon with this very real trend in education. It is important to evaluate both positive and negative aspects of the use of behavioral objectives. It is helpful, for example, to consider what we are trying to do in our classrooms. If we have clearer objectives in mind, we will be able to convey these objectives to our students so they, too, will know what is expected of them. Can we state objectives for affective elements of English education—for example, ability to write a haiku poem or participation in creative drama activities? Perhaps there is a way of measuring results in terms of performance without injuring the creative components of English that we want to emphasize.

The manner in which behavioral objectives have been presented has perhaps created more ill feeling than was necessary. If, for instance, the teacher is being punished, if behavioral concepts are imposed by state departments to judge teacher effectiveness, then it is natural for teachers to feel resentment. Clearly, however, we as English teachers do need to have well-defined goals in mind for our classes. We need to know also how we fit into the large picture of English education so that we can take a stand for or against philosophies and practices that are currently being advocated.

Books to Investigate

Borton, Terry. *Reach, Touch, and Teach.* New York: McGraw-Hill Book Co., 1970.

Greer, Mary, and Rubenstein, Bonnie. *Will the Real Teacher Please Stand Up?* Pacific Palisades, Calif.: Goodyear, 1972.

James, Muriel, and Jongeward, Dorothy. *Born to Win.* Reading, Mass.: Addison-Wesley, 1971.

Moustakas, Clark. *The Authentic Teacher.* Cambridge, Mass.: Howard A. Doyle Publishing Co., 1966.

Rogers, Carl R. *Freedom to Learn.* Columbus, Ohio: Charles E. Merrill, 1969.

Skinner, B. F. *Beyond Freedom and Dignity.* New York: Alfred A. Knopf, 1971.

Tiedt, Iris M., and Tiedt, Sidney W. *Readings on Contemporary English in the Elementary School.* Englewood Cliffs, N.J.: Prentice-Hall, 1967.

language study

chapter

Language is not an abstract construction of the learned.
Walt Whitman

"There is no such thing as the 'Queen's English.' The property has gone into the hands of a joint stock company and we own the bulk of the shares." So wrote Mark Twain in *Following the Equator* as he expressed a concept that for many of us today proves revolutionary.

During the decade of the sixties the study of linguistics added to the knowledge explosion, bringing to light new concepts of our English language which bear challenging implications for teachers of English. As a result of scholarly studies of language, we now realize that English is not only a language rooted in the past, but it is a live, and lively, language which is constantly changing, developed by the very people who use it in daily speech and writing.

The study of language, thus, is of direct concern to each of us, for language is a vital part of our existence. Spoken and written language, in which we are the senders, or language that is heard or read as we receive a message—all forms of language are important in the process of communication. The study of language focuses attention on:

The nature of language
Our linguistic heritage and its development
English in the world culture
Analysis of English grammar and usage concepts
Using language to communicate in varied ways

The specific purpose of this chapter is to explore new concepts of language that have been derived from developments in linguistics. We shall focus attention on contemporary concepts of grammar and usage and methods of presenting this information in the classroom. We shall also explore other fascinating language studies that offer much to the study of English in the elementary school—for example, dialectology, semantics, and word origins (the history of language).

What Is Linguistics?

There still remains much confusion about linguistics as a field of study. The term has been variously used and misused as textbook writers, for instance, sought to identify their materials with the "new English." "Linguistic readers" and "linguistic approaches" to teaching everything appeared. Use of these terms meant just as much or as little as saying that these readers used language because the adjective *linguistic* simply means: *belonging or pertaining to language.* The word originates in the Latin for tongue, *lingua.*

What then is linguistics? According to the college edition of the *Random House Dictionary of the English Language,* linguistics is: "The science of language, including phonetics, phonology, morphology, and syntax, and often divided into historical linguistics and descriptive linguistics." This field has been further defined as: ". . . the study, according to rigorously defined methods or principles, *of language as a system.* The linguist is concerned, not with the listing of miscellaneous items, as in a dictionary, but with the recurrent patterns and characteristic relationships." [1]

Linguistics has contributed the following new concepts of language and language study which have influenced English instruction:

1 Language constantly changes.
2 Change is normal.

[1] Hans P. Guth, *English Today and Tomorrow* (Englewood Cliffs, N.J.: Prentice-Hall, 1964), p. 25.

3 The spoken language *is* the language.
4 Correctness rests upon usage.
5 All usage is relative.[2]

AREAS OF STUDY WITHIN LINGUISTICS

Within the broad area of linguistic science there have developed subareas which focus attention on specific aspects of language structure, for example, historical linguistics, psycholinguistics, comparative linguistics, sociolinguistics, geolinguistics, and descriptive linguistics. It is within the last area of focus, descriptive linguistics, that the examinaton of the structure of the English language developed, bearing with it changed perspectives of our supposedly "familiar" language.

One of the prime movers of this development was Charles C. Fries, author of *The Structure of English,* who has been both praised and blamed for his attention to English structure and the resulting questioning of traditional grammar. There are those who preceded his work—Otto Jespersen, Edward Sapir, and Leonard Bloomfield—and there are others who have followed his lead in developing this study of the structure of English, but it is Fries who is credited with establishing important basic concepts such as the well-researched fact that there exist *social levels* of language usage rather than "right" and "wrong" usage. His chief contribution has been to lead the way toward a more realistic approach to the study of language and a more realistic approach to the teaching of English.

Emphasis in linguistics is clearly on the scientific approach to language. Ignoring existing concepts or *mis*conceptions, the linguist sets to work to examine the language as it is in operation. Subsequent statements about language are not derived from intuitive prescriptions for what language "ought to be" but are based firmly on direct observation of the language as it is used by the people. The study of English includes, therefore, direct research of this language as it is used by widely differing socioeconomic groups within the United States as well as the English of Great Britain and that of Africa, India, and other parts of the world.

To provide some insight into the significance of linguistic study, we can cite an interesting field project undertaken by a group of international linguists in the spring of 1966 when they met to create a new alphabet for the Mandingo languages which include, for example, Bambara (spoken in Mali), Malinké (Mali, Guinea, and western Senegal), Songhay-Jerma (Mali and Niger), Tamashek (Tuareg), Hausa (Nigeria and Niger), Kanuri (Nigeria and Niger) and Fulani (scattered from Senegal to north-

[2] Commission on the English Curriculum, National Council of Teachers of English, *The English Language Arts* (New York: Appleton-Century-Crofts, 1952), pp. 274–77.

ern Cameroon). As is true of many languages, these tongues existed primarily in spoken form, for efforts to write the languages had been unorganized and conflicting.

With contemporary emphasis on education, publication, and mass communication, however, came the need for a written language. Convened by UNESCO, the assembled linguists attacked these problems:

1 Proposing for these languages a common alphabet for all the consonants they share.
2 Creating an alphabet simple enough to avoid technical and economic problems disadvantageous to educational systems and publishing ventures.

What seems an impossible task was accomplished in one busy week, for the linguistic scholars developed a practical alphabet which encompasses the sounds of these six languages and deviates only slightly from the systems of most European languages. The creation of this alphabet will enable these African peoples to work more effectively toward mass education. As the UNESCO report states, "Six linguistic groups spread over seven nations now have alphabets that should enable them to start on the more and more urgent task of transcribing an immense heritage of oral literature." [3]

NEW TERMINOLOGY

One of the aspects of linguistics that has proved confusing for those who are new to the field, is the introduction of new terms. In many cases, too, familiar terminology has been redefined. Let us examine some of the linguistic terms that teachers need to be able to use.

Phoneme (fo′ nēm) The smallest unit of sound that makes a difference in meaning. Linguists can identify all the phonemes used in any language; for example, in English there are about forty phonemes, depending on the dialect examined. The sounds heard at the beginning of these two words—*fan* and *tan*—represent two phonemes because the meaning of each word depends on the particular phoneme used. The single sound change represents a change in meaning. Phonemes are written within slashes, thus: /*f*/ /*t*/. The phonemes in English and the symbols we use to write them are discussed in detail in Chapter 4.

Grapheme (gra′ fēm) The writing of a phoneme according to English spellings. One phoneme might, for instance, be represented by ten or more graphemes, whereas some sounds are spelled in only a few alternate

[3] Adapted from *UNESCO Features* No. 477, p. 1.

ways. The phoneme /f/ might commonly be spelled *f, ph, ff,* or *gh.* The vowel phoneme /*ey*/, the long *a,* might be spelled in many different ways: pl*ay*, th*ey*, r*ai*n, fl*a*m*e*, br*ea*k, n*eigh*, and so on. The relationships between phonemes and graphemes are also explored in Chapter 4 because they are related to teaching reading and spelling.

Morpheme (mor′ fēm) The smallest unit of meaning in the language. A morpheme is not necessarily a word although it might be. Notice the morphemes in these English words.

> One morpheme: words such as *dog* or *book,* past tense (as in walk*ed*), plurality (as in cat*s*)
>
> Two morphemes: *dogs, walked, playful, piglet*
> Three morphemes: *girls', unspeakable*

Can you identify the meaningful elements in each word?

Linguists have often used the term *free* to identify those morphemes that can stand alone as words—for example, *turn* or *light.* Morphemes that are part of a longer word and cannot stand alone are called *bound morphemes,* as *de* or *ful* in the word *delightful,* which contains three morphemes; or as *re* in the word *return,* which contains two morphemes. The study of morphemes is called *morphology.*

Grammar The terms *grammar* and *usage* have been clearly differentiated by the modern linguist. *Grammar* is defined as the study of the syntax of the sentence, the structure of the language. Traditional or Latin-based grammars were prescriptive in that people were told how language ought to be used. Prescriptive grammar was replaced by descriptive grammar that literally described how language is really used and allowed for linguistic change.

Usage Grammar had long been considered a study of how to use words and the learning of "proper" or "correct" English. When the definition of *grammar* was clarified as the study of syntax, usage was more accurately defined as "the choice of appropriate words." We began to recognize that we use language in different ways according to the situation and that the formal language of an academic lecture would be inappropriate in the bowling alley.

The changed concepts of grammar and usage caused great consternation in English classrooms, and many chose to continue teaching prescriptive rules for usage under the title of grammar. Fortunately, most English teachers now realize it is more important to use language in speaking and writing than it is to keep on teaching artificial rules which never helped anyone learn to use language effectively. Grammar and usage are such important topics that we will explore them a little more thoroughly in the following pages.

The Grammar and Usage of English

The change brought about by linguistic studies which has probably caused the greatest controversy for teachers is that of modern approaches to grammar. The only grammar which teachers have been taught is the so-called "traditional" grammar which linguistics has revealed as an inaccurate representation of English sentence structure. Naturally it is disconcerting to find that this knowledge is no longer useful, and there remains resistance to change as noted by W. Nelson Francis:

> The definitive grammar of English is yet to be written, but the results so far achieved are spectacular. It is now as unrealistic to teach "traditional" grammar of English as it is to teach "traditional" (i.e., pre-Darwinian) biology or traditional" (i.e., four-element) chemistry. Yet nearly all certified teachers of English on all levels are doing so. Here is a cultural lag of major proportions.[4]

Actually, several grammars have been developed for the English language: (1) traditional, (2) structural, and (3) generative or transformational.[5] It is interesting to note also that other grammars are in the process of being developed, for with new perceptive minds come new approaches to the structure of English; and too, the flexibility of our changing language may create a need for new descriptions. Each grammar has made its contribution as we will note in the following discussion.

Traditional grammar Traditional or Latin-based grammar has its roots in the eighteenth-century work of Joseph Priestley, Robert Lowth, George Campbell, and Lindley Murray, who were prescriptive, basing their precise rules on Latin, which they viewed as a perfect language, and on their own concepts of linguistic "correctness." The work of these early scholars is still evident in many English texts today as we observe the emphasis on "correct usage" and definitions of parts of speech—for example, "A noun is the name of a person, place, or thing."

Structural grammar Structural grammar is a descriptive grammar which began with the work of Leonard Bloomfield in the first half of the twentieth century. He attempted to separate structure of language from

[4] W. Nelson Francis, "Revolution in Grammar," *Quarterly Journal of Speech* (October, 1954), pp. 229–312.

[5] Owen Thomas, "Grammatici Certant," *English Journal* (May, 1963). Reprinted in: *Linguistics in the Classroom* (Champaign, Ill.: National Council of Teachers of English), p. 6.

its meaning, that is, he distinguished between study of syntax and that of semantics. The purely descriptive approach employed by the structural linguist caused panic among traditionalists who deplored the structural grammarian's failure to judge "correctness" of usage. Attempting to present language as it really exists are such linguists as Charles C. Fries, James Sledd, H. A. Gleason Jr., Archibald Hill, and many others.

Also ascribing to the theories of structural grammar was the editor of *Webster's Third International Dictionary*, Philip B. Gove, who was heavily criticized for "abdicating his responsibility." The literature is full of plaints—for example, that of *The New York Times:*

> Webster's has, it is apparent, surrendered to the permissive school that has been busily extending its beachhead on English instruction in the schools. This development is disastrous because intentionally or unintentionally, it serves to reinforce the notion that good English is whatever is popular.[6]

Philip Gove's letter in reply concluded with these words:

> Whether you or I or others who fixed our language notions several decades ago like it or not, the contemporary English language of the Nineteen Sixties—the language we have to live with, the only language we have to survive with—is not the language of the Nineteen Twenties and Thirties.[7]

Studies of the structure of English led to new concepts of (1) phonemes (the sounds of English, which number about forty), (2) morphemes (meaningful units of language), and (3) phrase structure. The structuralist also devised a new system of classifying the words in a language. Unlike the traditional grammarian, the structuralist bases definitions on syntax rather than on meaning. He has discovered, for example, that all nouns are distinctive from other words in that a noun can be made plural and possessive. This is not true of any other group of words—verbs, adjectives, adverbs, and so on. Here, then, we have a clear test for identifying nouns. Can all of the following words be classified as nouns? Might any of them also be included in other categories?

mother	winning	footstep	drive
pupil	score	telephone	parking
English	publishing	pencil	spelling

Compare this syntactic approach to classifying words with that of traditional grammar, which bases definitions on the meanings of words. Are

[6] *The New York Times,* October 12, 1961.
[7] *The New York Times,* November 5, 1961.

there words in this group which could not be identified as the "name of a person, place, or thing"?

Transformational-generative grammar The newest of the grammars is based chiefly on the work of Noam Chomsky whose works appeared in 1957 and 1960. Transformational-generative grammar extends the concepts of structural grammar, which was concerned with syntax devoid of meaning, to include the semantics of language. It seeks to:

1 Identify kernel sentences—simple, declarative, active sentences with no elaboration; for example, Joe has a dog.
2 Supply rules for transforming kernel sentences.
Judy ate a big hamburger.
Is Judy eating a hamburger?
Judy is not eating a hamburger.
What is Judy eating?
3 Identify obligatory transformations and optional transformations.
An obligatory transformation: agreement of subject and verb.
Mary is tall. (We cannot use *are* in this sentence.)
An optional transformation: any elaboration of a kernel.
The teacher is working. (We may add *tired* to describe teacher or *in her room* to designate the place, but these additions are optional.)

Transformational-generative grammar has developed very exact rules for transforming sentences, and these rules are usually stated in a formula. The changing of a kernel (simple, active, declarative) sentence into the passive form is stated in this formula:

Passive = Second noun phrase (+ auxiliary) + *be* + past participle + by + first noun phrase

Thus, the kernel sentence—Mrs. Parker called Joe—is made passive by applying the formula.

Joe (NP_2) was (form of *be*) called (past participle) by Mrs. Parker (NP_1).

QUESTIONS ABOUT GRAMMAR

There has been much confusion about grammar: comparisons of traditional grammar and that of the structuralist and transformationalist, the misconceptions about grammar and usage, and the amount of assistance which knowledge of grammar provides to composition ability. To clarify important concepts, we shall explore these questions.

1. What is grammar? The definition of grammar is somewhat difficult, for there are many conceptions of what grammar is, and far too many of these conceptions have been proved to be *mis*conceptions. We can begin defining grammar by pointing out, therefore, what grammar *is not.*

Grammar is not "usage." For many English instructors the problems of using "shall" or "will" or distinguishing between the use of "I" and "me" means the teaching of grammar. The linguist observes, however, that knowledge of this nature pertains to the manner in which English is used, to the selection of words according to appropriateness, not to the study of the structure of the English sentence, for grammar and usage are separate studies.

Grammar is not "good English." The placing of emphasis on the "correctness" and "incorrectness" is related to the study of usage. As we will point out in the discussion of usage, these concepts are relative depending on our personal values and the situation in which speech takes place.

Grammar is not "parts of speech." Some teachers have assumed they were teaching grammar as they drilled students on the identification of eight parts of speech. In the first place, linguists quickly teach us that there are more than eight categories of words in English, and that mere identification of each word as belonging to a certain category does not take note of the structural meaning of the sentence. We soon see, too, that many words fall into more than one category, for example:

His *running* of the race was unexpected.
The *running* water was cold.
John was *running* toward the school.

Jim hit a *home* run.
They were at *home.*
The family headed *home.*

Grammar is not "the mechanics of composition." Another interpretation of grammar has been the knowledge of punctuation, capitalization, and spelling—skills of composition. Although it is true that knowledge of juncture (the pauses in spoken language) has relevance for the study of grammar as well as for the use of punctuation, the study of punctuation is not the study of grammar.

How, then, shall we define *grammar* in accordance with modern linguistic concepts? One definition is "the system of devices in the English language which signal structural meanings." [8] Other writers note that grammar is a study of the way a language works encompassing morphology (meaningful forms); syntax (sentence structure), and phonology (sounds).[9]

[8] Metropolitan School Study Council, *Structural Linguistics; an Introduction for Teachers and Administrators* (New York: Teachers College, 1961), p. 2.

[9] Mary E. Fowler, *Teaching Language, Composition, and Literature* (New York: McGraw-Hill, 1965), p. 183.

It will be some time, however, before these definitions are assimilated by the teaching profession and even longer until the public understands, for example, that there is a distinction between grammar and usage. When critics of education cry, therefore, for a return to the teaching of grammar so that our young people will gain skill in composition, we can be certain that these representatives of the public really want the classroom teacher to stress the teaching of "correct usage." The assumption that knowledge of grammar *does* increase ability to write is the subject of the next question.

2. Does knowledge of grammar improve ability to speak and write? Research reports conclude:

> In view of the widespread agreement of research studies based upon many types of students and teachers, the conclusion can be stated in strong and unqualified terms: The teaching of formal grammar has a negligible, or, because it usually displaces some instruction and practice in actual comparison, even a harmful effect on the improvement of writing.[10]

Research indicates that skills of composition are learned through composing, not through learning to identify classes of words, rules of grammar, and so forth.

Paul Roberts, who authored a set of language books which feature transformational grammar for elementary school students,[11] asserted:

> It is not to be expected that study of the grammar, no matter how good a grammar it is or how carefully it is taught, will effect any enormous improvement in writing. Probably the improvement will be small and hard to demonstrate and for the large number of students who lack the motivation or the capacity to learn to write, it will be nonexistent.[12]

We should be cognizant also that researchers note the need for more extensive studies of composition, and this would certainly be true of the effects of instruction along the lines of structural and generative grammars which have only recently found their ways into the schools. It is our own observation that work in expanding basic sentences does increase student flexibility in writing by suggesting possibilities for more effective original sentences. Successful creation of interesting sentences stimulates student desire to write and composition skills do improve. Mere knowledge of terminology or ability to classify English words does not improve com-

[10] Richard Braddock et al., *Research in Written Composition* (Champaign, Ill.: National Council of Teachers of English, 1963), pp. 37–38.

[11] *The Roberts English Series* (New York: Harcourt, 1966).

[12] Paul Roberts, "Linguistics and the Teaching of Composition," *English Journal* (May, 1963).

position skills, but moving beyond that basic information to manipulation of words, phrases, clauses, that is, to composing, does improve ability to write. Again, however, research is needed to investigate this aspect of composition.

3. Why is traditional grammar no longer considered satisfactory? Linguistic studies have pointed out that, as can be readily proved, traditional grammar does not describe the English language. The following criticisms of traditional grammar have been made:

1 Prescriptive rules based on Latin, a dead language, had little effect on changing usage of a living language.
2 Traditional grammar did not recognize the changing nature of language.
3 Its definitions of word classes were based on meaning which changes for a word in varied contexts, and the definitions were ambiguous.

The emphasis on learning sterile rules which had no meaning for the student made the study of English boring and distasteful to students and actually inhibited learning. As Marckwardt observes, students tended to adopt a "classroom dialect, a sapless and super-correct form of the language employed only within the hearing of the English teacher and in written work subject to her scrutiny, and for the most part, dropped like a hot-cake as soon as the hour was over."[13] It is probable, too, that an excessive amount of time was spent, furthermore, on repetitious drill in usage when time might more wisely have been allocated for writing.

4. Does modern grammar offer something more effective than traditional grammar? Modern grammar (based on structural linguistics and transformational-generative grammar) emphasizes learning about grammar by engaging in the work of the linguist, that is, examining the language itself. Inductively, then, the student can discover word classes, for example, through learning processes advocated by Bruner.[14] He or she can also discover sentence patterns and methods of expanding them as we will discuss in more detail later in this chapter. The advantages of modern grammar include the following:

a Description of the structure of English is based on a study of this unique language as it is actually used.
b Grammar is differentiated from usage.
c The student acquires a more realistic attitude toward language and language study.

[13] Albert H. Marckwardt, "Grammar and Linguistics in the Teaching of English," *Illinois English Bulletin* (October, 1956), p. 3.
[14] *Ibid.*

d Modern grammar offers a more positive approach to study of the English language which appeals to students.

e Emphasis on creating original sentences after study of sentence structure patterns suggests a beneficial relationship between grammar study and composition.

QUESTIONS ABOUT USAGE

The usage of language, as we have noted, was stressed in traditional grammar, which prescribed detailed rules for usage and taught concepts of "correctness" and "incorrectness." New concepts of language based on description of language have altered attitudes toward usage, which is now viewed as changing along with the changing language. There are many questions about concepts of usage which merit our examination.

1. What is the difference between grammar and usage? Grammar, as has been explained, is the study of the structure of English speech, the language as it operates, the syntax. Grammar does not consider the meaning of individual words.

The syntax of a language tells us that, for example, the subject and the verb must agree in number. We say, therefore, "Tom and Sammy are going." Grammatically, we cannot say, "Tom and Sammy is going." We could, on the other hand, change our selection of words in other respects without changing the syntax, for example:

Tom and Sammy are running.
Thomas and Sam are walking.
Tom and Sam are playing.

Our choice of words may change the meaning, but it does not change the syntax or grammar.

2. What usage shall we teach? Linguists recommend that we teach the concept of varied levels of usage. Usage that is acceptable in an informal social situation may not be acceptable in a written composition and vice versa. We recognize, but don't condemn, the presence of varied social dialects among which *standard* English is only one, and even this dialect may vary regionally.

We teach, therefore, educated forms of standard English without undue stress on picayune points that really achieve little. Pooley recommends that we forget, for example, a number of specific items of usage which were formerly taught:

1 Any distinction between *shall* and *will*.
2 Any reference to the split infinitive.

3 Elimination of *like* as a conjunction.
4 Objection to the phrase 'different than."
5 Objection to "He is one of those boys who *is*."
6 Objection to "the reason . . . is because. . . ."
7 Objection to *myself* as a polite substitution for *me* as in "I understand you will meet Mrs. Jones and myself at the station."
8 Insistence on the possessive case standing before a gerund.[15] [Note that there is an example in this item.]

3. What is "good" English? The definition of good English written by Robert C. Pooley in 1933 has been widely quoted and remains a valid statement today:

> Good English is that form of speech which is appropriate to the purpose of the speaker, true to the language as it is, and comfortable to speaker and listener.[16]

Notice that there is no mention in this definition of "correctness" or of knowledge of rules of grammar.

4. Does memorization of rules improve usage? Meckel reports that "Improvement of usage appears to be most effectively achieved through practice of desirable forms than through memorization of rules." [17]

The child learns language through imitation from infancy, and it is true that many language patterns and much knowledge of English usage are formed before the child comes to school. Both home and the peer group are highly influential in determining usage. Changes will be brought about only when the student discovers a reason for changing speech, and learning of rules does not provide sufficient motivation.

5. Is slang "bad"? Here again we must rethink our concepts of correctness and usage. Slang is a vernacular which has a high interest value and often provides a means for snaring the interests of students in language study. Termed in French, *"la langue verte,"* slang represents the growth, the aliveness, of our language. Have students list as many slang words as they can. The words can be defined, categorized into word classes, used in sentence patterns, and compiled by several "lexicographers" into a dictionary of SLANGUAGE. Entries might read thus:

[15] Robert C. Pooley, "Dare Schools Set a Standard in Usage?" *The English Journal* (March, 1960), p. 180.

[16] Robert C. Pooley, *Grammar and Usage in Textbooks on English*, Bureau of Educational Research Bulletin No. 14 (Madison, Wis.: University of Wisconsin, August, 1933), p. 155.

[17] Henry C. Meckel, "Research on Teaching Composition and Literature," in N. L. Gage, ed., *Handbook of Research on Teaching*, American Educational Research Assn. (Chicago: Rand McNally, 1963), p. 981.

IN—accepted, popular—That's really *in!*
BOSS—good, nice, pretty—That convertible is boss!
CAMP—so old its *in*—His surfer outfit is really high camp!

The teacher does not teach slang but aims students toward standard English without authoritatively condemning slang. Students are taught the concept of varied levels of usage of which slang is one as is standard English. Sometimes words which originate as slang become elevated to a higher level of acceptability, and on rare occasions a slang word becomes acceptable as standard English.

Language Instruction

Our primary concern as teachers is the translation of our knowledge about grammar and usage into classroom experiences for the student. What are the implications of new concepts of language for English instruction? What knowledge shall we transmit to the elementary school student? How can we most effectively present information about language to the elementary school child?

"Perhaps of all the creations of man, language is the most astonishing," wrote Giles Lytton Strachey in *Words and Poetry*. As students are exposed to this astonishing language, to what J. Donald Adams has called "the magic and mystery of words," they will, it is hoped, gain some of this feeling for the English language. They will be intrigued by their ability to manipulate the language, to achieve astonishing results, to create beautiful arrangements. Teacher enthusiasm will serve to develop this feeling of deep involvement and interest in language that leads the student to independent investigation.

OBJECTIVES OF LANGUAGE INSTRUCTION

Toward what goals shall we direct instruction in language? We can direct language study in the elementary school toward the same concepts taught at other levels of education as we provide understandings in the following areas: (1) our literary heritage, the history and development of English; (2) the structure of the English language, its grammar; (3) the study of usage of American English; (4) composing (both oral and written) with English; (5) semantics; and (6) dialectology. We shall attempt to develop the major concepts to be taught in each of these areas.

1 History and development of the English language
   a. English is part of the Indo-European language family.
   b. Changes in spelling and pronunciation influence contemporary spelling and pronunciation; changing nature of language.

c. Origins of English words; continuing growth of English.
d. Comparison of American and British English.
e. English is part of the world culture.

2 Structure of the English language, grammar
a. Specific sounds (phonemes) can be identified for the English language; corresponding graphemes can be identified.
b. English words can be grouped according to their function in sentences; some words may belong to more than one group.
c. Word order helps to signal meaning.
d. English sentences are based on distinct patterns.
e. Basic sentence patterns can be elaborated through specific techniques.

3 Usage of American English
a. There are varied levels of acceptable usage or varied degrees of appropriateness of usage.
b. Usage concerns the selection of specific words to be used in any given speech situation.
c. Usage is not labeled "right" or "wrong," for the choice of usage is an individual operation. Usage may be judged on the basis of suitability to the context, whether it be a social context or a composition context.
d. Speech dialects differ according to region and social class. Even standard English allows for variety of acceptable speech.
e. We should develop sensitivity to language habits which are analogous to habits of eating and dress.

4 Oral and written composition in English
a. The purpose of using language is to communicate ideas and feelings.
b. The success of composition is evaluated on the basis of success in communicating.
c. Skills associated with written composition, for example, spelling, punctuation, and handwriting, facilitate communication.
d. In order to communicate one must first have an idea, or thoughts, to communicate.
e. We gain skill effectiveness in communication through practice in composing varied types of messages.
f. The study of other authors' attempts to communicate (literary models) can aid growth in ability to compose and communicate.

5 English semantics
a. Semantics deals with the meanings of words.
b. Words vary from the most concrete to those which are highly abstract.
c. We need to recognize more than the denotation of a word, for the connotation may have more significant effect.
d. In order to gain meaning we draw on more than words alone. For example, meaning is carried by intonation, body language, and so forth.

e. A special dictionary that deals with synonyms of words is the thesaurus.

6 Dialectology in American English

a. American and British English differ widely in many respects, yet the grammar is basically the same.
b. The study of dialectology includes both social and regional variation in language.
c. Language varies more widely in pronunciation than it does in syntax.
d. Many people in our country are bi-dialectal.
e. Each person speaks at least one dialect.

An exciting method for teaching students about their own language is through inductive activities or discovery techniques. In general children enjoy language and feel that it is something they know about. Let them examine their own language and the language of their classmates. Children can, for example, discuss the grammar of their own sentences. They can make a study of the dialects represented in their own classroom.

IMPACT OF LINGUISTICS ON ELEMENTARY ENGLISH TEXTBOOKS

Most elementary teachers need textbooks to assist them in presenting grammar to children in the classroom. If we are depending on the textbook for this input, it is important to know what textbooks are presenting. Tiedt's study of elementary English textbooks examined seventeen sixth-grade texts published between 1960 and 1970.[18] This content analysis focused on the following questions:

1 To what extent is each of three major grammar theories (Latin-based, structural, and transformational-generative) represented in the texts?
2 Which specific grammar concepts are presented by a majority of texts? How is grammar defined? What reasons are given for teaching grammar?
3 Which language concepts, in addition to those related to grammar, are presented?
4 What is the relative emphasis placed on grammar in each textbook?
5 What is the current trend in elementary English as exemplified by the textbook?[19]

The data collected for texts published during this decade revealed an interesting comparison between those published prior to 1966 (when the *Roberts English Series* was published) and those published after 1966.

[18] Iris M. Tiedt, *A Content Analysis of Grammar Presented in Elementary School English Textbooks Published between 1961–1970*, Unpublished doctoral dissertation, Stanford University, 1972.
[19] *Ibid.*, p. 31.

During the first half of the decade, traditional, Latin-based grammar dominated elementary school English textbooks. *Grammar* was synonymous with *usage,* and emphasis was placed on "correct" usage. The object in teaching grammar was to improve composition. Terms were drawn from Latin-based grammar, as were definitions based on meaning and function. *Sentence* was defined as a "complete thought," and sentences were classified according to analysis or the expected response. Concepts about language other than grammar were seldom presented.

Structural and transformational-generative grammar were first presented in the Roberts Series in 1966. Text writers who followed during the second half of the decade tended to de-emphasize "correct" usage, although 40 percent still included these concepts. A new aim for teaching grammar was to learn about the English language as a subject of study. There was a wide range in the percentage of the text used for presenting grammar (6 to 63 percent), which indicates controversy about how much grammar should be emphasized.

No texts defined *sentence* according to structural grammar, but 40 percent of the texts presented the transformational-generative formula: $S \longrightarrow NP + VP$. Four of ten texts published during the second half of the decade included structural patterns of predication and five presented the concepts *kernel sentence* and *transformation.* All of the texts used the terms *noun, verb, adjective, adverb, preposition, pronoun,* and *conjunction;* but these terms were usually defined according to both modern grammar and traditional grammar. Only three texts of ten avoided any use of the traditional definitions of terms. One hundred percent of the entire sample presented *subject, predicate,* and *object of the verb.* At least 50 percent of the texts published after 1965 included concepts about language in general, such as, "Language is always changing." They also taught concepts specific to English, such as, "Word order affects meaning in English." [20]

Interesting conclusions drawn from this study concern the effect of the publication of modern grammar in the Roberts Series in 1966. This series not only introduced "revolutionary" grammar concepts but also apparently opened the door to other linguistic studies such as dialectology, the history of English, and so forth. It is interesting to note that a single textbook author can have a tremendous impact on a field of study. This analysis also raised questions concerning the publication lag; for example, why did it take so long for modern grammar to appear in elementary school English textbooks, and what is the influence of theory on practice? [21]

[20] *Ibid.*, pp. 76–78.
[21] *Ibid.*, pp. 83–88.

Careful studies of textbooks are needed for textbook selection. How is a textbook selected? What are the criteria on which selection is based? Is there a clear rationale for decisions made, or is a textbook selection the "great experiment" that Robert Bennett, past president of the National Council of Teachers of English, termed it?[22] Textbooks should, moreover, represent what educators delineate as the curriculum, but texts will not do this until teachers can clearly state their own objectives and know what their priorities are for the English program in their classrooms.

WHICH "GRAMMAR" SHALL WE TEACH?

Our approach to grammar in the elementary school must clearly be eclectic, a synthesis of elements from varied approaches to English grammar. Which elements shall we select for instruction in the classroom? The following concepts, drawn from varied grammars, appear to contribute to the young person's understanding of the English language and its use:

1 Traditional grammar: terms for classifying words (plus others from structural grammar)
2 Structural grammar: identification of word classes, study of sentence patterns, expansion of basic patterns
3 Generative grammar: generating varied sentences from a core or basic sentence

What is the purpose of instruction in grammar? Concepts of grammar lead to a better understanding of English sentences and of "how language works." They also enable the teacher and student to communicate ideas about language as they use the vocabulary of the linguist to discuss more precisely the relationships of words. An eclectic approach to grammar leads to a greater interest in language activities as students compose sentences in paragraphs in stories. A limited amount of time should be spent on study specific to grammar or usage, for instruction time can be spent to greater advantage in actually using the language both orally and in written forms or in reading the language.

STUDENT KNOWLEDGE OF GRAMMAR

Elementary school students already know grammar before they enter school, for they have been using grammar since they began to speak. A

[22] Robert A. Bennett, "Roberts English: The Great Experiment," *Elementary English,* Vol. 47 (April, 1970).

wise approach to the study of grammar, therefore, is to impress the students with their own knowledge of grammar rather than to stress the esoteric, difficult nature of the study on which the class is embarking. Student knowledge of grammar can be brought out in many ways.

Before beginning any formal study of grammar it is important that students have had many opportunities to use English words and sentences. It is for this reason that stress is placed on oral language experience for beginning students, particularly those from disadvantaged backgrounds. These initial experiences will, however, reflect the teachings of linguistics. Young children can participate in language experiences like the following as they develop their abilities:

Selecting a sentence from an experience chart or dictated story, the teacher might say, for example, "We saw a movie. I wonder if we could do some interesting things with that sentence?" Using the analogy technique, she/he might lead the group to replace *movie* with other things that might have been seen (nouns), thus:

We saw a boy.
We saw two dogs.
We saw the teacher.

Then substitutions for the pronoun, *we,* might be explored:

The class saw the movie.
Joe saw the movie.

In this way, although the children don't know the terminology of grammar or even the fact that they are studying grammar, they are being introduced to the practice of substituting words in a common sentence pattern. INVENTING SENTENCES is a worthwhile oral activity that can be repeated with infinite variety.

Beginning readers can gain practice in reading while they are reinforcing their knowledge of English word order. Given words in confused order, they can construct a sentence that is grammatical, thus:

ran school to Tim
are going you where
new I a hat want

SCRAMBLED SENTENCES may sometimes contain an unnecessary word in this way:

visited car grandmother Polly her
happy is our neat room

CLASSIFYING PARTS OF SPEECH

Traditional grammar identified eight parts of speech; of these eight categories, seven are still useful, but structural linguistics has identified other function words which appear in English sentences.

MAIN WORD CLASSES

The four main word classes—noun, verb, adjective, and adverb—are open classes to which an unlimited number of words can be added.

Noun A noun is a word that can be made plural or possessive and may follow the words *the, a,* or *an.* A noun fits in patterns like these:

She has a ____________ (book, ball, pencil, dress, headache).
He looked at the ____________ (house, car, boy, dog, spot, movie).

Verb A verb is a word that can be changed from past to present and usually (except for forms of *to be*) adds *s* when patterned after *it, she, he.* The morpheme *ing* may be added to a verb. A verb fits in patterns like these:

The boy ____________. (runs, plays, speaks, shouts, ran, played).
They ____________ it. (found, chased, wanted, like, have, want).
What are you ____________? (saying, doing, missing, singing).

Adjective An adjective patterns with the word *very,* as *very lovely girl, very soft music, very small boy,* and the adjective can follow a linking verb.

She is very ____________. (happy, pretty, nice, healthy).
The very ____________ boy arrived. (tired, tall, unhappy, first).

Adverb Adverbs pattern like *often, up,* or *sadly.*

Mary sings ____________. (well, clearly, often, sweetly).
The baby climbs ____________. (up, eagerly, down, quickly).

Notice that many words may be placed in more than one word class according to their function in the sentence. Consider, for example, the various meanings and functions for these words:

check	book	trip
looking	walk	sound
leap	plane	root

FUNCTION WORDS

The other word categories are called *function* words or *structure* words. Included are: prepositions, conjunctions, subordinators, auxiliaries, intensifiers, pronouns, and determiners. These groupings are relatively limited in number, for only infrequently is a new word added to any of these structure categories.

Determiners The determiner signals that a noun follows. Included in this class are *the, a, an, every, each, this, that, these, those, my, one, two, three, four, most, more, either, neither, our, your, their, his, her, its, no, both, some, much, all, any, several, few.*

____________ cat chased ____________ dog.
____________ boys played with ____________ ball.

Pronouns *Pronouns* (like proper nouns) do not pattern with determiners, but they substitute for nouns or proper nouns.

The boy is tall. *Bruce* is tall. *He* is tall.

A special group of pronouns also function as determiners when followed by a noun, thus:

These boys are helpful. *These* are helpful.
That man is Mr. Sutter. *That* is Mr. Sutter.

Intensifiers Intensifiers (*very, quite, somewhat, rather*) pattern with adjectives and adverbs, thus:

Jim was *very* talkative. Jim walked *very* slowly.
He was *somewhat* uncertain. He was *rather* uncertain.

Auxiliaries The auxiliary signals that a verb follows. Some auxiliaries (*do, be, have, can*) may also serve as independent verbs, and only two (*be, have*) pattern with the past form of verbs.

I *can* go. He *did* help the teacher.
He *has played.* She *was* helping.

Subordinators Subordinators are connecting words that join subordinate subject-predicate word groups (clauses) with independent subject-predicate word groups (clauses). Included are *who, when, until,* *unless, that, since, if, what, which, whenever, while, although, as, because, whatever, whichever, whoever, how, before, whether, as if, unless, until.*

Their house is the yellow one *which* faces the park.
She is the person *who* called you.
When you return home, send me a copy of that book.

Conjunctions Conjunctions are linking words which join equal words or groups of words. Included in this group are *and, but, for, either . . . or, neither . . . nor, not only . . . but also, or, yet.*

Either David *or* I will come.
Her name is Joanna, *but* everyone calls her Jo.

Prepositions Prepositions signal that a noun follows, usually in a prepositional phrase which serves an adjective or adverb function. Common prepositions include *about, above, across, after, among, around, at, before, by, in, for, from, in, into, of, off, on, over, since, through, to, under, up, upon, with, within.*

The cat jumped *over* the box.
At noon we stopped working.
Walk *to* the corner *with* me.

What techniques can we use in the classroom to introduce students to these parts of speech? One of the most effective ways is the inductive approach through which students make linguistic discoveries for themselves. A class is asked, for example, to see how many words they can name in five to ten minutes as two recorders write the words on chalkboards. The students then examine the group of unsorted words to determine how these words can be sorted or classified. Varied methods may be explored—alphabetical order, length of words, meaning (animals, feelings, etc.—not all words will fit semantic groups), and so on.

Discoveries can be guided by the teacher who might ask, for example, after varied methods have been tried, whether any of the words can be made plural. After this identification of the noun class other groupings can be gradually introduced.

Additional practice in identifying words can be effected through the use of analogical patterns as words are supplied which fit given patterns, as in the first experiment:

- **Nouns and Determiners:**

  The ________ and the ________ followed the __________.
  ________ mouse is in ________ cage eating __________ cheese.
  I want to buy a __________ and two __________.

- Can you unite these sentences?
  Sheryl is pretty. She is popular. She studies hard.
  The siren shrieked. The car pulled over. The driver got out.
  This boy is the winner. He has long legs. He is in fifth grade.

- What word would you choose?
  We walked ________ the hill.
  ________ the assembly we returned ________ class.
  He sat __________ the table.
  The child was climbing _____ the box.

- Why is the meaning of these words uncertain?
  Plan moves ahead.
  City shelters poor.
  Ship sails today.

EXPLORING ENGLISH SENTENCE PATTERNS

The sentence merits considerable attention in the study of language and in developing composition skills. It is through study of the sentence that students can be made aware of grammar, for there is little justification in teaching grammar as an isolated subject. Grammar is not just a set of terms and rules to be learned; it is a study of the relationships of words and groups of words in the context of a sentence. These ideas should be taught, therefore, as students learn to write, to manipulate words and phrases, to create interesting, varied sentences.

Structural linguistics introduced the concept of the sentence pattern, of which there are many. In the elementary school, however, we might concentrate on working with five basic patterns. After introducing one pattern—for example, the simplest of all, Noun-Verb—let the students play with the pattern as they modify it in many ways. At any time, of course, they can still identify the basic pattern. Challenge class members to create a long sentence beginning with only two words, perhaps: *Horses run.* Compare the results.

The following five sentence patterns can be explored as you try experiments both orally and as written exercises. Students will enjoy developing the sentences according to specific directions. You can invent games based on working with these patterns—for example, HOW MANY SENTENCES CAN YOU WRITE IN FIVE MINUTES? Composing sentences is also a good activity for small groups, as students brainstorm sentences and develop them along specific lines together. Notice that terminology is taught and reinforced through use. The child who works with nouns and verbs begins to generalize what a noun is and what a verb is. Later the class might talk about nouns and how we know a word is a noun in a sentence.

N–V (SUBJECT–PREDICATE)

EXPERIMENTS:

Girls *giggle.* Girls *run.* Girls *sing.* (Analogical changes)
Boys *shout.* Boys *fight.* Boys *race.* Boys ____________
Cows *moo.* Cows *eat.* Cows *walk.* Cows ____________

The girls giggle. (Expansion–determiner)
Boys shout *loudly.* (Adverb)
In the morning cows moo. (Prepositional phrase)
The *amused* girls were giggling. (Adjective)

N–V–N (SUBJECT–PREDICATE–OBJECT)

EXPERIMENTS:

Boys run races. *Girls* run races. *Horses* run races.
Jane eats *ice cream.* Jane eats *sandwiches.* Jane eats *everything.*
Mrs. Barker *reads* books. Mrs. Barker *buys* books. Mrs. Barker *enjoys* books.

Boys and girls run races. (Expansion–compounding)
Jane eats *ice cream and cake* (Compounding)
Mrs. Barker reads books *about Africa.* (Modification)
A world traveler, Mrs. Barker reads books about Africa. (Apposition).

N–LV–N (SUBJECT–LINKING VERB PREDICATE–NOUN COMPLEMENT)

EXPERIMENTS:

This dog is a terrier, This dog is a collie.
My mother is a tall woman. My mother is a good driver.
Henry was a teacher. Henry was a barber.
This dog *which is lost* is a terrier. (subordinate clause)
Although my mother is a tall woman, she is thin. (subordination)
Henry was a teacher *in a small college.* (prepositional phrase)

N–LV–ADJ (SUBJECT–LINKING VERB PREDICATE–ADJECTIVE COMPLEMENT)

EXPERIMENTS:

Nancy is pretty. Nancy is intelligent.
Carnations are sweet. Roses are sweet.
Karl appears old. Karl appears unhappy.

Nancy and Susan are pretty (Compounding)
Carnations and roses are sweet. (Compounding)
Although Nancy is pretty, Susan is more intelligent. (Subordination)
Carnations are sweet, *but roses are lovelier.* (Coordination)

N–V–N–N (SUBJECT–PREDICATE–DIRECT OBJECT–INDIRECT OBJECT)

EXPERIMENTS:

Daddy gave me the book. (to me)
She read Peter a story. (to Peter)
The teacher told Larry the assignment. (to Larry)

Daddy gave me the ____________. (book, money, permission)
Daddy gave ____________ the book. (Mother, the neighbor)
____________ gave me the book. (Milly, A friend, My teacher)

Complete the formula:

$Noun_1$ verb $Noun_2$ $Noun_3$

CREATING ORIGINAL SENTENCES

The chief purpose of examining the structure of English sentences and experimenting with methods of expansion should be, as we have previously noted, the development of student ability to create, to compose, to generate original sentences. Experiments with sentence patterns and methods of expanding basic patterns should lead, furthermore, to greater skill and confidence in creating sentences that are not only interesting and effective but are also written with style, a style that is distinctive for each individual. To achieve this end we must provide many opportunities for the student to compose sentences and to discuss sentences. How can we work toward this end?

Helpful in teaching students to compose varied sentences is the process of expanding the basic pattern. Through many experiments in developing given sentences, the student acquires great flexibility in producing interesting original sentences. Note that as each sentence pattern was introduced, the experiments encouraged students to expand the pattern. After students have explored the possibilities for expanding sentences, have them examine the methods that have been used to expand a given sentence. Inductively, they can discover certain methods of expansion which can be repeated. At this time the common terminology for these methods should be supplied to provide the vocabulary for discussing sentence development:

MODIFICATION

Basic sentence–The boy went home.

The tired, but happy, boy went home. (Development of noun cluster)
The boy went home after school. (Prepositional phrase)
The boy immediately went home. (Adverb)
Having completed his work, the boy went home. (Participial phrase)

Combination: Having completed his work, the tired, but happy, boy immediately went home after school.

COMPOUNDING

Basic sentence—Debbie lives on Oak Street.

Debbie and Karen live on Oak Street. (Subject)
Debbie lives on Oak Street and goes to Maynard School. (Predicate)
Debbie lives on Oak Street, and she attends Maynard School. (Whole sentence)

APPOSITION

Basic sentence—Mr. Hadmon is an interesting person.

Mr. Hadmon, *our sixth-grade teacher,* is an interesting person.
Our sixth grade teacher, *Mr. Hadmon,* is an interesting person.
An interesting person is our sixth-grade teacher, *Mr. Hadmon.*
Mr. Hadmon, *well-read and informed,* is an interesting person.

SUBORDINATION

Basic sentence—Joe likes to play ball.

Joe, *who is in eighth grade,* likes to play ball. (Modifying subject)
Joe likes to play ball *whenever he has a chance.* (Modifying predicate)
Although Joe likes to play ball, he also studies hard.
Because Joe likes to play ball, he practices each Saturday.

THE STUDENT'S LINGUISTIC LIBRARY

Following is a bibliography of books which will provide supplementary reading in the area of language study. All are recommended for the elementary school library, for the elementary school student will find research intriguing as he or she studies early development of English, the work of the linguist, origins of English words, and discovers "word play."

Alexander, Arthur. *The Magic Words.* Englewood Cliffs, N.J.: Prentice-Hall, 1962. (Intermediate) [23] Language development.

Applegate, Mauree. *The First Book of Language.* New York: Franklin Watts, 1962. (Intermediate) Discusses use of parts of speech in writing.

Asimov, Isaac. *Words from the Myths.* New York: Houghton Mifflin, 1961. (Intermediate, Advanced) Explains origins of words which appear in the Bible.

———. *Words in Genesis.* New York: Houghton Mifflin, 1962. (Intermediate, Advanced) Excellent book on origins of words associated with mythology.

[23] Although it is impossible to "grade" books because student abilities vary widely, we have attempted to indicate difficulty and interest, thus: Primary (Levels 1–4), Intermediate (Levels 5–8), Advanced (Levels 9–Adult).

———. *Words of Science and the History Behind Them.* New York: Houghton Mifflin, 1959. (Intermediate, Advanced)

———. *Words on the Map.* New York: Houghton Mifflin, 1962. (Intermediate, Advanced).

Bach, Mickey. *Word-A-Day.* New York: Scholastic Book Services, 1972. (Intermediate)

Batchelor, Julie F. *Communication: From Cave to Television.* New York: Harcourt, Brace, 1953. (Intermediate) Explores the many ways of communicating.

Briggs, F. Allen. *The Play of Words.* New York: Harcourt, Brace, 1972. (Advanced) Excellent source for teachers.

Brown, Ivor. *Mind Your Language!* Chester Springs, Pa.: Dufour Editions, 1966. (Advanced)

Cahn, William, and Cahn, Rhoda. *The Story of Writing from Cave Art to Computer.* Irvington-on-Hudson, N.Y.: Harvey House, 1963. (Intermediate) Development of Language.

Cataldo, John W. *Words and Calligraphy for Children.* New York: Van Nostrand Reinhold, 1969. (Primary-Intermediate) Art and language.

Denison, Carol. *Passwords to People.* New York: Dodd, Mead and Co., 1956. (Intermediate) An entertaining introduction to the history of language.

Dugan, William. *How Our Alphabet Grew.* Golden Press, 1972. (Intermediate-Advanced)

Epstein, Samuel and Beryl. *The First Book of Words.* New York: Franklin Watts, 1954. (Intermediate) Beginning study of language.

———. *The First Book of Printing.* New York: Franklin Watts, 1955. (Intermediate) History of printing.

———. *What Is Behind the Word?* New York: Scholastic Books Services, 1964. (Intermediate) Word origins.

Ernst, Margaret S. *In a Word.* New York: Alfred Knopf, 1939. (Intermediate) Word origins; illustrated by James Thurber.

———. *Words.* New York: Alfred Knopf, 1936. (Intermediate) Development of the English language.

———. *Words: English Roots and How They Grew.* New York: Alfred Knopf, 1937. (Intermediate) Origins of English words.

———. *More about Words.* New York: Alfred Knopf, 1951. (Intermediate) An assortment of stories about word origins.

Evans, Bergen. *Comfortable Words.* New York: Random House, 1962. (Intermediate, Advanced) Stories of word origins.

Evans, Bergen, and Evans, Cornelia. *A Dictionary of Contemporary American Usage.* New York: Random House, 1957. (Advanced) Excellent reference and provocative information.

Fadiman, Clifton. *Wally the Wordworm.* New York: The Macmillan Co., 1964. (Primary, Intermediate) Wally's adventures as he eats his way through the dictionary.

Ferguson, Charles. *The Abecedarian Book.* Boston: Little, Brown and Co., 1964. (Intermediate-Advanced) Clever observations about words.

———. *Say It with Words.* Lincoln, Neb.: University of Nebraska Press, 1959. (Advanced)

Folsom, Franklin. *The Language Book.* New York: Grosset and Dunlap, 1963. (Intermediate) Explores all aspects of language development.

Friend, M. Newton. *Words: Tricks and Traditions.* New York: Scribner's Sons, 1957. (Intermediate, Advanced) Collection of facts and information about words.

Funk, Charles. *Heavens to Betsy.* New York: Harper and Row, 1955 (Intermediate) Humorous explanations of curious expressions.

———. *Hog on Ice and Other Curious Expressions.* New York: Harper and Row, 1948. (Intermediate). More about words in our language.

———. *Thereby Hangs a Tale.* New York: Harper and Row, 1950. (Intermediate) Exploration of clichés and idioms of English.

Funk, Charles E. and Funk, Charles E., Jr. *Horsefeathers and Other Curious Words.* New York: Harper and Row, 1958. (Intermediate) Word origins.

Funk, Wilfred. *Word Origins and Their Romantic Stories.* New York: Grosset and Dunlap, 1950. (Intermediate, Advanced) An excellent book about word origins; presents outline of affixes derived from Greek and Latin.

Hansen, Carl F., et al. *A Handbook for Young Writers.* Englewood Cliffs, N.J.: Prentice-Hall, 1965. (Intermediate) Paperback handbook covering grammar and usage.

Hanson, Joan. *Antonyms.* Minneapolis, Minn.: Lerner Publications, 1972. (Primary)

———. *Homographs.* Minneapolis, Minn.: Lerner Publications, 1972. (Primary)

———. *Homonyms.* Minneapolis, Minn.: Lerner Publications, 1972. (Primary)

———. *Synonyms.* Minneapolis, Minn.: Lerner Publications, 1972. (Primary)

Hofsinde, Robert. *Indian Sign Languages.* New York: William Morrow, 1956. (Intermediate) Presents Indian "vocabulary."

———. *Indian Picture Writing.* New York: William Morrow, 1959. (Intermediate) Symbols of Indian language.

Hogben, Lancelot T. *Wonderful World of Communication.* New York: Garden City Books, 1959. (Intermediate, Advanced) History of Communication.

Holt, Alfred H. *Phrase and Word Origins.* New York: Dover, 1961. (Advanced)

Hook, J. N. *The Story of American English.* New York: Harcourt, Brace, 1972. (Advanced)

Hudson, Peggy, comp., *Words to the Wise.* New York: Scholastic Book Services, 1971. (Intermediate)

Hymes, Lucia, and Hymes, James M. *Oodles of Noodles.* Glenview, Ill.: Scott, Foresman, 1964. (Primary) Introduction to word play.

Irwin, Keith G. *The Romance of Writing.* New York: Viking Press, 1957. (Advanced) Early developments of writing.

Jacobs, Frank. *Alvin Steadfast on Vernacular Island.* New York: Dial Press, 1965. (Intermediate)

Johnson, Wendell S. *Words, Things, and Celebrations.* New York: Harcourt, Brace, 1972. (Advanced)

Juster, Norton. *The Phantom Tollbooth.* New York: Epstein and Carroll, dist.

by Random House, 1961. (Intermediate) A fictional context presents many concepts about words and the dictionary.

Kaufman, Joel. *The Golden Happy Book of Words.* Golden Press, 1963. (Primary) Introduces many words.

Laird, Charlton and Laird, Helene. *Tree of Language.* New York: World Publishing Co., 1957. (Intermediate) Development of the English language.

Lambert, Eloise. *Our Language.* New York: Lothrop, Lee and Shepard, 1955. (Intermediate) History of our language.

Lambert, Eloise, and Pei, Mario. *Our Names: Where They Came from and What They Mean.* New York: Lothrop, Lee and Shepard, 1960. (Intermediate) Exploration of names.

Mathews, Milford M. *American Words.* New York: World Publishing Co., 1959. (Intermediate, Advanced) Origins of words.

Merriam, Eve. *A Gaggle of Geese.* New York: Alfred Knopf, 1960. (Primary) Explores unusual words for groups of things.

Moorhouse, Alfred C. *The Triumph of the Alphabet; A History of Writing.* New York: Abelard-Schuman, 1953. (Intermediate, Advanced) The story of writing.

Morris, William, and Morris, Mary. *Dictionary of American Word Origins.* New York: Harper and Row, 1963. (Intermediate, Advanced) Up-to-date words and their origins.

Ogg, Oscar. *The Twenty-Six Letters.* New York: Thomas Y. Crowell, 1948. (Intermediate) History of writing.

O'Neill, Mary. *Words Words Words.* New York: Doubleday, 1966. (Intermediate) Rhymes about words.

Osmond, Edward. *From Drumbeat to Tickertape.* New York: Criterion Books, 1960. (Intermediate) Development of writing and printing techniques.

Partridge, Eric. *A Charm of Words.* Hamilton, 1960. (Intermediate) Stories about words.

Pei, Mario. *All about Language.* Philadelphia, Pa.: J. B. Lippincott, 1954. (Intermediate, Advanced) Development of language.

———. *Our National Heritage.* New York: Houghton Mifflin, 1965. (Intermediate, Advanced) Cultural and linguistic heritage of Americans.

Provensen, Alice, and Provensen, Martin. *Karen's Opposites.* Golden Press, 1963. (Primary) Introduction to antonyms.

Radlauer, Ruth S. *Good Times with Words.* Chicago: Melmont Publishers, 1963. (Intermediate) Using varied words in creative writing.

Rand, Ann, and Rand, Paul. *Sparkle and Spin.* New York: Harcourt, Brace, 1957. (Primary) Enjoying words together; excellent illustrations.

Reid, Alastair. *Ounce, Dice, Trice.* Boston: Little, Brown, and Co., 1958. (Intermediate) Introduction to word play by an imaginative collector of words.

Rogers, Frances. *Painted Rock to Printed Page.* Philadelphia, Pa.: J. B. Lippincott, 1960. (Intermediate) How writing developed from primitive efforts.

Roget, Peter M. *New Roget's Thesaurus of the English Language.* Rev. by Norman Lewis. New York: G. P. Putnam's Sons, 1961. (Intermediate, Advanced) An excellent revised edition of the famous thesaurus.

Rossner, Judith. *What Kind of Feet Does a Bear Have?* Indianapolis, Ind.: Bobbs-Merrill, 1963. (Primary) Introduction to word play.

Russell, Solveig P. *A Is for Apple and Why.* Nashville, Tenn.: Abingdon Press, 1959. (Intermediate) How our alphabet developed.

———. *Peanuts, Popcorn, Ice Cream, Candy, and Soda Pop and How They Began.* Nashville, Tenn.: Abingdon Press, 1970. (Primary-Intermediate)

Sage, Michael. *Words Inside Words.* Philadelphia, Pa.: J. B. Lippincott, 1961. (Intermediate) Stresses enjoyment of words.

Schwartz, Alvin. *A Twister of Twists, a Tangler of Tongues.* Philadelphia, Pa.: J. B. Lippincott, 1972. (Intermediate)

Shipley, Joseph T. *Playing with Words.* Englewood Cliffs, N.J.: Prentice-Hall, 1960. (Intermediate-Advanced) Written for adults; provocative for better students.

———. *Word Games for Play and Power.* Englewood Cliffs, N.J.: Prentice-Hall, 1962. (Intermediate-Advanced) A second book about word play and the fascination of words.

———. *Word Play.* New York: Hawthorne Books, 1972. (Intermediate-Advanced)

Sparke, William. *Story of the English Language.* New York: Abelard-Schuman, 1905. (Intermediate) Interesting stories of the development of the English language.

Vasilu. *The Most Beautiful Word.* New York: The John Day Co., 1970. (Primary)

Waller, Leslie. *Our American Language.* New York: Holt, Rinehart, and Winston, 1960. (Primary) Introduction to the story of English.

White, Mary S. *Word Twins.* Nashville, Tenn.: Abingdon Press, 1961. (Primary) Fun with homonyms.

Wilbur, Richard. *Opposites.* New York: Harcourt, Brace, Jovanovich, 1973. (Intermediate)

Yates, Elizabeth. *Someday You'll Write.* New York: E. P. Dutton, 1962. (Intermediate) Specific information for the young writer on plot development, and the like.

Zim, Herbert S. *Codes and Secret Writing.* New York: Wm. Morrow, 1948. (Intermediate) Fascinating language activity.

The study of language can be exciting, or it can be tedious drill that is boring and meaningless to the student. The choice of how English is to be taught largely belongs to the teacher in each individual classroom. The choice is *yours*. The teacher who is "turned on" to the study of language delights in finding new words and interesting origins, ponders the more abstract ideas of semantics, and wants to share these ideas with the students. If you have nothing to share, how can you teach? Begin by reading some of the books listed in the Students' Linguistic Library. Here are enough ideas to last a lifetime. Your classroom will not be dull when you share your enthusiasm for language with the students you teach.

Books to Investigate

Eisenhardt, Catheryn. *Applying Linguistics in the Teaching of Reading and the Language Arts.* Columbus, Ohio: Charles E. Merrill, 1972.

Fries, Charles C. *Linguistics: The Study of Language.* New York: Holt, Rinehart, and Winston, 1964. Reprint of a chapter from *Linguistics and Reading.*

Hall, Edward T. *The Silent Language.* New York: Fawcett World Library, 1969.

Laird, Charlton. *The Miracle of Language.* New York: World Publishing Co., 1953. Excellent history of English, available in paper edition (Premier).

Lamb, Pose. *Linguistics in Proper Perspective.* Columbus, Ohio: Charles E. Merrill, 1967.

Littell, Joseph Fletcher, ed. *Coping with the Mass Media.* Evanston, Ill.: McDougal, Littell, 1972.

———. *The Language of Man.* Evanston, Ill.: McDougal, Littell, 1971.

Minteer, Catherine et al. *Teacher's Guide to General Semantics.* San Francisco: International Society for General Semantics, 1968.

Opie, Iona and Peter. *The Lore and Language of Schoolchildren.* New York: Oxford University Press, 1967. A fascinating book now in paperback.

Reed, Carroll E. *Dialects of American English.* New York: World Publishing Co., 1967.

Tiedt, Iris M., and Tiedt, Sidney, eds. *Readings on Contemporary English in the Elementary School.* Englewood Cliffs, N.J.: Prentice-Hall, 1967.

Wardhaugh, Ronald. *Reading: A Linguistic Perspective.* New York: Harcourt, Brace, Jovanovich, 1969.

chapter 3: the young child's language

The limits of my language mean the limits of my world.
Ludwig Wittgenstein

"What is this thing called 'Language'?" Language is so much a part of our existence that we are somewhat perplexed to attempt its definition. It is human speech in both written and oral forms, as a dictionary might briefly note, but it is more than that, for language connotes complicated processes of thought for both the speaker and the listener as well as for the writer and the reader. In a society as complex as our own the ramifications of language are extensive, for language is a means for social mobility, and it has become a weapon. The advertiser depends on persuasive powers to convince the buyer, and mass media bombard the individual with language in varied form.

As we ponder the nature of language, we can note characteristics of language. It is human, for it requires more intelligence and more complex vocal equipment than other animals possess. and it is universal. All peoples have developed languages (although not always with a written form), but the languages developed have been diverse, and even those that are clearly related are distinctly different. Language, furthermore, is learned anew by each human child. Language is highly flexible in that the human vocal apparatus is capable of making many more sounds than are ever used, and it is creative. As Barnett observes, "Alone of all creatures on earth, man can say things that have never been said before—and still be understood . . . man has the capacity to create every time he speaks." [1]

Acquisition of Language

How does the young child acquire language? Who teaches children to talk? How do children learn English grammar at such an early age?

Language is a human development, and normally all human babies learn to speak. Lying in their cribs, infants experiment with the physical movements of their bodies. They move their tongues and babble noises into the air. At this stage children make many strange sounds, some of which are not used in the language of their families. Gradually, however, they learn to focus on the sounds around them and to speak the language that they hear daily. They are highly motivated to learn so they keep practicing, talking, talking, talking. No highly trained teachers assist them, nor do we have books entitled *How to Teach Johnny to Talk.*

CHILDREN AND GRAMMAR

We can assume that all children have linguistic competence, the ability to learn language. Noam Chomsky argues that children must have an innate ability to grasp language, which is the only explanation of how they can learn the complex grammar system of a language at such an immature stage. They begin learning this system before the age of one when they are scarcely intellectually developed, and they learn without formal instruction. Children abstract syntactic generalizations, moreover, from a fragmentary, incidental presentation of language. Even dull children learn language, and they learn from children around them, rather than adults.[2]

Children have learned most of the syntax of their native language before entering school, and they have developed a large speaking and listening vocabulary. We can observe their knowledge of grammar through their linguistic performance, and many students of child language have now written grammars of specific young children to demonstrate this cognitive development. What is particularly fascinating about children's acquisition of language, however, is that they develop an approach to learning that is individualized in the truest sense. It is self-motivated and

[1] Lincoln Barnett, *The Treasure of Our Tongue* (New York: Knopf, 1964), p. 70.
[2] Noam Chomsky, "Language and the Mind," *Psychology Today,* February, 1969.

self-designed. Children select what they need from their language environment. They learn through:

real discovery techniques from the language environment
making and correcting their own "errors" or miscues
self-initiated and self-motivated learning
positive reinforcement and encouragement
feedback and expansion by children and adults around them

Notice, particularly, that there is no negative aspect to this early learning program. The child initiates it joyfully, feels successful and secure in learning, and would probably continue to approach learning positively if there were no interference. What happens to this enthusiasm when we adults design the program, select the input, and evaluate progress?

Many students of child language have analyzed the speech of young children to demonstrate the development of linguistic knowledge. Researchers note that dull children tend to lag behind brighter children at various stages—that is, a dull five-year-old may speak much like a bright four-year-old. Children of upper socioeconomic groups tend to develop at faster rates. Boys lag behind girls in development of speech, and children who are multiple births (twins, triplets, the famous quintuplets) tend to be retarded in linguistic development.[3] Excellent summaries of research in the field of child language can be read in the *Encyclopedia of Educational Research,* written by Dorothea McCarthy (1950), John Carroll (1960), and Robert L. Ebel (1969). A one-volume summary of developments in this field is *Child Language: A Book of Readings,* edited by Aaron Bar-Adon and Werner F. Leopold (Prentice-Hall, 1971).

Brown and Bellugi studied the development of syntax in two young children, Adam and Eve. They identified three processes in the children's acquisition of syntax:

imitation and reduction (repeating one or two words)
imitation with expansion (repeating a word or two plus additional idea)
induction of latent structure (demonstrating generalization about grammar)

Adam and Eve began with single word sentences—for example, "Bad." From these holophrases their speech progressed to two-word sentences, such as "See truck." Gradually additional words were added to the child's speech, and more complex syntactic structures appeared.[4] By the age of four, therefore, the child has acquired the basic syntactic structures of

[3] Dorothea McCarthy, "Language Development," in *Encyclopedia of Educational Research,* ed. by W. S. Monroe (New York: The Macmillan Co., 1950), pp. 165–72.

[4] Roger Brown and Ursula Bellugi-Klima, "Three Processes in the Child's Acquisition of Syntax," in *Language and Learning, Harvard Educational Review,* 34: 133–51.

English. McNeill notes that: "On the basis of a fundamental capacity for language, each generation creates language anew, and does so with astonishing speed." [5]

As Chukovsky listened to children's speech, he realized that it was not only fascinating "but also had an intrinsically high instructive value." He observed children's language "to discover the whimsical and elusive laws of childhood thinking." [6] He noted the child's creative use of language and invention of words and concluded that: "If his former talent for word invention and construction had not abandoned him, he would, even by the age of ten, eclipse any of us with his suppleness and brilliance of speech." [7]

Children learn language through hearing the speech of those around them; however, the process used is not imitation per se. The role of imitation in learning language needs clarification because children are not just repeating sentences they hear. Children actually construct a grammar based on the language they hear. They constantly test it by using it, polishing it over a period of years, until it closely approximates adult knowledge of the full syntax of English. What is amazing, furthermore, is that children all around the world learn their native language in much the same way. This fact supports the existence of linguistic universals, characteristics common to all language.[8]

THE LANGUAGE ENVIRONMENT

The language environment is highly influential in determining the quality of a child's linguistic development. Children who have many books and records and to whom stories are read frequently, will naturally develop a richer vocabulary and a greater facility with language than will children living in homes where books are not part of the life style and the language heard is very limited in quality. Parents can make a conscientious effort to provide varied language experiences, and child-care centers and nursery schools should stress the development of language skills in every way possible.

Picture books for children stimulate the child's thinking and broaden the concepts and experiences to which each child is exposed. ABC books, for example, usually contain pictures of various objects that children can enjoy looking at and name verbally. Children enjoy talking about the pic-

[5] David McNeill, "The Creation of Language by Children," in *Child Language*, ed. by Aaron Bar-Adon and Werner F. Leopold (Englewood Cliffs, N.J.: Prentice-Hall, 1971), p. 349.

[6] Kornei Chukovsky, *From Two to Five* (Berkeley, Calif.: University of California Press, 1966), p. xv.

[7] *Ibid.*, p. 7.

[8] McNeill, "The Creation of Language by Children," p. 350.

tures, especially if an interested adult or big brother is listening and will join in the commentary.

Reading aloud to children provides them with a richer environment from which to select for their own needs. As stories are repeated, the delighted children will "read" familiar phrases with the adult reader. "You wicked old rascal!" became a favorite line for all of us as we read "Little Red Riding Hood," and our daughter knew exactly when that phrase appeared in the sequence of the story.

Even at this young age children are beginning to collect their own libraries. It is during these years that attitudes toward reading and love of books will develop, but obviously adult attitudes are highly influential. It is the adult who takes the child to the library, points out the children's section, and leaves the child to browse and to make selections. It is the adult who buys books as gifts for children.

UNDERSTANDING CHILDREN

Have you ever really thought about the feelings of the young child who struggles to exist in our adult world? "As busy, pre-occupied adults we sometimes fail to realize the enormity of the perplexities which face children, perplexities which may never occur to us. Is childhood more complex than we adults can fathom?" [9]

It is truly difficult to understand the psychological development of children. We observe behaviors; we listen to speech; we question children—thus we obtain some information. Another fascinating means for gaining further insight into the development of children, however, is through reading literature written by skilled authors. James Agee's sensitive novel, *A Death in the Family,* for example, gives us insight into a child's reaction to the death of his father. All alone in his father's study, Rufus thinks:

> He has already been dead since way last night and I didn't even know it until I woke up. He has been dead all night while I was asleep and now it is morning and I am awake but he is still dead. . . .[10]

Frank O'Connor has written several short stories that reveal the young child's way of coping with the world. Five-year-old Larry, for example, has trouble adjusting to the return of his father after the war is over. He finds that his mother doesn't pay as much attention to him and tells him

[9] Sidney W. Tiedt and Iris M. Tiedt, "Secret World of Children," *Childhood Education* (February, 1968), pp. 363–65.

[10] James Agee, *A Death in the Family* (New York: Grosset and Dunlap, 1957).

to be quiet because she is "talking to Daddy." Naturally Larry resents this intruder and comments:

> At teatime, "talking to Daddy" began again, complicated this time by the fact that he had an evening paper, and every few minutes he put it down and told Mother something new out of it. I felt this was foul play. Man for man, I was prepared to compete with him any time for Mother's attention, but when he had it all made up for him by other people it left me no chance. Several times I tried to change the subject without success.[11]

Other selections can be discovered by referring to annotated bibliographies that list fiction appropriate for this purpose. The following titles will be helpful:

Landau, Elliott D. et al., eds. *Child Development through Literature.* Englewood Cliffs, N.J.: Prentice-Hall, Inc., 1972.

Tiedt, Iris M. and Tiedt, Sidney W. *Unrequired Reading,* 2d ed. Corvallis, Ore.: Oregon State University Press, 1967.

Contemporary Influences on Early Childhood Education

There have been several major influences on early childhood education which we should explore. We shall consider the contributions of Jean Piaget and Maria Montessori related to education of the young child. Another major influence that cannot be ignored is that of the British Primary Schools, which is not the work of a single individual, but rather represents a philosophy as well as important concepts in methodology.

JEAN PIAGET

The Swiss philosopher, Piaget, and his followers have attempted to describe the child's cognitive development. One of Piaget's major works, first published in French in 1926, is *Language and Thought of the Child* (available in a paperback edition from Routledge and Kegan Paul.) In this volume, Piaget explores the function of language for the child which appears to be composed of two elements: (1) the subjective element focused on the child's needs and desires, and (2) the social element that is more objective and concerned with the reality of the environment around the child. The young child is most concerned with the first ele-

[11] Frank O'Connor, "My Oedipus Complex," in *Child Language Development Through Literature,* ed. by Elliott D. Landau et al. (Englewood Cliffs, N.J.: Prentice-Hall, 1972).

ment, but gradually the second element imposes itself on the child's awareness.[12]

Piaget has clarified knowledge about the *quality* of the child's thinking, which he feels is more important than *quantity*. The child's intelligence undergoes a gradual change in character that has been observed by this psychologist-philosopher through the *methode clinique* (clinical method). Piaget observed children's use of language and their thinking by letting them talk while he observed the way their thoughts unfolded. He categorizes child language into the ego-centric and the socialized, which can be broken down as follows:

EGO-CENTRIC SPEECH

1 Repetition—sheer pleasure in talking, repeating sounds
2 Monologue—talking to themselves with no expectation of a listener
3 Dual or collective monologue—conversations between children which do not really involve the other person

SOCIALIZED SPEECH

1 Adapted information—telling someone else something that will interest that listener
2 Criticism—observations about behavior of others to specific audience
3 Commands, requests, threats—interaction between two children
4 Questions—call for an answer
5 Answers—replies to questions or commands[13]

The child begins with almost totally ego-centric speech, but gradually learns to operate with socialized speech. As Piaget notes:

> . . . for the understanding of other people as well as for the understanding of the outside world, two conditions are necessary: (1) consciousness of oneself as a subject, and the ability to detach subject from object so as not to attribute to the second the characteristics of the first; (2) to cease to look upon one's own point of view as the only possible one, and to co-ordinate it with that of others.[14]

This analysis of language development reflects the whole of cognitive development. Piaget categorizes child behavior in these developmental stages:

1 Sensory-motor stage (birth-two years)

[12] Jean Piaget, *Language and Thought of the Child,* trans. Marjorie and Ruth Gabin (London: Routledge and Kegan Paul, 1960), pp. 1–49.
[13] *Ibid.,* pp. 9–10.
[14] *Ibid.,* p. 277.

2 Preoperational thought stage (two-seven years)
3 Concrete operational stage (seven-eleven years)
4 Formal operational stage (eleven plus years)

During the sensory-motor stage, the child discovers objects in the environment. One significant concept that is developed at this stage is that objects do not cease to exist just because they are out of sight. Another concept is that of identity—that is, orange juice is orange juice whether it is in a bottle or a cup, and Mother is Mother no matter how she changes her attire.

The preoperational stage is characterized by rapid language development so that the child is no longer limited to motor activity. The child's thinking at this time, however, is limited by maturation or understanding. Piaget identified, for example:

animism—attributing life to an inanimate object that may move (leaves floating on water)
problem in conservation—child thinks a cup of water is more if it is in tall, thin bottle than when placed in wider jar
artificialism—everything was made by men for their own purposes
realism—dreams are real happenings

During the stage of concrete operation, the child develops logical thinking and learns to classify or categorize objects. Children develop abilities to recognize equivalence and can work with the concept of conservation which causes difficulty at the preoperational stage. They learn to reverse processes and to work with the principle of associativity.

MARIA MONTESSORI

Maria Montessori worked with retarded children in Rome around 1900. The first woman ever to receive the doctor of medicine in Italy, she applied her efforts to improve the education of ghetto children in Rome. She developed the concept that the learning environment had much to do with the effectiveness of learning and teaching. The Montessori method depends primarily, therefore, on the "prepared environment," which is designed to develop each child's fullest potential.[15]

The typical Montessori classroom is characterized by much child interaction and learning through discovery. The program focuses on:

Motor education
Sensory education
Language education

[15] Maria Montessori, *The Montessori Method* (New York: Schocken Books, 1964).

The three- and four-year-olds learn many basic skills through play activities selected to develop functional motor abilities. A variety of exercises are available to stimulate sensory awareness and discrimination among textures and forms. Visual and auditory training are provided as the child learns abilities of naming, recognition or identifying, and pronunciation or responding.

Gradually, as the child matures, activities focus more directly on writing, reading, and arithmetic. The child learns to associate the visual, tactile, and auditory impressions of the letters of the alphabet. Then, short words are learned. At the same time children are introduced to sets in mathematics through the use of colored rods and beads.

A concept that is essential to the Montessori Method is the Golden Rule, for throughout the program stress is placed on respect for the individual. The individual child is permitted much freedom of action, but at the same time the interests of the collective are protected. The child learns through discovery or inductive methods as opposed to deductive, teacher-controlled input.

Observations at a Montessori school are well worthwhile. Typical activities that are available at various Learning Centers in the large open classroom are the following:

Weighing and measuring
Counting objects
Listening to recorded stories
Painting
Working with clay
Learning to buckle, button, and zip
Cleaning or washing processes
Group exercises, following directions

Although children are operating as individuals throughout the classroom, there is no impression of noise or undisciplined behavior. A schedule is followed, and there is a sense of purpose and industry in the children's activities. Teachers and aides move about the classroom to serve as resources and to give assistance where needed. At times they conduct specific directed activities such as exercises or reading aloud to a circle of children.

BRITISH INFANT SCHOOLS

A third strong influence on early childhood education is the informal education typical of British infant (kindergarten-primary) schools and junior (elementary) schools. The Plowden Report, published in 1967, surveyed the needs of education of the young child in England and made definite proposals for specific changes.

Featherstone and others have observed the "tradition of revolution" which has developed in English schools.[16] This revolution is seen as:

1 encouraging innovation in curriculum development;
2 decreasing evaluation by government officials;
3 incorporating theories from developmental psychology, particularly that of Piaget, on how children learn.

L. G. W. Sealey, who reported on the Leicestershire County Schools in 1966, noted a number of characteristics of this informal education. One basic concept is the "integrated day" which eliminates scheduled blocks of time for specified activities. Learning takes place in Learning Centers that may focus on (1) reading and the language arts, (2) science and mathematics, (3) visual arts, and (4) general purpose activities. Learning is child centered, not teacher dominated. The child is expected to synthesize his or her own learnings in an atmosphere that encourages experimentation and exploration of immediate interests.

A second characteristic of this approach to education is the use of *vertical groupings,* which is sometimes referred to as "family grouping." This means that children are not classified in any way; they are not grouped by age, intelligence, or sex. The children group themselves by interests and mutual concerns.[17]

There is no emphasis on evaluation of academic achievement. It is considered more important that children grow in terms of self-motivation and discipline than that they be measured for knowledge of specific skills determined by the teacher. Nor is work clearly distinguished from play, for it is recognized that what adults might term "play" is actually meaningful learning for the child and, as such, is clearly not a "waste of time."

SUMMARY

In assessing these influences on early childhood education today, it is interesting to note the interrelationships among the theories and philosophies represented. Certainly there is a feeling of child-centeredness throughout, a way of thinking that is not entirely new in elementary education.

Elkind has pointed out related issues in the theories of Piaget and

[16] Joseph Featherstone, "Schools for Children," *The New Republic* (August 19, 1967), pp. 17–21.

[17] L. G. W. Sealey, "Looking Back on Leicestershire," *ESI Quarterly Report* (Spring-Summer, 1966), pp. 37–41.

Montessori. Both, he notes, see the duality of the nature-nurture relationship. In dealing with mental capacities, nature is dominant and nurture is subordinate. In dealing with content of thought, the emphasis reverses itself, with nurture dominating nature. Both of these writers recognize that mental capacity limits learning at any developmental stage. And, they both see the relationship between cognitive need and repetitive behavior. The latter may signal the development of a new cognitive element which is encouraged to grow through more repetitive behavior.[18]

The concepts represented in the Montessori schools and the British infant schools are also similar in nature. They are not unlike concepts proposed by writers who urge the use of methodologies that encourage creativity—the accepting classroom environment, use of discovery or inquiry thinking, and stress on divergent thinking as contrasted to convergent thinking (See Chapter 7). Ideas concerning evaluation of creative writing, the use of Learning Centers, and individualized approaches to instruction have permeated the literature for some time. There is, however, a distinctively new thrust in education in the seventies, which focuses more directly on individual growth.

School Language Programs

It is becoming increasingly common for young children to attend organized schools at the ages of three and four, even if only for two or three mornings per week. Almost all children enter kindergarten at the age of five and continue into first grade at age six. The number of years the child is in school, therefore, is increasing by beginning earlier.

NURSERY SCHOOLS

Compared to kindergarten education, the nursery school is a contemporary development. The first nursery schools appeared in the United States around 1920, but it was not until the 1960s that hundreds of thousands of children were enrolled in these schools across the nation. Nursery schools have sprung up on college and university campuses sponsored by early childhood education programs or in private homes or churches where parents volunteer for specified amounts of time as teachers. The quality and characteristics of these schools and their programs vary widely.

The Bank Street College of Education in New York City conducts perhaps the best known preschool program.[19] With the chief aim being to

[18] David Elkind, "Piaget and Montessori," *Harvard Educational Review* (Fall, 1966), pp. 535–45.

[19] Elizabeth C. Gilkeson, *Bank Street Approach to Follow Through* (New York: Bank Street College of Education, 1969).

develop positive self-concepts for each individual child, the learning environment is designed to promote social and emotional growth. This program stresses discovery learning through play activities. It also emphasizes language development through stimulating experiences common to the group—for example, pets in the classroom. It is not unlike the Montessori approach or that used in British infant schools.

Providing topics about which the child can talk is important, for the child's background may be limited. Varied experiences lead to vocabulary and concept development as the child seeks out the needed words to talk about something he or she has seen or done. Experiences which are common to the whole group stimulate conversation both in and out of the classroom. We can talk about:

1 *Pictures* are excellent, easily obtained sources of speech stimulators which can be used in a variety of ways:

Give children pictures about which they say a few sentences as they show the pictures to the other children. These pictures can be smaller than others.

Fasten one large picture on the bulletin board so that a small group can talk about it. They can ask questions about the pictured activity or answer questions asked by the teacher or an aide. The group can compose a story which the teacher records on tape or prints on a chart.

A listening activity can require the child to point to something in the picture as the teacher says:
"Can you find something yellow, Anabel?"
"Where is the big German Shepherd, Joey?"
"Is there a kitten in the picture, Bill?"

2 *Classroom experiences* can be planned to stimulate talking, for example:

An animal brought to the classroom can stimulate talking, and the children can dictate a story to the teacher.

Tommy, the hamster, is visiting our classroom.
He likes to run and play.
He eats seeds and carrots.

Eating an interesting food is exciting. Try fortune cookies, crisp Chinese noodles, or pretzels.

Recorded stories provide food for conversation, for instance, Kenneth Grahame's *The Reluctant Dragon* read by Boris Karloff or Carl Sandburg's reading of his *Rootabaga Stories* (both from Caedmon, distributed by Houghton Mifflin Co., 53 W. 43rd St., New York 10036).

3 *Field experiences* take the children out of the classroom to visit or observe things farther afield. Change in environment helps provide talking topics. Experiences might include:

Nature walks in a nearby park or around the neighborhood to make DIS-

COVERIES. Children might be directed to see how many different animals they can see on this Discovery Walk or they could notice specifically all the different SOUNDS heard.

A trip to the library serves to acquaint the children with the location of the library and to give them a chance to go inside for a Book Talk with the Children's Librarian.

Trips can be planned to varied facilities available in most areas:

Post Office
Fire Station
A museum or zoo
Airports, bus or train stations
A beach, the wharf

4 *Filmed materials* can present many interesting topics in the classroom. The short film or filmstrip, as well as slides, is useful in working with small groups who are encouraged to react to the pictures presented.

An interesting film is the wordless story, *The Hunter in the Forest* (Encyclopaedia Britannica Film Co.) which uses fine camera work to portray a sensitive story which can be discussed. The story can be told by the children.

The teacher who is aiming at developing linguistic fluency must plan a program that provides many opportunities for the *child* to talk, for our elementary school classrooms are more typically dominated by teacher talking. We can emphasize the use of oral language by:

1 Forgetting the desire for a quiet classroom
2 Encouraging children to ask questions and to react to classroom experiences
3 Using language laboratory equipment that involves listening and speaking activities
4 Working with small groups so that proportionately more children can speak at any one time
5 Planning for a high percentage of classroom time to be devoted to oral language

KINDERGARTEN

There has long been a controversy over the curriculum most appropriate for children in kindergarten. Should there be a formal program of instruction that includes "reading readiness" and encourages able children to begin reading and writing? Or, should kindergarten be reserved for congenial experiences and socialization?

We see no reason for enforcing the need to choose one focus over the other, for a kindergarten program should stress individual development. An individualized program will provide for the less mature child who needs much development at the experiential level. It must at the same time consider the needs of the more mature child who is intellectually ready to work with sounds and printed symbols and to begin reading and writing. There seems to be little reason to literally "hold back" the child who is ready to move to a more advanced level of stimulating and relevant achievement.

A strong emphasis in any kindergarten program will be on language experiences as children develop linguistic fluency. Fluency in using English can be achieved through (1) developing the child's desire to talk, (2) supplying topics for discussion, and (3) providing many opportunities for speaking.

How do we stimulate the kindergarten child to talk? There are many techniques which may prove successful, and we shall experiment with a variety of methods, for different children respond to different types of stimuli.

1 Humor tends to lend warmth to the classroom atmosphere. The teacher who laughs with the class will certainly break down barriers of reserve as children respond.

HUMOROUS POETRY. Have children paint pictures of strange animals they might imagine after thinking of "The Purple Cow."

I never saw a purple cow;
I never hope to see one:
But I can tell you anyhow
I'd rather see than be one.
GELETT BURGESS

Use a flannel board to present figures from the anonymous repetitive poem, "There Was An Old Woman." Keep it simple at first with only a few animals, but add others as the class becomes familiar with speaking together.

There was an old woman who swallowed a fly.

Class: Oh, my! Swallowed a fly?
Poor old woman, I think she'll die!
There was an old woman who swallowed a bird;
That's what I heard; she swallowed a bird!

Class: She swallowed the bird to kill the fly;
Oh, my! Swallowed a fly?
Poor old woman, I think she'll die!
There was an old woman who swallowed a cat;
Think of that, she swallowed a cat!

Class: She swallowed the cat to kill the bird;
She swallowed the bird to kill the fly;
Oh, my! Swallowed a fly?
Poor old woman, I think she'll die!

There was an old woman who swallowed a dog;
Jiggety, jog, she swallowed a dog!

Class: She swallowed the dog to kill the cat;
She swallowed the cat to kill the bird;
She swallowed the bird to kill the fly;
Oh, my! Swallowed a fly?
Poor old woman, I think she'll die!

(Other verses may be invented.)
There was an old woman who swallowed a horse!

Class (quickly): She died, of course!

STORIES THAT ARE READ ALOUD. Read stories aloud, showing the illustrations, explaining a word casually so children can understand, talking about the story and its characters.

The Fast Sooner Hound, by Arna Bontemps and Jack Conroy.
Slappy Hooper, the Wonderful Sign Painter, by Arna Bontemps and Jack Conroy.
Mr. Popper's Penguins, by Richard and Florence Atwater.
Freddy the Detective, by Walter Brooks.

Use finger puppets to encourage children to retell the stories heard, allowing free translation of the content. While several children manipulate puppets, the others supply guides to the development of the dialogue. What happened next? What do you think Mr. Popper might have said? In this way the whole of a small group participates. Audience and puppeteer roles rotate frequently.

JOKES AND RIDDLES. Tell simple jokes and riddles. Encourage children to tell riddles that they know, and print some on the board, for children are intrigued by seeing something they told in print and will be interested in reading it, for example:

What did the wallpaper say to the wall?
"I've got you covered!"

See: *Book of Laughs* by Bennett Cerf.
Riddles, Riddles, Riddles by Joseph Leeming.

2 Curiosity is natural to the child and can be useful in motivating speech.

CAN YOU GUESS? The teacher hides a familiar object (or a picture of one), saying, "I have something you can't see. Can you guess? It starts with *b*. Tell me words that begin with *b* like *box, boy*, and *boom*."

This activity can be varied to stress different learning experiences which require both listening and speaking, thus:

"I have something that sounds like (rhymes with) *ball*." (doll)
"I have something your mother uses in the kitchen." (pan)
Children can be guided to supply patterned responses, thus:

Is it a book? (All children will use this form for practice.)
Do you have a book? Do you have a pencil? Do you have . . .
I think it is a book. I think it is a pencil. I think it is a . . .

WHAT HAPPENED NEXT? Read a simple short story, stopping to ask, "What do you think happened next?" "Did Jack get caught by the giant, Bill?" "How did he get away, Mary?" Elicit many responses before reading the ending of the story.

THE TAPE RECORDER is a fascinating machine which arouses the curiosity of all children. A child who is usually reluctant about speaking will pay for the privilege of running the machine by asking the children questions or simply calling each child to come record a story. Again, the teacher can supply patterns, thus:

It's your turn now, Jane.
Please, come tell your story now, Jane.

What color is this book, Jane?
What color is this table, Nick?
What color is this paper, Susan?

3 Emphasize the game-like qualities of any learning experience.

WHO HAS A SENTENCE? Display a large picture before the group as you ask, "Who has a sentence about this picture?" A picture of a boy and his dog might elicit this type of response:

The dog is big.
The boy likes the dog.
The boy and his dog are running.

The teacher can print each sentence on an experience chart to lend importance to the composed sentences and to provide orientation to words and reading.

SINGING GAMES AND SONGS add to the enjoyment of speaking as words are repeated with relative ease. After hearing this song a few times, children will be able to supply the rhymed words and soon they can sing the whole song:

Hush little baby, don't say a word;

Mama's gonna buy you a ___________ (mocking bird).
And if that mocking bird won't sing,

Mama's gonna buy you a ___________ (diamond ring).
And if that diamond ring turns brass,

Mama's gonna buy you a ___________ (looking glass).
And if that looking glass gets broke,

Mama's gonna buy you a ___________ (Billy goat).
And if that Billy goat won't pull,

Mama's gonna buy you a ___________ (cart and bull).
And if that cart and bull turns over,

Mama's gonna buy you a dog named ___________ (Rover).
And if that dog named Rover won't bark,

Mama's gonna buy you a ___________ (horse and cart).
And if that horse and cart breaks down,

You'll still be the nicest boy (class) in town.

Other songs which offer excellent language practice include:

"Old MacDonald Had a Farm"
"The Farmer in the Dell'
"Go Tell Aunt Rhody"
"Are You Sleeping?"

An enjoyable record which combines words and motions is "The Hokey Pokey" which emphasizes Right and Left concepts and the parts of the body (Methodist Publishing House, 810 Broadway, Nashville, Tenn.).

Another interesting record is *Call and Response; Rhythmic Group Singing* by Ella Jenkins with children and instruments (Folkways/Scholastic Records, 906 Sylvan Ave., Englewood Cliffs, N.J. 07632).

BEGINNING COMPOSITION EXPERIENCES

In conjunction with listening and speaking activities the teacher consistently introduces the children to printed words as they dictate stories, list things seen, hear words in stories, and so forth. As their interest in classroom experiences gradually develops, many children will be ready to learn to print and to begin writing words and sentences independently. The advantages of working with small groups is again apparent, for one group may be moving much more quickly than are others; they will begin composing sentences and short stories which may form the basis of their first reading experiences.

Early experiences in composition will not emphasize grammar or spelling, but will focus on the thrill of recording an idea so that others can also share it. Beginning experiments will continue to stress the development of positive attitudes toward learning and feelings of success as a young writer. The chapters on Creativity and Creative Writing contain many suggestions which would work well with the young child, but here are a few we have selected as being especially suitable for these children.

Writing grows from talking After a discussion about a picture that the group is viewing, everyone will have many ideas that can be recorded. Let each write a word, a phrase, or a sentence or two which can be mounted on strips beside the picture. Children can "read" their own contributions.

Children enjoy rhymes Again, begin orally with rhyming experiences as you give a word and the child says one that sounds alike. Then you can give a word (choose one which has many rhymes) and print it on the board. Ask who could print a rhyming word—read challenge! Ignore misspellings at this stage.

After children are familiar with the making of rhymes, you can supply a short line, "Today the sun is hot," while they venture to supply a rhyming line, "Hunt for a shady spot." The poems produced should be printed on cards (by the teacher if necessary) for display and later taken home to share with parents.

Children can write their own experience stories Instead of dictating experiences to the teacher, these children will be able to write sentences to contribute to a group composition and gradually will write a story of several sentences independently. A group BOOK OF STORIES can be compiled.

Imaginative literature inspires writing Children often like to write their responses to a story they have enjoyed hearing or seeing on film. Again, these commentaries will grow from one sentence to a paragraph or more as abilities develop.

Children can write free verse and cinquains As children respond more freely to new experiences, they can be guided toward the writing of simple poetry. Group compositions are effective first steps toward individual writings. The month or season provides a topic familiar to all, for example, WINTER. The group talks about winter, the things they do, how it differs from other seasons; pictures may be shown. Then ideas are recorded by the teacher who prints them in poetry form, thus:

WINTER . . .
Snow falls on the street.
Children throw snowballs.
There is ice on the puddles.

The Cinquain *(Sánken)*, a five-line, unrhymed poem, is a poetry form which primary children find easy to follow as the emphasis is on words or syllables: Here is an example written on the same topic:

WINTER–	(One word; the subject)
Snow falling;	(Two words about subject)
Slipping, sliding, tumbling.	(Three words describing action)
Snowball fights and sleds–	(Four words; a feeling)
DECEMBER	(One word refers to subject)

READING AND LITERATURE

As Loban notes, "Schools are beginning to be aware that research shows a powerful linkage between oral language and writing or reading—one much greater than has previously been realized." [20] Although the strategies already presented do not involve direct instruction in reading, we have scarcely been ignoring reading skills; emphasizing the development of fluency in English, vocabulary growth, listening for auditory discrimination, and awareness of words are all preparing the child to read. Efforts to develop positive attitudes toward school and learning will serve to ensure the child's willingness to "try reading."

As with composition, reading is introduced as part of the total language experience. There is no traumatic moment when we suddenly begin to read, for experiences with language entice the children to begin reading as they begin writing. The teacher simply takes more time to talk about words, to see that more words are placed before the children and that they have opportunity to use them. Word cards become part of oral and written language experiences, and the child is encouraged to voice ideas, write them, and read them. Small group work continues to

[20] Walter Loban, "Oral Language Proficiency Affects Reading and Writing," *Instructor* (March, 1966), p. 97.

facilitate assistance of individual growth as children begin to read selections from literature that they, in many cases, will have already heard or viewed—for example, Ezra Jack Keats's *Snowy Day* (film from Weston Woods).

The Listening Center is extended to include books, and the children read along while they listen to the sentences read by an adult voice. They can "listen-read" the same story several times and can try to read the story themselves with assistance as needed. When they feel confident about ability to read that story, the book goes home to be read to anybody who will listen. Thus, through the experience-literature method, the child has learned to read with confidence and enjoyment. All children require now is the availability of more good books and guidance and assistance from the teacher or aide.

Another aspect of literature for young children is literature as a means of understanding themselves. Gradually, children's literature is reflecting concepts which society is beginning to acknowledge—all children are not white, not all families live in lovely suburban settings, few people speak standard English *all* the time. (Don't you sometimes say, "Yeah," "Whacha doin'?" "What got inta him?" and so on?) great effort is being made toward further understanding of minority groups (even by members of the groups themselves) by including titles which present a more realistic view of life. An excellent resource for this aspect of literature is *Reading Ladders for Human Relations*, edited by Virginia Reid and published by National Council of Teachers of English, 1111 Kenyon Road, Urbana, Illinois 61801.

Compensatory Education

The problem of compensatory education for the economically deprived child focuses on the alleviation of language impoverishment. The Head Start preschool programs have aimed at providing rich language environments that are designed to better prepare children for school.

What is deprivation? Is it synonymous with poverty? Is it always found in slums? Deprivation, or disadvantage, whichever term you prefer, connotes more than poverty alone, and it entails more than mere residence in a slum. The disadvantaged person, equated with no single ethnic or racial group, has been bypassed by the benefits which the average American has come to assume as a right, the American way of living; and this disadvantage usually has been accorded through no person's fault. Born in an economically depressed locality, a worker whose job disappears through automation, a migrant worker dependent on the vagaries of the crops, a small farmer striving to exist on exhausted land—these are disadvantaged members of our society who exist on substandard incomes. What chance do children born into these families have to obtain what for most of us are the necessities of life?

FACTORS FOCUSING ATTENTION ON THE PROBLEM

Poor people have always existed in our society. The slums have not sprung up overnight nor is deprivation a condition that is completely new to us (although the term may be). Why then are we suddenly concerned about deprivation and the needs of the disadvantaged child? A number of factors account for our unprecedented national concern for assisting disadvantaged Americans: (1) the unconscionable contrast between affluence and poverty, (2) civil rights activities, (3) high cost to the nation, (4) increasing numbers of unemployables, and (5) our national prestige.

The contrast between the impressive affluence of the majority of American citizens and the poverty-stricken, hopeless condition which is the present lot of others is difficult to justify. Americans are typically pictured as affluent individuals who might be described thus:

> They drive one or more cars, watch one or more television sets, own one or more telephones. They have added freezers to their refrigerators, automatic dryers to their automatic washers, swimming pools to their backyards, air conditioners to their homes and cars; and they have more time than ever to switch off the appliances and get away from it all.[21]

But is this image the picture for all Americans? No, for in the midst of apparent national wealth there still exist "pockets of poverty" whose depth is appalling when contrasted to the lives of middle-class Americans. The Bureau of the Census report in 1970 included the following depressing statistics:

> The median income for all families was $9870.
> The median income of non-white races was $6520.
> Of the 51.9 million families in the U.S., 8.9%, or approximately 4.6 million families, received incomes below $3000.
> 5.3 million families had incomes between $3000 and $5000 per year.
> 6.1 million, or 11.8%, had incomes between $5000 and $7000.

It is estimated that approximately one eighth of the United States' population was living in poverty in 1971. "These," states the Shriver Report, "are the people behind the American looking glass. Being poor is

[21] *The War on Poverty,* A Congressional presentation under the direction of Sargent Shriver, March 17, 1964.

not a choice for them; it is a rigid way of life. It has been handed down from generation to generation in a cycle of inadequate education, inadequate homes, inadequate jobs and stunted ambitions."

A second influential factor, the civil rights movement, has focused national attention on the plight of the black. Studies find that the black has been hardest hit by poverty, for the long history of racial discrimination, segregated educational facilities, and limited political representation has made the black truly a "second-class citizen" who has traditionally been "hired last, paid less, and fired first." One study reports that in 1963 nearly one-half of the American black population (8 million individuals) lived in families with less than $3,000 annual income.[22] It is small wonder that black Americans have at last revolted on a large scale. The increasingly responsive federal government has assumed a leading role in bettering educational facilities, assuring voting rights, and generally upgrading the status of this racial group as well as that of other submerged segments of society.

A third, highly practical, factor which has led to national concern for alleviating deprivation is the extremely high cost to the nation as a whole. The Department of Labor provides statistics relevant to the cost of unemployment to the nation. To maintain only one unemployed person through a lifetime, for example, can cost the nation a minimum of $40,000. Our annual bill for public assistance in 1963 (excluding costs of side effects leading to crime and delinquency) was $6 billion. It is pointed out, on the other hand, that full employment of the black portion of the labor force alone would add potentially $13 to $17 billion annually to the Gross National Product.

A fourth factor is that many of those who are unemployed are actually "unemployable." What is the high school drop-out prepared to do to earn a living? When our society permits the sixteen-year-old to leave school, untrained, unprepared to lead a useful life, we must immediately assume financial responsibility for maintaining this person. We can easily recognize the dollar and cents value of reaching each child long before the drop-out age. This need is further dramatized by the large number of draftees who are rejected on a literacy basis. It is incredible that illiteracy should exist in our society with its highly developed system of education.

Another factor which has placed the spotlight on the deprived fifth of the nation is our struggle for prestige in the eyes of the world. We are highly conscious, for example, of the disapproval of other nations as they view our treatment of the black. Extreme poverty contrasted to general affluence is also difficult to justify to a critical world. Even more pressing,

22 Vivian W. Henderson, *The Economic Status of the Negroes in the South* (Atlanta, Ga.: Southern Regional Council of Churches, 1963).

however, is the undeniable need in our complex industrialized society for a national labor force that is highly literate and capable of learning continuously so that we can continue to progress at top-level efficiency. It is imperative that all resources be explored and developed to the fullest potential.

WHO IS THE ECONOMICALLY DISADVANTAGED CHILD?

The disadvantaged child may be a Mexican-American boy living in California, an American Indian on a Utah reservation, a poor white from Appalachia, a Puerto Rican girl living in New York City or a black living along South State Street in Chicago. The point is that economic disadvantage is limited to no particular racial or ethnic group nor to any special locality; it is spread literally across our nation, for it is present in every city, in most small towns, and in many rural areas.

As Richard Corbin states in the excellent report published by the National Council of Teachers of English:

> Whatever the racial or ethnic background of these disadvantaged, their circumstances are much the same. They come from families that exist on annual incomes which fall below the established national minimum subsistence level, that have known little or no schooling, that have no job security. More than half have only one parent (generally the mother), and many have never known either parent. They come from families who seldom aspire, or when they do, aspire unrealistically, who are often idle because few jobs are open to them. They are the people who exist—one can hardly say "live"—on the wretched rim of an otherwise affluent world. And they number not fewer than one quarter of our total national population.[23]

Studies have identified certain characteristics which are typical of children of all ages who are classified as deprived or disadvantaged. The typical economically disadvantaged child can be described thus:

1 Lacks self-confidence. Insecurity may cause unruly behavior in the classroom or juvenile delinquency. Attitude toward self and possibilities for success in life is negative. Feels that others view him as "a worthless individual." Racial discrimination has accentuated the poor self-image for the black child. The disadvantaged child is afraid, ill at ease in the school situation. Lacks the security of a stable home. Frequently moves and has little opportunity to develop friendships.

[23] Richard Corbin, "Literacy, Literature, and the Disadvantaged," in *Language Programs for the Disadvantaged* (Urbana, Ill.: National Council of Teachers of English, 1965), p. 6.

2 The home does not provide educational stimulus. The family is economically poor as well as educationally impoverished. Money is not available for books, magazines, or the daily newspaper; and even were money available, there is little desire for spending it in this way. More likely, money would be used to buy entertainment, food, or clothing. Paper, pencils, and crayons are not available in the home, nor are varied toys to stimulate play. There is no precedent for obtaining an education, as parents and grandparents have had little formal schooling. A college degree or even a high school diploma is beyond the aspirations of this child. There may be hostility toward teachers and the school, with the latter viewed as a jail and the teacher as jailer. The child may enter school already looking forward to dropping out. The experiential background of this child is limited with little opportunity to travel, to be read to, to visit museums, or to explore the world in general.

3 Not physically well cared for, and in many cases undernourished. The child shows evidence of neglected illness and may have physical handicaps that need attention. Regular visits to the dentist have not been made, and the child's eyes have not been checked. Lack of parental supervision and adequate sleeping facilities may mean this child will come to school tired and may arrive hungry, having had no breakfast.

4 Language skills are impoverished. The speech heard at home is meager with little elaboration. Mother directs the child's activities by single-word commands, saying "Here," to the young girl to whom she hands the baby. She does not elaborate as a more educated person tends to, "Here; hold Manny while I start peeling the potatoes for dinner. He keeps crawling under my feet, and I'm afraid I'll step on him." The working mother, who herself may not be physically well, is tired and is preoccupied by providing the essentials—food, beds, clothes, a roof overhead. Although there may be many people living in the same apartment, the extent of the vocabulary to which the child is exposed is actually small, and no one has time to sit talking to a child about games or to tell stories nor is the child particularly encouraged to talk. The child is left largely alone, often having little contact with the English language, especially in its standard dialects. Mexican-Americans or Puerto Rican children may have the further disadvantage of not speaking English at all or of living in a home where English is not usually spoken. The English that this child learns is only that heard on the street. Proficient in neither language, entrance in elementary school requires the learning of English, therefore, as a foreign language for these children, who must become bilingual.

Our focus as teachers is not on the broad social problem of deprivation, however, but on helping the child who is the victim of deprivation; even more specifically, our concern in this book is for instruction in English as one part of the elementary school curriculum. In order to plan a program designed to aid the child in developing language skills, it is first necessary to determine the needs.

NEEDS OF THE DEPRIVED CHILD

The needs of the deprived child are varied, and they include more than academic knowledge, for this child comes to school psychologically handicapped, a factor which impedes learning. The objectives of any program for compensatory education must be cognizant of the child's need to develop:

1 Language skills: thinking, listening, speaking, writing, reading (in the order named)
2 Feeling of personal worth; confidence in ability to succeed
3 Recognition of school as pleasant and learning as pleasurable
4 Enthusiasm and interest in environment; wide experimental background
5 Interest in others and respect for them; ability to work and play with others

These skills, attitudes, and abilities are largely assumed to be part of a child's preschool development, and in a home in which the parents are concerned about the needs of the child and make a concerted effort to provide stimulating experiences for the child, it is probable that a foundation will have been built before entrance in school. The child usually enters school eagerly, confident about learning to read and about liking the teacher. We commonly take these factors for granted, proceeding immediately with readiness programs based on a preparation of five years directed toward helping the child grow and develop abilities. The disadvantaged child, however, requires a program directed toward providing experiences which will develop these attitudes and abilities which have not been developed in the home as well as concentration on compensating for language deficiencies.

THE IMPORTANT ROLE OF THE TEACHER

Is "disadvantaged" synonymous with "uncultured"? Are disadvantaged children to be regarded as potential delinquents? Must all teaching time be spent disciplining? Must creativity, discovery methods, and enrichment activities be discarded in favor of a rigidly teacher-controlled classroom? These are only a few examples of the fallacious thinking which teachers openly or unconsciously reveal.

A most influential factor in the deprived child's chances for success in school is attitude toward school, the teacher, and toward learning; and the three are encompassed in one complex feeling of uncertainty, hostility, and predestined failure. The burden for dispelling the child's fears lies on the classroom teacher. Authoritative tone of voice, aloofness, coldness of manner, the obvious view of the child as an inferior being—all serve to substantiate the child's preconceived idea of school; they do nothing to give a feeling of being welcome, wanted, warm.

Why should young Chuck wish to communicate with a teacher who talks to him only when pointing out his mistakes? Why should he try to read when he knows before he tries that he will fail as he has always failed? Isn't it natural that this child much prefers the familiar street on which he leads a relatively happy existence with others like himself who "speak his language" in an environment which accepts him for what he is? On what grounds can we meet these children, these "nonstandard" students?

We teachers must make a concerted effort to understand these children. We must realize that culturally different children don't understand us or our middle-class culture any more than we understand theirs. And we must overcome our own prejudices. As one young teacher of urban children describes it:

> I feel a part of the children; I know them, their spontaneity, enthusiasm, freedom, humor, innocence—all the childlike qualities that make them children. In these qualities, they are not deprived or disadvantaged. They are still children and can be reached as children. More important, they want to be reached and cared about and taught.[24]

The standard English which we speak is as foreign to these children as their dialects may be to us. The poem written by gifted Langston Hughes may provide insight for the teacher as well as the student:

> I play it cool and dig all jive.
> That's the reason I stay alive.
> My motto, as I live and learn,
> Is: "Dig and Be Dug in Return."

What personal objectives should the teacher (as well as courses for the teacher) of the deprived child consider when preparing to teach? We would direct the prospective teacher toward:

1 Understanding the lives and the learning styles of children in depressed areas
2 Understanding the psychological and sociological roots of prejudice and the problems within and between ethnic groups
3 Developing a positive attitude toward serving in programs for disadvantaged students

[24] Dorothy McGeoch, *Learning to Teach in Urban Schools* (New York: Teachers College, 1965), p. 4.

4 Developing, through study and supervised experience, teaching skills and patterns appropriate for working with culturally different children
5 Developing new curriculum guides and original teaching materials reflecting awareness of the needs and the special disabilities of disadvantaged children, but also capitalizing on interests and abilities of these children.

OBJECTIVES OF THE ENGLISH PROGRAM

It has been pointed out that language deficiencies are so pronounced for the deprived child that it is on oral language that primary stress must be placed. Beginning activities can be planned to work toward the dual objectives of developing security in the school situation and of developing language fluency. Our objectives are listed in sequential order based on the child's needs. The final objectives will not, therefore, be met until those listed first have been at least partially achieved.

1 Development of a positive attitude toward the school, the teacher, and learning
2 Development of a self-image that includes ability to succeed and a feeling of personal worth
3 Extension of experiential background involving all the senses and including many experiences with literature as well as field trips and classroom experiences.
4 Development of oral linguistic fluency and listening abilities; enjoyment of language; beginning study of English phonology
5 Development of abilities in composing through creative methods; enjoyment of language
6 Developing skills of reading which have already been introduced; sequential development of reading abilities; appreciation of literature through listening, viewing, reading

It is felt that achievement of the first four goals must begin immediately, for a positive attitude toward the school situation, a positive self-image, experiential backgrounds, and some degree of fluency in language are necessary before the skills of writing and reading will find adequate response. It is obvious, of course, that the third and fourth objectives are building foundations for both writing and reading, and that skills of composition and reading will continue to be introduced gradually as the group is ready to proceed.

It should be noted, too, that the objectives listed here are not particularly different for the disadvantaged child than they are for any child. How then is this program different from that planned for other children? It is largely a matter of degree or emphasis. For the child of a middle-class family the first three objectives would not require much special attention; these children are prepared to like school and the teachers, and they have no reason to doubt their ability to learn to read and write. They are prepared to succeed in school. The disadvantaged children, on the other hand, lacking this assurance, must be shown that they can succeed. They need repeated experiences which demonstrate to them and to their peers that they are able to cope with the school situation. They also need, as we have pointed out, to acquire language skills as tools to assist them in succeeding with these beginning steps and with increasingly more complex learning.

Where do we begin? We begin with children as they exist at any grade level and at any stage of language development. We accept their abilities and inabilities, one of which is their language, which we consider an ability although it may represent a disability in that it is probably a dialect other than standard English. Whatever the dialect, the teacher accepts it as a means of communicating which has been successful in the eyes of the child. Branding the child's language as being "wrong" or "unacceptable" accomplishes only adverse results—resentment, self-consciousness, fear, unhappiness, a sense of failure.

At the same time, aware of our long-term goals for improving the impoverished language abilities of each child, we direct activities and learning experiences toward achievement of the stated objectives. We provide a new environment for the elementary school student. Although initial activities may actually be directly focused on building up self-confidence and a positive attitude toward school, the child is immediately exposed to standard English as spoken by the teacher-model and classroom aides. The child is encouraged to begin talking about varied experiences. Instruction in composition and reading wait, for efforts to instruct are inefficient and ineffective until the child is psychologically ready. Attempts to teach students to read, while they still resent school and the teacher, have only meager ability with the English language, and have no personal motivation for reading, will surely produce definite antagonism toward reading.

The Task Force Report conducted by the National Council of Teachers of English stresses the necessity for developing abilities in oral language as the first step in helping the economically disadvantaged child: "Everything known about language suggests that the improvement of writing and reading must be built upon instruction in oral English. Even more obvious is the fact that if children are to develop skill in using English dialects other than their own, they need oral instruction."[25] The first school experiences for the child will be directed, therefore, toward developing oral language abilities and to meeting the psychological needs—

[25] NCTE Task Force Report, *Language Programs for the Disadvantaged* (Urbana, Ill.: National Council of Teachers of English, 1965).

confidence, positive attitude toward school, and a self-image as a successful learner and a worthwhile person.

DEVELOPING POSITIVE ATTITUDES

Both the first and second objectives involve the development of positive attitudes for the child in terms of (1) school and (2) self-concept. Just providing "more of the same" will not reach the child nor will it solve problems. We need to open new doors, and the entrance may not be through the front door. We will not limit ourselves, therefore, to the formal front door entrance which is more familiar to the beginning teacher. We will go around the house trying all the doors and even peering in windows. We may unexpectedly discover an opening through art, music, or science, for the child who once begins to smile, to ask questions, to answer "Yes," is responding; and in the beginning stages it matters not to *what,* for the initial steps toward communication have been taken.

As noted, one of the most important needs of the child is the experience of success in the classroom situation. Children need (whether a five-year-old in kindergarten or a ten-year-old in third grade) to participate in many simple activities or games which are easily handled and prove enjoyable in order to develop a feeling of self-confidence, a willingness to attack more difficult tasks. What activities are particularly suitable for this stage of development? Keeping in mind our dual aims, we stress enjoyable activities that involve language abilities, too.

Playing group games which include singing or chanting of simple familiar refrains:

Young children—"A Tisket-A-Tasket"
"Farmer in the Dell"

Older children—"What's Your Trade? Lemonade!"
Jumping rope

Oral activities which stress auditory discrimination:

Which words begin alike? Which one does not?
bird baby teacher

Which word begins like *horse?*
hospital apartment spoon

Enjoying a good story together.

The teacher reads aloud, showing the illustrations as the story proceeds.

Favorites with younger children include:

May I Bring a Friend?, Beatrice De Regniers
White Snow, Bright Snow, Alvin Tresselt
The 500 Hats of Bartholomew Cubbins, Dr. Seuss

Millions of Cats, Wanda Gág
Curious George, H. A. Rey
The Five Chinese Brothers, Claire Bishop

Films and records can also introduce excellent stories which provide topics for discussion and add to the child's experiences.

Weston Woods (Weston, Conn.) has produced films of familiar stories from children's literature, for example, "The Doughnuts" from *Homer Price* by Robert McCloskey and *Millions of Cats* by Wanda Gág. Of special interest is *A Snowy Day,* the film of a young Negro boy's adventures in the snow, and *Crow Boy,* the story of a boy who felt out of place in the classroom.

Positive reinforcement is essential to the child's success in school. As we teach varied content, therefore, our methods will reflect awareness of this need of the child for reassurance. It is especially important that the teacher display positive attitudes toward children and their abilities, for children soon sense the true feelings of the adult. Specifically, we can:

1 Praise liberally and sincerely, avoiding negative criticism
2 Avoid punishment by redirecting activities
3 Maintain contact with the child
4 Modify evaluation techniques

Praise liberally and sincerely Children respond to praise; doesn't everyone? The teacher's approval is actively sought by many children, and although it is not openly sought by those who are more reticent, it is an effective catalyst in the classroom which produces warmth and response. True praise must be dispensed in a natural, sincere manner without artificiality, but there are many opportunities in the day for the teacher to *appreciate* the students and their performances.

"Thank you for listening so attentively when Mrs. James read *Madeline.* "Would you like to have Mrs. James read you another story tomorrow?" (The whole class is happy and so is the new aide.)

"My goodness, Bill, what a nice straight back you have!" (As you pass him in a line for recess.)

"Lindy, that is the funniest clown I have seen in a long time. You must have enjoyed painting him."

"What a pretty dress, Anne. It must be your birthday."

Praise takes both direct and indirect approaches, and it can be addressed to the group or to individuals. However it is used, it adds a real feeling of warmth and congeniality to the classroom atmosphere which will lead to the concept that school is a good place to be.

Avoid punishment by redirecting activities The teacher must be unusually perceptive to spot trouble before it really gets started. Disciplinary action is seldom necessary in the classroom, however, if the children are (1) busy with varied activities, (2) stimulated to attack the task at hand, and (3) working at a task within their capabilities.

Varied activities must be planned, for excessively long periods of doing the same thing will naturally cause fidgeting and provide time for mischief. If the group has been listening to a recorded story, don't follow this experience with another listening activity, but select an activity which permits the child to move about. Remember, too, that attention spans vary and that the attention of the deprived child may be especially limited.

Are the children really interested in doing the task at hand? This may be influenced by the motivating techniques used by the teacher or by the abilities of the children to do the task. Disadvantaged children may show little interest in talking about life on the farm until they have seen pictures, viewed a film, or visited a nearby dairy farm. Before they will be motivated to talk, in other words, they need something to talk about, experiences to relate, some reason to try expressing themselves. The child who is not equipped to partake will be uninterested in the discussion and may cause disturbance in order to get a measure of attention. Remember, too, the background of disadvantaged children has not prepared them to accomplish many tasks which we would usually expect children at a specified grade level to perform.

Maintain contact with the child Children need to feel that the teacher as an adult really likes them and will take time for them as individuals. Joe may need actually to touch the teacher physically and to be touched by this adult who smiles and seems to be interested in what he says and what he does.

A practice we have recommended repeatedly for teachers at all levels is that of assessing daily personal contact with students with whom they are working. Is there some child to whom you did not directly speak during the day? During the last half hour of class make certain that you get to those children in some way so that for them the day spent in the classroom will have more personal meaning.

> Call Jose to your desk to help you sort a pile of papers.
> Walk past Sally's chair as you smilingly say, "You really worked hard today, Sally. Don't forget to take your story home to read to your mother."

The personal conference is a good device that also aids in maintaining direct individual contact with each child. The number of conferences per week with each child will depend on the size of the class and the number of assistants available to the teacher. The conference period (five to ten minutes) may be focused on needs specific to each child. When sitting with Buck at a small table, Miss Jordan may say, for instance, "I want you to play a game with me, Buck. It's called Echo. Do you know what an echo is?" After introducing Buck to the idea of repeating what she says, the teacher may say words or phrases that contain sounds with which this child has trouble. She will not use the entire conference period for the instructional game, however, but will ask Buck questions about his activities, members of his family, and so forth as a means of knowing the boy better, demonstrating interest in him as an individual, and perhaps most important, persuading him to talk. Conferences, designated less formally as Talking Time, may be rotated among the teacher and aides; or each adult working with the group may serve as personal consultant for a small number of students for a certain period of time, perhaps one month.

Modify evaluation techniques Evaluation must also exemplify positive reinforcement if it is to be helpful. The familiar techniques of red-penciling a child's composition have no place in this classroom, for the disadvantaged child already has a defeated air and a certainty of failure. If it is to be effective, evaluation must be positive in nature. The children must be praised for what they have accomplished, not criticized for what they *did not* do. As Joubert writes, "Children have more need of models than critics."

Nor can we measure the achievements of these children against nationally established norms provided with a commercial achievement test. Their achievement must be measured for them as individuals. Where were they before they began this program? How far have they progressed during a given period of time? We need new tests more appropriate for the child who is not verbally skillful. A checklist prepared by the teacher for a specific class may be more informative if completed at the beginning of the year and again at the end of the year's work. This checklist will reflect the skills the teacher is trying to teach, and the evaluation of each child's abilities at the end of the year will indicate the extent toward which these abilities have been taught to each child. It will also indicate the work that remains to be done so that the next teacher who works with Sam will know more clearly how to plan for him. This type of checklist does not necessarily reflect on the individual teacher's teaching ability, for there are many factors which, as we have noted, impede learning for the disadvantaged child.

The basic need of children during the early years is broad experience in using language. The verbal child usually succeeds with other language skills so that school programs should focus on building each child's linguistic abilities. At first these skills are developed through speaking and listening, and a large portion of the child's time will be spent in activities that stress these language abilities.

The use of language, however, is not the only concern being promoted through stress on speaking and listening. Through oral language, the child receives input in terms of information, new experiences, and concept and vocabulary development. Oral language also provides models of a second language or dialect.

Books to Investigate

Bar-Adon, Aaron, and Leopold, Werner F., eds. *Child Language: A Book of Readings.* Englewood Cliffs, N.J.: Prentice-Hall, 1971.

Cazden, Courtney. *Child Language and Education.* New York: Holt, Rinehart, and Winston, 1972.

Chukovsky, Kornei. *From Two to Five.* Trans. and ed. by Miriam Morton. Berkeley, Calif.: University of California Press, 1966.

Dale, Philip S. *Language Development: Structure and Function.* The Dryden Press, 1972.

DeStefano, Johanna S., ed. *Language, Society, and Education: A Profile of Black English.* Belmont, Calif.: Wadsworth, 1973.

Evans, Ellis D. *Contemporary Influences in Early Childhood Education.* New York: Holt, Rinehart, and Winston, 1971.

Gilkeson, Elizabeth C. *Bank Street Approach to Follow Through.* New York: Bank Street College of Education, 1969.

Montessori, Maria. *The Montessori Method.* New York: Schocken Books, 1964.

Northan, Saralie B., ed. *Child: Coordinated Helps in Language Development.* Northwest Regional Educational Laboratory, 1970.

Parker, Ronald K. *The Pre-School in Action.* Boston: Allyn and Bacon, 1972.

Piaget, Jean. *Language and Thought of the Child.* London: Routledge and Kegan Paul, 1962.

Weber, Lillian. *The English Infant School and Informal Education.* A Center for Urban Education Book. Englewood Cliffs, N.J.: Prentice-Hall, 1971.

spelling and reading english words

chapter 4

> **Language arts programs should offer both teachers and students the opportunity to explore their linguistic environment as an entity, rather than compartmentalizing the various language activities into spelling, handwriting, reading, composition, literature. . . .**
>
> ***Ronald Wardhaugh*** [1]

Current thinking indicates that skills involved in reading and writing English are more effectively taught in an integrated approach to language arts. Teaching reading and spelling as isolated subjects automatically builds in unplanned repetition that does not take full advantage of the reinforcement that would be part of a coordinated approach to the encoding-decoding process. Typical phonics instruction, for example, moves from printed symbols to spoken words, but fails to help children observe the opposite relationship.

Few teachers received formal college training or study of phonology, until courses in linguistics were recently required in credential programs. It is small wonder that there has been much uncertainty and many misconceptions about this aspect of language. It is essential that those who are teaching reading and writing skills in elementary schools have a

[1] Ronald Wardhaugh, *Reading: A Linguistic Perspective* (New York: Harcourt, Brace, and World, 1969), p. 149.

thorough understanding of English phonemes and the alternate spellings of each of these sounds. In this chapter, therefore, we explore possibilities for teaching phoneme-grapheme relationships through an integrated approach to language arts. We begin with a discussion of English phonology and the alternate ways of spelling the sounds of English. Emphasis is placed on the use of inductive methods to aid children in discovering the workings of the language they use daily as they become consciously aware of their own intuitive knowledge of English.

The Phoneme-Grapheme Relationship

> The use of all writing systems . . . necessitates the user's acquiring two closely related processes: (1) the mastery of the graphic symbols needed to set forth speech in writing (encoding or spelling), and (2) the ability to translate written or printed graphemes into the oral forms they represent (decoding or reading). But in American-English orthography, owing to the lack of a precise one-to-one correspondence between phoneme and grapheme, the encoding and decoding processes are sometimes disparate and confusing to the beginner.[2]

The learning of these relationships between phoneme and grapheme constitutes an important element of the basic learnings that usually take place in the primary grades. Concentration on these specific relationships is essential for beginning skills of writing and reading. Once students are aware of these relationships and can handle them easily, instruction can focus on vocabulary development, comprehension, and expression of ideas.

THE STUDY OF ENGLISH PHONOLOGY

The study of sounds made in our English language (phonology) is important in developing the ability to spell, pronounce, or read a word. Although researchers have pointed out that (1) regional pronunciations differ, (2) English sounds are frequently spelled in several ways, and (3) more than half of our words contain silent letters, others have found that a large percentage of English words are highly regular. For this group of regular words, phonology will prove especially helpful.

The study of the sounds of English introduces several terms related to phonology: *phonics, phonetics,* and *phonemics.* Sometimes these terms

[2] Paul R. Hanna et al., *Spelling: Structure and Strategies* (Boston: Houghton Mifflin, 1971), pp. 25–26.

are confusing to those beginning a study of the encoding-decoding system. They can be defined as follows:

Phonics—determining the sound that is represented by a set of given symbols, usually associated with reading

Example: *tion*—usually pronounced /*š* ə *n*/

phonetics—analysis of sound production in scientific detail developed in a code called the International Phonetic Alphabet, so that all linguists can reproduce the sounds

phonemics—identification of the sounds of a specific language such as English, which has about forty phonemes (sounds that change meaning)

Examples: The phonemes that begin these two words are different; the words mean something different.

/*fin*/ /*pin*/

The phonemes that begin these two words are the same although they are spelled differently in English.

phone /*fōn*/ *fun* /*f* ə *n*/

Is the spelling of English a completely hopeless task? Can it be taught? Many critics have pointed with ridicule to the peculiarities of English spelling and to the fact that spelling and pronunciation are not consistent. George Bernard Shaw, one of the more literate critics, gibed: "How do you pronounce GHOTI, if the letters are pronounced as follows: *gh* as in *rough*, *o* as in *women*, and *ti* as in *nation*?"[3]

Since the days of Chaucer, spelling and pronunciation have grown ever farther apart, with pronunciation tending to change more than does spelling. This tendency continues today. An anonymous poet records many oddities of English spelling ending with the conclusion that "sounds and letters disagree."

OUR QUEER LANGUAGE

When the English tongue we speak,
Why is "break" not rhymed with "freak"?
Will you tell me why it's true
We say "sew" but likewise "few";
And the maker of a verse
Cannot cap his "horse" with "worse"?
"Beard" sounds not the same as "heard";
"Cord" is different from "word";
Cow is "cow," but low is "low";
"Shoe" is never rhymed with "foe."

[3] The answer is FISH!

Think of "hose" and "dose" and "lose";
And think of "goose" and yet of "choose."
Think of "comb" and "tomb" and "bomb";
"Doll" and "roll" and "home" and "some."
And since "pay" is rhymed with "say,"
Why not "paid" with "said," I pray?
We have "blood" and "food" and "good";
"Mould" is not pronounced like "could."
Wherefore "done" but "gone" and "lone"?
Is there any reason known?

And, in short, it seems to me,
Sounds and letters disagree.

Although it is undeniably true that English contains many unusual and often inexplicable oddities, today's researchers are focusing attention on the fact that approximately 85 percent of English words have been found to follow regular patterns of spelling.[4] Few linguists claim that English spelling is easy, but it is not entirely without reason. There are many relatively consistent rules which bear teaching, and many concepts in phonics will assist students in attacking the large body of consistent spellings as they learn to read and write.

THE CONSONANT SOUNDS AND SPELLINGS

Linguists have identified twenty-four consonant sounds in spoken English. We teach these consonants first because they are more easily identifiable in the common initial position than are vowels which, usually surrounded by consonant sounds, are more difficult to distinguish. Consonants also serve to provide visual structure in printed words. Notice, for example, how easily you can read these words even though the vowels are completely eliminated:

g _ _ gr _ ph _
b _ rthd _ _
c _ ns _ n _ nt
ph _ n _ l _ g _

The more consonants that appear in the word, of course, the easier it is to identify. We recognize, at the same time, that we need vowel sounds because we can't pronounce the consonants without adding some

[4] Don H. Parker, et al., "Are We Teaching Creative Spelling?" *Elementary English* (May, 1963), p. 523.

vowel. This accounts for the fact that every syllable contains one vowel sound.

In order to work with an integrated language-arts approach, it is essential that the teacher understand the relationship between the sounds of English and the various spellings we use for these sounds in written form. The outline of consonant sounds includes numerous alternate spellings for many of the sounds. Obviously, we could not work with all sound-spelling relationships at one time, so we teach the simpler and more common spellings for each sound first. To assist the teacher, we have sorted the various spellings into three levels of difficulty. Those listed under Level 3 might not be taught until the upper elementary grades; in a few cases, these spellings might not be taught at all in the elementary school. Such a case is the *pf* spelling of /*f*/ as in pfennig and a few other words borrowed from the German language.

The positions in which the various spellings occur are also important to observe. There are certain spellings, for example, that never occur in the initial position. The *gh* spelling of /*f*/, for instance, never appears initially. The *gh* spelling in the initial position is an alternate way of writing /*g*/. These types of observations help us and the children we teach in writing and reading English words. This kind of observation would be a valid phonic generalization that children can be helped to recognize after they have been exposed to many English words.

As you read through the chart, identify each consonant sound by pronouncing the words listed under the Initial position. Then notice the variety of possible alternate spellings. Which sound-symbol relationships would be easiest to teach?

Contrast the pronunciation of these words. Hold your hand before your mouth as you pronounce each pair.

lid	lit
lab	lap
either	ether
have	half

When breath is released with the consonant, we say the phoneme is *voiced.* If there is no aspiration (breathiness), the phoneme is *unvoiced.*

CONSONANTS

PHONEMES	GRAPHEMES					
	Difficulty Level			Examples		
	1	2	3	Initial	Medial	Final
/b/	b			bill	tuber	cab
		bb			rubber	ebb
/d/	d			dill	coding	hard
		ed				pulled
		dd			sudden	Fudd
		ld				could
/f/	f			fill	fifer	loaf
		ph		phone	telephone	
		gh			roughing	cough
		ff			ruffle	off
			v			Chekhov
			pf (Ger.)	pfennig		
/g/	g			gill	tiger	bug
		gu		guest		
		gh		ghost		
		gg			logging	
			gue			catalogue
/h/	h			hill	unhappy	
		wh		who		
			j	Jose'		
/j/	j			jam		
		g		giant	imagine	wage
		dg			judger	judge
			di		soldier	
			du		graduate	
			de		grandeur	
/k/	k			kill	raking	look
		ke				lake
		c		cat	act	
		qu (1)*		quit	equinox	
		qu (2)*			liquor	
		ck			lacking	pick
		cc			accost	
		x			fix	
			cu		biscuit	
			cch		bacchanal	
			ch	chorus		

*In the initial position the grapheme qu(1) spells the blended phonemes /kw/; in other positions qu(2) is usually an alternate spelling for /k/.

CONSONANTS

PHONEMES	GRAPHEMES					
	Difficulty Level			Examples		
	1	2	3	Initial	Medial	Final
/k/ (Cont.)			kh	khaki		
			cqu		acquit	
			que (1)		barbeque	
			que (2)			plaque
/l/	l			like	failing	fatal
		ll (1)**	ll (2)**	llama	calling	doll
/m/	m			mill	timer	ham
		me				come
		mm			simmer	
		mb			climbing	lamb
			mn			hymn
/n/	n			no	lining	fun
		ne				line
		kn		knot		
		gn		gnat		feign
		nn			runner	
			pn	pneumonia		
/p/	p			pill	caper	top
		pp			copper	Lapp
/r/	r			rose	caring	fair
		rr			carry	Carr
		wr		write		
			rh	rhyme		
/s/	s			so		thus
		c		cell	receive	
		sc		scent		
		ss			classes	toss
		x				fox
			ps	pseudo		
/t/	t			to	later	hit
		tt			hotter	mutt
		bt			debtor	debt
		ed				licked
			pt	ptomaine		receipt
			dt			veldt
			th	Thomas		

**The grapheme ll (2) is very rare in the initial position. For that reason it is considered a difficult spelling while the ll (1) grapheme is rather common.

CONSONANTS

PHONEMES	GRAPHEMES					
	Difficulty Level			Examples		
	1	2	3	Initial	Medial	Final
/v/	v			very	cover	
		f				of
		ve				weave
			ph		Stephen	
			vv		flivver	
/w/	w			will	slower	how
		one		one		
		wh		while	awhile	
			qu (kw)		quit	
			ui		suite	
			oui	ouija		
/y/	y			yes	lawyer	
			j		hallelujah	
			io		onion	
			ll		bouillon	
/z/	z			zoo	dozing	whiz
		s (e)			miser	lose, is
		zz			dazzle	buzz
		ss			Missouri	
			sc		discern	
			x	xylophone		
			cz	czar		
/č/	ch			child		much
		tch			matches	hutch
			c	cello		
			cz	Czech		
			eou		righteous	
			t		nature	
/š/	sh			shoe	worship	rush
		s		sugar		
		ch		champagne		
			sch	schist		
			ce		ocean	
			si		mansion	
			ss		mission	
			sci		luscious	
			ti		patient	
			xi		anxious	
			chs		fuchsia	

CONSONANTS

PHONEMES	GRAPHEMES					
	Difficulty Level			Examples		
	1	2	3	Initial	Medial	Final
/ž/		g		gendarme (Fr)	adagio	garage
		s (i)			pleasure, Asia	
		z (i)			brazier	
			j	jejeune		
/θ/	th			thimble	ether	loathe
/δ/	th			the	either	breath
/η/	ng				ringer	wing
	nk				think	
			ngue			tongue

THE VOWEL SOUNDS AND SPELLINGS

The vowel sounds are more difficult to identify because they are commonly hidden in the middle of a word. Also there is much variation in regional dialects regarding the pronunciation of the vowel sounds. It is interesting to aid children in hearing varied ways of saying the same word—for example, *dog*. The teacher must be cautious, however, about evaluating the "correctness" of pronunciation. Your own speech represents only one speech sample in the classroom, and it may differ widely from the speech of children in the classroom.

Because the vowel sounds are usually internal or medial in position, they are not grouped according to position or difficulty level. They are divided, however, according to simple sounds and complex sounds called *diphthongs* (combinations of more than one vowel sound to make a clearly identifiable new phoneme).

Although many of us might say there are five vowels in English, linguists identify at least sixteen different vowel sounds in spoken English. We need to clarify our thinking about vowel sounds (not five letters of the alphabet) and learn to identify these sounds when we hear them. We will find, for example, that there is wide variation in the pronunciation of the vowel sounds used in specific words. For example, are the words—*Mary, merry,* and *marry*—homonyms for you? Do you pronounce them exactly the same? As you check with others, you will find that for some people, each of these words is pronounced differently; and, again, it is the vowel sound that varies.

DIPHTHONGS

PHONEMES	GRAPHEMES
/iy/ (long e)	see, sea, me, deceive, believe, carbine, ski, gladly, Aesop, people, quay, key, suite, equator, Phoenix
/ey/ (long a)	bay, rain, gate, they, gauge, break, neigh, rein, straight, care
/ay/ (long i)	kite, right, I, by, cries, find, buy, height, eye, stein, aisle, dye, aye, lyre, iodine
/ow/ (long o)	lone, road, foe, slow, dough, beau, sew, yeoman, whoa, odor, oh, solo, soul, brooch
/yuw/ (long u)	use, few, view, beautiful, queue
/oy/	toy, moist
/aw/	now, out, bough
/uw/	too, blew, tune, suit, lose, flu, do, canoe, through, tomb, blue, group, prove, maneuver

SIMPLE VOWELS

PHONEMES	GRAPHEMES	Unaccented Syllables
/i/	give, pit, myth, quilt, busy, women, England, sieve, been	
/e/	red, said, breath, friend, any, leopard (leisure), says, aesthetics, their, foetid	
/æ/	had, have, laugh, plaid	
/ə/	nut, flood, rough, son, of, dove, was, does	cattle ahead fountain parliament
/a/	ah, halt, hot, mirage, cart, heart, fault, sergeant	moment happily burgeon porpoise
/u/	good, full, put, wolf, could	
/ɔ/	caught, jaw, talk, fought, daughter, watch, broad, toss, otter, Utah	
/ɨ/	her, sir, fur, work, satyr, journey, heard, grammar	

We need to be aware of varied dialects as we teach, for we should not expect the speech of all children in the classroom to be the same. This can, for example, be a problem as you dictate to children or pronounce spelling words. Studies of dialectology can be helpful with children of all ages as they learn to observe these variations with interest. Notice, however, that dialectal variations are not labeled as "wrong," nor do we try to make children change their prounciations to match our own.

We aim instead at awareness of speech variation in our own speech as well as that of children.

Observe the sixteen vowel sounds and their alternate spellings as outlined on the chart. Say each word aloud as you listen carefully to the vowel sound your voice is making.

Compare your pronunciation of these words with that of other members of your class:

house	Mary	child	park
merry	garage	here	bath
log	idea	because	fire
were	right	of	Harvard

Listen to the record *Our Changing Language* by Evelyn Gott and Raven I. McDavid, Jr. (McGraw-Hill, 1965) for further comparisons of speech samples across the country.

Rethinking Spelling

Spelling is probably one of the most regularly taught areas in the elementary school English curriculum. Literature may be discussed only spasmodically by the teacher; creative writing may be totally ignored; but a daily spelling period is rigorously included in the classroom schedule by most teachers.

It is not too difficult to point out reasons for this attention to spelling instruction. The most obvious is that the subject matter to be taught is familiar to every teacher. It is also relatively easy to present to students, and it is easily evaluated. The teacher feels secure with the content as it is usually taught. The routine nature typical of spelling instruction provides a comfortable niche in the curriculum, for on Monday we always introduce the words, on Tuesday we test. . . .

There are few uncertainties involved in spelling instruction; but there are few excitements; and there is actually an example here of ineffective teaching. In many cases the routine becomes a "rut" which makes spelling a dull subject with little real learning taking place and much valuable school time wasted. As Horn reports, "Weekly time allotments are still much larger than can be justified either by the relative value and difficulty of spelling as compared with other subjects or by the results obtained." [5]

The task at hand, therefore, is to investigate the objectives for teaching spelling and to determine efficient and effective ways of reaching

[5] Ernest Horn, "Spelling," *Encyclopedia of Educational Research,* 3rd ed., Chester Harris, ed. (New York: Macmillan, 1960), p. 1346.

these objectives. Spelling is a tool, a skill that is closely allied with composition, or the writing of words. The prime objective in teaching spelling is, therefore, to teach children to spell words which they now need in order to write. Another phase of this objective is the teaching of words which these children will need as adults. We find that these two needs overlap and that many of the words needed by the adult are also needed by the elementary school child.

As we strive to determine more effective means for teaching spelling, we would do well to analyze the task at hand. What is it that we are trying to teach? What are the obstacles that we will encounter? What is the role of the teacher in spelling instruction? Who is the teacher of spelling?

SELECTING THE WORDLIST

What words shall we teach? On what basis should they be selected? How many words should be taught each week? Published wordlists, that is, series of spelling books each of which contains a portion of the total list, are most commonly based on the above criteria although the lists vary widely. Betts found, for example, when studying twenty-five spelling series, that the total number of different words included was about 10,000.[6] Since each series usually presents about 4000 words, the variation was obviously great.

All lists include a nucleus of words which are used repeatedly in everyone's individual writing, for it has been estimated that approximately 50 percent of our writing consists of only 100 words used in varied combinations. Three thousand words comprise approximately 98 percent of those words most commonly used.

> Students could conduct an enlightening and rewarding study of papers written over a period of time to determine what group of words is most commonly used. Their study would motivate student interest in learning these needed words, for the list would be composed of words which they themselves have discovered that *they* need to know.

How do we decide which words shall be taught at any grade level? Although it was once thought that the difficulty of spelling a word was a superior method of placing it for study by grade level, more recent studies find that, though a word may be difficult, the child's early need of the word may warrant its inclusion at a lower grade level. Horn cites

[6] E. A. Betts, *Spelling Vocabulary Study: Grade Placement in Seventeen Spellers* (New York: American, 1940), p. 143; and *Grade Placement of Words in Eight Recent Spellers* (American, 1949).

the word *receive* as one which is consistently difficult for adults to spell, but which is presented in the elementary school because young children use the word widely. Words are selected for placement at specific grade levels usually on a basis of:

1 Permanent value
2 Difficulty of spelling
3 Use by children
4 Type of logical grouping [7]

CAUSES OF SPELLING DIFFICULTY

In order to teach spelling effectively it is helpful to examine the causes of deficiency in spelling. Why do some students require little teaching of spelling, while other children have repeated difficulty in mastering spelling skills? Following is a list of deficiencies compiled from several sources: [8]

Lack of interest Noted frequently as the most influential factor in learning spelling skills, the interest factor can provide a point of attack for the teacher. See the discussion of motivation of student interest.

Physical defects Disability of the eye or ear can cause a child to be unable to perceive the word visually or aurally. Either handicap results in misconceptions about the spelling of a word.

Intelligence Although a high intelligence quotient does not guarantee ability to spell, the child with a low IQ is handicapped in learning any skill, including spelling. He or she brings less ability to the task at hand and therefore cannot be expected to achieve at the same level as the more able child.

Poor memory ability We need to focus attention on memory abilities as the child learns to perceive the word in varied ways. Memory will be assisted by the development of other skills: listening, speaking, knowledge of phonology, and so on.

Speaking and listening skills How do we hear a word? How do we speak a word? Both skills are essential to correct spelling. Improved speaking and listening abilities will aid auditory discrimination, which is an essential aspect of correct spelling.

[7] James A. Fitzgerald, *A Basic Life Spelling Vocabulary* (Milwaukee, Wis.: Bruce, 1951).

[8] James A. Fitzgerald, *The Teaching of Spelling* (Milwaukee, Wis.: Bruce, 1951), p. 193. See also: Ernest Horn, "Spelling," in *Encyclopedia of Educational Research*, 3rd ed., Chester W. Harris, ed. (New York: Macmillan, 1960), pp. 1347–49.

Poor study habits How is spelling presented? How is the child directed to study? Is he or she assisted in any way with the study of spelling? A large percentage of the time spent on studying spelling by any child is in the classroom, and therefore study habits can be directed by the teacher. The poor speller needs special attention to this aspect of learning spelling and may work better in a small group situation.

THE TEACHER'S ROLE

The chief responsibility of the teacher, as we see it, is that of establishing positive attitudes toward spelling. Presented as a problem for investigation about which the teacher is obviously knowledgeable and enthusiastic, spelling can be incorporated in a rewarding study of the English language. (See Chapter 2 for more ideas.)

Research indicates that the classroom teacher frequently dislikes teaching spelling, an attitude which would inevitably be projected to the student. If the techniques used in teaching spelling become so routinized as to be dull and uninteresting to the teacher, it is unlikely that children will display any genuine liking for this study. The individual teacher must analyze the methods employed to determine their effectiveness. The following questions should be explored:

1. Are the words studied of interest to the students?
2. Are able spellers being held down to a low level of achievement?
3. Am I spending too much time on spelling activities?
4. Are poor spellers receiving help as needed?
5. Am I reinforcing spelling learning through use of composition?
6. Do I vary techniques of teaching spelling? Is spelling "dull"? Are student attitudes positive?
7. Am I really "teaching" spelling?
8. Do I permit spelling to inhibit creative writing?
9. Are techniques of teaching spelling based on the findings of research?
10. Are spelling and reading skills introduced together so children see the relationships?

The teacher has a responsibility for knowing about English spelling and about the English language in general. Knowledge of the development of the English language, and American English in particular, will enable the teacher to include information about changes in spelling, the origins of words, variations in British and American spellings, and so on. This information adds "spice" to the learning situation and will aid in motivating student interest.

Teacher concepts of correctness should be examined, too, for a rigid, uninformed concept of correct spelling can cause confusion, and at times, embarrassment. We must be prepared to allow for differences in spelling as in these examples:

1 Which spelling is correct: *Viet Nam* or *Vietnam*? Both are seen in reputable newspapers and journals. Does one spelling *have* to be wrong?
2 Which spelling is correct: *labor* or *labour*? The first spelling is more common in the United States whereas the latter is the common British spelling. British spellings often occur in children's literature, for example, *Children of Green Knowe* by Lucy Boston (Harcourt, 1954).
3 Which is correct: *ax* or *axe, fulfill* or *fulfil*? For these and many other words, two equally acceptable spellings are listed in reliable dictionaries.
4 Which is correct: *catalog* or *catalogue*? Both are acceptable; one is obviously a shortened, simplified form of the other.

Caution must always be exercised to avoid teaching which permits *only one right answer*. The discovery of such differences in spelling should be utilized by the skillful (or is it skilful?) teacher to add interest to the spelling lesson, and the child who discovers variations in spelling should be highly praised. The teacher who is aware of spelling variations will not be disconcerted by the child's questioning attitude nor will the questions be regarded as threatening teacher authority.

If you feel guilty about permitting a child to use the shorter spelling of such words as *dialog*, perhaps an examination of your attitude is in order. Why do you object? Is it that you had to learn the longer, older (and, therefore, more respectable) spelling? Are these modern students "getting by with something"? Is there something inherently better in one of the two variations? Don't they both communicate? Discussions of this nature can prove highly stimulating for a class of alert elementary school students.

Individualizing spelling What is individualized spelling? No single approach has been determined although most authorities agree that the practice of teaching for individual needs which allows for individual differences is desirable. The use of a pretest is one way of allowing for individual differences, as some individual needs are immediately determined by the test. Another method is the use of programmed material, although a student might be required to study words already known. A completely individualized approach would consist of each child's developing a list of words misspelled from his or her compositions. Perhaps the most commonly used technique combines the use of the standard word-list with the pretest to which are added a number of words which the child as an individual needs to learn. These words may be dictated by pairs of children who work together to check the individual portion of the spelling lists.

Inductive or discovery methods An effective technique of teaching understanding about spelling is through the inductive method in which the student is led to make the discovery. Have students name, for example, words which end with the common suffix, *tion* (šən). As the words are named, write them on the board: *nation, convention, impression, examination, vacation, fission, confession, relation, aggravation, completion.* After twenty or more words have been named, ask the class what they notice about these words (that is, about the spellings of this sound in English). Have them form generalizations about the spelling of this suffix. One might expect a class to suggest statements similar to these:

1 The suffix which sounds like SHUN is spelled SION or TION.
2 -TION occurs after A.
3 -SION occurs after the letter S which is then double.

Record the findings of this particular study on a chart to which additional findings can be added. The generalizations may be revised as new findings are noted; for example, someone may discover the group of deceptive words which terminate in SION which sounds /žən/ as in DECISION and REVISION. Also watch for the word COERCION.

Generalizations may also be made after exploring the spelling of other commonly used affixes or phoneme groups. Have students examine these examples in the manner described:

1 boner, honor, sulfur, grammar, recorder, splendor (How about martyr?)
2 ease, marry, teens, piece, detour, sardine, pique, rainy, wee, fear
3 mended, scored, shocked, crooked, hoped, spelled

Study steps Almost every set of spelling texts includes a list of steps for learning to spell a word. The steps usually are something like these:

1 Look at the word.
2 Say the word.
3 Say the parts of the word.
4 Try to write the word without looking at it.
5 Compare your spelling with that in the book.

These steps would undoubtedly be helpful if they were applied, but it has been found that the child studying spelling independently does not follow the prescribed steps. His failure to follow these steps may be attributed to the complexity of the steps or perhaps to sheer boredom with a less than exciting routine.

MOTIVATING STUDENT INTEREST

The most important task of the spelling instructor is to develop student interest and concern for spelling. What are the reasons for learning to spell words? The discussion of this topic proves beneficial at the beginning of a school year as a means for motivating student interest in learning this skill. The listing of student-contributed reasons often is more influential in affecting student opinion than is a teacher-prepared list, although both lists might include the same point:

1 People can understand what you have written.
2 You make a better impression on those reading your work.
3 You make better grades in school on written work.
4 There is personal satisfaction in doing something well.

Why do we need standardized spelling? Why not permit everyone to spell as he chooses? This sentence written on the board will bring laughter, but should make your point:

Noo Girzee lize ahn thu koste.

The next problem in motivating interest is to select techniques which are stimulating rather than routine. Moving from the usual method of test-study-test-study-test, the perceptive teacher will find varied ways for teaching spelling, methods which will have more lasting effects on ability to spell. In selecting stimulating activities the teacher must be discriminating, for many Spelling Games are of little real value in teaching children to spell or even in motivating interest. The Spelling Bee is one example of an activity which has little benefit, for its emphasis on oral spelling is of questionable value in teaching the written skill of spelling and too few children are actively involved at one time.

- **BEWARE OF THE SILENT LETTER** is the caption of a display featuring words (contributed by students) that contain silent letters which are printed in contrasting colors, for example:

gnat knob debt cupboard column slide

HOW DO YOU SPELL IT? Why, i,t, of course!

- Practice spelling words which are not known. Even the longest word can be spelled readily if it follows regular phonic patterns. Familiarity with common prefixes and suffixes is also helpful. Pronounce words carefully as children write them and build confidence through success. Aren't these words easy?

plantation	equitable	surrounding
fantastic	explanatory	blameless
convention	discovery	alliteration
insistent	reputation	equation

How would this exercise assist children in composition skill? Would you grade these words? What would you say if a child left out one L in alliteration?

• Unusual characteristics of words lend interest to the study of spelling as they do the study of words (See Chapter 5). This poem can be read aloud, although each person should be looking at a copy, as an introduction to a study of Homonyms:

A TAIL OF WHOA

Iris M. Tiedt

(Two bee red allowed)

Eye stood before the window pain
To stair out on the stormy seen.
The wind it blue
With grown and mown
As rein pored threw the lain.

Eye razed my head to view the cite
And new my hart wood brake
Four rested from hour would
Were awl the furs sew tall and grate
Know more too waive the see.

Aisle ne'er forget that dreadful knight—
A quire of desolation maid
Buy hale and creek of bows—
Yet still no paws or lesson.
The whether it was fowl!

Then shown at last the mourning son.
The heir now boar the fare suite cent
Of rows and hair belle whet.
At piece the wind; knot sew my sole,
Fore their the land lei waist.

• To give practice in using capital letters with names of cities and states conduct an Alphabet Search as each person tries to find a city beginning with A (Akron, Ohio), then *B* (Baltimore, Maryland), and so on.

- WHAT WORD IS THIS? might be the title of these riddles which focus attention on the spelling of specific words as in this example:

I like green but I don't like purple.	(G)
I like house but not mouse.	(H)
I like autos but not cars.	(O)
I like sheet but not blanket.	(S)
I like night but not nigh.	(T)

(GHOST: one letter indicated by each line. Each letter is within the first word but not the second.)

- This humorous poem by an unknown poet may serve to interest students in discovering examples of plurals which follow a similar pattern and those which deviate.

AN ENGLISH TEST

We'll begin with box, the plural is boxes,
But the plural of ox should be oxen, not oxes.
One fowl is a goose, but two are called geese,
Yet the plural of mouse is never meese.
You may find a lone mouse, or a whole nest of mice,
But the plural of house is houses, not hice.
If the plural of man is always men,
Why shouldn't the plural of pan be called pen?
The cow in the plural may be called cows or kine,
But a bow, if repeated, is never called bine;
And the plural of vow is vows, not vine.
If I speak of a foot and you show me two feet,
And I give you a boot, would a pair be called beet?
If one is a tooth and a whole set are teeth,
Why shouldn't the plural of booth be called beeth?
If the singular's this, and the plural these,
Should the plural of kiss ever be written keese?
We speak of a brother, and also of brethren,
But though we say mother, we never say mothren.
Then the masculine pronouns are he, his, and him,
But imagine the feminine, she, shis, and shim!
So the English, I think you all will agree,
Is the funniest language you ever did see.

- Teach any of these skills and spelling itself through the technique of dictation. Compose (or have students compose) sentences which illustrate the use of capitalization, plurals, contractions, and possessive forms, thus:

Mary's mother said, "Please, Mary, set the table."
Your three cats won't stay out of Mr. Handy's garden.
Harry's coming home for his grandfather's birthday.

Present these sentences without previous study to see how many students can write them correctly. Have students write them on the board as class members point out any errors, and each corrects his own sentences. Repeat the testing procedure.

METHODS OF STUDY

Most of the words which are included in a spelling list are words which are already present in the child's speaking or reading vocabulary. Only occasionally, therefore, is it necessary to present detailed information about the meanings of words presented. When presenting a new list of words, on the other hand, it is motivating to note with the class the interesting characteristics of the words being presented. What aspects of this list might the teacher use to add interest to spelling?

coal	goal	foal	hole	whole	mole
bowl	pole	role	roll	soul	roll

An inductive approach to this lesson will lead the children to identify several spellings for the sound *ōl: oal, ole, owl, oll, oul.* This list has been grouped according to a common sound with only the initial sound changing in each word. Extend learning by having children experiment with changing the vowel or the ending sound; for example, "If you know how to spell *coal,* what other word might you spell?" (coat, cool) What will be noticed about the pairs of words: *hole* and *whole, roll* and *role?*

An assorted group of words might be presented to a group of fourth graders.

huge	rather	spoken	hopeful	crimson
bicycle	control	present	examine	complete

We might begin with the first word by asking, "Who recognizes this word?" "Who knows what it means?" There would follow a discussion of other synonyms for *big.* What sound does the *g* make in this word? If we removed the *e,* what word would we have? Why is the *e* there? (To keep the *g* soft; to make the *u* long.) The word bicycle might initiate a discussion of the prefix *bi,* and *control* would warrant a comment on the prefix *con.* The word *present* is a heteronym which can lead to an interesting discussion (Who will present the present?).

Pretesting As noted previously, many spellings are learned incidentally, therefore before any study takes place the teacher should dictate each word to the group as a test, having each student attempt to spell the words correctly. The purpose of this pretesting technique is simply to determine which words are already known by each individual student. This test is marked (not graded) by the teacher, who may circle the part of each word which has been incorrectly spelled. The student can then compare the incorrect spellings with the list in the spelling book or on the board. This test-study-test method has been found more effective than study followed by testing without a pretest.[9]

The student who already knows the spellings of the words presented should spend his other time with some other profitable activity rather than wasting time pretending to study. Students who need help, on the other hand, can be assisted in learning the spellings not known.

When marking student papers, accent the positive by noting the number right rather than always marking those wrong.

Moving from Symbol to Sound: Reading

In developing the chart of phonemes and the corresponding graphemes that occur in written English, we first identified the forty sounds of English. Working with each phoneme, we noted the alternate spellings or symbols associated with each phoneme. As the child learns to read, the process is reversed. The beginning reader views the printed symbols and must decide with which sound each set of symbols is associated. Children learn, for example, that *ph* is an alternate spelling for the phoneme /*f*/. If they see the words, *phone, elephant,* or *graph,* they must learn to supply that phoneme in the appropriate position. This aspect of learning to read is called *phonics.* The fluent reader seldom stops to decode in this manner.[10]

The ideal integrated language-arts program will include a built-in reinforcement of the writing (encoding) and reading (decoding) of individual phonemes and the graphemes, beginning, of course, with the least difficult relationships and the most commonly used words. In order to teach the phoneme-grapheme relationship, we deliberately choose words that are fairly regular and represent the easiest and most common spellings for each phoneme—for example, *man, make, miss, mad, map.* We recognize the fact that many short, commonly used words such as *does, one,* and *who,* are not regular, so they are taught as "sight words" that the child learns without analysis (see Chapter 12).

[9] Gerald C. Eichholz, "Spelling Improvement through a Self-Check Device," *Elementary School Journal* (April, 1964), p. 376.

[10] Frank Smith, *Understanding Reading* (New York: Holt, Rinehart, and Winston, 1971), pp. 221–28.

A DEVELOPMENTAL SEQUENCE

To facilitate this type of presentation, we have created a developmental sequence that is designed to aid the child's ability to associate phoneme with grapheme and grapheme with phoneme. Activities suggested begin orally and aurally and move to writing and reading.

STEP I: Initial Consonant Phonemes

/b/, /d/, /f/, /h/, /j/, /k/, /l/, /m/, /n/, /p/, /r/, /t/, /v/, /w/, /y/, /z/

Bird begins with the letter *b, bird.* (Print on board.)
Can you tell me other words that begin like *bird?*

(Later) Who can tell me what sound we hear at the beginning of ball?
Can you tell me other words that begin with *b?*
Which word in this group does not begin with *b?*
boy barn cow

CAUTION: Do not introduce too many sound-letter correspondences at one time. Begin as shown with only one sound. Review this sound the next day, and introduce one new sound, and so on. Call attention to the known sounds as they occur in other activities for excellent reinforcement.

Never present a consonant sound isolated from a word, for children may later have difficulty blending the beginning consonant and the following phonogram. The child who has been taught to say *buh* for the sound of /b/ may pronounce the word *bent* as *buh ent.*

After children know a number of consonants, a valuable practice requires them to substitute consonants to make new words:

With which letter-sound does ball begin? *(b)*
Who can make a new word by changing */b/* to */t/*? Substitute other known sounds: */f/, /h/, /w/.*

What letter-sound do we hear at the beginning of *hold? (h)*
Can you make a new word that begins with */t/?*
Let's see if we can put */b/* in front of these little words: *and, eat, ad, in, at.*
Can anyone put */b/* in front of *ring?* in front of *right? link? low? lame?*

Repeated oral practice with sounds will later aid a linguistically sound approach to independent writing of words as the child learns to print in first grade.

STEP II: Uncomplicated vowel sounds

"Short vowels": */e/, /æ/, /i/, /ə/, /a/,*
as in: hen, sat, pit, nut, got

The short u, /ə/, is called the schwa. It is also made by other vowels in *un*accented syllables as the *i* in family. Some authors differentiate between the short u sound and the schwa, but there seems to be no reason to do so as the sound is a single phoneme /ə/.

"Long vowels" */iy/, /ey/, /ay/, /ow/, /yuw/* [11]
as in he, hay, ice, go, use

The linguist's designation of long vowels is confusing for the student unfamiliar with Romance languages. The first sound above, for example, is *ē;* because the *i* has that sound in Romance languages. (The letter *e* sounds like *ā;* the letter *a* sounds like *ah;* the *u* is pronounced *o͞o*). The *y* and *w* which follow each sound indicate a gliding sound which we make faintly after the first sound. Try saying words containing these vowel sounds to notice this effect.

Although the vowel sounds are presented orally in kindergarten and first grade, their real study waits until writing and reading experiences. Again we can make use of substitution.

> What vowel sound do we hear in *hat?* Can you put another *short* vowel sound in place of the *a?* What words can you make?
>
> hit, hot, hut. Does *het* make a word?
>
> If you know how to spell the word *luck* (write on the board), how would you spell *lock? lick? lack?*
>
> Can you read this word? (Print *miss.*)
>
> If we change the vowel *(moss),* what word do we have?
> If we change the vowel *(muss),* what word do we have?
> If we change the vowel *(mass),* what word do we have?

Use inductive or discovery methods to introduce concepts of phonology also. Ask the children, for example, to begin naming words which contain *long* vowels. List twenty to thirty words on the board for examination:

[11] Linguists do not include the sound */yuw/* as a separate phoneme because it is actually two sounds, */y/* and */uw/,* but we find it helpful to teach *ū* with the other vowels because in practice they really do "say their own names."

name	boat	hope	slide	many
see	heel	use	seed	might
leaf	speedy	diet	write	sadly
right	kite	light	late	speech

Use a large number of samples so the class will note variations in spelling of long vowel sounds. They can make generalizations like the following derived from their observations:

1 A double *ee* is pronounced *ē*.
2 When a silent *e* is on the end of a word, the vowel before the *e* is long.
3 The letters *igh* signal a long *i* sound.
4 When two vowels are together, the first is long and the second is silent. (The group will find exceptions to this "rule" later, for example, *diet* does not fit this statement.)
5 The *y* on the end of a word is usually pronounced *ē*. (This statement may later be amended to "a word of two or more syllables" and even that generalization has exceptions. Also see the note on page 110.)

This kind of discovery activity causes the students to think as they observe language. The teacher must permit students to make their own discoveries (and their own mistakes), although the "correctness" of a recorded statement previously made by the class may be questioned when new cases are discovered. Students should be encouraged to share and to record any LINGUISTIC DISCOVERIES made as the study progresses.

STEP III: Initial Consonant Blends

Blends: *bl, cl, fl, gl, pl, sl*
br, cr, dr, fr, gr, pr, tr
sc, sk, sm, sn, sp, st, sw, tw
scr, shr, spr, str, spl, sch, thr

The blends are introduced in the same way as the initial consonants and are expanded through substitution and induction or discovery techniques.

Give students difficult words they could scarcely know how to spell. What blend do you hear at the beginning of FLUCTUATE? SMITHEREENS? STRIPLING? PRIMROSE? GROUSE? STIPEND? This is an effective way to encourage students to try spelling unknown words as well as to introduce them to some interesting words which can be explained or used in a sentence by the teacher as seems appropriate.

STEP IV: Irregular Consonants

Letters that do not represent a sound of their own: C, X, Q

C represents /s/ in *cent* and /k/ in *cow;* there really is no *c* sound.

X sounds like /*ks*/ in *fox* and *excuse* and /*z*/ in *xylophone.*
Q is usually followed by U and sounds like /*kw*/ as in *quit.*

Letters that represent two or more sounds: G and S

G represents a "hard" sound /*g*/ as in *gave* and represents the "soft" sound of /*j*/ as in *age.*

S represents several sounds as in *sit* /*s*/, *rose* /*z*/, *measure* /*ž*/, and *sure* /*š*/.

A WORTHWHILE RULE: C represents /*s*/ before I and E (and Y when Y substitutes for *I* and *E*), but it represents /*k*/ before other letters—*cake, coat, creek, cure, clean.*

STEP V: Consonant Digraphs

CH as in *chest, chorus* (Greek), *champagne* (French)
SH as in *short, patient, nation, ocean*
TH as in *the, thing*
WH as in *where, who*
GH as in *ghost, laugh*
PH as in *phone*
PS as in *psalm*
NG (an ending sound) as in *hang*
NK (an ending sound) as in *think*

What is the difference between a blend and a digraph? In a blend you can hear the letter sounds which blend, but in the digraph the identity of individual sounds is lost and a new sound is produced.

STEP VI: Silent Letters

W as in *wrist*
K as in *knot*
B as in *comb*
C as in *sick, scene*
L as in *walk*
G as in *gnaw*
H as in *honest*
T as in *witch, often*
U as in *guide* (The *u* serves to indicate the /*g*/ phoneme.)
GH as in *light*

STEP VII: Vowels Followed by *R*

AR as in *car*
ER as in *her*
IR as in *sir, mirror*
OR as in *for, favor*
UR as in *nurse*

The R causes the vowel to produce a sound that is neither long nor short, yet is relatively common; for example, *er*.

An E following the Vowel + R signals a long vowel, thus:

car = care fir = fire her = here

STEP VIII: Vowel Diphthongs

A	E	I	O	U
ai gain	*ee wee*	*y by*	*oa goat*	*u(e) use*
ay may	*ea meat*	*uy buy*	*ow own*	*ew few*
ei neigh	*ei receive*	*ei height*	*oe doe*	*en queue*
ey they	*ie believe*	*igh high*		

The diphthong is a single blending sound produced by two vowels usually ending in a gliding sound (y or w). Notice the spelling and pronunciation of this word (diphthong). Do you hear the phoneme /f/? See the vowel chart for more examples of spellings of the various diphthongs.

OW as *now, slow*
OU as *house, rough, slough, dough, could*
EW as *few, knew*
OO as *food, good*
AU as *caught*
AW as *saw*
OI as *oil*
OY as *boy*

STEP IX: Phonograms

at	ed	it	ot	un
ate	et	in	ote	ung
ail	eat	ip	oat	ub
ain	ean	id	oar	ug
ait	eed	ing	ore	unt
an	eet	ind	on	ule
ang	end	ine	one	up
ap	ent	int	ong	ull
ag	eam	ick	ort	um
ab	en	iss	oon	uss
ad	eg	ite	ool	ut
ack	ell	ice	oom	ute

The list of phonograms is almost inexhaustible. These ending sounds may be used in conjunction with learning of initial consonants and blends. How many of the above phonograms will form a word if the letter s is placed before them: *sat, sail, sang, sap,* and so on?

In teaching the vowel sounds many teachers find it practical to emphasize three sounds for each vowel, always carefully noting that these sounds are not the *only* sounds associated with each vowel. A chart like this one is helpful in clarifying what may otherwise be a most confusing subject of study for those who are just beginning to use phonic skills in reading and spelling:

	LONG		SHORT		FOLLOWED BY R	
A	make	/ey/ *	at	/æ/	car	/ar/
E	eat	/iy/	let	/e/	her	/ɨ/
I	ice	/ay/	hit	/i/	sir	/ɨ/
O	no	/ow/	got	/a/	for	/or/
U	use	/yuw/	nut	/ə/	purr	/ɨ/

Instructors often teach rather odd concepts about letter sounds. One can only assume that these misconceptions were taught them as children and continue to remain as part of their store of "knowledge," which points up the need to rethink or re-evaluate our thinking periodically or, more precisely, *constantly*.

One teacher, when using the illustrated vowel chart, for example, cited the word YOU as an example of the long U sound. Why is this example incorrect? A well-known linguist equates the vowel sounds in WHO and PUT, although the sounds are made in different parts of the mouth and throat. It is plain that one needs an attentive ear to distinguish differences in sounds.

Another letter which causes much confusion is Y, which represents both consonant and vowel sounds. The consonant sound is clearly identified in words like YELLOW, YACHT, YONDER. It is Y as a vowel, however, which bears clarification.

Y represents no vowel sounds of its own, but serves as an alternate spelling for I and E sounds. It would be inaccurate, therefore, to designate long and short sounds for Y, for it actually appears as both long I */ay/* and long E */iy/* as well as short I */i/*. We know of no cases in which Y takes the short E */e/* sound; perhaps you will find one. Note the following examples:

* When presenting to a class, do not use the phonemes provided for your use.

LONG I	LONG E	SHORT I
dye	sadly *	crypt
my	playfully *	analysis
cry	happy *	tryst
lyre	baby	cygnet
lying	theology	nymph
hyphen	identity	lyric
cypress	sticky	lynx
scythe	St. Cyr (Fr.)	rhythm
why	Ypres (Belg.)	oxygen
modify	Yperite (a gas)	Ypsilanti (Michigan city)
hygiene	Elysian	lynch
type	Lyons (Fr.)	catalyst
thyme	embryo	gypsy (the first Y)
gyrate		gymnasium
hyacinth		hymn

As we scan the list of the sounds used in speaking English, we can readily note that some sounds are less confusing in that only one grapheme is usually used to denote this sound—*/p/, /t/, /b/, /d/, /m/, /n/, /l/, /v/*. These consonant sounds are among the first to be identified, and they cause little difficulty in spelling. For this reason we can safely teach words combining these consonants with the simpler vowel sounds—*/i/, /e/, /æ/*—in early spelling lessons.

Display pictures of objects with the word printed below. Omit the beginning consonant so that children can determine which grapheme should be placed at the beginning of each word. Provide a variety—*vase, table, pony, baby, dog, mother, number, picture, log, dancer.*

Practice locating blends which occur in different positions in a word as: SK in *skip, risk,* and *whiskers.* Other sounds may also be located as: SH in *shape, overshoe,* and *brush,* and CH in *chatter, branch,* and *unchain.*

As students advance in ability to identify sounds, they can explore the diphthongs and those consonant phonemes which are made by varied graphemes. Often the inductive method can be used to encourage student discovery.

The phoneme */š/* is spelled with a wide variety of graphemes. Students can pursue a search for as many different examples as they can find. Discoveries

* The Y in the suffixes *ly* and *y* was long designated in dictionaries as a short I */i/*. Usage, however, denies this pronunciation, for do we not use a *long E* to end such words? It is interesting to note that *Webster's Third New International Dictionary* (1961) lists for the first time the long *E* as the first pronunciation, thus: 'sadlē or 'hapē. Teaching this Y as a short I is confusing to students and should be avoided when the /iy/ pronunciation is used.

may include: *shell, ocean, racial, sugar, delicious, vacation, fission, schwa, champagne, tissue, omniscient.*

Write twenty to thirty words containing the letter C on the board; for example, *coal, accident, block, accuse, scale, sick, crime, custom, concave, circumstance, circle, circus, cell, cactus, cane, cigar, ace, accept.* Have the words pronounced as the class examines the list. Ask them what they notice about the group of words. They can make generalizations which will lead to the observation that C represents no sound of its own and might be considered to be a useless letter.

Write a few words from one extensive family; for example, *lack, back, pack, rack, sack, Jack.* After observing the similarity, have the students expand this family as much as possible, adding: *track, clack, knack,* etc. (If the word *plaque* is suggested, send someone to the dictionary.) Examine the list when completed; have children pronounce the words. Then experiment with changing the vowel to I or O. How many of these words will make words with the new vowel? Will spelling change at times?

PHONIC FALLACIES

Phonics has been severely criticized by the linguists, and some of the criticism has been justified. The fallacies that have been included in most presentations of phonics have largely, however, been the result of lack of information. The persons who have worked with reading instruction have, heretofore, had little or no knowledge of the phoneme and were unable, therefore, to consider the phoneme-grapheme relationship in detail as we have done in this chapter.

In many cases teachers teach as they were taught without considering the exceptions that exist for most of the phonic generalizations that have been handed down from earlier instructors. Many examples of fallacious thinking appear in print and continue to be taught (1) in classrooms by teachers who have not been taught contemporary linguistic concepts, (2) by professors writing textbooks, who should be better informed, and (3) even by linguists who are supposed to be experts but who do not know the field of reading. Careful examination of presentations of phonics leads us to the following conclusions:

1 Very few "rules" are consistent enough to warrant teaching. Several that are consistent have been inserted within the phonics sequence. As soon as there are many exceptions, rules have little value and serve only to confuse the beginning reader.

2 Sounds of single phonemes or combinations of phonemes should be pronounced in the context of a word. A consonant cannot be pronounced alone. The minute we try to say a consonant phoneme, we put a vowel sound behind it, which explains the presence of a vowel in every syllable.

The number of vowel sounds heard indicates the number of syllables in a word.

3 We need to be certain of our linguistic knowledge and our ear for sounds, and we may need to reassess our understanding of phonology and the concepts we are teaching (even though they may appear in a textbook).

4 Regional variations in pronunciation exist. Because varied pronunciations are used does not mean they are "wrong." We bring them to the level of awareness because they are interesting phenomena in our language, not to evaluate them or to change the child's native speech.

Children should develop their own generalizations about language just as an adult does. The phonic concepts that we try to teach children may have meaning only to the fluent reader who has already been exposed repeatedly to written language.

The use of phonics has been aimed at aiding the beginning reader. As Smith points out, however, the language rules needed to enable a reader to predict the pronunciation of even common words are highly complex; and, even if you knew them all, you couldn't be certain a word would be correctly identified by use of phonics alone. Smith notes, furthermore:

> The question that cannot yet be answered concerns the *effectiveness* of phonics: is the limited degree of efficiency that might be attained worth acquiring? Other factors have to be taken into account related to the *cost* of trying to learn and use a phonic system. Our working memories do not have an infinite capacity and reading is not a task that can be accomplished at too leisurely a pace. Other sources of information exist for finding out what a word in context might be, especially if the word is in the spoken vocabulary of the reader.[12]

It is true that fluent readers obviously know many phonic generalizations. They use them intuitively usually without conscious thought. In fact, it is unlikely that they could verbalize these rules if requested to explain how to pronounce specific words. For example, how would you pronounce these words?

clique	diphthong	lachrymose
coupon	dilatory	impious
athletics	albeit	slough

Can you explain the rules on which you based your selection of a pronunciation? Work in small groups as you compare your pronunciation with that selected by other students in the class. Which pronunciation is listed in your dictionary?

[12] Frank Smith, *Psycholinguistics and Reading* (New York: Holt, Rinehart and Winston, 1973), p. 90.

Another point to consider about phonics is the expectation that the child will figure out how to pronounce a word. Reading does not necessarily include verbalization. Unless you use the above words in a speech, you have no real need to know their exact pronunciations. The children literally do not have to pronounce a word to gain meaning. They do have to associate a set of symbols with a meaning, but they do not have to say the word aloud as we often think. We must have our objectives clearly in mind in teaching. Are we aiming at fluent reading with comprehension, or are we concerned about oral performance with language and effective communication?

Integrating Spelling and Reading

Obviously, there is much overlap in the related skills of spelling and reading. There is little justification, therefore, for presenting these areas of study as totally unrelated subjects as is done in the elementary school curriculum and in textbook publication. If these subjects are taught in isolation, the child may never be aware of the interrelated nature of reading and spelling. An examination of spelling and reading textbooks, particularly workbooks, reveals that there is also a great deal of repetition without the benefit of coordination.

Individualized instruction and the language-experience method of teaching language-arts skills permit children to discover the ways of English without this repetition. These approaches encourage children to make their own generalizations and to integrate the learnings through experimenting and observing. Here are ways of teaching that remove any stigma from English and spelling and break down the barriers among the various language arts. It is time for us to rethink old methods, to question the efficacy of time-honored tradition, and to risk letting children make choices about how and what they will learn.

TEACHING THE PHONEME-GRAPHEME RELATIONSHIPS

The primary grade child usually knows the full set of English sounds but is probably not aware of these sounds until formal instruction in auditory discrimination begins in the classroom. Jerry learns to relate the sounds he has learned to the written symbols that we use to represent these sounds. He learns that it is possible to write the words he can speak and, conversely, that anyone who knows the sound-symbol code can read a coded message that he has written or that someone else has written.

How can we best aid the English-speaking child who is learning to read and write? The first step is awareness of the sounds of English at the auditory level. The child needs practice in discriminating likenesses and differences among the sounds that he uses regularly. We give practice like this:

Which words begin like Tom? tiger, dog, tough

Which word does *not* begin like Tom? table, tool, dust

How many words can you name that begin like Tom? toast, tub, tick, turtle, tease, tooth, . . . and so on

As the child learns to work with sounds orally and aurally, we introduce the written symbol that we commonly use to represent a sound that we can make. Tammy is beginning to work with the sound-symbol relationship as she learns to associate the sound she says with a symbol she can write. She then associates the written symbol that she sees with the sound that she can make.

We begin, of course, with the most commonly used relationships between phoneme (the sound) and grapheme (the spelling of the sound). The child soon learns, for instance, that the sound heard at the beginning of *take* or the end of *sat* is spelled in the same way with one *t* symbol. Then he or she might be introduced to the less common grapheme that appears at the end of *mitt* or *mutt*. Upper grade students will delight in discovering even more unusual alternate spellings of this sound as in:

ptomaine	Thomas	veldt
pterodactyl	debt	Tiedt

The same process is followed for each of the sounds of English as the child learns to associate the sounds of the spoken English language with written symbols working back and forth with encoding and decoding—that is, writing and reading. Through this discussion, it is easy to see how important it is to teach reading and writing together as two aspects of the same process—that is, learning to use the English code.

How can we develop the child's awareness of the sound-symbol relationship in the English language? This is a continuous process beginning with the simplest relationships that can be easily handled by first graders to more complex ones that some of you may discover as adults.

Minimal pairs One method the linguist uses to identify the existence of different phonemes in a language is the comparison of words that are exactly the same except for one sound, as /*pin*/ and /*fin*/. A native speaker could pronounce the word *pin* loudly, softly, with very little breath, or heavy aspiration. If, no matter how Harry says the word, he still points to a safety pin as he says /*pin*/, there is no change in meaning.

When he says /*fin*/, however, he no longer points to the safety pin but indicates the fin of a fish. Clearly he acknowledges different meanings as he says /*pin*/ when pointing to the safety pin but /*fin*/ when talking about the fish. Here is phonemic difference or two different sounds, /*p*/ and /*f*/.

Children can observe these differences in minimal pairs, too. At first present the pairs orally, thus:

Which word is an animal? *cat, hat*
Which word is something to eat? *ham, hat*
Which word tells time? *clock, click*

Rhyming words is another way of working with minimal pairs, a series of them. Ask children to name words that rhyme with *ring*. Only the initial consonant phoneme is changed as they name *sing, king, wing*.

If children name such words as *sting* or *strong*, of course, they are no longer working with minimal pairs because more than a single phoneme has been introduced. Contrast the phonemic spelling of these words: /*riŋ*/, /*stiŋ*/, /*striŋ*/. There are three, four and five sounds in these words, respectively. Notice, however, that *ring* and *thing* contrast minimal pairs because the grapheme *th*—as in *thing, thin, thimble*—represents a single English sound /*θ*/. *Ring* and *thing* are spelled phonemically, thus: /*riŋ*/, /*θiŋ*/.

A sound-symbol chart A chart of sounds with corresponding symbols can be developed at varying levels of sophistication as soon as children begin associating spoken sounds with written symbols. Encourage children to discover these sounds of English themselves as they work first orally and aurally. Then have them supply the common grapheme(s) for each sound as you begin a chart like this:

SOUND	SPELLING		
	BEGINNING	MIDDLE	FINAL
/*t*/	ten	after	hat
/*b*/	box	about	cab
/*p*/	pat	upon	cup
/*f*/	fat, phone	before	half, laugh
/*n*/	not, knot	inside	pin

More advanced children can expand this chart fully in an exciting study of the English language. Their discoveries may include the following additions to the sample chart above.

SOUND	SPELLING		
	BEGINNING	MIDDLE	FINAL
/*t*/	ten, ptomaine, Thomas	after	hat, debt, veldt
/*b*/	box	about, Dobbs	cab, Dobb
/*p*/	pat	upon	cup, Lapp
/*n*/	not, knot, gnat pneumonia, mnemonics	inner, another, unknown	inn, on
/*s*/	seen, cent science, psalm	also	class, hats, ax
/*g*/	go, ghost, guess	legal, ago	bag, vague
/*k*/	cat, kite, khaki chorus, quit	act	pick, plaque

Development of these charts will lead students to make many observations regarding patterns of English orthography. Notice, for example, that the grapheme *gh* occurs in two places on the chart. Have students make a list of examples of these two sound-symbol relationships:

laugh	ghost
rough	ghastly
enough	ghetto
tough	
cough	

It is easy, of course, to develop a list of words that begin with a given initial grapheme. Here is a real incentive for using the dictionary. Development of such lists also exposes children to new vocabulary; for example, *ghastly* or *ghetto,* which may be learned incidentally by many children.

After these lists are completed, children can examine the sample words and derive generalizations regarding the appearance of this grapheme in English words.

1 When the sound /*f*/ is heard at the end of a word, this sound might be spelled GH.
2 When the sound /*g*/ is heard at the beginning of a word, this sound might be spelled GH.
3 When GH appears at the beginning of a word, it has the sound /*g*/.
4 When GH apears at the end of a word, it has the sound /*f*/.

Notice the very limited number of examples of each of these phoneme-grapheme relationships. Obviously, this spelling is not the most common spelling for either phoneme. Children can compare the number of words listed for /*g*/ spelled GH with those in which initial /*g*/ is spelled G.

They may also prepare a list of words beginning with /g/ spelled GU. In this way, students will begin to observe the frequency of the various spellings. When they are uncertain about which spelling to use for this sound, the educated guess would select the most frequently used.

Students are also becoming aware of the specific words that use the less common spellings. It is not essential that children memorize these lists of words. Gradually, however, reinforcement through exposure to this knowledge will help students learn to associate certain spellings with specific words.

INDIVIDUALIZED APPROACHES

There are many individualized activities that students can pursue as they enjoy playing with language in varied ways. Through these activities they will learn far more about language than through any formal presentation followed by drill. Use some of the following on TASK CARDS that children can select for independent study.

- ARE YOU TEED OFF? asks the caption of a display which features words containing the sound TEE with emphasis again on student discoveries:

  teeny teepee eternity teasing society teaspoon

- Student-prepared word quizzes can feature interesting pairs of words that will prove intriguing to others:

  quiver, quaver stunt, stint boner, banner

- TWENTY-SIX SCADOO! has all students racing to write a word for each letter. Specify rules according to the ability level: each word must be at least six letters; each word must contain three syllables, etc.

- BEAT THE CLOCK requires each student to write ten (set the number according to the group) words beginning with any given sound before the second hand goes all around the clock. As the second hand approaches twelve, write the letters *tr,* for example, on the board. Each student immediately begins writing: *Treat, Trust, Truth,* etc.

- SELF-DIAGNOSIS is an excellent means for interesting the student in bettering his spelling. At the beginning of the year give the students a test (never too long at any one time) of words which all should know how to spell—*said, what, who, and, that, which, them, she, can, like,* and so forth. If you don't have a list compiled, ask several students (poor spellers will be motivated by assuming this responsibility to prepare a list of words they think all should know). Repeat the test several times during the year as each tries to master the group of words. Refer to these words incidentally also to keep them in everyone's mind.

- **CATTY WORDS is the caption which accompanies a group of words which contain the syllable CAT. Encourage students to discover words with a similar relationship to introduce to the class: THESE WORDS ARE DOGS! (*doggerel, dogged, dogma*), HAVE YOU PAID YOUR FEES? (*fealty, coffee, phenomenon*), CAN YOU SEE? (*season, deceive, seep*).**

- **Each student develops a CHAIN REACTION as he or she creates a new word by changing one letter at a time, thus: *tear, dear, deaf, leaf, loaf, loan, loon, noon.***

A WORD WHEEL is useful in the primary classroom as students try to combine initial consonant sounds with varied phonograms. Simple wheels can be made, as in the diagram, or commercial varieties are available.

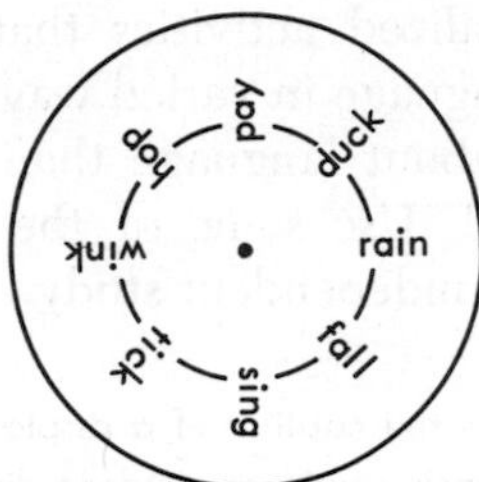

More advanced work in phonology can introduce students to examples of foreign language in English which affects our pronunciation and causes supposed irregularities in English pronunciation. Why, for example, do we look at the word *cello* which might be pronounced *sello* and say *chello?* It's an Italian word, of course, which requires the *ch* sound according to Italian linguistics. We can observe many *loan* words: *plaza, prima donna, tempo, séance, requiem, mirage, per capita, piñata, boudoir, cuisine*. Often we have retained the original pronunciation, but sometimes we anglicize the borrowed words as in *detour, bonbons, ensemble, adroit.*

DICTIONARY STUDY

Although this skill has direct relevance for spelling, it is also vital to other subject area studies. The use of the dictionary throughout the curriculum tends to reinforce learning and also increases the value of construction. Dictionary skills range from the most elementary to advanced skills involving specialized dictionaries with a sequence of abilities developing something like this:

1 Ability to say the alphabet letters in order
2 Use of alphabetical order in arranging words
3 Examination of the dictionary and its parts
4 Opening the dictionary to a specified letter
5 Finding a specified word

6 Using the dictionary to find acceptable spelling, pronunciation, and meaning
7 Using the dictionary to increase vocabulary (synonyms)
8 Making discoveries about words; studying etymology

Many kindergarten children come to school already able to recite the alphabet in order. Practice should be given in the use of this skill during kindergarten and first grade as the children become increasingly aware of the letters through phonics studies and beginning writing skills.

- **Display the alphabet in the room in varied ways. An alphabet chart is helpful because all can see it, and the chart is available for reference as needed. Display letters in connection with appropriate pictures as knowledge of the alphabet is integrated with increasing vocabulary. A,B,C,D might be featured on a bulletin board with large pictures of an apron, baby, cat, and dog.**

- **Having children line up for recess in alphabetical order is a way of introducing alphabetical order. (Specify either first or last names.) As you call out, "A," all those with names beginning with A may get in line, then B, and so on. Later introduce the concept of alphabetizing the group of A names by the second letter.**

- **WHO CAN FOLLOW ME? is a simple game for stimulating use of alphabetical order. As the teacher (or leader) says one letter, he or she points to a student who must name the following one or two letters of the alphabet. If D is named, for example, the player must name E and F.**

The use of a dictionary can be started in first grade as children become accustomed to refer to a picture dictionary. Gradually the coverage of the dictionary used expands until students are introduced to the library's copy of an unabridged volume. The teacher should again beware of employing monotonous study techniques which decrease student interest.

- **Opening the dictionary to a specific letter can be an enjoyable game as well as a learning experience. Which letters are in the middle of the alphabet? Which are near the end? Discussions of these ideas will aid the child in opening the dictionary to approximately the right place as any letter is called.**

- **Encourage interest in word study by encouraging student discovery. Are there words which have two pronunciations? Does the meaning change with the pronunciation? (As in the heteronyms, for example, en*trance* and *en*trance.) What words have two acceptable spellings? Do some words have many meanings? Make illustrated charts of some words which have many diverse meanings—*run, horn, hand, fly, field, beat, stock.***

- **Explore synonyms for familiar words by referring to the short list of words included in many dictionary entries or by using the specialized synonym dictionary**

(Roget's *Thesaurus* and others). Prepare a synonym dictionary for use by class members including pages for overworked words: *walk, say, look, big, little.*

- **Prepare a class book of WORD DISCOVERIES in which is included an assortment of interesting facts about words—the longest word found, words which read the same backwards and forwards (palindromes), less common homonyms (*right, wright, write, rite*), and creative uses of words in advertising.**

The study of the English language is fascinating even when children are becoming aware of English spelling. As they discover patterns and generalizations in the language, they will begin to feel a sense of power, a feeling of control over language in a manner they may never have felt before. Language is not an esoteric subject for the study of scholars. Language belongs to all of us, and we can wield it to perform many functions. This concept is important for children to understand.

It is essential also that teachers assess the reading process, the purpose of spelling, and the validity of our own information about linguistics. What are our objectives? What are the concerns of our students? Are we really using the best means to achieve the most desirable ends? Both spelling and phonics instruction are areas that deserve careful scrutiny.

Books to Investigate

Briggs, F. Allen. *The Play of Words*. New York: Harcourt Brace Jovanovich, 1972.

Durkin, Dolores. *Phonics, Lingustics, and Reading*. New York: Teachers College Press, 1972.

Groff, Patrick. *New Phonics*. Boston: Allyn and Bacon, 1973.

Hall, Robert A., Jr. *Sound and Spelling in English*. Philadelphia, Pa.: Chilton Book Co., 1961.

Hanna, Paul, and Hanna, Jean. "The Teaching of Spelling," in *Readings on Contemporary English in the Elementary School*, Iris M. Tiedt and Sidney W. Tiedt, eds. Englewood Cliffs, N.J.: Prentice-Hall, 1974.

Hanna, Paul et al. *Spelling: Structure and Strategies*. Boston: Houghton Mifflin, 1971.

Hodges, Richard E., and Rudorf, E. Hugh. *Language and Learning to Read*. Boston: Houghton Mifflin, 1972.

Horn, Thomas D. "Spelling," in *Encyclopedia of Educational Research*, Robert L. Ebel, ed. New York: The Macmillan Co., 1969, pp. 1282–99. An invaluable reporting of research in spelling.

Johnson, Jean, and Tamburrini, Joan. *Informal Reading and Writing*. New York: Citation Press, 1972.

Smith, Frank. *Psycholinguistics and Reading*. New York: Holt, Rinehart, and Winston, 1973.

Wardhaugh, Ronald. *Reading: A Linguistic Perspective*. New York: Harcourt Brace Jovanovich, 1969.

chapter 5 wordplay

> **We think with words.**
>
> ***Anatole France***

Words, the basic symbols which make up any language, are the tools of the writer and speaker. Spoken, written, read, or heard, they affect the lives of every person from birth. Words are so integral a part of our way of living that the early development in children of a positive attitude toward words and word study is important, for it is through this pleasurable feeling for words that the young student will learn to use them with effect.

How can we promote this feeling for words? We certainly cannot accomplish this end through the assigning of lists of words to be learned, no matter how interesting they are or how useful we know them to be. The approach to student involvement with words must be rather through discovery and inquiry techniques, for it has been found that young people tend to remember and to be interested in those discoveries which they themselves make. It is this approach to word study which we shall explore in this chapter.

Words in Perspective

There are certain aspects of any word which can be studied—structure, sound, meaning, history—any one of which may provide the avenue toward reaching student interest and developing pleasure in the use of words. The presentation of varied perspectives of words will teach students to view words in different ways. As they learn to examine words from many angles, they will learn to use words with imagination.

STRUCTURE

Structure, in the case of a word, has multiple meanings. Looking at a word as a whole we note its shape, its appearance, its configuration. Examining the word further, we find that it is made up of individual letters and that longer words are composed of groupings of letters or syllables. We note, too, that many syllables appear frequently, as in the case of affixes (suffixes and prefixes) or other common groupings of letters. Examining the structure of varied words can be most enlightening and enlivening as in these suggestions:

- **Word Shapes—Primary level children are easily taught to observe the shape of words. They trace the form of the letters with their fingers in an effort to familiarize themselves with the word. Each student can select a word which interests them. Each person then prints or writes this word in as many different ways as they can imagine to see how the word changes in appearance. Here is the word *train,* for example:**

train TRAIN *train* *niart*

After students select the type of print or script to use, they execute the word on a half sheet of colored paper using large letters. (Words containing many ascending and descending letters provide more interesting shapes.) The word shape is outlined with a contrasting crayon to emphasize the shape before it is cut out. The shape is then examined to determine what it suggests—an animal, a human figure, a building, a plant—and a picture is drawn with the shape as the center of interest.

- ***Word Ways*—Encourage students to relate the meaning of words to their appearance in a humorous type of word play. Each student can produce an example like those shown on here, to be displayed on a bulletin board captioned WORDS WITH IMAGINATION. There could be a small learning center set up near the bulletin**

board with stacks of construction paper and felt pens so that boys and girls could let their imaginations soar as their feeling for words grows.

Word Ways

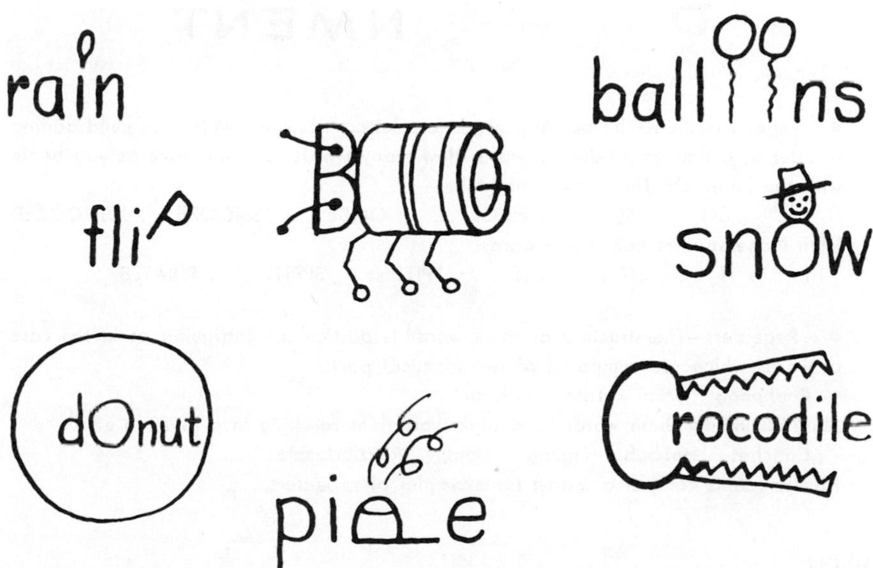

What is the value of this type of word play? Is time spent in this manner justified? The chief argument for presenting word play activities in the classroom is that these activities promote a feeling for words, a liking and respect for words. Words should never frighten or be considered dull, dutiful responsibilities. Rather they should intrigue and fascinate, inviting the young writer to play with them, to manipulate them. Intrigued by words met in this fashion, the child reaches out to discover other words.

- **Word Architecture—The study of prefixes and suffixes which can be attached to root words can lead to the construction of magnificent edifices by young architects. Given a root word, each can see what words can be built. The root LIGHT, for instance, might be built into the following structure:**

LLY
E U G
N F N I N
L I G H T
E E
D NMENT

- Letter Addition—The building blocks are letters this time, with each child adding a letter at a time to produce a word. How many words can you make as you begin with the letter O? The answer might be:
  O . . . SO . . . SON . . . NOSE . . . NOOSE . . . SNOOZE . . . SNOOZED
  With I one student built these words:
  I . . . IT . . . SIT . . . SITE . . . SPITE . . . SPRITE . . . PIRATES

- Repeaters—The structure of some words is particularly intriguing as in the case of words which are composed of two identical parts:
  Poohpooh Mimi Tata Rahrah
  More commonly these words have slight variations resulting in a rhyming effect.
  Chitchat Hubbub Zigzag Tiptop Razzledazzle
  Have students conduct a search for examples of repeaters.

SOUND

The sound of words—the way we say them, pronunciation, musical effects—also lends stimulus to word study. Activities focusing attention on the sound of words can be oral so that the differences can be more readily discerned by students who may miss the full significance of these differences if the words are read silently.

- Homonyms—Students are usually familiar with some examples of the words which sound alike but are not spelled alike—*to, too, two,* and *for, four, fore.* The class can conduct a Homonym Hunt, however, to discover hundreds of less familiar homonyms —*aisle, isle, I'll; council, counsel; marry, merry, Mary; carrot, carat, caret.* Each can present a set of homonyms on a poster illustrating the differences in meaning.

- Heteronyms—Introduce students to the group of words which have different pronunciations and meanings although they are spelled exactly the same. Provide a number of examples and then encourage students to discover as many other examples as possible. Each can prepare a page for a class wordbook entitled HETERONYMS, which includes examples like these:

SEPARATE—Please separate the completed pages.
SEPARATE—Each child had a separate room.
SUBJECT—Don't subject me to that experience.
SUBJECT—What is the subject of your talk?

Beginning with oral activities and developing into written activities, word study emphasizing initial sounds in words is helpful. Not only do these activities lead to the discovery of new words, but they also assist in the learning of phonics skills which aid spelling and reading. Here are examples of varied approaches:

- Print a large *B* on the board. "Let's see how many words we can name in ten minutes that begin with *B*." Everybody takes a turn suggesting words which are printed on the board—*baby, bird, book, bus, Billy, Boston, ball, balloon. . . .*

- Print a large *P* on the board. "Let's see how many words we can name in ten minutes that begin with the *P sound*. Every word must contain more than four letters today." More advanced students can suggest—*princess, pleasant, plaster, paradise, pounce*. (*Pony, pheasant,* and *pea* would not be accepted according to the restrictions set.)

- "How many words can you write which begin with the first syllable RE?" Have students, without the aid of dictionaries, list as many words as possible which begin with this prefix—*refund, renew, refuse, repeat, research, reside*. Compare results after ten minutes, writing examples on the board. Later, dictionaries may be explored to discover the numerous words which might have been included in this list. (*Reptile, rescue,* and *red* are not examples of this prefix.)

- "How many words can you name that begin with the sound CAT?" Students may be able to suggest *catalog, catsup, catacomb, catch, catcher, catechism, category, catfish, cattle*. After sharing any contributions have each one explore these words in the dictionary. (Would *cathedral* be acceptable this time?)

Continuation activities, using these and other variations, can be made available at one or more learning centers about the classroom.

MEANING

The meaning of a word, its definition, includes both the word's denotation and its connotation. In order to communicate successfully in our complex world, we must be aware not only of the meaning of a word for us, but what that same word might mean for the person to whom we are speaking. Our world would be most confusing if we were all like Humpty Dumpty in Lewis Carroll's *Through the Looking Glass,* who said:

> ". . . There's glory for you!"
> "I don't know what you mean by 'glory,'" Alice said.
> Humpty Dumpty smiled contemptuously, "Of course you don't—till I tell you. I meant, 'There's a nice knock-down argument for you!'"
> "But 'glory' doesn't mean 'a nice knock-down argument,'" Alice objected.
> "When I use a word," Humpty-Dumpty said in rather a scornful tone, "it means just what I choose it to mean, neither more nor less."
> "The question is," said Alice, "whether you *can* make words mean so many different things."
> "The question is," said Humpty-Dumpty, "which is to be Master—that's all."

The exploration of varied meanings for both common and uncommon words offers an excellent opportunity to introduce extended use of the dictionary. Vocabularies will grow as students delve deeply to discover the ideas behind the words they encounter. Your use of intriguing words in the classroom will cause students to stretch to meet your challenge, for they love new words, big words, unusual words. So speak of homonyms, clichés, palindromes, and acronyms and alert young minds will question, understand, and use these interesting words, too. There is a need to explain, but never to "water down" the English language for children of the twentieth century.

- **Confusing Words—There are many words which are frequently confused; for example, *affect* and *effect*. Displaying groups of words and encouraging a search for groups of confusing words will assist students in familiarizing themselves with the use of these words. Here are a few to initiate the search:**

  accent, ascent, assent (Which two are homonyms?)
  dessert, desert (Can these words be homonyms?)
  loose, lose, loss
  accept, except
  they're, there, their
  you're, your
  whose, who's

- **Writing Definitions—Have students be *lexicographers*. Imagine their amazement when you question, "How would you like to be lexicographers today?" Each student can select several common words to define so that there is no question about its meaning, A chair, for example, may be defined as "something to sit on," but what about a bench or a stool? Definitions can be tested by a board of examiners.**

• Unfamiliar Words—Present a word that is likely to be unfamiliar to almost everyone. Have each person write the definition of this word. Then use the same word in a sentence context. Each will rewrite the first definition. Then check the dictionary definition. How many had a correct definition the first time? Did context aid others in discovering the correct definition? This is especially fun when done as a class game. The teacher reads aloud a puzzler such as *antedeluvian*. Children in each team try to guess the meaning. A dictionary monitor checks the correctness of all responses. This is an exciting way to enlarge vocabularies.

• Long Words—Students are fascinated by enormous words. Share some of the following impressive examples and encourage students to submit any others they find.

sesquipedalian
sesquicentennial
hippopotomonstrousesquipedalian
pneumonoultramicroscopicsilicovolcanoconiosis
floccinancinihilipilification
antidisestablishmentarianism
ptertiaryoctylphenoxyethyoxyethylodimethylbenzylammoniumchloxide

---

What is the longest word in the dictionary?
SMILES—There is a mile between the first letter and the last.

• Jingo Lingo—Jingo Lingo consists of a two-word verse (sometimes called Terse Verse or Hinky Pinkies) plus a humorous definition. Students will delight in composing *Daffynitions* to accompany the verse which might include the following:

SPINAL FINAL:	The big examination for medical students.
VOTER QUOTER:	A public opinion poll.
STOUT SCOUT:	An overgrown cub.
TIGER GEIGER:	Necessary equipment for every big-game hunter.
FEATHER WEATHER:	It's for the birds!

• Context and Definition—Encourage the use of the context to reveal the meaning of a difficult or unfamiliar word. Present new words in sentences which provide some clue to the meaning, having students write the definition of the underlined word before checking themselves with the dictionary.

It was a *picayune* matter, but he insisted on proving the statement.
The *enormous* dog frightened the small girl.
They felt it was *expedient* to hold the meeting immediately.
The food was completely *unpalatable* although we were hungry.
Can you trace their *itinerary* on the map?

- **Reworded Proverbs—Able students will especially enjoy disguising familiar proverbs by rewording them. These proverbs are then presented to the class which can try to identify the original saying. What proverbs are being stated in these examples?**

  Were desires stallions, mendicants would be equestrians.
  The absence of prevarication proves to be an advantageous plan of action.

HISTORY

Another aspect of word study is the origin or history of a word, its *etymology*. Where do words come from? How do words get into our language? The histories of words make fascinating reading, and a number of books have been written about the origins of words. Most of the following can be used by the better student in the middle grades through the adult reader. The information provided can be retold for younger students. Additional books are listed on page 44.

Epstein, Sam and Beryl. *What's Behind the Word?* New York: Scholastic Book Services, 1964.
Ernst, Margaret, and Thurber, James. *In a Word.* New York: Alfred Knopf, 1939.
Evans, Bergen. *Comfortable Words.* New York: Random House, 1962.
———, and Evans, Cornelia. *A Dictionary of Contemporary American Usage.* New York: Random House, 1957.
Ferguson, Charles W. *The Abecedarian Book.* Boston: Little, Brown and Co., 1964.
Funk, Charles. *Horsefeathers and Other Curious Words.* New York: Harper and Row, 1958.
———. *Thereby Hangs a Tale; Stories of Curious Word Origins.* New York: Harper and Row, 1958.

In examining the origins of English words, students will soon notice that there are a number of specific sources of words: (1) coined words, (2) borrowed words, (3) adapted words, (4) names of inventors or persons associated with certain objects or ideas, (5) imitations of sounds, and (6) fusions of known words. Students can make individual studies of words which originated in different ways, or the class can work together in compiling collections of words which fall into the listed categories. Described here are additional activities to stimulate learning about word histories.

- **Portmanteau words—Students will be intrigued by these new words which have been created from two words pressed together as in these examples:**

  chortle—chuckle + snort (Lewis Carroll)

slanguage—slang + language
slithy—slimy + lithe (Lewis Carroll)
smog—smoke + fog

• Word Inventions—Introduce students to Lewis Carroll's poem, "Jabberwocky," which is composed of invented language. Students can invent words for objects or ideas which they think need new words. What words could be invented for the following?

A chair with a broken leg.
A letter that has been opened by mistake.
A book that no one enjoys reading.
A trip to the oceanside.

• A second-grade child wrote this poem after a class discussion of words and how they are used:

WORDS [1]
by Cindy Rowland

Words are sometimes gentle and sweet;
Words are sometimes nice and neat.
Words are sometimes mean or cruel;
Some are slang, not according to rule.

Some are common words like *if* and *and;*
Some are words from a foreign land.
But words always have to mean something—
A robin's egg or a blue jay's wing.
How many words there are nobody knows.
When a word comes, it never goes.

• Acronyms—Where did words like *radar* or *snafu* originate? Many contemporary words have been derived from the words used to define a concept, but most people have long since forgotten (or never knew) the definition. Words composed of the first letters or syllables of a longer term are called *acronyms;* many organizations known by a series of letters which have become the name itself are also examples.

SNAFU = *S*ituation *N*ormal: *A*ll *F*ouled *U*p
RADAR = *Ra*dio *D*etecting *a*nd *R*anging
UNESCO = *U*nited *N*ations' *E*ducational, *S*cientific, and *C*ultural *O*rganization
SCUBA = *S*elf-*C*ontained *U*nderwater *B*reathing *A*pparatus

• People and Places—Students can conduct a search for words in common usage which are based on place names or the names of people, as in these examples:

[1] Cindy Rowland, Second Grade, Coventry School, Campbell, California.

PEOPLE	PLACES
camellia	frankfurter
Fahrenheit	hamburger
macadam	italics
pasteurize	marathon
pompadour	shanghai
victorian	waterloo

The book, *Word People,* written by Nancy Caldwell Sorel, illustrated by Edward Sorel, and published by American Heritage, 1970, includes biographies of people whose names have become common words in the English language. They include such individuals as Boycott, Cardigan, Chauvin, and Bloomer.

- Word Cartoons—Encourage the investigation of word origins which can then be shared through the drawing of illustrative posters depicting the origin of especially interesting words. Here are a number of words which have intriguing histories.

agony	gargantuan
alphabet	journey
anecdote	magazine
bombast	milliner
bonfire	pedigree
canopy	quixotic
chivalry	queue
deliberate	uranium

- Synonym Bingo—The children match the called word with its synonym printed on the card. The first player or team to get five words in a row wins. For example, the teacher might call the word "Large" and the child would respond with "Gigantic." Synonym bingo can also be played in pairs at a learning center.

The Teacher and Words

What do you know about words? Have you ever read a page in the dictionary? Do you notice words as you read? Do you find yourself jotting words on slips of paper for further investigation? We hope that you share the feeling expressed by Evelyn Waugh, who wrote: "Words should be an intense pleasure just as leather should be to a shoemaker. If there isn't that pleasure for a writer, maybe he ought to be a philosopher."

Although it is true that most teachers are not writers, it is equally true that the teacher who knows little of the lore of words and has no real enthusiasm for experimenting with words and the effects they produce will never instill a love for words in the student. For this reason it is imperative that you examine your own knowledge of words and explore means to acquire additional knowledge.

SELF-EVALUATION

One of the simplest methods for assessing your knowledge of words is through a vocabulary test intended for adults. Of the ten common words presented below, for how many can you select the correct meaning? If you correctly identify nine or ten, you're on the right track, but less than five correctly identified would certainly indicate that you need to concentrate on becoming more aware of words.

1 ambiguous: (a) having two separate parts, (b) desiring fame, (c) uncertain in meaning, (d) talkative
2 chastise: (a) punish, (b) chase, (c) virtuous, (d) help
3 effervescent: (a) efficient, (b) bubbly, (c) hopeful, (d) quiet
4 garrulous: (a) small, (b) rapid, (c) wordy, (d) completed
5 implacable: (a) misplaced, (b) hurried, (c) insolent, (d) relentless
6 mien: (a) bearing, (b) definition, (c) rudeness, (d) place
7 petulant: (a) soothing, (b) flowerlike, (c) fretful, (d) stopping
8 sagacious: (a) wise, (b) unhappy, (c) green, (d) fastened
9 timbre: (a) lumber, (b) tone, (c) shy, (d) time
10 writhe: (a) inscribe, (b) right, (c) twist, (d) anger [2]

As a teacher of English, it is important, too, that you know words commonly used in the study of the English language. It is surprising to find teachers who mispronounce or use incorrectly terms that should be well known to a teacher in the language arts. Can you identify the following terms? Can you pronounce them easily?

homonym	obsolete	linguistics
antonym	archaic	phonics
synonym	colloquial	phonetics
cliché	onomatopoeia	phoneme
euphemism	alliteration	etymology

ACQUIRING KNOWLEDGE

How does one improve one's knowledge of words? Just as for the elementary school student, the answer is not the learning of long lists of words; this type of study might result only in killing any real interest in words. Rather you must develop habits of inquiry and an awareness of words, so that you notice words that sparkle, words that are peculiar, words that offer something to you personally. The steps are three: (1) desire, (2) explore, and (3) experiment.

[2] ANSWERS: 1-c, 2-a, 3-b, 4-c, 5-d, 6-a, 7-c, 8-a, 9-b, 10-c.

We shall assume that the desire is present or you would not be reading this paragraph, and so we can safely proceed to the exploration. A good place to begin exploring words is in books. Here are several we would recommend:

- *Playing with Words* by Joseph T. Shipley. (Englewood Cliffs, N.J.: Prentice-Hall, Inc., 1960).

"You should enjoy words, play with them, make them familiar. Then they will respond to you, and let you command them. And the right word will come for your need." You will meet many fascinating words and ideas about words while browsing through this small book.

- *Word Origins and Their Romantic Stories* by Wilfred Funk. (New York: Funk and Wagnalls, 1951).

This book is particularly recommended because the histories of words are grouped in an interesting manner. Also worth careful study is the last section, which presents the many Latin and Greek affixes and common roots which compose a large percentage of the words in the English language.

- *Ounce, Dice, Trice* by Alastair Reid. (Boston: Little, Brown and Co., 1958).

Although this book was written for children, it is equally delightful for the adult who is being introduced to word play. What is a Hamburgler? What is Oose? You'll know after reading this book.

- *Word Play* by Joseph T. Shipley. (New York: Hawthorn Books, 1972).

Written for young people, this book by Shipley is a fine collection of word games and examples of many kinds of word plays, riddles, palindromes, acrostics, and much, much more.

- *Phantom Tollbooth* by Norton Juster. (New York: Random House, 1961).

A wonderful book to read aloud, it might spark all sorts of word activities, including a Dictionopolis Word Fair. The illustrator is Jules Feiffer.

- *Words and What They Do To You* by Catherine Minteer. San Francisco: (Institute of General Semantics, 1965).

A book of beginning lessons in general semantics for junior and senior high school. The program developed in this book is in the area of communication; the lessons provide pupils with a new, strong motivation for careful listening, critical reading, accurate speaking, and effective writing.

Next let's turn to the dictionary. When purchasing a dictionary, try to obtain one that provides the etymology and gives synonyms. Get in the habit of using the dictionary to find the meanings of words which puzzle you. Use a file card as a bookmark when reading so that you can jot words down easily for later investigation. A special type of dictionary which is also very useful for anyone who is interested in words is the thesaurus (there's a word for investigation), which is simply a dictionary of synonyms. Several synonym dictionaries are now available in paperback editions.

To become well acquainted with words you must do more than explore—you must *experiment.* You must *use* words, for using a word makes it truly yours. The many word activities described for use in the classroom throughout this chapter will provide ideas for experimentation for you, too. Your experimenting with the activity will lead to your better understanding of the technique as well, so that you will be better able to teach students. Here are other ideas about words to assist your individual experimentation.

- List ten common adjectives. Can you name two synonyms for each adjective?

- Open the dictionary to any page. Which words do you know on this page? Read the definitions of the words you don't know. Which of these could you add to your every day vocabulary?

- Purchase a small spiral notebook in which to jot interesting words or ideas about words. You will meet intriguing ideas in the most unusual places—billboards, magazines, conversation, a menu, the newspaper.

- Have you ever heard of an OXYMORON? This esoteric word means the use of two apparently incongruous words to produce an epigrammatic effect as in these examples:

sweet sorrow	broadly ignorant
cruel kindness	trained incapacity

Conduct a search for *oxymora* (plural) and you will have a rare collection, a conversation stopper.

Classroom Strategies

Planning experiences with words is a worthwhile effort, for not only are you teaching specific information about words presented, but you are also generating interest in language, its study, and its use. Word study, too, is appropriate to the entire elementary school curriculum, for words are an integral part of any subject matter taught. We shall explore in this section a wide variety of word activities which might be used in the classroom.

CONCEPTS TO BE TAUGHT

What concepts are we trying to teach as we present words in the classroom? There are many concepts to be considered, and they range widely in complexity. Listed here are some ideas to teach about words which we have presented in a developmental sequence. Consider the background of the group with which you are working before deciding what concepts to present, for within this sequence each concept can also be introduced at varying levels of difficulty.

1 Words may name people, places, and things.

Begin with rather ordinary names, moving quickly to more exotic, exciting names. Maps, almanacs, and dictionaries will suggest fascinating examples. Do names make a difference? Shakespeare wrote: "A rose by any other name would smell as sweet." Do you agree?

Discuss the ways we have changed names in our society as marks of status. A janitor is now a custodian; an undertaker is now a mortician; a hairdresser is now a beautician; a barber is a hair stylist; the garbage man is a sanitary engineer; and so it goes. These and other euphemisms can instigate interesting studies by able students.[3]

2 Words may tell that action is taking place.

An excellent oral exploration of words focuses on the concerted effort of a class to compile a collection of synonyms for a verb which is overworked in common usage. Have students suggest substitutes, more exact words, for WALK as these synonyms are listed on the board:

slip	trip	stride
rush	waddle	steal
stroll	skip	bounce
strut	creep	limp

Varied types of walking can then be demonstrated. A discussion of situations which require certain kinds of walking may ensue. When would you creep? When would you rush? Who might waddle? Who might bounce?

Then try SAID, ASK, FIND, and other common verbs and compile lists of synonyms for each. These could be combined in a class thesaurus and referred to during creative writing periods. You should soon see the results of these verbal explorations in student writing.

In Other Words . . . A Beginning Thesaurus by W. Cabell Greet, William A. Jenkins, and Andrew Schiller. (Glenview, Ill.: Scott, Foresman, 1969.)

A book on synonyms and antonyms, including one hundred entry words; its purpose is to give a youngster some new words to use rather than the worn-out ones.

---

[3] Read the chapter on "Euphemisms" in H. L. Mencken's provocative work, *The American Language* (New York: Alfred Knopf, 1936).

3 Words may describe people, places, and things.

The study of adjectives is fascinating as you begin thinking of synonyms for commonly used examples. List a variety of phrases to be explored together:

A PRETTY GIRL	A TIRED MAN
vivacious lass	weary worker
charming miss	exhausted fieldhand
attractive girl	exasperated father
chic mademoiselle	fatigued scholar

4 Words may describe actions.

Show a picture which depicts action, perhaps a boy throwing a ball. How does he throw the ball—carefully, wildly, accurately, swiftly? Introduce sentences in which adverbs may be inserted to influence the meaning of the writer.

Mildred spoke ____________________________.
The author wrote ____________________________.
They ran ___________________________________.

5 One word may have many meanings.

Explore *Multiple Meanings* of many common words. "Words are like those insects that take their color from their surroundings," remarked Elihu Root, and it is interesting to explore the influence of context on the meaning of even a simple word like *run:*

He can *run* fast.
The rabbit's *run* was small.
The politician will *run* for office.
It is a short *run* to the city.
She has a *run* in her stocking.

Each student can choose one word—*trunk, list, swing, plant, catch*—which has multiple meanings that can be depicted on pages for a class book of words. Students might also write verses about words to illustrate their varied meanings as in this example:

WHAT IS A TRUNK?

A trunk is sometimes
An elephant's nose.
It's part of your body
Or a large case for clothes.
A tree has a trunk,
And so does your car.
And a telephone trunk line
Carries messages far!

IRIS TIEDT

6 Different words may mean almost the same thing.

Explore words which describe color. How many ways can you express RED, for example? Have students conduct searches for varied examples displaying the discoveries on a large color wheel. Near red would be some of the following:

cherry, vermillion, rose, ruby, scarlet, flame, crimson.

Which word does not belong?

glisten, glitter, shine, round
aid, help, lame, assist
increment, coffers, addition, increase

7 Words are often made of distinct parts.

Discuss prefixes—*pre, ex, in, de,* etc. Select one prefix, having the class name as many words beginning with the syllable as possible (without dictionaries). For EX, words might be listed thus:

example	exercise	examine
examination	exit	excellent
explain	exclaim	exciting

Examine a variety of words to discover the parts which compose them.

entangle	respectfully
recruitment	remarkably
hopelessness	delighted
insightful	inscription

8 Two words may be put together.

An intriguing activity with compound words is a type of CHAIN REACTION in which students try to name a compound word which begins with the last half of the previous word named, in this way:

Hangman, Manhole, Wholesome (permit liberties), Somewhere, Wherever, Everlasting.

The object is to make the chain as long as possible, so students try to use words which have possibilities. EVERLASTING, above, will break the chain.

9 Some words are more colorful than others.

Have students collect words which fascinate them for a variety of reasons. Have each present a favorite word telling the class about it. You can share favorites, too. Words like these are interesting to us.

Shibboleth	Potpourri	Caravansary
Scrimshaw	Quixotic	Effervescent

Why do you like certain words? Who knows? The meaning may intrigue you or just saying the word which has a certain rhythm may be pleasant.

10 Some words have unusual characteristics.

Palindromes are words which form the same word (or even a whole sentence) when read either forward or backward as:

RADAR MADAM LEVEL EYE KAYAK
Rise to vote, sir.
Able was I ere I saw Elba. (words reputedly spoken by Napoleon)
Too bad I hid a boot.
A man, a plan, a canal: Panama.

Present a group of words like these:

ABSTEMIOUS, FACETIOUS, ABSTENTIOUS, ARSENIOUS

Do you notice any peculiarity about these words? Display them for a day or two if necessary to permit students to think about them. (They contain the five common vowels in alphabetical order.) Others contain the five vowels, but not in order—AUCTIONEER, GRACIOUSNESS, CAULIFLOWER, EQUATION, and so on.

11 Many English words have been borrowed from other languages.

Conduct a search for words borrowed directly from Spanish, French, Italian, German, and other languages. French words might include:

boudoir	ballet	entrée
encore	souvenir	en route
fiancée	vogue	parole

12 Words develop and change in meaning.

Have students investigate the meaning of words as they develop historically. Try some of these:

bureau	rankle	heckle	stink
garret	tawdry	magazine	patter
virtue	fancy	bury	starve

13 Words are often invented or coined to meet needs.

Students can investigate the origin of words which have been coined as BLURB, GERRYMANDER, ALPHABET, MAVERICK, OK, MACKINTOSH.

Are there objects or ideas for which we need new names in our society? (See the section on "History" at the beginning of this chapter for more ideas about Word Inventions.)

14 Some words and phrases become worn out.

Clichés are fascinating and humorous. Consult Eric Partridge's *Dictionary of Clichés* for explanations of the origins of many of these diverting expressions. Taken literally they provide motivation for stories and illustrations. What happens, for example, when someone interprets these expressions literally?

That boy is a *dog in the manger*.

Do you always *beat around the bush?*
Come, let us *bury the hatchet.*
They were *head over heels in love.*
Be careful, you're *skating on thin ice!*
Poor John isn't *out of the woods yet.*

PLANNING EXPERIENCES WITH WORDS

Many experiences with words develop by accident when something said in the classroom suggests a brief discussion about words or when students ask questions about words encountered which then leads to further research or study. In addition to these highly beneficial incidental experiences, there is also a need for teacher-planned lessons about words. Planned experiences with words frequently focus attention on the use of the dictionary, which is certainly a most essential tool for even the youngest student. The teacher must be cautious, however, when planning dictionary studies to ensure that these activities are not dull, drill-type lessons which may actually kill student interest in words and in using the dictionary. Too many dittoed sheets read something like this:

> Here are twenty words. Find each word in the dictionary.
> Write the definition of each word and use it in a sentence.

A little ingenuity will serve to heighten student interest while at the same time providing for teaching dictionary skills. Using a title for the activity makes it sound more enticing. A different method of indicating whether the child has found the required definition will also relieve the monotony of just "finding words in the dictionary." The following examples are taken from a duplicated sheet entitled: TAKE YOUR CHOICE, which is one way of enlivening dictionary usage.

Which would you rather be—a SPELUNKER or a PHILATELIST? ____________
Why? ____
Which would you rather have—a QUIRT or a SACHET? ____________
Why? ____
Would you rather be a PRINCIPAL or ruler of a PRINCIPALITY? ____________
Why? ____

In the type of questions used in this example there is no *one* right answer. The answer to the question *Why?* is an individual response which may differ from those made by other students. We need to emphasize this kind of individuality through open-ended questions and the encouragement of more creative answers.

INDIVIDUALIZED APPROACHES TO WORDS

Word study can often be pursued individually. The gifted student is particularly well prepared to investigate varied aspects of words. Games and puzzles are diverting and informative as before-school activities or for the student who completes an assignment ahead of schedule.

Word activities are well adapted to the Learning Center concept and can be used at a Word Center or a Writing Center however the teacher wishes to organize the class. The following word games are suggested for use in the classroom. Students should be encouraged not only to solve examples given but also to create word games to share with other members of the class. We have noted that more actual learning and enjoyment is derived from the development of the game itself than from its solution.

- Scavenger Hunt—This variety of word quiz, and others, can be prepared by students who often display real skill in writing provocative types of word activities. The students' dictionaries are needed for these discoveries:

  What is the word following *murder*? ____________
  Find two birds. ____________ ____________

- Yes or No—Again dictionaries are needed to determine the right answer.

  Is a bird fond of eating limericks? ____________
  Is a lion carnivorous? ____________
  Might a lady be garrulous? ____________

- Introduce students to Spoonerisms, speech slips of the type made by the Reverend W. A. Spooner of Oxford University. Have students invent these slips and create situations around them for fun with words and writing. Here are two remarks supposedly made by this illustrious gentleman:

  "Is the bean dizzy?"
  When a parishioner complained, "Someone is occupewing my pie," he rejoined, "I'm very sorry, Madam. I'll sew you to another sheet."

- Add an A to the following words to produce a new word. Each student should try to find additional examples.

  rod—road
  pry—pray
  red—read
  fir—fair
  slam-salaam (2 A's)

bird—baird
bred—bread, bared
shred—shared

• The interest of this type of puzzle depends on its form, DIAMOND O. Definitions will usually need to accompany the unsolved example.

c o t
s n o w y
u n d o i n g
r e s t o r i n g
s u b f l o o r i n g
d e p l o r i n g
s p r o u t s
p r o u d
t o n

• Many commercial games found in most toy and stationery stores can be well put to use in a language-arts interest center. These would certainly include Scrabble, Spill 'N' Spell, and Password.

A student teacher [4] in a third-grade classroom used a number of word activities with the children. Then she encouraged each child to construct an activity. Geoff produced a group of scrambled words:

MAKE WORDS OF THESE

1. sdnuo—noise s__________
2. npduo—hit p__________
3. inur—to wreck r__________
4. urn—flee r__________
5. lsraya—fee s__________
6. yco—shy c__________
7. mjup—pep j__________
8. stsasi—help a__________

Michelle developed a group of antonyms with the instructions: "Draw lines to their antonyms."

dog	glad
white	sea
mad	south
happy	cat
land	girl

[4] Mrs. Bonnie Manley teaching with Mrs. Young, Booksin School, San Jose, California.

FUNNY PHRASES

①	②
sgge sgeg gegs	Your nose right
③ once 2:30	④ don't eat
⑤ ME AL	⑥ he art
⑦ y y y men	⑧ Lawyer

Answers:

1. scrambled eggs
2. right under your nose
3. once upon a time
4. dont over eat
5. square meal
6. broken heart
7. 3 wise men
8. crooked lawyer

north	sad
west	stand
boy	black
sit	east
father	work
sister	out
in	brother
play	mother

• **Word Brackets** [5]—For this game print a word vertically on the chalkboard. Choose a holiday word, one connected with a subject being studied, or an interesting new word you wish to introduce. To the right, print the same word with its letters reversed in order as shown. The object is to insert letters between those given to make new words, the longer the better, for every letter inserted gives the player a point. Students will enjoy challenging each other.

G	n		a	T
H	i		s	S
O	h		i	O
S	m	a	s	H
T		a		G

Score: 10

G		i		a		n	T
H		e		a		r	S
O		l		e			O
S		p	e	e		c	H
T	e	a	c	h	i	n	G

Score: 18

After you have played the game a few times with the above rules, try this simple variation. Work for the lowest score rather than the highest score by using shorter words. This time you are playing golf instead of baseball.

• **Double Tactics**—Two students can play a word-forming game on a frame as in the illustration. As the players alternate turns, each tries to form a word by adding only one letter at a time. Each word formed scores one point.

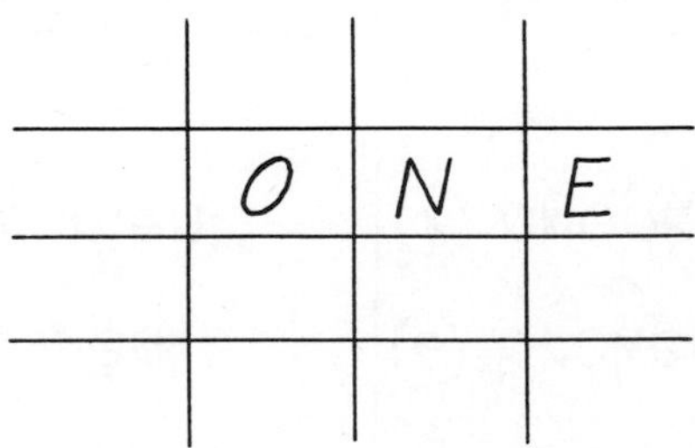

[5] Sidney and Iris Tiedt, *The Elementary Teacher's Complete Ideas Handbook* (Englewood Cliffs, N.J.: Prentice-Hall, Inc., 1965), p. 76.

In this example Jill started with the letter O, Tony added N to score with ON. Then Jill added E to form ONE. We readily see that Tony can place a letter before ONE to form BONE, TONE or CONE.

- Name acrostics—Each child can make an acrostic based on the letters of his or her name. Some names are difficult, so allow plenty of leeway.

Carol might write: Coughs
Are
Really
Old
Laughs [6]

Students can use the letters in their names to begin words that describe themselves.

James Teel might write:

Joyful	
Ambitious	Talker
Massive	Effective
Evasive	Efficient
Saving	Lover

- Tom Swifties—The Tom Swifty was a twentieth-century contribution to word play. Small books quickly appeared illustrating the use of adverbs especially appropriate to the quotation in a sentence as in these examples:

"I'll have seafood salad," she muttered crabbily.
"What a beautiful piece of wood," he remarked craftily.
"My, I'm terribly hoarse today," she whinnied.
"That song is too long," he announced curtly.

Students can invent Tom Swifties and portray a situation in which someone is making this remark. The humorous illustrations can be displayed for enjoyment by all and later compiled in an entertaining book.

- Wordbooks—Encourage individuals or groups of students to conduct searches for interesting categories of words. The types of words collected may reflect an individual interest—SPACE WORDS, WORDS AND NUMBERS, HORSES AND WORDS, WORDS ABOUT DOGS—or a collection may be focused on WORD ODDITIES, SPANIARDS IN OUR LANGUAGE, ANTONYMS, WORD PLAY, MY FAVORITE WORDS.

- Word Puzzles—Here is another variety of word puzzle which can be developed by students. What is the secret word?

[6] Mary Yanage George, *Language Art, An Ideabook* (San Francisco: Chandler Publishing, 1970), p. 42.

S	a	f	e	t	y
s	**C**	o	l	d	s
s	a	**H**	a	r	a
t	h	r	**O**	a	t
h	o	l	l	**O**	w
s	p	r	a	w	**L**

- Some students with a ready wit might enjoy tackling "I Could Have Been."

I could have been a secretary but it's not my type; a garbageman, but it's not up my alley; a mortician, but it's too much of an undertaking; a sausage maker, but I haven't got the guts.

After these examples they should be able to make up their own "I Could Have Been . . ."

WORD STUDY IN ALL SUBJECT AREAS

Word study is of particular importance in that it permeates the entire elementary school curriculum. A student who has developed an inquisitive attitude toward words will reach out to the words of science, the words of history; each one will be constantly aware of the intrigue of words. The alert teacher will utilize opportunities that arise to further word interest whether they occur during the language period or in the middle of a mathematics lesson. Included in this section are suggested activities which relate interest in words to subjects other than English itself.

SCIENCE is a subject which offers many fascinating new words. Begin a study of words that are related to space, medicine, birds, cats, insects, and so on. Display a group of words with related pictures.

- *Words of Science* by Isaac Asimov (Houghton Mifflin) is an excellent collection of words in this field. The story behind each word is explained in readable fashion by a reputable scientist whom some will recognize as a writer of science fiction.

- CATEGORIES is an interesting word game that can feature knowledge in science, thus:

	Space	Biology
A	astronaut	ant
T		
O		
M		
I		
C		

- **Word Quizzes can focus attention on scientific knowledge. Have students compose questions like these:**

With what word does the name of this animal rhyme? GNU ________________
Where would you expect to find an EGRET? ________________
What is the origin of our word HELICOPTER? ________________
What does the prefix TELE mean? ________________

MATHEMATICS can be helpful in furthering interest in word study as we begin thinking about the words which denote number and the processes used in computing. The study of numerology also provides fascinating words which are intriguing to the young student.

- **THE ORIGIN OF NUMBER WORDS can be the title of an interesting collection of words related to numbers. Have a page for each numeral, on which are presented words related to that numeral. The page on which a large 1 is printed would bear some of these words with information about their origin:**

one	**primary**	**prime**
first	**unison**	**unicorn**
solo	**unity**	**primer**
sole	**unanimous**	**lone**

This number booklet might be part of a learning center. Students could use dictionaries to expand the lists of number-related words. Later there could be an interesting class discussion of the number-word discoveries.

• The magic powers with which numbers were supposed to be endowed can provide material for challenging research. Information gathered might be presented on a bulletin board, for example, bearing a large cut-paper 3, around which is mounted information about the magic properties of this number and its influence.

It is related to the Holy Trinity.
Three strikes in baseball.
Three magic wishes.
I'll give you three guesses.
Third time's a lucky charm.

SOCIAL STUDIES provides a wealth of word-centered activities as we discuss words in history, the history of words, words related to travel and the map, words we have borrowed from other lands and languages, words in propaganda, and so on.

• WORD CROSSINGS are provocative ways of showing relationships between words. The main word is supplied while definitions are given for the other words to be identified as in this example:

			F					
1.	N	O	R	M	A	N	D	Y
2.		P	A	R	I	S		
			N					
			C					
3.		S	E	I	N	E		

The word FRANCE would be printed in place with spaces for the other letters. Definitions might be: (1) section, (2) city, (3) river. Students can construct Word Crossings for names of people, regions, countries, etc.

• ACROSTICS also lend themselves to words in social studies. An acrostic can be developed for a person's name, a country, river, city, and so on. Here is an Acrostic for FRANCE:

F	R	A	N	C			
R	H	O	N	E			
A	L	P	S				
N	A	P	O	L	E	O	N
C	A	L	A	I	S		
E	I	F	F	E	L		

What is the secret of this puzzle? (The first letter of each word read vertically spells a word.) Definitions are written to assist the solution of the puzzle.

• *Words on the Map* and *Words from the Myths* (Houghton Mifflin) are two titles by Isaac Asimov which explore words related to areas in the social sciences.

ART offers not only an interesting vocabulary of its own but also techniques and media for enhancing the study of words related to other subjects.

- WORD CUTTINGS are made by writing a word on the fold of a sheet of paper as indicated. The word is then cut out without disturbing the fold. Opened flat, the word cutting forms an attractive design, thus:

- WORD COLLAGES provide an unusual method for displaying words which interest students. Each student clips words from magazines selecting words on one particular theme—FRENCH WORDS, SPRING WORDS, PROVOCATIVE WORDS, R WORDS—or a potpourri of words can be included. The collection of words is then arranged over a poster with pieces of colored paper used to unite the clipped words and to add color and interest to the collage.

- WORD INTERPRETATIONS can be made by each individual. Each person selects a word—FREEDOM, MUSIC, COLOR, BLUE, TRADE, LANGUAGE, SCIENCE, HEAT, and so on. He then develops a poster on which the word appears as well as drawings which interpret the meaning of this word for the individual.

- WORD BOOKS can be tastefully enhanced by the addition of an attractive cover prepared through simple art techniques—stenciling, crayon resist, dribbling of paint in

patterns, etc. The form of a booklet can also add interest to the project—the long, slim form; paper cut in an unusual shape; varied types of ties. Attention to printing and the arrangement of a title on the page will assist students in preparing a more effective booklet, a work in which they can take pride.

Books to Investigate

Bellafiore, Joseph. *Words at Work.* New York: Amsco School Publications, 1939, 1968.

Bombaugh, C. C. *Oddities and Curiosities of Words and Literature.* New York: Dover Publications, 1961.

Briggs, F. Allen. *The Play of Words.* New York: Harcourt, Brace, Jovanovich, 1972.

Opie, Iona, and Opie, Peter. *The Lore and Language of School Children.* London: Oxford University Press, 1959.

Tiedt, Sidney W., and Tiedt, Iris M. *Exploring Words.* San Jose, Calif.: Contemporary Press, 1963.

creativity and the child

chapter

A man's life is dyed the color of his imagination.

Marcus Aurelius

What is creativity? Why is creativity significant? Who is the creative individual? How can we encourage creativity in the classroom? Creativity is an elusive, and at times all-inclusive, term which many have found difficult to define. Writers in this field offer varied interpretations that will help us determine a working definition for the word *creativity*.

J. P. Guilford, author of *Personality* and one of the leading authorities in this field of research, was the first to use the term *divergent thinking* as a necessary component of creativity. He states further: "Creative thinking is distinguished by the fact that there is something novel about it." [1] Donald W. MacKinnon, a pioneer in the study of creativity who conducted extensive studies of creative adults, defines creativity as "the ability to make original significant responses to a

[1] Joy P. Guilford, *Personality* (New York: McGraw-Hill, 1959), p. 115.

problem."[2] E. Paul Torrance has studied many aspects of creativity, providing particular insight into the problems of the creative child at the elementary school level. His book, *Guiding Creative Talent,* defines creativity as "the process of sensing problems or gaps in information, forming ideas or hypotheses, testing and modifying these hypotheses and communicating the results."[3]

It is interesting to note that each of the men quoted defines creativity in terms of the process rather than the product produced. This is an important distinction, for many misunderstandings arise between those who conceive of creativity in terms of a painting or a novel and those who view it as an ability, a way of thinking or perceiving. For purposes of our discussion we shall define creativity as "the ability to produce something original, to see new relationships, and to use imagination and inventiveness."

"Creativity at its highest level has probably been as important as any human quality in changing history and reshaping the world," writes Calvin W. Taylor, editor of *Creativity: Progress and Potential.* "As few as three or four highly creative minds can make a crucial difference."[4] Historian Arnold Toynbee states, in the same vein: "To give a fair chance to potential creativity is a matter of life and death for any society."[5]

Creativity has something to offer all persons as an area of study. It is important to stress the point that *every* person is creative; it is the *degree* of creativity which varies. We are concerned here not only with the highly creative individual but also with the *least creative child.* Our aim is to stimulate creativity in all children, and this aim will influence our methods and even the content we teach. As Torrance notes:

> One of the most revolutionary changes I foresee is a revision of the objectives of education. Today we proclaim that our schools exist for learning. We say that we must get tougher and make pupils learn more. Schools of the future will be designed not only for *learning* but for *thinking*. More and more insistently, today's schools and colleges are being asked to produce men and women who can think, who can make new scientific discoveries, who can find more adequate solutions to impelling world problems, who cannot be brainwashed—men and women who can adapt to change and

[2] Donald W. MacKinnon, ed., *The Creative Person* (Berkeley, Calif.: University of California, General Extension, 1962), p. 203.

[3] E. Paul Torrance, *Education and the Creative Potential* (Minneapolis, Minn.: University of Minnesota Press, 1963); and *Guiding Creative Talent* (Englewood Cliffs, N.J.: Prentice-Hall, 1962), p. 16.

[4] Calvin W. Taylor, ed., *Creativity: Progress and Potential* (New York: McGraw-Hill, 1964), p. 2.

[5] Arnold Toynbee, "Has America Neglected Its Creative Minority?" *California Monthly* (February, 1962), p. 7.

maintain sanity in this age of acceleration. This is the creative challenge to education.[6]

Identifying the Creative Child

One of the problems related to creativity which holds great significance for the school is that of identifying creative students. How can the teacher in the classroom recognize the creative individual? What characteristics are typical of the creative person? Can we test for creativity?

RESEARCH IN CREATIVITY

Identifying creativity in the child is not easy, which may account for our failure to recognize this type of giftedness. The commonly use IQ test, it has been found, does not indicate creativeness. Although most researchers find a positive correlation between intelligence and creativity, the high scorer on the intelligence test may not score high on tests of creativity. Nor is the student who receives the highest grades necessarily the most creative child.

MacKinnon studied more than 500 famous people—writers, architects, composers, and so on—who were judged by their peers to be creative. In studying these famous artists MacKinnon found that in general they (1) had disliked school, (2) did not identify with teachers, and (3) had in many cases dropped out of school. These findings have great implications for teacher education.[7]

This study and others which followed resulted in a body of generalizations about the creative person which may prove helpful as we attempt to identify and to understand the creative student. The creative person has been found to possess the following traits:

1 Nonconformity of ideas, but not necessarily of dress and behavior
2 Egotism and feelings of destiny
3 Great curiosity, desire to discover the answer
4 Sense of humor and playfulness
5 Perseverance on self-started projects
6 Intense emotions, sincerity
7 Tendency to be shy
8 Lack of rigidity

Victor Goertzel and his wife, Mildred Goertzel, studied the childhoods of 400 of this century's best-known men and women. Their book, *Cradles*

[6] E. Paul Torrance, *Education and the Creative Potential* (Minneapolis, Minn.: University of Minnesota Press, 1963).

[7] Donald W. MacKinnon, ed., *The Creative Person* (Berkeley, Calif.: University of California Press, 1962).

of Eminence, describes findings relevant to the study of the creative: (1) most of those people studied did not like school, (2) most of the parents had a love for learning and determination to reach goals, and (3) the creative child was not a contented child.

The latter finding has particular relevance for the classroom, for studies show that the teacher may find the creative student is not always the well-liked child, the agreeable, conforming child; he or she may impress the teacher as a disagreeable, uncooperative child who is mischievous, who daydreams when supposed to be completing assigned work. The suppression of creativity, it is believed, may lead to learning disabilities, behavior problems, and even serious neurotic conflicts, or psychoses.[8]

The Minnesota study of elementary school youngsters identified three characteristics which differentiated the highly creative child from the less creative but equally intelligent children:

1 Reputation for having wild or silly ideas
2 Work characterized by the production of ideas off the beaten path
3 Work characterized by humor, playfulness, relative lack of rigidity and relaxation.[9]

Many researchers have observed a decline in imagination as the student advances through the grade levels. Further research indicates an increase in creativity in the primary grades followed by a gradual slump at the fourth-grade level with another at the seventh grade. This finding has significance for those who are designing elementary school curricula.

Guilford, in his research at the University of Southern California, found the creative individual to be:

1 Sensitive to problems
2 Fluent in ideas
3 Mentally flexible
4 Divergent in thinking.[10]

TESTING FOR CREATIVITY

Although a variety of tests have been devised for testing creativity, they are largely in experimental stages requiring further development and

[8] Victor Goertzel and Mildred Goertzel, *Cradles of Eminence* (Boston: Little, Brown, 1962).

[9] E. Paul Torrance, *What Research Says to the Teacher: Creativity* (Washington, D.C.: National Education Assn., 1963).

[10] Joy P. Guilford, *Personality* (New York: McGraw-Hill, 1959).

use to increase reliability and validity. It is interesting, however, to note the types of tests which are being developed.

Barron utilized incomplete drawings as well as interpretation of ink blots as a basis for determining creativity. He found the creative person to be especially observant, with greater independence of cognition.[11]

Guilford developed a variety of tests including word associations, for which the subject is given twenty-five pairs of words which have only remote associations. The task is to provide a third word which relates the pair. Given cat and fish, for example, a person might supply words like animal, food, or pets. The test score is determined by the number of associations made in four minutes. He also used tests for flexible thinking such as listing many uses for a common object (a brick, a tin can) or supplying plot titles for given stories.[12]

A number of tests have also been developed at the University of Minnesota by Torrance and others. These tests consist of both verbal and nonverbal forms. One verbal form (B) is entitled "Just Suppose—" and consists of six tasks for the student to perform, each of which is a written composition based on a picture and an improbable situation as in this example:

> JUST SUPPOSE: Our shadows were to become *real* . . . WHAT WOULD BE THE CONSEQUENCES?

The directions which accompany this test form appear on the front cover, reading as follows:

> INSTRUCTIONS: On the pages which follow are six improbable situations or conditions—at least they don't exist now. This will give you a chance to use your imagination about all of the other exciting things which might happen IF these improbable conditions might come to pass. In your imagination JUST SUPPOSE that each of the situations described were to happen. THEN think of all of the other things that would happen because of it. What would be the consequences? Make as many guesses as you can.
>
> Write your guesses as rapidly as you can in the blank spaces on the page opposite the picture. You will be given five minutes for each of the improbable situations. As soon as time is called, turn the page and proceed immediately to the next situation. Do not worry too much about spelling, grammar, and the like, but try to write so that your ideas can be used.

[11] Calvin W. Taylor and Frank Barron, *Scientific Creativity: Its Recognition and Development* (New York: Wiley, 1963), pp. 227–37.

[12] Joy P. Guilford, "Creativity: Its Measurement and Development," in *A Source Book for Creative Thinking*, Sidney J. Parnes and Harold H. Harding, eds. (New York: Scribner, 1962), pp. 151–68.

This type of test is scored on three points: (1) fluency, or the number of responses; (2) originality, or uniqueness; and (3) flexibility, or variety.

In addition to the Just Suppose Test there are other verbal varieties which include:

Unusual Use: Name all the possible uses for (a tin can).
Improvement: How would you improve (this toy pictured)?
Impossibilities: Name all the impossibilities you can.

It is enlightening to observe the differences between the test of creativity and tests which are more commonly constructed. The student is instructed in the creativity test to (1) write as many different answers as possible and (2) think of answers which no one else will include. The test of creativity gives the high score to the person who can think of answers which are different (divergent thinking); the student is never required to guess the *one right answer* which the instructor has in mind. There is no one right answer, for these open-ended questions require the student to think, to invent, to imagine. Getzels and Jackson found, on the other hand, that the IQ test stresses "convergent, retentive, conservative" cognitive processes.[13]

OBSERVING CREATIVITY IN THE CLASSROOM

It is admittedly difficult to score tests of creativity when such scoring requires the skill of an expert. This fact does not, however, exclude classroom teachers from identifying creativity characteristics in the children with whom they work, nor does it eliminate the teacher from teaching *for* creativity.

Through observation the teacher can discern signs of creativity. Awareness of the many facets of creativity will lead to watchfulness and recognition of creative characteristics. A child's possession of one or two of these characteristics may or may not signal creativity. Robert's asking many questions may merely indicate that he needs more training in listening skills or that he wants attention. There are always a multitude of factors to be considered. The asking of probing, discerning questions, on the other hand, is an excellent indication of the creative thinker. Here is a list of characteristics which can be readily observed by the classroom teacher:

1 Probing, discerning questions

[13] Jacob W. Getzels and Philip W. Jackson, *Creativity and Intelligence* (New York: Wiley, 1962).

2 Avid interest in a specific topic or project
3 Unusual ideas and ways of expressing ideas
4 Great curiosity and a need to explore the answers
5 Playfulness in behavior and in use of words

Encouraging Creativity

It is our belief that everyone is creative. Although some question the teachability of creativity, the atmosphere of the classroom can stimulate, encourage, and make every effort to avoid stifling whatever creativity may exist in any child. The development of a classroom environment which is conducive to creativity, then, is the first step toward promoting creativity. There are a number of specific attitudes which you can develop both in yourself and in students to encourage the growth of creativity.

RESPECT UNUSUAL QUESTIONS AND IDEAS

Too often we are busy and hesitate to take time for questions which to us appear nonsensical, poorly timed, or not pertinent to the subject under discussion. How do we develop the necessary respect for the questioning attitude both in ourselves and in our students?

1 Make it plain to the class that good questions have value. A large box can be covered with question marks in which a child can at any time insert a card or sheet of paper on which a puzzling question is written. Each week a time can be allocated for answering these questions or for discussing them with the class. Those questions which do not produce a ready answer can be researched by volunteers who report their findings at the next question period.

2 Students can write questions which they might ask about any unknown object, person, or place. About an unknown object, for example, students might ask:

Is it large or small?
What color is it?
Is it a useful object?
Would it be found in a kitchen?

A SENSE OF WORTH FOR EACH INDIVIDUAL AND HIS CONTRIBUTIONS

In a sense the teacher must often act as a buffer between the highly creative child and the peer group, for these peers may represent the severest critics. They can stifle creativity through ridicule, rigid insistence on the exact truth, and on conformity to group standards. The attitude of the students toward imaginative ideas and divergent ways of thinking reflects the attitudes of adults who influence their thinking; the teacher's own attitude is reflected here, too. How can we promote this sense of the worth of each individual?

1 Accent the positive in evaluating student work. There is always some aspect of any student effort which can be praised, and it is for that praiseworthy bit, no matter how small, that we should search. Circle it, underline it, draw attention to it in some way; under the light of praise it will grow.
2 When displaying student work, display something by everyone. Must only "perfect" papers be given the limelight? Extract unusual uses of words, effective phrases, new words from student writing to display with the caption, WORD WIZARDRY. When featuring poetry, select a line or poem by every student.

STIMULATION OF CREATIVE THINKING

The teacher needs to aim at stimulating creative thinking rather than mere memorization of miscellaneous facts. We sometimes have a tendency to "stuff" students like sausages rather than to concentrate on developing their abilities to think. It has been said that "we never step in the same stream twice." The facts and figures which we teach students today may prove virtually useless, outdated in our fast-moving society. Margaret Mead states this idea thus: "No one will live all his life in the world into which he was born and no one will die in the world in which he worked in his maturity." The ability to think creatively, however, will prove worthwhile no matter what the developments of the future. How can the teacher stimulate creative thinking?

1 Provide the student with many opportunities for problem solving. The problem may actually exist, as, "How can we decrease the noise in our lunchroom?" or it may be purely hypothetical, "If you were eight feet tall, what problems would you face; how would you solve them?" These problems can be attacked by the group orally in discussion or by the individual through writing.
2 An interesting and rewarding technique for stimulating the imagination of your people is Brainstorming (designed by Alex Osborn), which produces a multitude of ideas within a short time. The entire group works on the solution of a problem, the improvement of an object, or the exploration of a topic in a joint effort to suggest solutions, changes, ideas. The rules for Brainstorming include:[14]

a No criticism or ridicule is allowed.
b Any idea is acceptable, no matter how fantastic.
c New ideas can be based on previous suggestions.

[14] Alex F. Osborn, *Applied Imagination* (New York: Scribner, 1957).

Students must be introduced to this technique with the teacher acting as the leader. Later, however, when the technique is more familiar, small groups can brainstorm ideas on specific problems. In beginning a brainstorming session the teacher may have to suggest a few ideas to get the group started. It is best to begin with a problem or topic that is familiar to the entire group. An interesting topic for an elementary classroom is the improvement of the student desk, something which is familiar and of concern to each individual. Suggestions might include: a personal pencil sharpener, a padded seat, a built-in television set.

3 Show short, provocative films designed to stimulate the imagination of young people. Follow up with discussion, creative writing, or art activities.

Ten Short Films for Creative Teaching

Why Man Creates, 1968, Pyramid Film Producers, 30 min.
The Red Balloon, 1956, Brandon Films, 34 min.
Dream of Wild Horses, 1962, Contemporary/McGraw-Hill, 11 min.
Clay, 1964, ACI Productions, 8 min.
*The Adventures of an **, 1957, Contemporary/McGraw-Hill, 11 min.
A Chairy Tale, 1957, International Film Bureau, 10 min.
Pigs, 1967, Churchill Films, 11 min.
The Loon's Necklace, 1964, Britannica Films, 11 min.
Up Is Down, 1970, Morton Goldsholl Design Association, Inc., 6 min.
Genius Man, 1970, ACI Productions, 2 min.

4 Many children's books are highly creative in their story content, their illustrations, or their humor. Open books for children by reading aloud, or use some of the ideas presented as the basis for stimulating experiences that encourage children to use their imaginations. After reading *The Wing on a Flea,* for example, children can find other examples of various shapes in the environment around them. *Hailstones and Halibut Bones* often serves to motivate children to write poetry, too, much to the delight of author, Mary O'Neill. Children can paint wild, wonderful fish after reading about those in *McElligott's Pool.*

Children's Books for Creative Learning

Barrett, Peter, and Barrett, Susan. *The Line Sophie Drew.* New York: Scroll Press, 1972.

Borten, Helen. *Do You See What I See?* New York: Abelard-Schuman, 1959.

———. *Do You Hear What I Hear?* New York: Abelard-Schuman, 1960.

Bradfield, Roger. *There's an Elephant in the Bathtub.* Chicago: Albert Whitman, 1964.

Emberly, Edward. *The Wing on a Flea.* Boston: Little, Brown and Co., 1961.

Fago, Vincent. *Here Comes the Whoosh!* San Marino, Calif.: Golden West Books, 1960.
Garelick, Mary. *Where Does the Butterfly Go When it Rains?* Glenview, Ill.: Scott, Foresman, 1961.
Joslin, Sesyle. *Dear Dragon . . .* New York: Harcourt, Brace, and World, 1962.
———. *What Do You Say, Dear?* New York: Harcourt, Brace, and World, 1962.
Juster, Norton. *The Phantom Tollbooth.* New York: Epstein and Carroll, 1961.
Krauss, Ruth. *A Hole Is to Dig.* New York: Harper and Row, 1952.
Munari, Bruno. *Who's There? Open the Door.* New York: World Publishing Co., 1957.
O'Neill, Mary. *Hailstones and Halibut Bones.* New York: Doubleday, 1961.
Roberts, Cliff. *The Hole.* New York: Franklin Watts, 1963.
Seuss, Dr. *McElligott's Pool.* New York: Random House, 1947.
Waber, Bernard. *How to Go About Laying an Egg.* New York: Houghton Mifflin, 1963.
Wolff, Janet, and Owett, Bernard. *Let's Imagine Thinking up Things.* New York: E. P. Dutton, 1961.

A POSITIVE ATTITUDE TOWARD FAILURE

When a student makes a mistake or a project fails to produce the expected results, the student should not experience a sense of personal failure. Mistakes should be viewed as stepping stones toward success much in the manner of Thomas A. Edison's often quoted remark as he continued to discover methods that did not achieve the desired electric light bulb. How can the teacher develop positive attitudes toward failure?

1 Assist the student by not overburdening him or her with corrections. A composition which is returned to the student blushing with red pencil marks may prove an insurmountable obstacle to ever writing anything of worth. Praising wholeheartedly that which is of value in student's work has been proved to result in more effective development of writing skills. If a correction needs to be made, concentrate on one or two items which can be readily assimilated at one time by the young writer.

2 Encourage experimentation with the clear understanding that the results are never guaranteed successful. Students should be encouraged to play with words, to invent new forms for poetry, to attempt new effects in their writing without any fear of so-called "failing." These experiments add to the feeling for discovering, exploring, trying the wings of originality.

3 Assume the role of a guide and consultant rather than of one who knows all the answers and stands ready to point out punctuation errors, faulty construction, or misspelling. Teachers need to become admirers of student ideas, accepting them and enjoying them. We should celebrate the achievements of young people.

ACCEPTANCE OF THE NONCONFORMIST

As studies have pointed out, the highly creative child has problems functioning as part of a group. For this reason he or she may cause disturbance or refuse to conform to our standards of behavior. It is difficult for the teacher of thirty-five children to condone or understand this type of behavior, and the first inclination has been to chastise the child with the entire class listening. The teacher must make a conscious effort to investigate the child's reasons for causing disturbance or for failing to conform. If the child is creative, some understanding on the part of the teacher may lead to rewarding solutions of this problem.

Although we grant the relative ease of writing about the classroom situation as opposed to actual operation in the classrom, a better approach to this type of problem involves talking to the child privately. Questioning behavior and discussing the reasons for some measure of conformity in any group situation has proved beneficial. But provision must be made for some outlet for creative abilities and an opportunity to become part of the group. The teacher can assist the child in reducing isolation from peers by letting him or her share results of individual experimentation. James might "teach the class" for fifteen minutes as he explains the project which he is developing.

The class must be helped to understand the creative child. As Plato wrote: "What is honored in a country will be cultivated there." The teacher's obvious approval and interest in the activities of the child will make the child's work take on interest and value for peers. Introducing creative activities for the entire class will lead them to understand the need for divergent thinking and the challenge of producing original ideas. Students can read and discuss creative people of the past, pointing up the fact that their ideas were not always acceptable to people of their times. These approaches may lead to a measure of admiration for the child who formerly was tagged with having "wild ideas."

PARENTS WHO UNDERSTAND THE CONCERN FOR CREATIVITY

Parents, like teachers, have trouble understanding the nonconforming child. What we adults value is not always manifested by the child, and therein lies a conflict that may well be disastrous for the germ of creativity. Studies show that the home influence has great effect on the development of creativity; whether creativity is stifled or nurtured, therefore, is not the sole responsibility of the school. It is the concern of the school, however, to promote understanding of the creative child, and the teacher and the school work to this end as they assist the parent in understanding the need for concern about creativity.

A communique from the school to the home can feature creativity, briefly outlining the significance of this element of human intelligence and stating the concern of the school for encouraging creativity in children. This information sheet can draw attention to articles in general magazines or books which parents may be interested in reading.

Ways can also be suggested for parents to encourage creativity in their own children in much the same manner that the school does:

1 Respect questions and ideas of the child.
2 Encourage experimentation and exploration.
3 Give the child time to think and to express ideas.
4 Accept the child for what he or she is.
5 Help children understand themselves.
6 Recognize and value the talents of the creative child.
7 Provide materials.

Discussion or study groups can also be helpful in promoting understanding of creativity. Speakers can be obtained to present this topic to the group. Parents of unusually creative children should be invited to come to school to discuss the problems of the individual child. The film *Adventures of an* * (McGraw-Hill) is excellent to use with parents, especially with fathers.

Teaching English Creatively

English is an area of the elementary school curriculum that lends itself to creative approaches. The teaching of English creatively, however, requires the teacher to develop new perspectives of English and of the objectives we are trying to achieve. It is important, observes Kneller, "to recognize that if a person is to make full use of his talents, he should learn to think creatively in a range of situations and on a variety of subjects. The mind, in other words, should be trained to think creatively at the same time that it is trained to think logically." [15]

CRITERIA FOR A CREATIVE ENGLISH PROGRAM

In order to determine the degree of creativity of any English program, we must first establish some type of criteria. These criteria will reflect what we know about creativity in general as applied to the various areas

[15] George F. Kneller, *The Art and Science of Creativity* (New York: Holt, Rinehart, and Winston, 1965), p. 78.

included in the English curriculum. Let us examine some of these criteria:

1 Is the program different in some way from that of the past year?
2 Do the children enjoy English activities?
3 Is stress placed on use of the imagination, playing with words, inventiveness?
4 Is the child praised for that which is accomplished rather than criticized for the mistakes made?
5 Are many opportunities provided for writing, speaking, and reading creatively?
6 Does the teacher function as a guide rather than a judge?
7 Is there evidence in the room that children are creating?

We can apply the concepts of creativity to all areas included in the broad term of English. Particularly adaptable to creative approaches are writing and dramatics, but we can also apply these stimulating concepts to listening, speaking, and even to spelling and the mechanics of writing.

In many respects English has pioneered specific aspects of creativity through creative writing and creative dramatics. Hughes Mearns, writing in 1929, for instance, stated: "Good teaching is not solely the business of instructing; it is also the art of influencing another. Primarily, it is the job of uncovering and enlarging native gifts of insight, feeling, and thinking."[16] The revised edition of his challenging exploration of the creative potential of youth, *Creative Power,* is being widely heralded by contemporary writers who are now cognizant of the import of the methods used by Mearns in stimulating creativity. Mearns admonished his young writers in these words.

> You have something to say. Find out what it is. That is the beginning. Once really started, it will carry you through life; for you will be doing for yourself all that education can ever do for anybody, encouraging that deeper and powerful self to rise within you and take possession.[17]

METHODS TO PROMOTE CREATIVITY

Methods can be used in the English program to encourage creativity rather than stifle it. In the past, instruction in English relied chiefly on the authoritarian approach to learning. Studies in science and mathe-

[16] Hughes Mearns, *Creative Power: The Education of Youth in the Creative Arts,* rev. ed. (New York: Dover, 1958), p. 267.

[17] *Ibid.,* p. 260.

matics have led the way toward the use of questioning, experimenting, exploring, discovering–inductive methods of learning. The following approaches allow for individual development and, therefore, permit the creative child to operate in a freer environment:

1 Use of open-ended topics which encourage thinking
2 Independent study and research
3 Free selection of topics for speaking and writing
4 Less emphasis on form, more emphasis on ideas expressed
5 Reward of diverse contributions
6 Guidance through individual conference or consultation
7 Tests which emphasize divergent thinking

MATERIALS THAT STIMULATE CREATIVITY

There is a dearth of materials now available which truly exemplify the concepts embodied in the study of creativity, for instructional materials still chiefly reflect authoritarian methods of teaching and convergent thinking. What is needed now are books, films, records, and other teaching aids which will assist the teacher in emphasizing diverse contributions, encouraging questions, stimulating new ideas, providing opportunities for problem solving.

Creative approaches to spelling, listening, and speaking need to be developed. There is a need, too, for material which permits the individual to advance according to his or her ability, flexible material which meets the needs of the child and the teacher. A wide variety of instructional aids must be designed specifically to promote creativity.

Teachers can also experiment with their own materials as they develop devices for motivating creative writing, adapting materials which are presently available. Students, too, can be motivated to create materials which can be used by the class.

Materials to Foster Creativity

Covington, Martin V.; Crutchfield, Richard; et al. *The Productive Thinking Program.* Columbus, Ohio: Charles E. Merrill, 1973. Designed to help all students in the upper elementary grades develop their potential for effective thinking.

Making It Strange. New York: Synectics, 1968. A series of four books to motivate students to think creatively.

Torrance, E. Paul, and Cunnington, B. F. *Sounds and Images: Elementary Version* and *Sounds and Images: Adult Version.* Boston: Ginn and Co., 1965.

Torrance, E. Paul, and Myers, R. E. *Can You Imagine?* Boston: Ginn and Co., 1965. Workbook of exercises and teachers' guide.

———. *For Those Who Wonder.* Boston: Ginn and Co., 1966. Workbook of exercises and teachers' guide.

———. *Invitations to Speaking and Writing Creatively.* Boston: Ginn and Co., 1963. Workbook of exercises and teachers' guide.

———. *Invitations to Thinking and Doing.* Boston: Ginn and Co., 1964. Workbook of exercises and teachers' guide.

———. *Plots, Puzzles, and Ploys.* Boston: Ginn and Co., 1966. Workbook of exercises and teachers' guide.

CURRICULUM REVISION IN ENGLISH

Not only is there a great need for new methods and materials in English, but the curriculum itself needs re-examination. If we accept the concepts offered by researchers of creativity, then courses of study will require revision. Activities which stress creative thinking and allow for originality must be incorporated in the entire program.

We hear primary teachers say securely, "That's fine for the upper grades, but our children don't write well enough." We object wholeheartedly, for first-grade children *do write,* as will be discussed in more detail in Chapter 7. These children discuss, they dictate, and they print their own stories as their ability progresses through the year. Young children, begin developing many creative abilities through speaking, listening, and dramatics. This problem is only one of those which must be considered by curriculum revisers. We must begin stimulating creativity in children as early as possible, for there are those who remind us that the school has already missed the most crucial early years.

Curriculum revision is not easily effected, but it must come if we are to reach our goal of developing each child to the fullest extent of his abilities. What are the blocks to revision? In most cases they are rigid thinking, refusal to accept change, and even actual fear of the new approaches entailed in changes proposed. One hears remarks such as these which represent the immovable force:

"We tried that years ago and it didn't work."
"Why, that would cost the district too much money."
"Those ideas would never work with my class."
"That's another one of those *progressive* ideas."

In order to overcome these inhibiting factors to curriculum revision one must first understand these opposing viewpoints. Fixed ideas and values represent the direct opposite of open-mindedness and divergent thinking, the very things the creative teacher would promote in children. It is difficult to change these ways of thinking which have developed over long periods of time.

Many people feel threatened by the thought of doing something different. They fear being wrong or making a mistake. Conformity has been so much a part of them that they wouldn't think of making a change unless it was already nationally accepted. Others actually feel threatened by the creative child himself; they need to dominate the child they teach. These teachers fear that which remains mysterious and incomprehensible to them. They fear loss of control.

Changes will not be made overnight, but those which are considered advantageous to the student are coming and will continue to gain acceptance with time. We can already find evidence of the tendency in this directions as more and more school systems include creative activities in their English programs. Creative teachers are leading the way.

Developing Your Own Creativity

It is generally conceded that the teacher who is creative will be better able to teach creatively and to establish empathy with the child who is creative. Creative teaching promotes creative behavior in students. How can you evaluate your own creativity? How can you stimulate your personal creative development?

GET ACQUAINTED WITH YOURSELF

The first step in developing personal creativity is the acceptance of ourselves as we exist, for as individuals we often fail to become acquainted with our own personality. We never think about ourselves. What are our strengths? What are our weaknesses? We need to make an honest appraisal of our behavior patterns. Why do we do the things we do? Why do some things irritate us? We need to gain some understanding of ourselves and to accept ourselves as we really exist.

Try this list on for size. Which of these experiences have you had during the past month?

Creativity Checklist

________ 1 Acted in a play.
________ 2 Wrote a poem.
________ 3 Kept a diary.
________ 4 Recorded on a tape recorder.
________ 5 Made up a recipe.
________ 6 Wrote a song.
________ 7 Solved the problem of getting along with my peers.
________ 8 Wrote a letter to someone in another country.
________ 9 Made up a game and played it.

_______ **10** Sketched a picture.
_______ **11** Kept a record of my leisure reading.
_______ **12** Cooked a foreign food.
_______ **13** Made jewelry.
_______ **14** Took color photographs.
_______ **15** Collected anything.
_______ **16** Took a walk in the woods.
_______ **17** Drew cartoons.
_______ **18** Helped organize something.
_______ **19** Designed greeting cards or invitations.
_______ **20** Made a toy for a child.
_______ **21** Performed with a group—danced, sang, played an instrument.
_______ **22** Wrote a short story.
_______ **23** Made a play on words.
_______ **24** Wrote a letter to an editor.
_______ **25** Told a child an original story.

We can prepare for the further expansion of creative abilities by viewing ourselves in the role of the learner, of one who is ready to make discoveries, to explore. Are we truly interested in exploring new territory? Isn't life too short to waste on boredom? Being creative does not mean that every person should immediately write a poem or short story and send it off to *Harper's*. Creative abilities and interests may lie in diverse areas—landscaping a garden, flower arranging, designing a bookcase, solving a problem, organizing a work area, preparing new teaching materials, ad infinitum. One school we know of has a display of teachers' creative efforts.

Many persons are stymied when creativity is mentioned, for they immediately reject the possibility that they can create, saying helplessly, "I am just not creative." One of the requisites for creativity is the "open mind," the willingness to explore possibilities. We shall operate, therefore, on the premise that every individual has some elements of creativity.

EXPLORE CREATIVE ACTIVITIES

Creativity can be expressed in widely varied ways—experimenting, planning, organizing, writing, speaking, constructing, thinking. We wish to dispel the narrow view that immediately associates creativity with a product of the acknowledged arts—a painting, a novel, a symphony.

Begin thinking about events, objects, ways of doing things, in new ways. Examine your own school or room. Can you explore the possibilities for organizing, decorating, or arranging it for more efficient and enjoyable living?

Consider the time that lies before you each day. Can you discover ways of planning your activities more effectively? Are there periods of time which can be used creatively? You can think, plan, and organize while doing rather mundane tasks such as walking, ironing, or cutting grass. Keep a notebook handy for jotting down ideas which originate during these periods. The teacher can look at teaching creatively. Examine the problems in the classroom with a new eye toward solving them, for problems were made to solve. Explore a variety of possibilities, keeping the mind open for varied answers to problems which arise.

The teacher can create a finger play story to tell to students, introducing this story by saying, "Here is a story which I made for *you*." They will take special interest in this gift, perhaps responding by making a story themselves.

The teacher can also participate in creative activities which are introduced to the students. This is one of the most effective methods of interesting students in creative activities, for it immediately demonstrates the teacher's value for these activities. If composing poetry is fun, enriching, and worthwhile for students, might it not also prove rewarding for the teacher? What could be more inspiring to the class, as the teacher tells them about Haiku, than the presentation of a Haiku written by the teacher? It immediately involves the class far more than would the Haiku of Buson or Shiki, who are only names to the child.

Invent creative ways to teach. New and different methods lend a sparkle to teaching for both the teacher and the students. If the teacher is bored with the method used in teaching spelling, think how bored are the students. Experiment with different approaches, exploring possibilities for effective teaching without dull routine. Don't be afraid to be different. There are too many conformists and not enough nonconformists in the teaching ranks.

Creativity has much to offer the elementary school classroom; it has much to offer the teacher of English. The findings of researchers in this area should lead to the re-examination of the objectives and aims of the elementary school English program. These objectives should encompass efforts not only to avoid the stifling of creativity which exists in each child but also to stimulate the growth of that creativity in varying degrees.

Taking into consideration the findings of research in creativity and that knowledge which we now possess about teaching and learning processes, the classroom teacher can best stimulate creativity through:

1 Rewarding diverse contributions; encouraging questions and new ideas
2 Accepting the creative child for what he or she is, a child with all the usual problems of childhood plus an active thinking brain

3 Reducing the overemphasis on sex roles. Boys can enjoy poetry, art, music; girls can enjoy science and things mechanical
4 Helping the creative child adjust to the group situation, reducing isolation and helping him or her participate
5 Helping the child solve personal problems; helping parents understand the creative child and the significance of creativity
6 Recognizing the talents of the creative child, making obvious the value of the contributions of each child by praising sincerely
7 Using a variety of stimuli in the form of methods and materials and developing an atmosphere conducive to creativity
8 Assuming the role of a guide, not a chastiser-corrector; avoiding rigid thinking and evaluating
9 Developing a positive attitude toward failure
10 Encouraging experimentation and divergent thinking

Books to Investigate

Darrow, Helen F., and Van Allen, R. *Independent Activities for Creative Learning.* New York: Teachers College Press, 1961.

Getzels, Jacob W., and Jackson, Philip W. *Creativity and Intelligence.* New York: John Wiley, 1962.

Kneller, George F. *The Art and Science of Creativity.* New York: Holt, Rinehart, and Winston, 1965. An excellent overview of creativity.

Koestler, Arthur. *The Art of Creation.* New York: The Macmillan Co., 1964.

Lowenfeld, Viktor. *Creative and Mental Growth.* New York: The Macmillan Co., 1957.

Mearns, Hughes. *Creative Power: The Education of Youth in the Creative Arts.* New York: Dover, 1958.

Shumsky, Abraham. *Creative Teaching in the Elementary School.* New York: Appleton-Century-Crofts, 1965.

Smith, James A. *Setting Conditions for Creative Teaching in the Elementary School.* New York: Charles Scribner's Sons, 1962.

Tiedt, Sidney W. *Creativity.* Morristown, N.J.: General Learning Corp., 1975.

Torrance, E. Paul, and Myers, R. E. *Creative Learning and Teaching.* New York: Dodd Mead and Co., 1970.

Torrance, E. Paul. *Guiding Creative Talent.* Englewood Cliffs, N.J.: Prentice-Hall, Inc., 1962.

creative writing

chapter 7

**Tell me, where oh where is fancy bred—
In the heart or in the head?**

Shakespeare

What do we mean by "creative writing?" How does it differ from other writing? Of what value is creative writing? These are questions raised frequently by teachers. It is our purpose in this chapter to introduce the various facets of creative writing as part of the English program in the elementary school. We shall explore the following areas of concern as we investigate the possibilities for encouraging creativity through writing:

How can we define creative writing?
Why should we teach creative writing?
How can we plan for teaching creative writing?

Defining Creative Writing

The term *creative writing* has long been used by teachers and writers. Substitutions have been suggested by those who shy away from the *creative* terminology, for example, personal writing, writing for fun, expressive writing, free writing. It is our feeling, however, that these phrases remain mere substitutes which are not quite as descriptive as the original term.

What are the elements of creative writing which make it different from other writing? As we begin listing these characteristics, you will soon note that they are similar in nature to attributes of creativity, for creative writing is usually characterized by original, individual expression and imaginative, experimental thinking that is guided but not confined by direction.

TYPES OF CREATIVE WRITING

There are many types of creative writing which are appropriate to the classroom; indeed, almost any kind of writing is appropriate for exploration.

Sentence stories, descriptive paragraphs
Jokes and riddles
Diaries and letters
Skits, plays
Fables and myths
Short stories, books
Poetry
Songs

Creative writing, you will note, includes both poetry and prose. We feel, however, that since poetry is so very important and since the techniques used differ sufficiently from those of prose, this type of creative writing should be discussed in a separate chapter, with the present chapter focusing on the writing of prose.

Why Teach Creative Writing?

> Children are creative persons, not scholiasts; they use language as the artist the world over and in all ages has used his medium, not as an end in itself but as a means for the expression of thought and feeling. Language in itself, they sense, is comparatively unimportant; if the vision is steady and the feeling is true these will find their proper vehicle. The attention is never on the word but upon the force that creates the word.[1]

[1] Hughes Mearns, *Creative Power: The Education of Youth in the Creative Arts* (New York: Dover, 1958), p. 9.

So writes the imaginative and sensitive teacher Hughes Mearns in a charming and enlightening book, as he describes his attempts to stimulate creativity.

Writing is only one area of the elementary school curriculum in which we can stimulate creativity. It is, however, an area which requires very little in the way of equipment and materials and, therefore, is perhaps an area in which many teachers find themselves more at ease, more prepared to encourage creativity. It is also, as stated by McCarthy, an area of a child's development in which more striking degrees of individual variation can be observed than in almost any other phase of growth.[2]

"Language is the dress of thought," wrote Samuel Johnson, and it is this concept we wish to stress in encouraging the young writer. When the student views language as a means for achieving a desired end—that is, the recording of ideas and the communication of these ideas to others—then he/she will become concerned with the learning of the skills of writing. Students will have a reason for learning these skills, but emphasis should remain on the stimulation of creative thought.

THE OBJECTIVES OF CREATIVE WRITING

We need to examine the objectives of teaching creative writing to help us direct these learning activities toward the achievement of the greatest good for each student, and therein lies the primary objective of all teaching—to assist each child in developing to the greatest extent of his/her abilities. More specifically, however, the objectives of teaching creative writing might be stated thus:

1 Stimulation of the creative expression of ideas
2 Development of a sense of potency and personal worth for each child and his/her contributions
3 Establishment of rapport among children and teachers to encourage freedom of expression
4 Development of writing skills and vocabulary to facilitate writing as a form of communication

---

How do I know what I think 'til I see what I say?

These objectives are focused on the child and that child's personal development, for we are not overly concerned with the product of this

[2] Dorothea McCarthy, "Language Development in Children," in *Manual of Child Psychology*, L. Carmichael, ed. (New York: Wiley, 1954), pp. 492–630.

process. We have not stated, therefore, as an objective: "The production of a short story with full development of characters, plot, and setting," for it is not our purpose through teaching creative writing to discover child prodigies or to encourage students to produce work which compares favorably with that of adult writers. We would hope rather that at the end of any year each child would be writing more sentences, using new words, and expressing ideas more freely than was true at the beginning of the school year.

Planning Writing Experiences

Planning for writing experiences is essential if this part of the English program is to be effectively carried out. Without careful attention to planning it is easy to lose sight of long-range goals. There is also the danger that writing experiences will never materialize, lost in the multitude of other areas which demand time in the busy elementary school classroom. We shall examine three aspects of planning for writing which frequently perplex the teacher: (1) time for writing, (2) sources of new ideas, and (3) lesson plans.

TIME FOR WRITING

One of the aims of the creative writing program is frequent opportunity to write, but classroom teachers sometimes complain that they just do not have this time for creative writing. Admittedly the elementary school schedule is a crowded one, but writing can be included without excluding other subjects. There are a number of ways for finding more time for writing as we begin to think about this problem:

1 Scheduled writing periods

Example: Several thirty to forty-five minute periods are scheduled each week for introducing new writing tasks. This amount of time is usually allotted by the course of study.

2 Relating writing to other subjects

Example: Writing an adventure set in Brazil which utilizes knowledge of the geography and history of that country; or writing a diary of a founding father or an early pioneer.

3 Writing before school

Example: Designate the five or ten minutes before the bell rings as the WRITERS' WORKSHOP when each writes a daily entry in his personal Idea Book.

4 Writing at home

Example: Encourage able students to continue writing activities at home. Writing done at home is also placed in the Writing Folder and can be the subject of an individual conference.

5 Writing clubs meeting after school

Example: Those students who are especially interested in writing can form a club called PEN POINTERS or WRITERS, INC. They can meet once or twice a week using the time to write, to discuss their writing, or to learn about writing. With a chairman, the club can be student-managed.

6 Writing when other work is completed

Example: Writing is an excellent individualized activity which can be pursued independently by a student who has completed assigned work in social studies, and so on. The student is free to get a Writing Folder at any time. Tom might, for example, be publishing a collection of poems at the Publishing Center at the back of the room.

"Imagination is like any muscle, it improves with use."
William Faulkner

SOURCES OF NEW IDEAS

To sustain continued interest in writing the teacher needs varied ideas for motivating student writing. The regularly scheduled writing period should usually be designated for beginning new writing tasks although at times these periods will be needed for completion of longer writing projects. Several new ideas will be required each week, which at first may appear to be too much to expect of a teacher. Let us consider, therefore, ways of finding new ideas or of making *old* ideas appear *new*.

1 *Alternating the writing of prose, poetry, and word study.* A class may work on poetry for a week or two, then concentrate on forms of prose for a period of time. As different forms of prose and poetry are introduced, students will have a wider range of ideas for independent writing. The study of words adds to interest in writing both prose and poetry.

2 *Adapting ideas so that they appear new the next time they are presented.* If the technique of drawing several lines on a blank sheet of paper has been used to intrigue students' imaginations as they complete the drawing and write about it, several weeks later interesting shapes can be cut from colored paper which students arrange in any fashion on a larger sheet adding lines as they wish to complete a drawing about which they write.

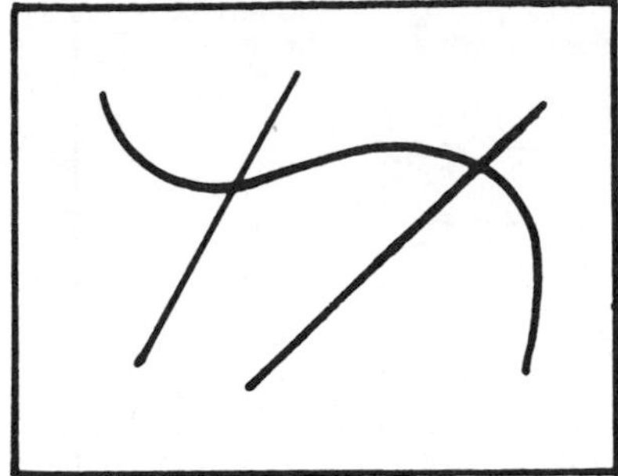

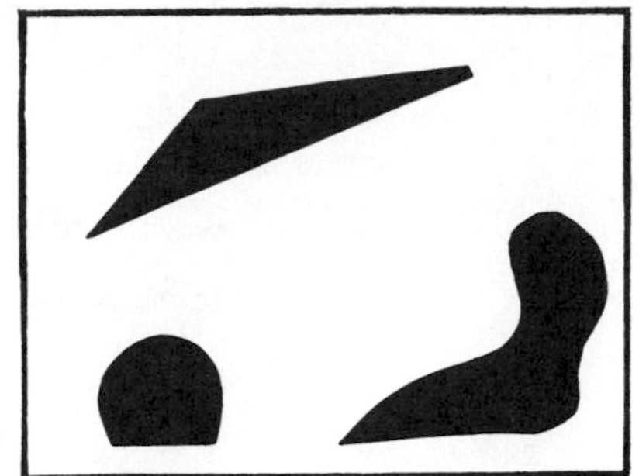

lines shapes

3 *Repeating the same idea after a period of time has elapsed.* A good idea is worth repeating if it is not worn out. If one day the students based their writing on three unrelated nouns which were written on the board, the same technique can be used several weeks later; they will welcome the assignment as something familiar but still challenging especially if three different words are used. Instead of three nouns, three adjectives, three verbs, or a combination of noun, verb, and adjective can be suggested. The students can also select the words to be used, for another slight change.

4 *Alternating the type of motivating devices used.* One day a device is used which appeals visually, such as a picture about which the children write. The next day a record is played, or the sense of touch is the stimulus through the use of an unknown object concealed in a paper bag which all have a chance to feel.

5 *Inventing ideas for motivating student writing.* A writing period can be allocated for "brainstorming" exciting first lines about which to write. These lines are then used to motivate writing.

> It was sinking, but there was nothing I could do.
> "One, two, three. Go!" he shouted.
> He looked and looked but it was nowhere to be seen.

6 *Collecting new ideas from varied sources.* The teacher must always remain alert to new ideas which are described in journal articles about creative writing. Check copies (even old issues) of *Elementary English, Instructor, Grade Teacher*. Often ideas are gathered from fellow teachers who describe techniques they have tried. It is an excellent practice to jot each new idea on a file card so these ideas are readily available when needed. We use this form in recording ideas briefly on file cards:

Title of Activity: Jigsaw Story

Area of Study: Creative Writing

Description of Technique:

Cut a square of construction paper in four irregular pieces on which are written:
2 characters, 1 setting, 1 noun
Each student gets an envelope containing a Jigsaw Story which he assembles; he then writes a story relating the four parts.

7 *Journals for and by children. Cricket, Kids,* and *Stone Soup* are the provocative titles of new magazines for children which suggest many possibilities for writing.

Cricket, The Magazine for Children. An illustrated journal of children's writing. Published monthly except June, July, and August by Open Court, 1058 Eighth St., La Salle, Ill. 61301. Single copy $1.50.

Kids, The Magazine by Kids for Kids. Contains articles and pictures done by children. Published by Kids' Publishers, 77 Third Ave., New York, NY 10017. Single copy 60¢.

Stone Soup, A Journal of Children's Literature. Collection of stories, poems, plays, and illustrations by children and adults. Published in November, February, and May by Big Trees Press, Box 83, Santa Cruz, Calif. 96063. Single copy $1.50.

LESSON PLANS FOR CREATIVE WRITING

Each writing experience should be carefully planned. The lesson is sure to be more effective if the teacher is certain of the motivational device to be used, the method for its introduction, and follow-up activities. It is also helpful if suggestions are noted after the activity has been completed, for we continuously learn as we teach. We find that a simple lesson plan form like the one illustrated for Traveling Tales provides the necessary guidelines for a successful writing activity. This form aids the teacher in thinking through the creativity from start to finish, clarifying the development of the teaching technique.

LESSON PLAN FOR CREATIVE WRITING

Title: Traveling Tales

Time: 45 minutes

Technique:

Questions:
"Have you ever traveled?"
"Have you ever heard of a Traveling Tale?"
"What does this kind of tale mean?" (write on board)
"What would a traveling tale be?

Directions:

Today we are going to write Traveling Tales, stories that move from place to place. Each one of us is going to begin a story. When I say TRAVEL TIME, you will pass your story to the person behind you. Then each of you will read what is on the paper and add what you think would happen next. We'll have our stories travel several times so that each of you will work on several different stories. Then we'll read the stories to see how they grew as they traveled.

Tips:

Stop writing soon enough so a number of students can read their tales.

At each passing allow enough time for passing as well as for writing.

Each child can finish one of the stories next day.

Compile stories in a book: Traveling Tales

Notice that the activity has been given a *Title*. Students respond more readily to an activity which bears an intriguing name so that, if possible, an imaginative name should be used rather than Writing Activity Number Twenty-Seven. Students may apply an apt name to the activity which can be adopted for future use.

The amount of *Time* required for this activity may appear to be too long. Experience will prove, however, that an effective warm-up period requires perhaps ten minutes, that students need about twenty minutes to write using this technique, and that fifteen minutes is not too long a time to allow for reading some of the results. Other activities may not require as long a period of time; certainly forty-five minutes will usually be the longest writing period needed. The second day of this activity, for example, does not require as much motivation because students do not have to read new material as it is passed to them. Thirty minutes would suffice. As experience is gained in teaching, the teacher is better able to judge the amount of time required for varied activities.

Under the heading *Technique* should be included the exact words that will be said to the class as the writing project is introduced. The teacher may begin with a question, by showing the class an object of interest, by writing something on the board, or by pinning words or a picture on the bulletin board. The objective of the opening procedure is to arouse the interest of the class immediately.

In the example described, Sue Johnson has chosen to begin by asking the question, "Have you ever traveled?" which she is sure will elicit a positive response to involve the entire class. She follows that question with another, "Have you ever heard of a Traveling Tale?" which she assumes will mystify the class of third graders. She may then write the word *tale* on the board, asking someone to identify the homonym *tale* as a story, leading them further to identify a traveling tale as a "story which moves around or goes from place to place." The teacher can then proceed by saying:

> "Today we are going to write Traveling Tales, stories that move from place to place. Each one of us is going to begin a story. When I say, TRAVEL TIME, you will pass your story to the person behind you. Then each of you will read what is on the paper and add what you think would happen next. We'll have our stories travel several times so that each of you will work on several different stories. Then we'll read the stories to see how they grew as they traveled."

If the children have not written much before this experience, they may be assisted in getting started by supplying one or two first lines which can be used by anyone who needs help:

I ran happily down the beach, but stopped suddenly when I saw . . .
It was eleven o'clock one evening when the telephone rang.

Sufficient time is allowed for the children to write a few sentences before calling "Travel Time." If you walk around the room during the writing period, you can easily ascertain when most students have written enough. The time allowed must be progressively longer, for the growing story requires more time to read. Time must be allotted, too, for some of the stories to be read aloud before the writing project is put aside for the day. The reading of these efforts shows the class the wide variety of possibilities for developing stories. It also points up the value placed on their work as all enjoy it together. (Tip: If one child from each row is called to read, probably something written by almost every child will be read.)

On the following day each child may be given one of the partially completed stories with the instructions to read the story, make any changes desired, and complete the story. Again some stories can be read. The entire group of stories can be compiled (by one or two students) in a book entitled TRAVELING TALES. Other students can illustrate the volume. If the stories are especially good, ten to fifteen copies can be made on ditto, collated, and combined by students to create "readers." This set can be given or loaned to other classes later on.

Perhaps the most important single aspect leading to successful creative writing experiences is the motivation of the student. The child who lacks motivation may find the writing period a chore and a bore, and there will be little that is creative about the writing.

There is a great need for research regarding the techniques of motivating creative writing. Many people question, for instance, whether this type of writing can be motivated effectively. Through questionnaire, interview, and observation in forty elementary schools, Smith compiled a list of ten factors in motivating creative writing.[3]

1 Providing attractive classrooms rich in materials
2 Encouraging pupils to write from their own interests and needs
3 Providing rich experiences about which a child can express himself
4 Developing sensitivity to good writing which in turn helps a child improve
5 Using real needs of children or helping them to develop new ones
6 Providing freedom from fear and helping pupils gain confidence in their ability to create
7 Providing abundant time and opportunity for writing in many areas and in many forms

[3] Ethel Smith, *Procedures for Encouraging Creative Writing in the Elementary School* (Doctoral dissertation, Northwestern University, 1944).

8 Developing skill in mechanics without sacrificing spontaneity
9 Sharing the end products of writing
10 Evaluating the writing in terms of the total growth of the child

How can the teacher best implement the findings of research about the motivation of creative writing? How can effective motivation be achieved in the classroom? We have found that the teacher of language arts best stimulates creative writing through (1) creating a climate for writing, (2) providing a warming-up period before writing, and (3) using varied techniques for motivation.

"The pen is the tongue of the mind."
Cervantes

CREATING A CLIMATE FOR WRITING

If we wish students to write creatively, we must provide an atmosphere in the classroom which is conducive to writing freely without fear or concern for criticism, an atmosphere which clearly communicates the feeling that whatever each child writes has value. What do we mean by "an atmosphere conducive to writing?" This concept is so vital to successful writing in the classroom that we need to examine the components of this atmosphere—teacher attitude and student attitude.

If we truly value writing as a means to learning and self-expression, we must operate on the theory that there is *worth in the writing of every child,* some small item that rates a favorable comment, something for which to praise the child, which will in turn encourage efforts.

As a teacher, what would be your comment after reading the following short composition written by a second-grade girl?

Judy
My dog is blak.
He is a good dog.
We play ball after
skool.

Judy was eager to share this story with "Teacher," who would surely like it. Her teacher might have made any number of remarks:

1 "Your story is not very long. Why not add more to it?"
2 "I see two words that are misspelled. See if you can find them."

3 "Why, Judy, I didn't know you had a dog. I'd like to hear more about him."

The first two statements are certainly justifiable and are not unkind, but the third would be made by a teacher who understood, a teacher who was concerned for the development of a child. The focus remains on the child and her ideas, not on her mistakes, and carries a warmth and interest in the child as well as the writing. The use of the student's name is also an excellent device for adding to her security in the classroom situation. The teacher's desire to know more about Judy's dog suggests obliquely that Judy write more while at the same time approving subject matter which is familiar to the child. It is this type of teacher enthusiasm and understanding which stimulates the child to write freely.

In order for children to write effectively, creatively, they must feel *a sense of freedom.* By freedom we do not, however, mean license. We would borrow the words of Robert Frost who defined this type of freedom: "Freedom is feeling easy in your harness."

The child functions well in the harness which in this case is the controlled situation of the classroom but also needs this feeling of being at ease, of being free to experiment with language, of daring to disagree or to try something different from that which others are doing. To feel free to be original, the student must know that originality or difference will not be condemned or ridiculed by peers.

The young writer, too, must be reassured that intimate emotional revelations will not be tacked on the bulletin board for all to read. There must be some way of protecting privacy, or Tim will never risk putting these words on paper; certainly he will never ask his teacher to share them. Some teachers have employed the practice of telling students early in the year that anything they write which is not for reading aloud may be marked NOT TO BE READ or PERSONAL. A child's Writing Folder can also be clearly designated as Personal Property with the understanding that no writing *has* to be shown to anyone else, even to the teacher.

Anyone entering a classroom will know that *writing is important* if there is evidence that children are writing. Writing is displayed around the room—on bulletin boards, compiled in booklets, on the classroom reading table. The Writing Center also serves to add to the importance of writing. The purpose of this activity center is to encourage writing and to provide a place where students can work undisturbed and undisturbing. This helpful addition to the classroom requires few materials which are not readily available. Suggested here are types of equipment and materials which add to the Writing Center:

Table and chairs to accommodate about six students
Paper supplies, pencils, erasers

Dictionaries suitable to grade level
File of individual writing folders
Typewriter (a motivating addition if available)

Sometimes the Writing Center can be supplemented with a Publishing Center, with the emphasis still on writing. The student is encouraged, however, not only to write but also to publish work in simple form with an attractive cover. The publication may consist of a leaflet with appropriate illustrations by the author. The more ambitious, prolific author may produce a book which can be properly stitched and bound. Publishing lends an additional note of value to the writing of each child. Published works of individual children make excellent gifts for parents and provide a good way to let the public know what the school is doing.

Writing must be *an integral part of the child's learning activities.* A regularly scheduled daily writing period provides time for the development of language abilities. A student who completes assigned writing tasks is then free to develop any writing project in the writing folder, which may include the following:

1 An assignment that the student wants to develop from a previous writing period
2 A topic which has been noted for exploring
3 A long story or book written independently
4 Checking definitions for words accumulated in the WORD BOOK
5 Preparing a copy of selection to discuss during individual conferences
6 Preparing a final draft of writing to be published or displayed

An interesting technique for providing daily writing practice is that which we call Timed Writing. This technique is especially suitable to the classroom in that it can fit into any small amount of time you may have available—before school, the last five minutes before recess or lunch. These regular writing periods add to the student's fluency or ability to get words on paper. The object of the exercise is to write for five or ten minutes without ceasing no matter what is written. It is usually most effective to direct students to write about something of personal interest—what they do at home, something they saw on the way to school, something they would like to do. These writings can be done on single sheets of paper which are filed in the Writing Folder or they can be written in a spiral notebook in the form of a journal, diary, or log.

WARMING-UP BEFORE WRITING

There is little likelihood that students will be stimulated to write interesting, creative stories if the teacher passes each student a clean sheet of composition paper and says, "Now I want each of you to write an interesting story." The situation will be little remedied even if you state, I want each of you to write an interesting story about a cat."

The writing experience can, however, be rescued if the teacher allots just a few minutes for a warming-up period before the students have a sheet of paper before them. Suppose, for example, we use the suggested topic of cats. The teacher might begin something like this:

> "How many of you have a cat at your house? What kind of cat do you have, John?" (Students name the species, color, size of their house pets.)
>
> "Are there other types of cats than those which have already been described?" (She elicits the naming of wild animals in the cat family—tiger, lion, jaguar—which are listed on the board as named.)
>
> "Where would you see cats like these?" (Jungle, circus, zoo—pictures can be shown.)

By beginning the writing period with this type of discussion, students become involved with the topic. Each one has begun to think of some sort of cat in a specific situation. A wide variety of possibilities have been opened up by the discussion. Each child is ready when the teacher continues:

> "Today I want each of you to write a story about a cat, any kind of cat that interests you. While I pass paper to you, you can begin thinking of the cat you will describe. Where is this cat? What does it look like? What is its name? What is it doing? Is it with a human being or another animal?"

Some of the resulting stories will be about the common feline, but others will describe leopards, panthers, or Bengal tigers. Some will be based on real experiences whereas other young authors may stretch their imaginations as they track the jungles of Kenya or sail down the Ganges. At any rate each student will produce a story, long or short, which can be included in a class book of CAT TALES.

Another important aspect of preparing for writing is the *development of the student's self-image as a writer.* It is infrequent that the home environment provides students with the image of themselves as writers, for parents usually regard any type of writing as an undesirable task. To develop Larry's interest in writing, it is helpful if he can visualize himself as a writer, secure in the knowledge that his writing has value. Although it is true that the objective in teaching students to write is not that they produce writing of commercial quality, we wish to promote the concept that writing, like reading, is a desirable occupation whether one earns a living through writing or merely writes for personal enjoyment.

One good method for strengthening the desirability of writing is the knowledge that the teacher writes. Students are greatly impressed by this fact. If Miss West can share personal writing experiences of any nature with the class, they will respect her not only as a teacher but also as a writer who really knows what writing is all about.

Another effective device for developing student interest in writing is to acquaint them with published authors in a variety of ways. At times there will be a local author who can be invited to visit the school to talk with the class about writing. In lieu of the real person, books can be found which tell about an author's views of writing. Portions of *Writers at Work,* edited by Malcolm Cowley (Viking), which is a collection of interviews of famous authors—Joyce Cary, Dorothy Parker, James Thurber, William Faulkner, and many others—can be read. Authors describe their writing experiences and their feelings toward writing.

A page of biographical information as well as a picture is included for each writer, which further humanizes the members of this profession. Revealing also is the sample sheet of each author's manuscript which is shown with corrections and changes as made by the writer. Even the young child will be interested in hearing some of the comments about writing such as those of Frank O'Connor who recommends, "Get black on white . . . I don't give a hoot what the writing's like. I write any sort of rubbish which will cover the main outlines of the story, then I can begin to see it." [4] In conjunction with this same author's comments it would be interesting to play his recording of one of his best stories, "My Oedipus Complex" (Caedmon, TC 1036) which appeals to both child and adult. His pleasant Irish voice reads the humorous story of five-year-old Larry who resents the return of his father from war.

USING VARIED TECHNIQUES FOR MOTIVATION

One of the surest methods of maintaining a high level of interest in writing is the use of widely varied approaches in stimulating student thinking. Devices used may appeal to different senses—auditory, visual, olfatory, tactile—or they may involve the use of varied materials—pictures, records, books, films, words. The writing of prose can also be alternated with word study or the composing of poetry to achieve greater variety. We shall examine here types of motivational devices (with examples of each) which have been used successfully in the elementary school classroom.

[4] Malcolm Cowley, ed., *Writers at Work* (New York: The Viking Press, Inc., 1964), p. 167.

"An experience isn't finished until it's written."
Ann Morrow Lindbergh

Words—A single word or a group of words can provide stimulus for writing.

- The teacher writes the word HAPPINESS on the board and asks the class to identify the word and questions the meaning of this word for them. Each class member then writes a brief essay on the meaning of happiness. This idea originated with the publication of *Happiness Is a Warm Puppy* by Charles Schulz (San Francisco: Determined Press, 1963), which can be used to stimulate discussion. Other abstract ideas can also be explored in this manner—LIBERTY, LONELINESS, LOVE, TEACHER, SCHOOL, MISERY, SUMMER, and many, many more.

- A group of words can be written on the chalkboard or printed on cards around a picture displayed on the bulletin board. The words focus on one theme—*ship, ocean, suitcases, vacation, porthole, exploration, engine trouble*—to motivate student thinking about a possible story.

Titles—The title (or several titles) can be provided by the teacher or written by the class.

- The teacher asks each student to write two titles at the top of a paper. Each student then passes the paper to another person, or the papers are collected and redistributed. As students receive a paper, they select one of the two titles and write a story based on that title.

- Three provocative titles can be written on the chalkboard (it is best to use a limited number). Each student may then select one title about which to write. Titles should allow for many possibilities:

Do You Know What I Saw?
Early in the Morning
I Couldn't Believe My Eyes!
What I Like to Do Best
It Happened at Six O'Clock
Was I Embarrassed!

Sentences or Phrases—Either first or last lines can be suggested by the teachers or students.

- A sentence is written on the board. After a discussion about the possibilities for story material based on that beginning sentence, each student is directed to write the sentence on a paper and to create a story situation. A comparison of results is especially effective when all begin with the same line, for it demonstrates the many approaches to one topic and also the differences in individual thinking.

When I heard the door open, I turned around quickly.

What could be the meaning of the words I had just heard?
"Tell me where it is," he begged.

- The last line for the story can be supplied in the same manner. Each student writes his story so the given line will be an appropriate ending.

Was I ever relieved to see Mom and Dad!
I had no desire to enter that house again.
That was the last time I ever saw the big dog.

Paragraphs—A short paragraph can be the stimulus for the development of a story.

- A descriptive setting can be typed for duplication. Each student then writes a story using that paragraph to set the action.

It was dark in the woods at eight even though it was July. We walked slowly along the path guided by the light of Jim's flashlight. The tall trees grew thick along the narrow stream, but the path was wide. As we approached a familiar outcropping of rock, we knew we were almost to our camping spot.

Stories—Stories that are read by students often supply ideas which motivate writing.

- A story that is unfamiliar to the class is read to the students. The reader stops at a crucial point in the story, asking, "What happened next?" Each student writes a conclusion for that particular story. Student endings can be read and later that of the original author, not to set the author's work as a model, but again to demonstrate differences in thinking. Try:

Lindgren, Astrid. *Pippi Longstocking* (Viking).
McCloskey, Robert. *Centerburg Tales* (Viking).

- Often students express the desire for a story to continue. After reading a story together, the class may write stories based on the same characters telling of further adventures. These adventure stories can be compiled as a class book.

- Students can write their own Story Starters. These can be put in a box at the Writing Center, and other youngsters can use them for starters.

Books—We read books to children; children read books to themselves. Often the ideas and illustrations of these books are highly provocative. Described here are several books which have been found especially effective in motivating student writing.

- Young children are fascinated by *The Hole* by Cliff Roberts (Watts), which explores the many possibilities of a single shape, the crescent. A large crescent-shaped hole is cut from cover to cover in this book forming part of each illustration—a piece of watermelon, the body of a crane, and so on. Children can expand this idea by drawing pictures based on other given shapes—cone, triangle, cylinder. After the drawings have been completed, each child can write a story to accompany the picture.

- Another charming book is *Here comes the WHOOSH!* by Vincent Fago (Golden Press). "Here it comes . . . WHOOSH . . . there it goes and in such a hurry, no one could see it . . ." and the reader never does see the mysterious creature, whatever it is. We are introduced, however, to many other interesting animals—the pigadoon, the snakearoo, and a whole family of be-whiskers. This book can lead to the invention of many unusual animals as children describe their habitats, appearances, and behavior.

- Both of the above books are picture books, but they are used successfully with older children who appreciate the imaginative humor of these modern authors. Others which we recommend for use in similar fashion include:

Younger Ideas:

Borten, Helen. *Do You See What I See?* (Abelard-Schuman).
Borten, Helen. *Do You Hear What I Hear?* (Abelard-Schuman).
Joslin, Sesyle. *What Do You Say, Dear?* (Harcourt).
Krauss, Ruth. *A Hole Is to Dig* (Harper).
Munari, Bruno. *Who's There? Open the Door* (World).

More Mature Ideas:

Piatti, Celestino. *The Happy Owls* (Atheneum).
Rand, Ann. *Umbrellas, Hats and Wheels* (Harcourt).
Reid, Alastair. *Supposing* (Little, Brown).
Straight, Dorothy. *How the World Began* (Pantheon).
Wolff, J., and B. Owett. *Let's Imagine Thinking Up Things* (Dutton).

Pictures—Pictures and drawings represent one of the most often used techniques in motivating creative writing. Pictures, both large and small, should be collected by the teacher and students so that a good collection is always available. Parents will contribute magazines for classroom use.

- Excellent sources of pictures that encourage writing are Sierra Club books such as *The Gentle Wilderness* or *Time and The River Flowing.*

- One large picture can be displayed before the class, which discusses the action depicted, suggesting names for characters, possibilities for the settng, and so forth. The use of a large picture is a good beginning activity in writing as it provides excellent stimulation of ideas and an opportunity for the teacher to observe with the class the author's right to name the characters, to have events develop as he or she chooses, that is, the possibilities for original, divergent thinking.

• Smaller pictures can be distributed to students for use as illustrations for stories. Each student writes about one picture, mounting the story and picture on one large sheet. The next writing is based on another picture which again is mounted on a large sheet together with a story. After this activity has been repeated several times, the sheets can be stapled together with an attractive cover to form individual story collections.

• Some questions that help generate ideas about a picture are: How many things can you see? What is happening now? What happened in the past? What will happen in the future? What does the picture make you think of? How does it make you feel? Finally you can ask students to imagine that they are part of the picture.

• A more advanced type of motivation is an incomplete drawing which requires students to complete a picture based on several given lines or shapes. They then write about the completed drawing. Inkblots are used in this manner also, with students interpreting what they see in the blot or what the shape brings to mind.

incomplete drawing

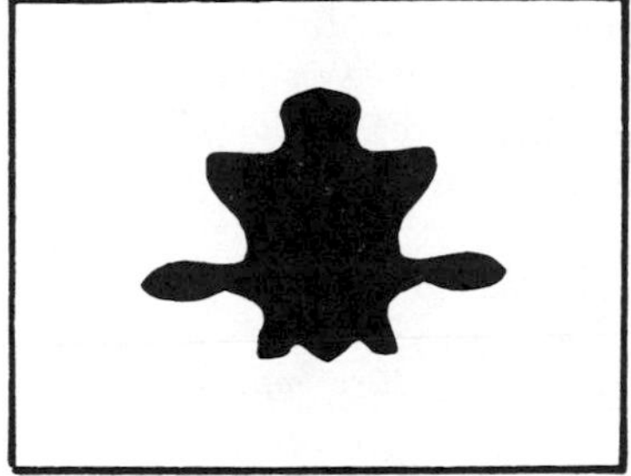

inkblot

• Again a picture collection can be filed in a box that becomes the focus of another Learning Center. At specified times or during free time, students can go through the file of pictures and choose an appealing picture creating a paragraph or story around it.

Bring in a small Oriental Rug (3 × 5 or smaller) or carpet scrap. This is a magic carpet. Discuss where you might fly with it. Write the names of the cities, countries, imaginery places on the board. When the enthusiasm is high, pass out paper and encourage the children to pick the place they'd most like to go on the magic carpet and tell all about the trip.

Objects—Both familiar and unfamiliar objects lend themselves to use as stimuli in writing.

- A delightful type of motivation is achieved through hiding an object in a large paper bag. Each child in turn feels the unfamiliar object without seeing it and then writes about it. It is interesting to compare results and then to display the object for all to see—a coconut in the hull, an eggplant, an empty plastic bottle, a wooden animal, pumpkin seeds, and so on.

- Another somewhat unusual device which elicits a good response from students is the use of an old bottle which has a cork or cap. Inside this bottle the teacher places a note. The bottle containing the note is shown to the class as the teacher excitedly explains that the bottle was found on a local beach (or sent by a friend). The class speculates on the contents of the note, its origin, etc. in writing. That night the teacher "breaks" the bottle and the next day reads the note to the class.

- An inanimate object can be given life with each student playing the role of a chair, a pencil, a book, or, to be more imaginative, a picture frame, a traffic light, a crown, a building in the city. The student imagines the feelings of the chosen object, describing the activities of the day, reactions to the behavior of people, and so on.

  A good way to start thinking about making inanimate objects come alive would be to use the film, *A Chairy Tale,* available from the International Film Bureau. Harper and Row's *Making It Strange* series of workbooks also has many good ideas for becoming an inanimate object, including a series on being a bullet—in the gun of a trigger happy outlaw or in a policeman's holster. The possibilities of exploring being inanimate objects can add great variety and sensitivity to your creative writing program.

  This idea integrates well with units on ecology—for instance, practice being a redwood tree about to be cut down, or standing majestic in the forest; or try being a waterfall or a dam, a smokestack, or a building built too close to its neighbors. Besides encouraging interesting writing experiences these ideas can help develop insight.

Recorded Materials—Both recorded music and recorded sound add real variety to the writing experience. Tapes can be prepared by students or the teacher to fit specific needs of the class.

- The playing of recorded music for the class is often used as a stimulus to writing. The mood of the music may suggest settings for stories or the music may actually suggest action. Several effective musical selections are:

Danse Macabre, Saint-Saëns
The Moldau, Smetana
Flight of the Bumblebee, Rimsky-Korsakov
Capriccio Italien, Tchaikovsky

• There are excellent recordings of stories which can also be utilized in stimulating writing. Rudyard Kipling's *Just So Stories* (Caedmon) will interest young writers in producing original stories which explain how animals came to be made as they are in similar fashion to Kipling's explanation of "How the Camel Got His Hump." This writer's wonderful imagination and his way of playing with words serve to inspire students.

• The tape recorder, too, offers the teacher a way of motivating. Taping "sound situations" is an interesting experience for the teacher or students. The sound situation consists of the combination of several intriguing sounds—a clock ticking, footsteps, a door slamming—which suggests a situation, the basis for a story.

Films—Slides, filmstrips, and movies challenge the imagination in a visual manner and serve to vary the more routine approach.

• Eight films for creative writing are listed here. Show the short film; discuss; then write.

Hunter and the Forest, 1955, Encyclopedia Britannica, 8 min.
Rainshowers, 1965, Churchill Films, 14 min.
Leaf, 1962, Pyramid Films, 7 min.
Concrete Poetry, 1970, Pyramid Films, 15 min.
Cosmic Zoom, 1969, McGraw-Hill, 8 min.
Neighbors, 1952, International Film Bureau, 9 min.
Pigs, 1967, Churchill Films, 11 min.
Story of a Book, 1962, Churchill Films, 11 min.

• Filmstrips of stories such as *Alice in Wonderland* and *Bambi* (Encyclopaedia Britannica Films) are used also as introductory material for imaginative writing. Students can write more adventures about the same characters, or they can imagine changes in the action—"What would have happened if . . . ?"

• The teacher's personal collection of colored slides will also offer pictures to inspire writing. A group of pictures on varied topics can be shown while students rapidly suggest titles for each picture. Two or three related pictures can be shown to furnish material for a class discussion which leads to writing. The picture of an old house will lead students to imagining the past of this house, the people it has known, and so on.

Students as Authors—Student writing is motivating.

Kohl, Herbert. *36 Children.* New York: The New American Library, 1968. Illustrations by Robert George Jackson, III. A young teacher's account of his revolutionary, unforgettable year in a ghetto classroom; includes children's writings.

Joseph, Stephen M., ed. *The Me Nobody Knows.* New York: Avon Books, 1969. Children's voices from the ghetto.
Lewis, Richard. *Journeys.* New York: Simon and Schuster, 1969. Prose by children of the English-speaking world.
Mirthes, Caroline. *Can't You Hear Me Talking to You?* New York: Bantam Books, 1971. Writing from and about children from the ghetto.

Other Ideas for Motivation—The ideas that follow do not necessarily fall into any particular category but are excellent motivators.

- What I like about myself or what I dislike about myself. Students can select one of these or write about both. This enables them to gain some insight into their problems and their image of themselves.

- If I can talk to anyone living or dead, who would it be and what would I say to them? They can describe who they might want to talk to; and, then, they can write out some of the ideas that they would want to explore with that individual. This can be someone from fiction or someone who has lived or is presently living.

- What if?
  Everyone was invisible.
  You had two lives to live.
  Children didn't have parents.
  You lived on the moon.
  You could be any animal you wished to be.
  Everyone looked alike.
  We could change our size.
  People could fly.
  The more we ate, the smarter we became.
  We had no friends.

- What bugs you? What is your pet peeve? Or another way of putting it, might be—a situation I could do without. Students, then, have a chance to explore this idea.

- What would you do if you had the whole day to spend in any way you wanted? How would you spend it? What would you do?

- What five headlines would you like to see in tomorrow morning's paper? The students are asked to list the five headlines. And, then, possibly take one of the headlines and write a story as it might appear in the paper.

- Have youngsters write their favorite dream or fantasy. This might lead to a discussion of dreams or daydreams—and, that it is all right to dream, that it is all right to fantasize, and that this helps us create a richer life.

- Playing with time. Students might pretend that they have invented a time machine that can go a hundred years back or a hundred years forward. They can then pretend that they are in that time period. Another variation on this is: the teacher asks the youngsters to write their autobiographies for the next ten years, rather than for the last ten years. Finally, playing with the future—how will your life be different in the twenty-first century?

Through the stimulation of creative writing in the elementary school classroom we are attempting to apply the theories of research in creativity to practices in the teaching of the language arts. Although there remains some doubt about the possibility of teaching creativity itself, it is accurate to state that we can teach *for* creativity, making every effort to encourage creative endeavors, and above all, avoiding the stifling of these germs of creativity. Creative writing offers an effective means for stimulating creative thinking and the creative use of language. To encourage creative writing the teacher should:

1 Provide many opportunities for writing,
2 Establish a relaxed atmosphere conducive to free expression,
3 Encourage students to experiment with forms and subjects for writing,
4 Use varied approaches to motivate writing,
5 Use evaluative techniques which encourage rather than discourage.

Books to Investigate

Applegate, Mauree. *Easy in English.* Evanston, Ill.: Row, Peterson, and Co., 1960.

Carlson, Ruth Kearney. *Writing Aids Through the Grades.* New York: Teachers College Press, 1970.

Evertts, Eldonna L. *Explorations in Children's Writing.* Urbana, Ill.: National Council of Teachers of English, 1970.

Hennings, Dorothy Grant, and Grant, Barbara M. *Content and Craft.* Englewood Cliffs, N.J.: Prentice-Hall, 1973.

Mearns, Hughes. *Creative Power: The Education of Youth in the Creative Arts.* New York: Dover, 1958.

Myers, R. E., and Torrance, E. Paul. *Invitations to Speaking and Writing Creatively.* Boston: Ginn and Co., 1965. One of a series of workbooks designed to stimulate creativity.

Petty, Walter T., and Bowen, Mary E. *Slithery Snakes and Other Aids to Children's Writing.* New York: Meredith, 1967.

Tiedt, Sidney W., and Tiedt, Iris M. *Creative Writing Ideas.* San Jose, Calif.: Contemporary Press, 1964.

exploring poetry

chapter

Poetry is when you talk to yourself.

Hughes Mearns

How does poetry fit into the classroom? How do you find time for poetry? What does poetry teach a child? Does poetry have to rhyme? What is poetry anyway?

These are the questions we hear which represent the teacher's dubious approach to the use of poetry in the classroom. We must admit that poetry does present problems, for the very definition of poetry is nebulous as is indicated by the following quotations from poets who are acknowledged masters of the art:

> "Poetry is a search for syllables to shoot at the barriers of the unknown and the unknowable," said Carl Sandburg.[1]
>
> "Another definition of poetry is dawn—that it's something dawning on you

[1] Carl Sandburg, *Good Morning America* (New York: Harcourt, Brace, 1928), p. viii.

while you're writing. It comes off if it really dawns when the light comes at the end," remarked Robert Frost.[2]

"A poet's autobiography is his poetry . . . The work of a true poet is not only a moving, breathing, sound-filled portrait of his time—it is also a self-portrait, just as vivid and just as comprehensive . . ." wrote the Russian, Yevgeny Yevtushenko.[3]

If poetry escapes definition, if poetry is that elusive, how can we present it to children? How can we tell them what it is? Our response is to surround them with poetry—read poetry, listen to poetry, write poetry. Go to poetry to find out what poetry is. We would not confine poetry by a stereotyped definition, but would attempt instead to develop a feeling for poetry like that expressed by Eleanor Farjeon:

What is poetry? Who knows?
Not the rose, but the scent of the rose;
Not the sky, but the light of the sky;
Not the fly, but the gleam of the fly;
Not the sea, but the sound of the sea;
Not myself, but something that makes me
See, hear and feel something that prose
Cannot; what is it? Who knows?[4]

Discovering Poetry

"Poetry belongs in the lives of children—all children," writes May Hill Arbuthnot in her introduction to *Time for Poetry*. She comments further:

> It is not so much the adult's job to put it there as it is to keep it there. For the newborn baby is a rhythmic being. His first cries of distress and his first gurgles of delight are cadenced. He responds to the melody and the meter of sung and spoken words long before he knows the literal meanings of those words. His early vocalizations are unworded chants that accompany his own increasingly rhythmic body movements and express the state of his being.[5]

[2] Edward C. Lathem, ed., *Interviews with Robert Frost* (New York: Holt, 1966), p. 204.

[3] Yevgeny Yevtushenko, *A Precocious Autobiography* (New York: Dutton, 1963), p. 3.

[4] Reprinted by permission from *Poems for Children* by Eleanor Farjeon, Lippincott, 1951.

[5] May Hill Arbuthnot, *Time for Poetry* (Glenview, Ill.: Scott, Foresman, 1968), p. xv.

Here is a poem that has long been a favorite of both teachers and children.

Whisky, frisky,
Hippity hop.
Up he goes
To the tree top!

Whirly, twirly,
Round and round,
Down he scampers
To the ground.

Furly, curly
What a tail!
Tall as a feather,
Broad as a sail!

Where's his supper?
In the shell.
Snappity, crackity,
Out it fell!

Only forty-six words, and what do they say? A little squirrel is running up a tree to find a nut for supper. Then it runs down the tree and cracks open the nut. There is no comparison between this prosaic translation and the gay lilt of the lines in verse form. Children will find themselves repeating the poem, but the prose statement of the same ideas would barely catch their attention.

"A performance in words," is another of Robert Frost's succinct descriptions of poetry. It is perhaps this approach which can be used in bringing children and poetry together, for in poetry we see a poet performing with words and we admire the performance. Delight in words brings delight to us. Thoughtful contemplation of the sky, the earth, or humanity creates a responsive thoughtfulness in us. Poetry speaks to the emotions in a way that most prose does not.

What understandings are we trying to impart to children as we present poetry in the classroom? It is important that we examine these understandings ourselves in order that our presentations will work toward furthering these understandings in students. There are a number of attitudes or values which we are attempting to nurture, a few of which we shall examine here:

1 Poetry is personal.
2 Poetry is related to music.
3 Poetry is communication.
4 Poetry can discuss any subject.
5 Poetry takes many forms.
6 Poetry contains imagery.

POETRY IS PERSONAL

Poetry is written by widely differing poets and it is read by widely differing readers. It is inevitable, therefore, that some readers will not care for some poetry. What appeals to ten-year-old Jim, whose mind is usually traveling far from the classroom, may ring a discordant note for the teacher, whose interests are obviously not those of the boy.

As teachers, we must constantly remember the varied backgrounds of age, sex, knowledge, and experience which we and the students bring to the same poem. It is important that we present poetry that appeals to varied segments of the membership of the class. It is our responsibility, furthermore, to refrain consciously from inflicting our own preferences on the students with whom we work. Certainly it is natural for you to share a favorite poem with the class, for teacher enthusiasm and participation adds to that of the students, but a wide variety of poetry must also be presented, directed toward capturing the interest of all.

Divergent interpretations of a single poem should also be stressed as each student is encouraged to form individual opinions of a selection, to react to it freely. We must refrain from tagging a poem as *good* or another one as *bad* so that students learn to determine for themselves whether a poem has something to offer them.

POETRY IS RELATED TO MUSIC

Poetry is the music of language. Its meters are related to the measures of the musical score, and many terms are common to both music and poetry; for example, *composing*. We also stress the rhythm and the music of the words as we arrange them to achieve effects similar to those of music—figures of speech, repetition, themes, patterns, rhythm. What other words are common to both poetry and music?

To write good poetry, children must hear and see great poetry.

Onomatopoeia, a Greek word that has a certain enchantment of its own, adds to the music of poetry. "Imitative words," words that imitate natural sounds, add to the effect of writing in both poetry and prose. Vowels and consonants produced toward the back of the mouth may combine to produce a sound effect that is broad, low-pitched, and rough as in these words: *rumble, growl, gong, howl, croak, chug, snarl.* By contrast, vowels and consonants produced toward the front of the oral cavity are often higher in pitch, giving sharper onomatopoetic effects as in: *ouch, hiss, click, bounce, whistle, jingle, rasp.* The short *u* sound combines with *l* and *m* to form soft words; for example, *lull* and *hum.*

- A committee of students can prepare a bulletin board display featuring onomatopoetic or "echoic" words. Using the caption, ECHOES, this committee can display examples contributed by class members.

tinkle	creak	splash
blare	bark	purr
whoosh	buzz	murmur
whisper	snore	patter
mutter	whine	shriek

- Encourage students to invent new words which imitate sounds. They should provide a definition for each invented word, thus:

CLONK: the sound of a hammer on wood
SWIZZLE: the sound of water spurting from a sprinkler

What, for example, would you call the sound made when your soda is almost gone?

- Find examples of onomatopoeia used in poetry as in these examples:

"The slippery slush
As it slooshes and sloshes,
And splishes and sploshes . . ."
"Galoshes" by Rhoda W. Bacmeister [6]

. . . "He bumps
And he jumps
And he thumps
And he stumps . . ."
"The Goblin" by Rose Fyleman [7]

Alliteration is another poetic device which adds to the melodious effects of poetry. "The repetition of the initial sound of a word in one or more closely following words" is a provocative technique if it is not overworked. Remember that alliteration is based on *sound,* not just on the repeated use of a letter—*sticks and stones, phonics fun, chic shape* (don't slip on the French *ch*).

[6] In May Hill Arbuthnot and Zena Sutherland, *The Arbuthnot Anthology of Children's Literature,* 3rd ed. (Glenview, Ill.: Scott, Foresman, 1972), p. 167.
[7] *Ibid.,* p. 125.

• Have students experiment with writing descriptive alliterative phrases as in these examples:

Slippery, slithery sleuth
Proud princess Prudence
Gloomy glowering glance
Shining, shimmering shells

• Set out on an EXPLORING TRIP to discover uses of alliteration in poetry. Each student will need a book of poetry unless small groups work on this project at different times. This type of exploratory browsing introduces students to much poetry as they search for examples like these:

"ribbon roads"
in: "The Rock" by T. S. Eliot

"camel caravan" "mosque and minaret"
in: "Travel" by Robert Louis Stevenson

"Slowly, silently, now the moon
Walks the night in her silver shoon."
in: "Silver" by Walter de la Mare

"Sing a song of seasons!"
in: "Autumn Fires" by Robert Louis Stevenson

Poets have long been considered "makers of music" with language as their medium. Wrote A. W. E. O'Shaughnessy:

"We are the music-makers,
And we are the dreamers of dreams . . ."

• Print the above lines on a large piece of construction paper for use with a display of children's poetry. The words MUSIC MAKERS or DREAMERS OF DREAMS supply excellent captions for displays or titles for collections of student writing.

• Play the recording of Dylan Thomas reading his beautiful poetic prose selection, "A Child's Christmas in Wales" (Caedmon TC 1002). You might also consider the film of the same title produced by Marvin Lichtner.

POETRY IS COMMUNICATION

Poetry is "Man speaking to men," wrote the English poet, William Wordsworth. What is the poet trying to say? It may be a feeling or an experience. In some poetry he or she may try to teach a lesson. The main point is that poets differ in the type of "speaking" each one does, and the message varies as does the poet and the intent.

- Examine poetry together to decide what the poet's message is, what the poet is trying to communicate. Point out the interesting fact that poems continue to communicate the thoughts of their originators even after the poet has died.

What, for example, is Carl Sandburg telling us in "Phizzog"?

This face you got,
This here phizzog you carry around,
You never picked it out for yourself, at all, at all—did you?
This here phizzog—somebody handed it to you—am I right?
Somebody said, "Here's yours, now go see what you can do with it."
Somebody slipped it to you and it was like a package marked:
"No goods exchanged after being taken away"—
This face you got.[8]

- As a way of interpreting a poem, each student can prepare a booklet with one line of the poem written on each page. An appropriate illustration is drawn or mounted with each line. These booklets can then be shared as a way of exchanging ideas about favorite poems.

POETRY CAN DISCUSS ANY SUBJECT

"The poet gathers fruit from every tree," observed poet Sir William Watson, and this statement can quickly be substantiated as we read poetry about widely varied topics such as "The Drugstore" by Karl Shapiro and "Fresh Air" by Kenneth Koch. Stress the variety of subject matter particularly to dispel the mistaken impression that poetry is associated only with flowers and love. Read a variety of poems with the class—for example, the following: [9]

"The Dentist" by Rose Fyleman
"My Dog" by Marchette Chute
"Cockpit in the Clouds" by Dick Dorrance
"A Modern Dragon" by Rowena Bennett
"This Happy Day" by Harry Behn
"The Cowboy's Life" by James Barton Adams
"The Kangaroo" by Elizabeth Coatsworth
"Skating" by Herbert Asquith
"The Man Who Hid His Own Front Door" by Elizabeth MacKinstry
"Snow in the City" by Rachel Field

[8] From *Good Morning, America.* Copyright 1928, 1956 by Carl Sandburg. Reprinted by permission of Harcourt Brace Jovanovich, Inc.

[9] The poems here are included in: May Hill Arbuthnot, *Time for Poetry* (Glenview, Ill.: Scott, Foresman, 1968).

Introduce students to Robert Burns, who has written delightful poetry about homely topics, as in "To a Mouse" or "To a Louse." The Scottish words when read aloud often resemble our modern English closely. Students will have little difficulty with these two stanzas from "To a Louse" which was written as the poet supposedly watched the small bug crawl on a lady's bonnet in church:

Ha! Whare ye gaun, ye crawlin' ferlie?
Your impudence protects you sairly:
I canna say but ye strunt rarely
  Owre gauze an' lace;
Though, faith! I fear ye dine but sparely
  On sic a place.

Ye ugly, creepin', blastit wonner,
Detested, shunned by saunt an' sinner,
How dare you set your fit upon her,
  Sae fine a lady?
Gae somewhere else, and seek your dinner
  On some poor body . . .

After reading from Burns' work students may try to write poems addressing some lowly creature, for the humor of this approach has great appeal.

POETRY TAKES MANY FORMS

The variety of form is closely related to the variety of subject, and we endeavor again to expose children to many different types of poetic forms so that their view of poetry is in no way limited. Forms of poetry will be discussed in more detail as we progress to the writing of original poems, but here are suggestions for furthering the concept that forms of poetry vary widely:

- Read poems that represent varied forms—long, short, rhymed, unrhymed—as in these examples: [10]

  "Automobile Mechanics" by Dorothy Baruch
    Unrhymed free verse

  "Newspaper" by Aileen Fisher
    Couplets

  "How Doth the Little Crocodile" by Lewis Carroll
    Quatrains (*abab* rhyming)

[10] The poems listed here appear in Mary C. Austin and Queenie B. Mills, *The Sound of Poetry* (Boston: Allyn and Bacon, 1963).

"A Fairy Went A-Marketing" by Rose Fyleman
Octaves (2 quatrains, *abcb* rhyming)

"The Jumblies" by Edward Lear
Use of a refrain

"The Old Pond" by Basho
Haiku

- Have each student collect favorite poems to produce a personal anthology of poetry. Each student-editor can try to include a variety of forms which may be listed by the class before the editors set to work.

- Show children various kinds of concrete poems such as that printed here.

- Encourage students to experiment with highly individualized forms for their poems as in this example:

PICTURES ON THE FLYING AIR [11]
Scott Alexander

A
poem
can play
with the wind
and dart and dance
and fly about in the mind
like a kite in the cloudy white
sky at so dizzy a height it
seems out of reach but
is waiting to be
very gently
pulled
down
to
the
page
below
by a
string
of
musical
words.

[11] Reprinted by permission. Copyright 1966, *The Instructor*, F. A. Owen Publishing Company.

POETRY CONTAINS IMAGERY

The imagery—the pictures, the petite vignettes of poetry—is the most important element distinguishing poetry from prose. Prose that is rich in imagery comes close to being poetry whatever the form, as in "A Child's Christmas in Wales" by Dylan Thomas. The image may be achieved through the use of simile, metaphor, or an extension of the latter. As poetry is read aloud or silently, it is most rewarding to encourage the sharing of imagery that is discovered.

- **Prepare a bulletin board with the caption, POETIC IMAGES, where students can mount copied words, phrases, or whole poems which contain particularly effective imagery. The title of the poem and the poet's name should appear with each example, thus:**

". . . a road with a mountain tied to its end,
Blue-humped against the sky. . . ."
From: "Roads" by Rachel Field

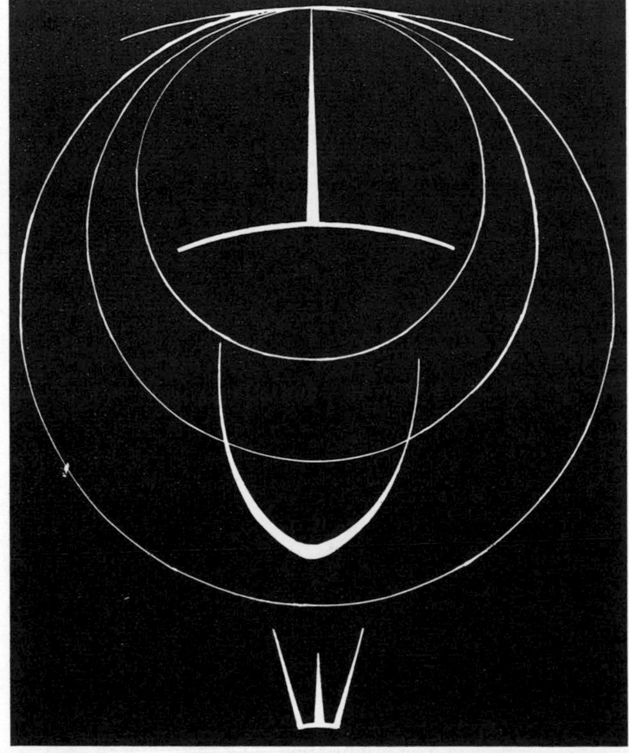

"Echo" by Richard Kostelanetz, from *Visual Language* (Brooklyn: Assembling Press, Box 1967, 1970). Reprinted by permission of the author.

". . . He is a conscious black and white
Little symphony of night."
From: "The Skunk" by Robert P. Tristram Coffin

". . . the big, big wheels of thunder roll . . ."
From: "The Woodpecker" by Elizabeth Madox Roberts

- Have students illustrate images that have been found in the above activity. Fold 9 x 12 sheets of drawing paper in half to form folders on the front of which can appear the illustration while the poem or a portion of the poem is written inside.

- Read Emily Dickinson's poem, "I Like to See It Lap the Miles," as an example of excellent imagery and the use of intriguing words:

I like to see it lap the miles,
And lick the valleys up,
And stop to feed itself at tanks;
And then, prodigious, step

Around a pile of mountains,
And, supercilious, peer
In shanties by the sides of roads;
And then a quarry pare

To fit its sides, and crawl between,
Complaining all the while
In horrid, hooting stanza;
Then chase itself down hill

And neigh like Boanerges;
Then, punctual as a star,
Stop—docile and omnipotent—
At its own stable door.

After reading this poem aloud, ask questions to stimulate the students' thinking:

What is Emily Dickinson describing in this poem?
How do you know she is writing about a train?
Does the word ever appear in the poem?
To what is the poet comparing a train?
What words make you think of a horse?

Draw attention to the provocative words: *supercilious, prodigious, omnipotent.* Have the students try guessing their meanings from the context of the poem before checking with the dictionary.

Introduced here, too, is a reference to mythology, a technique which is not often found in children's poetry. Have one child investigate Boanerges, the Sons of Thunder.

- Compare Emily Dickinson's poem about a train with poems about trains by other poets. Other poets have compared the train differently. Rowena Bennett, for example, wrote: "A train is a dragon that roars through the dark . . ." in "A Modern Dragon." Frances Frost gives the trains human characteristics as she describes trains that ". . . whistle softly and stop to tuck each sleepy blinking town in bed!" in "Trains at Night."

POEMS CHILDREN ENJOY

Brooks, Gwendolyn. *Bronzeville Boys and Girls.* New York: Harper and Row, 1956.

Ciardi, John. *You Read to Me, I'll Read to You.* Philadelphia: J. B. Lippincott, 1962. Poems read by the poet and his children.

Cole, William, ed. *Beastly Boys and Ghastly Girls.* Illustrated by Toni Ungerer. New York: World Publishing Co., 1964. Wry selections.

Dunning, Stephen et al., comps. *Some Haystacks Don't Even Have Any Needle.* Glenview, Ill.: Scott, Foresman, 1966. For older children and youth.

Gordon, Alvin. *Brooms of Mexico.* Illustrated by Ted DeGracia. Palm Desert, Calif.: Best-West Publications, 1965. Poems of the Indians beautifully illustrated in the DeGracia manner.

Hoberman, Mary Ann. *A Little Book of Little Beasts.* New York: Simon and Schuster, 1973. Verses about small animals. In a beautiful picture book for younger children.

Huston, James. *Songs of the Dream People.* New York: Atheneum, 1973. A beautiful book of chance and images from the Indians and Eskimos of North America.

Jordan, June, and Bush, Torri, comps. *The Voice of the Children.* New York: Holt, Rinehart and Winston, 1970. Poems written by children from nine to seventeen years old in New York.

Livingstone, Myra Cohn. *The Moon and a Star and Other Poems.* New York: Harcourt, Brace, Jovanovich, 1965.

Merriam, Eve. *There Is No Rhyme for Silver.* New York: Atheneum, 1962. Imaginative use of words and many coined words childrens will love.

Problems in Poetry

Why is poetry not present in all classrooms? Why do some teachers have much greater success with poetry experiences than do others? There are a number of problems related to the use of poetry in the classroom, and a discussion of these may in part answer some of the questions which arise and may assist the beginning teacher in developing a successful approach to poetry with young people. The problems, as we see them, revolve around the following:

1 Teacher knowledge of poetry

2 Attitudes toward poetry
3 Methods of presenting poetry

TEACHER KNOWLEDGE OF POETRY

The teacher who knows poetry and enjoys it finds time for poetry in the classroom. It emerges in the classroom in many subtle, unexpected ways, for this teacher is prepared to open the door when poetry knocks.

How can you, as a prospective teacher, develop a knowledge of poetry that will lead to this type of *poetry readiness?* An introductory course to poetry in a college English department may develop the requisite attitudes toward poetry as adult poetry is explored, but it is not likely that you will come to know Eleanor Farjeon, Walter de la Mare, or the many other wonderful poets who have written poetry especially for children. A course in Children's Literature will probably introduce some of the poetry for children but not in the quantity necessary for the challenging opportunities of the elementary school classroom.

In order to become really familiar with the marvelous poetry available to you and to the young people whom you will teach, you should *explore* independently in order literally to steep yourself in poetry for children. This is not a laborious chore, for you will find that children's poetry is not only charming, delightful, and thoroughly enjoyable, but it also offers a pleasant variety ranging from the nursery rhyme to poems by John Ciardi or T. S. Eliot.

Every teacher should have at least one good anthology of poetry for personal use so that it can be underlined and marked with marginal suggestions for using poems that have been particularly successful or ideas about presenting a poem. Listed here are a number of collections which are recommended for your perusal and possible purchase:

Arbuthnot, May Hill, and Root, Shelton L., Jr. *Time for Poetry.* Glenview, Ill.: Scott, Foresman, 1968.

Austin, Mary C., and Mills, Queenie B. *The Sound of Poetry.* Boston: Allyn and Bacon, 1963.

Bissett, Donald J., ed. *Poems and Verses about Animals.* San Francisco: Chandler Publishing Co., 1967.

de Reginiers, Beatrie Schenk; Moore, Eva; and White, Mary Michaels. *Poems Children Will Sit Still For.* New York: Citation Press, 1969.

Dunning, Stephen; Lueders, Edward; and Smith, Hugh, eds. *Reflections on a Gift of Watermelon Pickle.* Glenview, Ill.: Scott, Foresman, 1966.

Larrick, Nancy, ed. *On City Streets.* New York: Bantam, 1968.

Withers, Carl. *A Rocket in My Pocket.* New York: Holt, Rinehart, and Winston, 1948.

Delight children with a poem to lighten up a gloomy day—for example, this jingle from the last book listed:

I've got a rocket
In my pocket;
I cannot stop to play.
Away it goes!
I've burnt my toes.
It's Independence Day!

ATTITUDES TOWARD POETRY

How do you feel about poetry? Do you conceive of poetry as language which is somewhat frilly, frothy, and feminine? Do you think every student ought to memorize poetry? Would you assign the memorization of a poem as a type of punishment? Do you feel that you know which poetry is "good" contrasted to that which is "bad"? The attitudes of both teacher and student are based on past experiences with poetry. They may represent the attitudes expressed by parents and peers.

The attitude, for example, that *poetry is feminine* has led to the feeling, particularly among boys, that poetry is not something which should rightfully interest a man. Is poetry "sissy stuff"? It is if you present only poems about the blue sky, lovely flowers, pretty girls, and LOVE. To snag the boys' interest we must clearly demonstrate that poetry is for boys; poetry is for men; poetry is for all people.

- Point out that many poets have been men. Conduct a small research study by having several boys examine six to ten anthologies of poetry, first counting the number of poets listed in the index. Then they can count the number of these names which are masculine to determine the percentage of male poets. Conducting this study themselves will impress some students who would scarcely believe your own statement of the same fact.

- Read a variety of poetry written by men: Carl Sandburg, Robert Frost, Walt Whitman, Walter de la Mare, John Masefield, James Whitcomb Riley, James Tippett, Robert Louis Stevenson, Lewis Carroll, Edward Lear, to mention only a few of the many.

- Display pictures of men and women who write poetry. Record albums, magazine covers, articles will provide pictures which can be mounted on a bulletin board with samples of poetry as well as quotations from these men and women.

  Robert Frost: "Poetry is my kind of fooling."
  Paul Laurence Dunbar: "What's so fine as being a boy?"
  Eleanor Farjeon: "What is poetry? Who knows?"

The *memorization of poetry* as an end in itself has long been discarded as a method of enjoying poetry and certainly as a means of punishment. Many students voluntarily choose to memorize a poem which has particular meaning for them. Poetry is also memorized incidentally through repetition as it is recited in chorus or read frequently by individuals as a result of its appeal. Often, too, students will learn first lines or lines which are repeated in poems although the whole poem has not been memorized. Examples of lines which many children come to know include:

"The fog comes on little cat feet . . ."
  Carl Sandburg: "Fog"

"You can't go to court in pajamas, you know."
  Beatrice C. Brown: "Jonathan Bing"

"If I had a hundred dollars to spend
Or maybe a little bit more . . ."
  Rachel Field: 'The Animal Store"

"Some one came knocking
At my wee, small door . . ."
  Walter de la Mare: "Some One"

"The Owl and the Pussy-Cat went to sea
In a beautiful pea-green boat . . ."
  Edward Lear: "The Owl and the Pussy-Cat"

"I'm hiding, I'm hiding,
And no one knows where . . ."
  Dorothy Aldis: "Hiding"

The *analysis and evaluation of poetry* should not be heavily stressed with the child, for our stress is on the enjoyment of poetry. There is little doubt that the poem loses something as it is pulled apart line by line. This is not to say, on the other hand, that students should not discuss the meaning of unusual words used by the poet or that effective imagery should not be pointed out as an object of admiration. Certainly, if the class shows particular interest in the subject treated by the poem, discussion will logically develop, but we then return to the poet's "performance" as a whole.

Poetry is an experience, not a form.
Karl Shapiro

METHODS OF PRESENTING POETRY

How do you introduce a poem to the elementary school child? There are numerous ways, but all of them revolve around the technique of "setting the stage" or creating a "receptive mood." How is this mood created by the teacher? It can be developed subtly by first introducing a familiar incident related to the poem or presenting an object or picture which will then suggest the poem. Sometimes we begin by writing several provocative words on the board which will lead us into the poem or we may ask several questions to stimulate a discussion.

"Now I am going to read a poem about colors," states the teacher, and the children immediately squirm. You will be more certain of a positive reaction to the poem if you provide a brief "warm-up" session. To present Christina Rossetti's lovely poem, "What Is Pink?" the teacher might effectively begin with a discussion about colors which would arouse interest thus:

"What color is Jill's dress?" (pink)
"And what color is this flower?" (pink)
"What other things come to mind when you think of pink?
What is pink?"
(powder, ice cream, a kitten's tongue, chilly cheeks)

From this point the discussion could easily move to several other colors and the objects they recall. Participation in the discussion has started minds working and the reading of the poem is a natural consequence.

WHAT IS PINK?

Christina Rossetti

What is pink? a rose is pink
By a fountain's brink.
What is red? a poppy's red
In its barley bed.
What is blue? the sky is blue
Where the clouds float thro'.
What is white? a swan is white
Sailing in the light.
What is yellow? Pears are yellow
Rich and ripe and mellow.
What is green? the grass is green
With small flowers between.
What is violet? clouds are violet
In the summer twilight.
What is orange? Why, an orange,
Just an orange!

Color in Poetry

Hailstones and Halibut Bones. Sterling Educational Films (241 East 34th St., New York, N.Y. 10016). Part I, 1964, 6 min., color. Part II, 1967, 7 min., color.

Both parts are excellent short films that combine artful design and color with the reading of the poems from the book by Mary O'Neill and published by Doubleday. Hailstones and halibut bones are things that are white.

A natural setting for poetry is often provided by the weather. Children who have just come in with snow still on their mittens and in their minds will be quite ready to tell the teacher excitedly of their feelings about snow. "What words can you use to describe snow?" queries the teacher. Soft, white, fluffy, cold, light, sparkling. "Let me read you a poem that talks about snow; we'll see how this poet describes snow."

Rain, wind, and sunshine can each provide an effective mood for poetry. A holiday, the season, the blooming of flowers suggests poems on varied topics. Subjects studied in the classroom will provide opportunity to relate appropriate poetry. The teacher who knows poetry, who has "the right poem at the right time," will be able to take advantage of these times for poetry and will be able to plan the right setting for an exciting experience with poetry.

Poetry is meant for the ear as well as the eye. Here is a list of records to promote listening pleasure focused on poetry. Include them in a Listening Center to which children can go to hear their favorite poems.

Carl Sandburg's Poems for Children. Read by Carl Sandburg. Caedmon TC 1124, n.d.

Miracles. Poems written by children. Collected by Richard Lewis. Read by Julie Harris and Roddy McDowall. Caedmon TC 1227, 1967.

Reflections on a Gift of Watermelon Pickle . . . and Other Modern Verse. Stephen Dunning, Edward Lueders, and Hugh Smith, comps. Read by Ellen Holly and Paul Hecht. Scholastic Records FS 11007, 1967.

Experiences in Writing Poetry

Perhaps one of the most rewarding outcomes of a child's familiarity with poetry will be the writing of their own original verse. The creation of a person's own poetry augments interest in the poetry of others. At the same time, knowledge of poetry written by others increases the student's desire and ability to write poetry. As they see that poetry comes in a wide variety of sizes and shapes, and that poets "talk" about any topic that appeals to them, young persons will feel at home with poetry and will be able to conceive of themselves as poets. The development of this image is the key to stimulating student-composed poetry.

As teachers, we must be ready to take advantage of natural opportunities that arise. When a child expresses a thought or an apt bit of imagery, we must be alert to say, "I like the way you said that, Phil. Let's write it on the board so everybody can enjoy it." Some teachers keep strips of manila paper on which phrases or sentences can be lettered quickly with a felt pen so that the children's words can be recorded for display on a bulletin board. Displayed with the caption POETRY PLEASES in one first grade room were these examples:

quiet as a flea at work

SALLY

soft, secret sound

PHIL

Our earth is round,
All water and ground

STAN

walking and talking

MARGIE

The bear clumped and humped,
thumped and bumped.

BOB

Poetry is a word, two words, and more. The teacher must be aware of the possibilities for poetry as it occurs in natural form. When Dave brings his frog to school, for example, and calls it "my funny, funny frog," the mere repetition of Dave's phrase leads children to add other lines to produce a spontaneous class composition. " 'My funny, funny frog' —that sounds like a poem. Who can add another line?" As the first words are written on the board, someone suggests, "Hippety, hippety, hop," and another child cries excitedly, "Will he ever stop?" and there is a poem!

My funny, funny frog.
Hippety, hippety, hop.
Will he ever stop?

The teacher cannot, of course, wait patiently for the unplanned experience in writing poetry to come. We must plan experiences which seem as natural and desirable as those which are initiated in the manner just described, but we must provide the stimulus. A sequence of experiences in the writing of poetry can be readily developed, beginning with the least complicated types of poetry for primary grades and progressing in difficulty through the grades. The emphasis in the *writing* of poetry remains on enjoyment, as was true in the *reading* of poetry. The elementary school child who is steeped in poetry will find writing original poetry a natural means for expressing thoughts.

What forms of poetry are suitable for the elementary school student? There really is no limit, for able students will reach out to try almost any form of poetry which they meet and they will even create original forms. Although the simplest forms can continue to be used in upper grades, more mature students will be challenged by exploring further if they have had a background of experience in writing poetry. Listed here is a sequence of poetry forms which seem appropriate to ability levels:

Words and phrases
Free verse
Couplets
Triplets
Cinquains
Haiku and tanka
Limericks
Quatrain
Diamante
Septolet, Quinzaine, Quintain
Additional poetry forms

WORDS AND PHRASES

Experimenting with words and the writing of phrases will encourage a feeling of freedom in the use of written language. It will also stimulate the student to think while concentrating on producing inventive imagery. Experiments in using alliteration and onomatopoeia have already been discussed and many activities presented in the chapter on words will be appropriate to stimulate the use of words and phrases in poetry. Presented at this point are ideas specifically directed toward the first steps in poetry:

- Have students list words which fit a certain mood or theme. To stimulate thinking you may show a picture; for example, a dark, stormy scene, a little child crying, a family picnic (to mention only a few possibilities). Questions asked by the teacher will assist the flow of thought.

"Is this picture of something happy or sad?"
"Would you use *dark* or *light* words to describe this scene?"
"How does this picture make you feel?"

• Introduce children to the idea of the simile (an expressed relationship between objects of different classes). A good way to begin is to write a trite simile on the board—as black as night, as quiet as a mouse, as happy as a lark. Students can think of *fresh* comparisons as in these samples:

as happy as . . . a hot boy running toward the pool.
. . . a rabbit that has eluded the hounds.
. . . three ladies trying on hats in April.

FREE VERSE

The type of poetry which many teachers have found highly successful with children who have had little experience with the writing of poetry is *free verse*. Beginning poets may write only one line, whereas the more able or experienced child will soon write two, three, and and more lines. Why is free verse especially suited to inexperienced writers? The key word is *freedom,* for in free verse there is:

1. No rhyming to lend artificiality.
2. No set pattern of rhythm or meter.
3. Free variation in length of lines, form, and content.
4. Emphasis on the thought expressed.

The fact, too, that free verse may consist of one or many lines provides a built-in accommodation for individual abilities. The child for whom writing is laborious finds success in composing one line whereas the child for whom writing comes with greater ease may extend ideas into ten lines. For this reason the following suggestions for motivating the writing of free verse may be used at any level of ability.

• Display a large picture of a boy and girl. Ask some provocative questions: "What are these children doing? What are they thinking? Can you imagine that you are the boy or girl in the picture?" Pretending that he or she is one of the figures in the picture, each student writes the thoughts that come to mind. Again, suggest that each thought begin on a new line, thus:

I wish I could get a new bike.
Then I'd go like the wind—

Down Madison Street,
Across the Highway–
No place would be too far for me
If I had a bright shiny new bike.

• Use the senses to motivate the writing of poetry by providing an object that is concealed within a box or a large paper bag. To feature the concept of SOFTNESS, for example, use a piece of soft fur or velvet. After students have felt the concealed article, ask them how it felt.

When someone mentions the adjective *soft,* ask the question, "What is soft? How would you tell someone what you mean by softness?" Have each one write ideas on paper as they try to think not of how many thoughts they can write, but of *how interesting* or *unusual* each thought is.

What is Soft?

Softness is a feeling.
Softness is velvety fur.
Softness is a small kitten's paw.
Softness is my mother's cheek.

• Show the class a series of slides or a group of pictures about one theme—the ocean, mountains, the city. Ask each one to write thoughts about the group of pictures shown. A series of ocean scenes resulted in the following effective response from a sixth-grade student:

Break waves,
Fruitlessly challenging flexible shores.

Kenneth Koch includes many excellent ideas in his book, *Wishes, Lies, and Dreams.* One of his ideas is the "I Wish Poem."

Each child writes one line starting with "I wish" and including things such as a color, a comic strip person, and a city or a country. For example, an "I Wish" poem of this nature might be: "I wish I lived in gray San Francisco with Dick Tracy."

The youngsters turn these in, and then they are read by the teacher as a poem.

There are many other ideas for motivating youngsters to write poetry in Koch's book and also many excellent examples of children's poetry.

• Read poems to children which do not require rhyme. Poems by Hilda Conkling, Carl Sandburg, E. E. Cummings, and Walt Whitman provide excellent examples. This passage from Whitman's *Song of Myself* describes a handsome stallion which could inspire students to write poems about an animal they know.

A gigantic beauty of a stallion, fresh and responsive to my caresses,
Head high in the forehead, wide between the ears,
Limbs glossy and supple, tail dusting the ground,
Eyes full of sparkling wickedness, ears finely cut, flexibly moving.
His nostrils dilate as my heels embrace him,
His well-built limbs tremble with pleasure as we race around and return.

• Write these words on the board: "Rain is . . ." (Use this idea on a rainy day for best results. As appropriate, try "Snow is . . ." or "Sunshine is. . . .") Then ask the class what rain means to them. Have them write their ideas on paper beginning each new idea on a fresh line (the poetry form). When completed, each child will have a poem of varied length about rain.

Type each poem on a large raindrop shape for display encouraging children to read the differing ideas about rain.

Rain is . . . patter on the roof.
. . . a day for hiding behind furniture.
. . . the flower maker.
. . . the producer of umbrellas.
. . . the washer of leaves.
. . . the frizzies.

If it doesn't happen to be raining, you can show the film *Rainshowers* which expresses many thoughts about rain (distributed by Dimensions Films). Here are poems children wrote using this idea, beginning with "The moon is . . ."

The moon is a white rabbit
Jumping up and down.
While we are asleep,
It jumps up;
And when we wake,
It jumps down.

ROBERT ROGERS

The moon is a sun drowsing,
but never going to sleep
The stars are faces in the sky.
Time is how long it takes you
to do your homework.

PHYLLIS DYER
Teacher: Mrs. Norville

COUPLETS

The couplet is the simplest type of rhymed verse, and therefore offers possibilities for introducing rhyme to young writers. Many couplets are produced incidentally as children experiment with language—"Jean, Jean, your hair is green," or "Pink, pink, she drank some ink"—the jingles and rhymes of childhood. An excellent way to begin composing couplets is through group composition.

• To introduce students to the couplet and the techniques of writing rhymed poetry first discuss rhyming if the class members are not already familiar with the making of rhymes. Oral activities will quickly familiarize the class with the skill of rhyming as lists of rhymes are developed. Stress the following understandings:

1. Rhymes are based on the sound, not the appearance of a word.

   day, neigh, lei, prey
   theme, dream, seem
   sane, gain, reign, rein
   rhyme, climb, time, I'm

2. Not all words have rhymes. (silver)

3. You must pronounce a word correctly and listen carefully to determine whether words really rhyme:

   sand—tan   few—too   kind—fine

• Try making a class rhyming dictionary. Small groups of students could take different sounds and work together to think of all the words ending with that sound. One page might be headed "ite." It would include in alphabetical order words such as bite, fight, light, right, rite, sight, site, tight. Then as groups finished the various pages they could be dittoed and collated to create ten to fifteen copies of class rhyming dictionaries—great for your Poetry Learning Center.

• After a class has learned to rhyme easily, the teacher can select an appropriate theme—the month, season, weather, state, event, person—about which the class will compose a poem together. For a beginning experience lines can be provided as in this example of a poem about Halloween.

The subject of Halloween is introduced through a discussion or the singing of Halloween songs, after which the teacher says, "Let's write a poem about Halloween. Will you help me?" She then writes a first line on the board being sure that the line ends with an easily rhymed word "Ghosts and goblins are all around." Class members then suggest possible second lines as indicated here:

Ghosts and goblins are all around. (Teacher)
An owl is hooting with mournful sound. (A child)

There are devils and demons and cats of black (Teacher)
And each one carries a great big sack. (A child)

Aren't you afraid to be out this night, (Teacher)
For devils are fearsome and cats might bite? (A child)

Oh, no, not I, for don't you know, (Teacher)
The cat is Susan, and that devil is Joe! (A child)

- Hints about group composition:

1. Have several lines suggested each time before selecting a best one to be written on the board.
2. Select lines by different people each time so that as many as possible have contributed to the finished product. You may also choose to have two poems produced at the same time so more than one line can be used; simply work on two boards inserting a different student line after the given first line each time.
3. Children can learn to tap out the rhythm of the given line as they try to produce similar rhythm in the second line—the beginnings of meter.

- After a class has composed couplets together orally, the teacher can supply a variety of beginning lines as each student writes one or more ending for each line supplied. For the line, "Flowers now are growing," these examples were written:

Flowers now are growing.
And the grass is showing.

Flowers now are growing.
Gentle winds are blowing.

Flowers now are growing,
And the grass needs mowing.

Flowers now are growing,
Baseballs we are throwing.

TRIPLETS

The triplet, an intriguing verse form which is not widely used, offers interesting possibilities as a form of rhymed poetry which young writers can create effectively. These three-line poems tell a brief story and are often humorous. As with the couplet, the initial experience can be a group composition. Teachers who have used this verse form have found that students are more successful if each first produces a rhyme list.

- Each child selects a word that interests him. The word selected must be one that

rhymes easily, so you may choose to provide a list from which each person selects his word; for example, PLANE, JET, TRAIN, CAR, SWIM, FISH, PLAY, BOOK, SKY, RIDE, GAME, SING, BOX, FORT, EAT, DOG, CAT, BALL, SEA. The word chosen is then written at the top of a sheet of paper and a column of rhyming words is developed. Three related words are used to compose a triplet.

From a list of words rhyming with GAY one person produced the following triplet:

Our cat likes to play;
His antics are gay.
"See me?" his eyes say.

Another poet used the word SEA to inspire this triplet:

Standing silent before the sea
I thought the water talked to me
Then laughed aloud with sudden glee.[12]

• An interesting variation which we developed to add to the enjoyment of writing triplets as a verse form is the TRIANGULAR TRIPLET.[13] As in the example, the reader may begin reading at any point of the triangle. The poem must be composed so the lines may be read in any order.

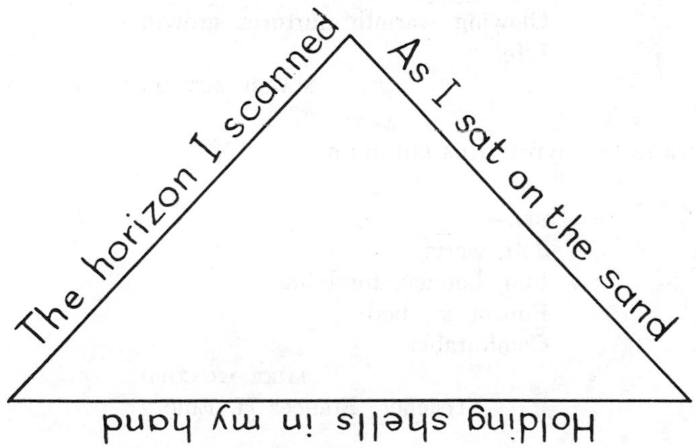

[12] Sidney Tiedt and Iris M. Tiedt, *The Elementary Teacher's Complete Ideas Handbook* (Englewood Cliffs, N.J.: Prentice-Hall, 1965), p. 93.
[13] Sidney Tiedt and Iris M. Tiedt, *Creative Writing Ideas* (San Jose, Calif.: Contemporary Press, 1964, p. 19.

CINQUAINS

Cinquains are, as the name reveals, poems of five lines. Although there are many varieties possible for five-line poetry (the limerick is one), the cinquain is a form more akin to Haiku. The stress should still remain on the thought to be expressed, but the unrhymed lines of the cinquain fit these specifications, according to one version.

Line 1: One word (which may be the title)
Line 2: Two words (describing the title)
Line 3: Three words (an action)
Line 4: Four words (a feeling)
Line 5: One word (referring to the title)

Here are examples written by college students who, like you, were venturing into poetry:

RAINBOW—
Sky's umbrella
Turned upside down
Lovely splash of color
Aftermath.

KAYE HAWLEY

SUN—
Fiery orb
Shooting golden arrows
Glowing warmth nurtures growth
Life.

MARGE SUTTON

A third-grade boy wrote this cinquain:

BED—
Soft, warm,
Fun, bouncy, tumbling,
Fun on my bed;
Comfortable.

MIKE MC CORD
Teacher: Frances H. Emery

Another form of the cinquain [14] is as follows:

Line 1: Two syllables

[14] This form has been attributed to Adelaide Crapsey, a minor American poet and author of *Verse* (Rochester, New York: Manas Press, 1914).

Line 2: Four syllables
Line 3: Six syllables
Line 4: Eight syllables
Line 5: Two syllables

Following is an example of the cinquain written in the syllable format:

FUNNY—
People can seem
So different to me
As when they are so far away
From me.

EVELYN LOUIE

HAIKU AND TANKA

Perhaps one of the most delightful unrhymed poetry forms used in the elementary school classroom is that of the ancient Japanese poets, haiku. Discovered by America as a result of translations, this poetic form has become very popular.

Haiku is a three-line verse form which originated in thirteenth-century Japan. Early masters of the form include Buson, Boncho, Moritake, Bashō, Sōkan, and many others. Authentic haiku has several distinct characteristics which have been followed rather consistently by Japanese writers and those who have translated their work:

1 The poem consists of only three lines totaling 17 syllables.
  Line 1: 5 syllables
  Line 2: 7 syllables
  Line 3: 5 syllables
2 The season, location, and references to nature are included.
3 There is no rhyme and few articles or pronouns are used.
4 The poem contrasts diverse ideas, is subtle, symbolic.

Here are two examples of haiku translated from the original Japanese:

BASHŌ

First cold showers fall.
Even little monkey wants
A wee coat of straw.

HASHIN

All sky disappears
The earth's land has gone away;
Still the snowflakes fall.

In popular use today many poets have taken liberties with this versatile verse form. American haiku have been written about a wide variety of topics, and lines have not always remained the prescribed length. Translator and poet, Harry Behn comments, "Any translation into English should be, so I believe, what the author might have done if English had been his language." These rules that have grown out of Zen should be followed as much as possible in "the same packaging," but writing haiku is not a game. "It is not easy to be simple." [15]

An excellent source of information for the teacher who wants to know more about haiku is *An Introduction to Haiku* by Harold Anderson (Doubleday).

Children are most successful with this brief verse form if emphasis is rightly placed on the thoughts they are expressing rather than on the confining form. The beauty of haiku for children is that they do succeed in producing charming examples which compare well with those created by adult writers. The following examples corroborate this point: [16]

The sun shines brightly.
With its glowing flames shooting
It goes down at night.
RICKY

The old cypress tree,
So beautiful by the rocks,
Has been there for years.
MARJORIE

After first thinking about an idea they wish to express, the students are encouraged to write it on paper. They can then examine their own written thought to determine how it can be divided into three parts. Experimentation with word arrangement, imagery, changing the order of the lines, and choice of words used should be encouraged as the poem is developed. The deceptively simple form requires more delicate handling than does free verse. Here are ideas for working with Haiku in the classroom:

- **One way of introducing a class to haiku is through the reading of a number of examples such as those found in the artistic little volume *Cricket Songs* by Harry Behn. After reading a number of these short poems, provide each student with a**

[15] Harry Behn, *Chrysalis; Concerning Children and Poetry* (New York: Harcourt, Brace and World, 1968), p. 39.
[16] Fourth-grade children at the Van Meter School, Los Gatos, Calif.

duplicated sheet (or write on the board), containing several examples of haiku. Let them discover the haiku pattern, the subject treated, and other characteristics by rereading the poems, thus:

Count the number of syllables in each line. How many syllables does each line contain?

1________________ 2________________ 3________________

Is this true of each poem?______________________________

What season of the year is indicated in each haiku?

____

- Japanese poetry makes us think of cherry blossoms or other spring blossoms. Use a twig of any flowering fruit tree to prepare an attractive display to motivate the writing of haiku. The flowers may be combined with pictures mounted on a bulletin board or music may be played to assist the development of a mood for haiku.

- Type haiku written by a class on a duplicating master using two long columns so that the folded sheets will produce two long, slim pages. Cut the duplicated sheets to form pages of an attractive booklet which can be encased in a decorative cover.

- Motifs for booklet covers should be appropriate to the poetry. Students can experiment with brush stroking to produce Japanese writing or the reeds, bamboo, flowers, and so on, associated with their art.

The word HAIKU can be printed using letters that have an oriental appearance.

- **Two films on haiku well worth investigating are:**

In a Spring Garden. Pictures by Ezra Jack Keats. Weston Woods Studios, 6 min., color, n.d. (See the book on which this film is based, too: *In a Spring Garden* by Richard Lewis.)

The Day Is Two Feet Long. Weston Woods Studios, 9 min., color, 1968.

- **A most rewarding art experience which correlates well with the writing of haiku is the blowing of ink with a straw. Washable black ink is applied in a swath near the bottom of an unlined file card (or any nonabsorbent paper). The wet ink is then blown with a straw to direct the ink in the desired direction. Blowing across the ink causes it to branch attractively. When the ink is dry, tiny dabs of bright tempera may be applied with a toothpick to add spring blossoms to the bare branch. The student then writes the Haiku on the card below the flowering branch, and the card is used for display or as a gift for parents.**

Winter wind whistles;
Rude, crude, arrogant pusher.
Bow, gracious silk tree.

• For an authentic presentation of haiku use rice paper (or thin onion skin or tissue paper) mounted inside colored paper. The poem is written (a felt pen will write on thin paper) together with an oriental motif—reeds, moon over water, flowering branch—and the author's name. The cover is folded so that the front flaps overlap slightly as in the sketch. A ribbon is then tied around the folder which is ready for presentation as a gift, as shown.

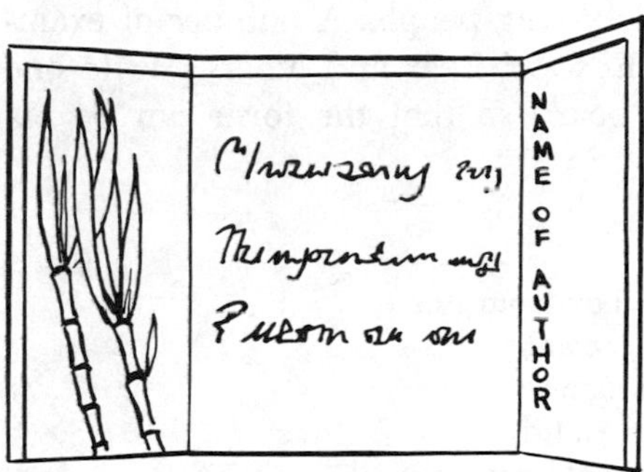

Folded slightly overlapping...
...tied with ribbon

Tanka are five-lined Japanese poems which contain a haiku (the first three lines). Like the haiku, they are unrhymed and follow a well-defined syllabic pattern with a total of 31 syllables for the entire poem:

Line 1: 5 syllables
Line 2: 7 syllables
Line 3: 5 syllables
Line 4: 7 syllables
Line 5: 7 syllables

Following is an example of tanka:

Silver raindrops fall:
A puddle of water stands.
Ocean before me,
All the world is reflected.
Look hard and you see black mud.

IRENE TABATA

A beautiful book on tanka is *The Seasons of Time,* edited by Virginia O'Baron and published by Dial Press.

LIMERICKS

"Did you know there is a city in Ireland named Limerick through which flows the River Shannon?" The limerick, which actually consists of a triplet and a couplet, is a form of verse which students usually enjoy. The form has consistently been used for humorous, nonsense verse which perhaps explains its appeal for young people. A number of examples can be read from the verse of Edward Lear and others. Write one example like the following on the board so that the form can be examined together:

There once was a boy from Rome
Who never used a comb.
   His hair was a sight;
   It never looked right!
A boy like that should stay home!

IRIS TIEDT

The triplet consists of lines 1, 2, and 5, whereas lines 3 and 4 form a couplet. Students will soon observe, too, that limericks often begin with the words, "There once was . . . ," which is helpful to the beginner, but the use of these words is not mandatory. Remind students to arrange the wording so that easily rhymed words end each line.

- **Limericks can be written about characters from familiar literature—Tom Sawyer, Jack Horner, Charlotte, Henry Huggins, Homer Price, Ellen Tibbets—to relate interest in reading to that of writing verse.**

Tom Sawyer was a barefoot lad;
Far from good, not really bad.
   Aunt Polly he teased,
   Sid and Mary displeased.
His story will make your heart glad.

IRIS TIEDT

- **Have students invent the strangest animal they can imagine. They can draw or paint pictures of the animals as well as write a limerick to accompany their art.**

There once was a kangeroogo,
Who would only go where you go.
He ate jam and bread
And could stand on his head.
He constantly read Victor Hugo.

IRIS TIEDT

QUATRAIN

The quatrain is the most commonly used verse form, perhaps because of its versatility. You can readily find examples of varied rhyme schemes —*aabb, abab, abcb,* and others. An effective method of introducing the quatrain to a class is to write several on the board with the class commenting on the similarities and the differences:

1 Quatrains contain four lines.
2 The lines are of uniform length.
3 There is rhyme.
4 The rhyme pattern varies.

Students who have had experience in writing poetry will not find the quatrain particularly difficult. One rhyme pattern develops naturally from the couplet as the quatrain is composed of two couplets. The other patterns are not unlike the couplet as the rhyming is still in paired lines although lines may intervene.

- **Biographical sketches of authors, historical figures, or other famous people can be depicted through the quatrain with one or more stanzas being written as in this example:**

A silversmith I was by trade,
But that does not explain my fame.
By lighting a lantern I warned of a raid
Have you guessed? What is my name?

IRIS TIEDT

- **The quatrain can be arranged in varied forms for added interest. Have students create QUADRANGLES which, like Triangular Triplets, can be read from any starting point.**

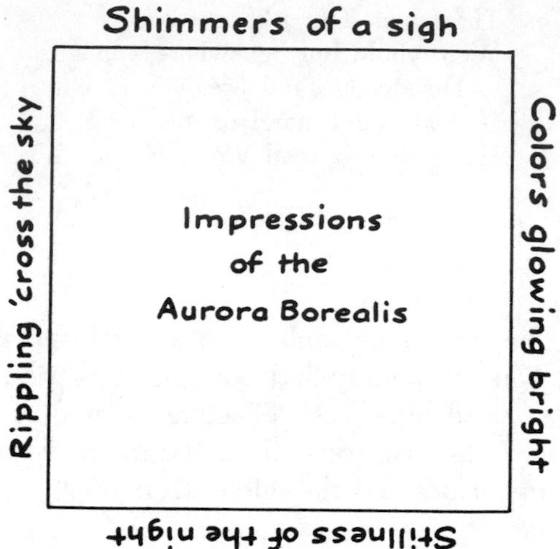

- Encourage students to combine forms of poetry which they know. A completed poem, for example, may consist of three quatrains and a couplet (a sonnet) or a series of quatrains may be used to form a poem of any length.

DIAMANTE

The Diamante (dee ah mahn' tay) was invented by Iris Tiedt who wrote in an article on exploring poetry patterns:

> If you become enthusiastic about having students write poetry, as I have been, you will find yourself searching for additional patterns to challenge students who have become involved in the composition of poetry. It was this search that led to my creation of four new poetry patterns that have proved to be very successful frames for ideas. While lending some structure, a pleasant patterning, the framework is not dominant or confining.[17]

The diamante, which many teachers have tried successfully with elementary school children, is a seven-line diamond-shaped poem that follows this pattern:

____

____

____

____

____

____

____

[17] Iris M. Tiedt, "Exploring Poetry Patterns," *Elementary English* (December, 1970), pp. 1082–85.

It is suggested, furthermore, that the poem be developed according to the following specifications:

Line 1: subject noun (1 word)
Line 2: adjectives (2 words)
Line 3: participles (3 words)
Line 4: nouns (4 words)
Line 3: participles (3 words)
Line 2: adjectives (2 words)
Line 1: noun-opposite of subject (1 word)

Notice that this poem creates a contrast between two opposite concepts as in the following example:

Air
Balmy, soft,
Floating, wafting, soothing,
Typhoon, wind, gale, cyclone
Twisting, howling, tearing,
Bitter, cold
Blast.

VERA HARRYMAN

SEPTOLET, QUINZAINE, QUINTAIN

Three additional forms invented by Iris Tiedt are the septolet, quinzaine, and quintain. These forms are described here with examples. You and students in your class are invited to create other new poetry forms.

The septolet consists of 7 lines (14 words) with a break in the pattern as indicated in this diagram.

____
____
____
____

____
____
____

Kitten
Padding stealthily
Amongst green grasses
Most intent.

Bird
Ascends rapidly
Causing great disappointment.

BEVERLY OLDFIELD

The quinzaine (kan zen′) consists of 15 syllables in 3 lines (7, 5, 3) which make a statement followed by a question, thus:

Boys screaming in the distance—
When will they drop to stillness
On this dusk?

IRMA JOHNSON

The quintain (kwin ten′) is a syllable progression: 2, 4, 6, 8, 10, as illustrated here:

Poems
Read for pleasure
Before the bright firelight
Words meant for all those who enjoy
Delightful, soothing, lovable music.

L. WILLE

ADDITIONAL POETRY FORMS

In addition to the more common varieties of poetry forms already discussed, additional forms have been developed which can be introduced to the more able student or to a class which shows unusual interest and ability. Familiar forms include:

1 Octave: Eight-line stanza (varied rhyme pattern)
2 Sonnet: An octave plus a sestet (6 lines)—Italian
Three quatrains plus a couplet—English
3 Blank verse: Unrhymed iambic pentameter

To further the more talented student's interest in poetry, there are a number of other intriguing forms of poetry which can prove most challenging. Acrostic poems, for example, are poems of varied length and rhyme scheme. The unusual aspect of such poems is that the first letter of each line is part of a word which can be read vertically. Poems have occasionally been written in this fashion to spell the name of a famous person who is being honored by the poet, and in at least one case the name of the poet himself is spelled. Following is a short example which spells the subject of the poem—SPRING. (Note the rhyme scheme in this poem.)

Silent the winds come a'bringing,
Primroses, dogwood and heather.
Rapidly winter has vanished;
Into the past it is banished.
Now in bright Aprilly weather,
Go we to work lightly singing.

IRIS TIEDT

Ways with Poetry

Poetry can become an integral part of the elementary school classroom in many different ways. Why, then, is poetry not evident in many rooms? The reasons given are numerous:

"I don't read well."
"The children aren't interested."
"We don't have time for poetry."

These excuses are far from valid, however, for the teacher or prospective teacher can learn to read poetry. The children will be interested in poetry if the teacher is interested and if stimulating experiences are planned. And time for poetry can be found by the resourceful teacher who introduces poetry in varied ways.

READING POETRY ALOUD

The teacher is the logical person to introduce the reading of poetry to the class, selecting poems which have proved popular with children for many years. Good poems for reading aloud can be about almost any topic, but they must have appeal—rhythm, humor, narrative. Some poems which we have enjoyed reading aloud in the classroom include:

The Elf and the Dormouse	Oliver Herford
The Clown	Dorothy Aldis
Whisky Frisky	Anonymous
There Once Was a Puffin	Florence P. Jaques
The Woodpecker	Elizabeth M. Roberts
Trains	James S. Tippett
Who Has Seen the Wind?	Christina Rossetti
Sneezles	A. A. Milne

Sea Fever	John Masefield
Eletelephony	Laura E. Richards
Daffodils	William Wordsworth
Antonio	Laura E. Richards
My Shadow	Robert Louis Stevenson
I Think Mice Are Nice	Rose Fyleman
The Road Not Taken	Robert Frost
Child on Top of a Greenhouse	Theodore Roethke

Children are very much impressed by poetry which their own teacher has written. Have you tried any of the suggestions for writing poetry discussed in this chapter? If you do, you will be more familiar with the technique described, and you will also have samples of your own poetry to share with the class you teach. Following our own sagacious advice, here are poems which we have written as we experimented with varied techniques—it's fun!

Cherry blossoms white
Adorn aseptic classroom—
Touch of rare beauty.

SWT

(Written after college class
learned to write haiku.)

FREE

One day I walked
Beside the sea.
  I looked for shell;
  I looked for stones;
And all of them were free!

it

After children become familiar with a variety of poetry, they, too, can choose favorites to read to the class. Discuss the qualities of effective reading of poetry, pointing out the fact that sentences appear in poetry just as in prose, and that punctuation must be observed so that the poem "makes sense."

- A class can practice reading poems orally together after hearing the teacher read. Stress the reading of sentences rather than lines to avoid a sing-song effect which is often associated with poetry. Try these with middle graders:

Theme in Yellow	Carl Sandburg
A Story in the Snow	Pearl R. Crouch
Brooms	Dorothy Aldis

• Children can prepare a tape recording of their reading of poetry. Each child reads one poem, either original or by known poets, which may be grouped on one theme—the season, a holiday, favorite things, vehicles, traveling. Music can be played softly to produce a pleasant background for the recording.

The Voice Choir The reading of poetry has much the same attributes as the singing of songs in a group. The values of the Voice Choir include:

1 Participation by even shy children
2 Sharing of enjoyable language experience
3 Group empathy developed
4 Improvement of pronunciation
5 Vocabulary development
6 Enjoyment and appreciation of poetry.

The Voice Choir does not have to be an extremely complicated matter. Almost any poem offers potential for group enjoyment. Students will become interested in experimenting with different effects with spoken poetry. Encourage suggestions of possible effects to be achieved through varied grouping of voices, different ways of interpreting lines, or even the use of sound effects when appropriate. Poetry interpretations can be varied through these techniques:

1 Use of one solo voice for a few lines
2 Division of the class into two to four groups that alternate lines or stanzas
3 Boy and girl groups (light and dark voices) speak lines to vary tonal quality
4 Varied speed of lines
5 Experiment with varying pitch for unusual effect

Treat the group as a chorus, using some of the same techniques which you might use in singing. Some poems can be read in unison, but others lend themselves to part work—many verses, repetitive lines or refrains, conversation, contrasted stanzas. Students have fun saying poetry together just as they do singing songs together; they soon build up an excellent repertoire.

• A poem which is effective with older elementary school students is Lewis Carroll's "Father William," which consists of a conversation between a father and his son. The girls, with their higher voices, can speak the young man's part with sprightly rhythm while the boys use their lower voices to portray the part of Father William, speaking slowly and impressively until the final verse.

FATHER WILLIAM

"You are old, Father William," the young man said,
  "And your hair has become very white;
And yet you incessantly stand on your head—
  Do you think, at your age, it is right?"

"In my youth," Father William replied to his son,
  "I feared it might injure the brain;
But, now that I'm perfectly sure I have none,
  Why, I do it again and again."

"You are old," said the youth, " as I mentioned before,
  And have grown most uncommonly fat;
Yet you turn a back-somersault in at the door—
  Pray, what is the reason of that?"

"In my youth," said the sage, as he shook his gray locks,
  "I kept all my limbs very supple
By the use of this ointment—one shilling a box—
  Allow me to sell you a couple?"

"You are old," said the youth, "and your jaws are too weak
  For anything tougher than suet;
Yet you finished the goose, with the bones and the beak—
  Pray, how did you manage to do it?"

"In my youth," said his father, "I took to the law,
  And argued each case with my wife;
And the muscular strength which it gave to my jaw
  Has lasted the rest of my life."

"You are old," said the youth, "one would hardly suppose
  That your eye was as steady as ever;
Yet you balanced an eel on the end of your nose—
  What made you so awfully clever?"

"I have answered three questions, and that is enough,"
  Said his father. "Don't give yourself airs!
Do you think I can listen all day to such stuff?
  Be off, or I'll kick you down-stairs!"

LEWIS CARROLL

• **Even the youngest of children enjoy repeating the lines of poetry if the poem has rhythm, repetition, and some humor. Other poems which are especially suitable for speaking in a group are:**

Puppy and I: A. A. Milne (Conversation)
Poor Old Woman: Anonymous (Refrain and Repetition)
The Mysterious Cat: Vachel Lindsay (Repetition)

The Owl and the Pussy-Cat: Edward Lear (Repetition)
The Monkeys and the Crocodile: Laura E. Richards (Repetition, Conversation)

MUSIC AND POETRY

Many familiar poems have been set to music; for example, some of the nursery rhymes, "Grandfather's Clock," Christmas carols, "Twinkle, Twinkle, Little Star," "The Star-Spangled Banner," "Home, Home, Sweet Home," and many others. Children are intrigued by seeing the verses of the songs in the form of a poem.

Interest in singing poems that someone else has set to music can lead to the selection of a poem by each child for which a melody can be written. A piano, small xylophone, or tonette will assist the students in producing the music they feel is appropriate to the poem selected. They will want to learn something about musical notation in order to write their songs with the words placed below the notes, thus:

The original poetry of children can also be set to a melody which they can sing for the class or teach to other members of the class. This technique lends further importance to the poetry produced by the child. Their own poem set to music can be mounted inside a decorated "song sheet" to be used as a gift for their parents. Music can also be used to assist the development of an experience in either reading or writing poetry.

- **Play appropriate music before reading a poem. Before reading the poem "Sea Fever," for example, play music which suggests the surf. Oriental music can set the stage for the writing of haiku.**

- **Music can also be played while poetry is being read. A soft musical background serves to provide a theme and unites a group of poems. Play Christmas music softly while Christmas poetry is read.**

- **Play records of Bob Dylan, the Beatles, or Pete Seeger. These modern poets and song writers will be very familiar to youngsters.**

ART AND POETRY

Art techniques offer varied, challenging ways to enhance the pleasure of poetry.

- Each student can select a poem to portray in a poetry broadside (poster). The poem can be typed or printed on a card or sheet of paper which is mounted on the broadside in some appropriate place. One youngster chose to print his poem, "The Balloon Man," on a bright yellow balloon which floated through the air above a town.

  Another concealed several poems about clouds beneath cloud shapes which were lifted to reveal the poems, "White Sheep," "The Cloud," and "Clouds."

- The collage, an abstract presentation of an idea or theme, is another excellent medium for presenting a poem. In order to construct a collage the student must first examine the poem selected for elements which can be portrayed. Some poems, for example, "The Owl and the Pussy-cat," contain many concrete references which can be included in a collage. Other poems which convey a mood will require a thoughtful use of color, texture, and shapes to help convey that mood.

- Crayons can be used to tell the story of a poem read. "See if you can draw a picture which will make the class know which poem you have in mind." Each picture can then be presented to the class to see if anyone can guess which poem is pictured. The artist can read the poem he/she selected.

POETRY AND THE SOCIAL SCIENCES

Much good poetry treats topics related to the areas of history and geography. One immediately thinks of Stephen Vincent Benét and his wife, Rosemary Carr Benét, who have written many fine poems depicting the figures of American history. A collection of these poems is entitled: *Book of Americans* (Rinehart, 1933). Poems can be read aloud by either the teacher or a child to add interest to a study of history. "Abraham Lincoln" and "Nancy Hanks" are two titles which could be featured during a study of the Civil War. Other ideas relating poetry to social studies include:

- An exciting way to present background material for a study of foreign countries is through the reading of poetry by poets from these countries. Good translations of many poets are available, and it is interesting, too, to use short passages in the original language.

  Here is the refrain of a poem by Spanish poet José de Espronceda, "Canción del Pirata."

Que es mi barco mi tesoro;
Que es mi Dios la libertad;
Mi ley la fuerza y el viento;
Mi única patria la mar.

SONG OF THE PIRATE

My boat is my treasure;
Liberty is my god;
My law the force and the wind;
My only homeland the sea.

TR. BY IRIS TIEDT

- Other poets can be explored as different countries are featured in a truly humanistic approach to the social studies. Suggested here are poets whose work is available in translation from a variety of countries:

  France: Victor Hugo.
  Scandinavia: Dag Hammarskjold, *Markings* (Knopf, 1964).
  Russia: Yevgeny Yevtushenko.
  Japan: Haiku, tanka (See earlier discussion).
  England: Wordsworth, Shelley

POETRY ON DISPLAY

Poetry can be brought into the classroom also as part of an attractive display—bulletin board, poster, mobile, table exhibit. Poetry is a suitable addition to a display on almost any topic. A poem or two can be typed or printed (let students help select and prepare) to be mounted on a bulletin board which features Mexico, England, The West, Exploring; even mathematics topics can include a poem such as Carl Sandburg's "Arithmetic." Here are a few suggestions for incorporating poetry in displays:

- For a seasonal display print a short poem on light colored paper or poster board. Around this poem can be scattered appopriate motifs on which are printed words related to the season, thus:

  In October use the poem, "Autumn Woods" by James S. Tippett or "Fall" by Aileen L. Fisher.

  Around the printed poem scatter large leaves cut from colored construction paper on which are printed words and phrases which connote autumn.

falling leaves	Columbus Day	frosty grass
Halloween	chilly nights	fall flowers
football	pumpkins	shorter days
crisp air	colored leaves	Indian summer

- Lines of poetry, phrases from poems, or titles of poems often provide excellent captions for a display. The whole poem may then be included as part of the display. Try these suggestions:

  THE FLAG IS PASSING BY!

  A patriotic display about citizenship might feature this poem, "The Flag Goes By," by Henry H. Bennett.

  SING ME A SONG

  This phrase, which appears in "Sea Shell" by Amy Lowell, can be used to feature the poetry written by the class.

  SEA FEVER

  The title of John Masefield's familiar poem makes an effective caption for pictures or writings about the sea.

  A WORLD OF WONDERS

  This caption comes from a line of Walter de la Mare's "Dream-Song" which could be used with children's writing about their own dreamings.

Collections of Poetry by Children

Baron, Virginia Olsen. *Here I Am!* New York: E. P. Dutton and Co., 1969.
Kohl, Herbert, and Cruz, Victor Hernandez, eds. *Stuff*. New York: World Publishing Co., 1970.
Lewis, Richard. *Miracles*. New York: Simon and Schuster, 1966.
Pellowski, Anne; Sattley, Helen; and Arkhurst, Joyce, eds. *Have You Seen a Comet? Children's Art and Writing from Around the World.* New York: John Day Co., 1971.

- Frequently display the poetry written by the class even though individual contributions may be very short.

  The three-line haiku can be printed on small paper fans or colored butterflies which are scattered over a board.

  Triangular Triplets can be written on bright construction paper triangles of varied size. Glue two of the same size on a triangle of cardboard so that poems appear on both sides of the triangle. Suspend these triangles mobile fashion.

  Cut a large tree shape from black or brown paper and fasten to a bulletin board. Short poems can be written on flower shapes which are placed on the branches of the tree.

  Use a large paper map as the background for a display of poetry about travel or exploration. Each poem can be written on a ship or plane shape (let each student design one).

- Collections of student compositions can be exhibited on a table. Each child may compile an individual booklet of poetry written over a period of time or the class may combine efforts to produce one or more books of poetry. Have students prepare an attractive design for the cover with a title, for example:

POETRY PLEASES
THE POETRY OF GREG WESTON (the child's name)
OUR POETRY
OCTOBER VERSES
ARE YOU WELL-VERSED?

Books to Investigate

Applegate, Mauree. *When the Teacher Says, "Write a Poem."* New York: Harper and Row, 1965.

Arnstein, Flora J. *Poetry and the Child.* New York: Dover Publications, 1970.

Hoffman, Marvin, director. *Teachers' and Writers' Collaborative Newsletter.* New York: Pratt Center for Community Involvement.

Koch, Kenneth. *Wishes, Lies, and Dreams.* New York: Chelsea House, 1970.

Walter, Nina. *Let Them Write Poetry.* New York: Holt, Rinehart, and Winston, 1962.

Wolsch, Robert A. *Poetic Composition.* New York: Teachers College Press, 1970.

the listening child

chapter

The hearing ear is always close to the speaking tongue.
Ralph Waldo Emerson

Of the four facets of language ability—reading, writing, speaking, and listening—listening is the primary skill, for it is as a listener that the baby is first aware of speech. Through imitation of the sounds heard he or she learns to form words, and through listening continues into adult life learning new ways with pronunciation, inflection, sentence patterns, and the many complexities of adult speech.

It is perhaps this primary nature of listening which has made us consider it a natural skill, one that is known by everyone, one that does not require teaching. It has been only in the last 20 years that researchers have investigated the nature of listening and the success with which we as individuals are able to listen. Russell questions this attitude toward listening instruction when he writes: "Can we assume that listening will take care of itself? Few deny the importance of listening, but it is not incorporated in curricula. Studies have consistently proved that instruction in listening improves listening abilities."[1] Research should make a difference in the classroom, yet Anderson notes:

> Except in isolated instances, virtually the only instruction in listening that children and young people receive in the schools is the quite useless admonition of "pay attention" and to "listen carefully." Listening, at all educational levels, has been the forgotten language art for generations.[2]

Listening as a Receptive Skill

Listening is to speaking as reading is to writing, for both listening and reading are receptive skills. The listener receives the spoken word. The skills of listening and speaking are, therefore, interdependent; the success of one depends on the success of the other. The speaker is usually trying to reach a listener, who may present blocks to reception which the speaker must overcome if he or she is to convince the listener of an argument, share an idea, or raise a question. The listener, on the other hand, is dependent on the speaker for the content of what is heard, the rate of speaking, and the clarity of enunciation and pronunciation.

Listening has been defined as a:

> . . . learned receptive skill. It is a personal, often private absorption of ideas and attitudes expressed through oral language. To listen implies attention and responsive thinking, sometimes only casual, often quite intent and indeed critical. Listening differs from hearing, which is a physiological process and does not involve interpretation.[3]

DIFFICULTIES OF LISTENING EFFICIENTLY

Listening is not a facile skill, for there are many factors which impede listening efficiency. The listener, for example, has no control over the rate of speed of the speaker. In *vis-à-vis* conversation it is perfectly permissible to request a friend to speak more slowly, but Dr. Thomas addressing a group of 400 has his audience literally at his mercy. He not only may speak rapidly, but he may also possess speech characteristics which prevent effective listening. As is pointed out in the chapter on speaking, the speaker has a responsibility to those who are listening, but this responsibility is not always recognized and assumed.

[1] David H. Russell, "A Conspectus of Recent Research on Listening Abilities," *Elementary English* (March, 1964), p. 263.

[2] Harold A. Anderson, "Needed Research in Listening," *Elementary English* (April, 1954), pp. 215–24.

[3] Ralph C. Staiger, "Defining the Terms, *Children and Oral Language* (Washington, D.C.: Joint Committee of the ACEI, ASCD, IRA, NCTE, 1964), p. 3.

The speaker may mispronounce words or he may place words in odd contexts (we hesitate to say that he may not always know the meanings of words he uses), which cause confusion in the listener's mind. While floundering to grasp one point, the listener is no doubt missing the next. He is forced to skip ahead mentally with the speaker and hope that the points missed were not vital to understanding the total message.

The organization of the speaker also influences listening efficiency. The well-organized speech is followed with relative ease, whereas the discussion which flits from topic to topic with no obvious framework may lose many listeners en route to the main point.

Usually the listener has no written guide to assist his task of listening. The provision of a script or type of libretto for material to be heard will aid listening efficiency. Reading a play or story which is to be presented on record will greatly aid comprehension when the recording is played for the first time. An outline of the material to be heard enables the listener to follow the report of detailed information.

Another factor which impedes comprehension is that there is seldom an opportunity for repetition in the speaking-listening situation. A line that is not "caught" in a play, a television program, or a speech is not likely to be repeated. If time and circumstance permit, a record may be replayed to permit listeners to hear portions of a selection again. The tape recorder has the further advantage of permitting the listener to stop the recording immediately in order to replay lines which he would like to hear again.

The group listening experience contains hindrances to effective listening which are not present in an individual listening situation. As a member of a group, John may hesitate to request that the speaker repeat a statement or that a portion of the tape be replayed. He may hesitate to expose his failure to understand, or he may fear disapproval of his request for repetition. Listening abilities vary as do other abilities, and it is for this reason that we would not expect all students to listen with the same efficiency. Individualized approaches, as in any other area of the curriculum, will also prove effective in teaching listening skills as each child develops abilities according to individual capacity. Listening stations in individual classrooms or in a central library will assist individual development of listening abilities.

Successful listening also depends on the maturation of the listener. A child of five will usually be unable to listen with comprehension to a lecture intended for an adult audience. No doubt the child will quickly "tune out," as he attempts to listen but discovers that he cannot understand. Children who become bored with adult conversations often attempt to gain attention by creating distractions clearly meant to annoy the adult until he pays attention to the child.

The experiential background and the knowledge of the listener also influence ability to listen with comprehension. This is one of the basic problems of the economically disadvantaged child whose background has not prepared him or her to understand ideas presented with a middle-class white child in mind. The urban child who has never seen a cow or pig may be totally unconcerned by a discussion of the farm.

Background or previous knowledge may also distort meanings if they cause the listener to conceive of something entirely different from that intended by the speaker. When Father queries, "Where is that new pipe?" Terry may begin searching for a pipe his father might smoke, whereas his dad is preparing to repair the kitchen sink.

Insecurity may also prevent a student's listening. The need for attention may be so great that Ted is concentrating on waving his hand for permission to say something. His own needs and desires disable him as a listener, for he is actually unable to sit quietly listening while someone else talks. Unless he is talking, he is not interested. He would dominate a conversation or discussion if permitted to do so.

LISTENING TASKS

We are impressed by the large percentage of our time spent directly or indirectly in listening, but just what skills are involved in this complex subject or ability? Incorporated in the broad term of *listening* are the following categories of specific skills: (1) Reception, (2) Comprehension, and (3) Assimilation.

RECEPTION:

Hear sounds made externally
Distinguish variety in sounds (auditory discrimination)
Decide to listen or not to listen

COMPREHENSION:

Follow words used
Understand ideas expressed
Recognize purpose for listening
  Note details
  Receive new ideas and information

ASSIMILATION:

React to ideas expressed
  Disagree
  Ask questions
  Make additions
  Evaluate

Reinforce learning through use
- Follow directions
- Repeat information to another
- Develop given information
- Adapt ideas presented

Each stage of listening development is important to the total listening experience. Receiving sounds is essential, for lack of reception clearly eliminates any possibility for comprehension and assimilation of what is heard. The three tasks of the listener are interdependent and self-generating, for reception leads to comprehension, which in turn leads to assimilation and reaction, and the cycle begins again as the question or commentary is in turn received, comprehended, and reacted to.

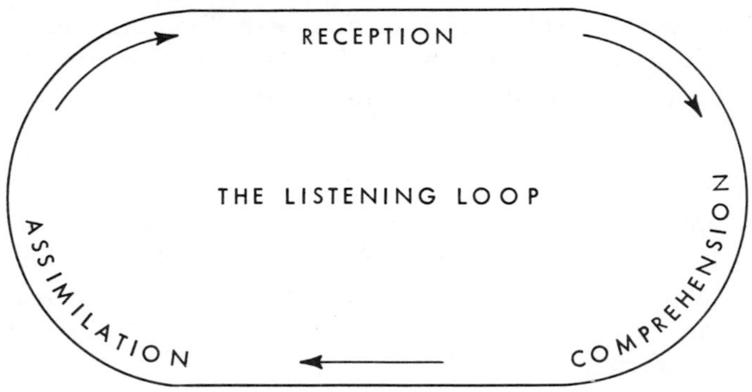

We can design specific techniques of classroom instruction which will tend to increase listening efficiency. Although each focuses on only one aspect of the complex of listening skills, increased efficiency in one task increases over-all efficiency.

1 Auditory discrimination between sounds

Which of these words does *not* begin like BIRD?
balloon brother case

2 Appreciation or oral interpretation of others

Play recordings, for example, *Alice in Wonderland* (Caedmon, TC 1097) for enjoyment.

3 Location of central theme or idea

Read or play recorded passages to provide practice. The student may be asked to state the main idea or several possible themes may be suggested from which a selection is made.

4 Discovery of new word meanings from context

Talk about words after reading aloud, for example, "Armies in the Fire" by Robert Louis Stevenson.

5 Awareness of the power of words

Tape passages which propagandize; have students identify examples of slanting, loaded words, glittering generalities, etc.

6 Discovery of specific details

In what state did Philip live?
Where was Linda going?
How did Mr. Pepper obtain a penguin?

7 Recognition of imagery in writing

Discuss types of figurative language—simile, metaphor, etc. Try to remember several images or figures of speech while listening to "The Daffodils" by William Wordsworth.

8 Comparison of two or more examples

Have all students write descriptions of a single item or event. These passages can be recorded, or several may be read by one person. (It is best for this purpose if the writer does not read his own passage.) Discuss the variety of treatment.

9 Recognition of fact and opinion

After the student talks on assigned topics, discuss the presence of both fact and opinion in the speech. Was fact substantiated? Was opinion qualified?

10 Learning needed information

Provide many opportunities for students to take notes on taped or read passages which explain how to do something. Ability to follow directions may fall in this category.

11 Selection of pertinent data

Provide experience with passages which include directions for doing something as well as a number of bits of extraneous information. Students record the information necessary to perform a specific operation.

12 Repetition of what has been heard

Read short stories such as *The Mean Mouse and Other Mean Stories* by Janice Udry (Harper, 1962). After each story ask someone to see if they can retell the story while the class listens to determine which details are omitted.

Developing Skills of Listening

"Now listen carefully," says the teacher, almost automatically as she begins a classroom presentation. Do students obey this perfunctory admonition? How can we tell? When we ask children to write or to speak, we can immediately ascertain the degree to which the direction is being followed, but a child may appear to be listening intently when in reality his mind is relishing thoughts of a promised trip to the zoo or reliving the mad adventures of Batman. The teacher has competition, and in many cases it is "stiff" competition.

EXAMINING PRESENT PRACTICES

Studies by Ralph B. Nichols and others point out that without training in listening most of us operate at only 25 percent efficiency.[4] Research also indicates that direct instruction in listening does increase listening effectiveness.[5] It is obvious that training in this essential skill should be included at all levels of education.

We find, according to Wilt's study, that children actually spend half their school time listening, but at what level of efficiency? Is this a wise use of student time? How might their time be better used? Does the teacher spend too much time talking when students should be more directly involved? Does the fact that only one child usually speaks while more than thirty listen indicate a low level of direct participation? Does it indicate a need for varied grouping techniques or individualized approaches to learning?

Is listening as practiced a guided, purposeful experience? We say the class is listening; but are the children really auding, or are they merely waiting their turn to participate? Are they literally wasting their time? Could teaching techniques be more exciting, more stimulating, if greater use were made of visual aids—films, filmstrips, pictures, direct observation, experimentation, field excursions? Perhaps some periods of "listening" should be eliminated from the daily schedule.

Consider, for example, the practice called "Show and Tell" or "Sharing Time" which is common in many elementary school classrooms. One teacher wrote, "I hate Show and Tell," and the reasons were that this method had become so stereotyped that the time was wasted and children were actually being taught poor listening habits.[6] It is essential that we reconsider the value of what we are doing in the classroom and how this basically good idea can be used more constructively. Here are suggestions that may help you make Sharing Time more worthwhile.

Don't have Sharing Time every day or always at the same time.

Select a theme for the Sharing period—My Best Friend, Was I Scared!, Work Can Be Fun, An Exciting Moment. Announce the theme the day before.

Use an unusual seating arrangement—circle, semicircle, sitting on the floor. Tape the speaking occasionally for evaluation by students.

[4] Ralph B. Nichols, "What Can Be Done About Listening?" *The Supervisor's Notebook,* Vol. XXII, No. 1 (1960).

[5] Sister Mary Kevin Hollow, "Listening Comprehension at the Intermediate Grade Level," *Elementary School Journal* (December, 1955), 158–61.

[6] Pat Timberlake, "I Hate Show and Tell," *Elementary English* (April, 1973).

You listen, too, and comment with interest. (Don't be obviously busy with paperwork.)

If a child has something exciting to share, let him, even if Sharing is not on your schedule. Take advantage of this show of interest.[7]

Let us turn to listening experiences that are better planned, more purposeful, and, therefore, more stimulating and more effective. Children need specific practice, for example, in critical listening. They need to listen to each other and to combine speaking and listening skills. We need positive approaches to listening instruction based on provocative material, new ideas, something the child can become excited about; otherwise, slovenly listening habits will be encouraged along with justifiable disinterest, apathy, and boredom with school.

OBJECTIVES OF TEACHING LISTENING

What is the purpose of the classroom teacher in teaching listening? Toward what objectives are listening activities directed? The general goal is the improved efficiency of the teaching-learning experience in the elementary school. More specifically, however, listening instruction is directed toward:

1 More efficient use of classroom time through increased effectiveness of reception
2 Awareness of the significance of listening as a skill and the value of increasing effectiveness
3 Provision of extensive practice in listening for varied purposes

These objectives can all be accomplished through carefully planned classroom experiences. Consider the value of these types of activities.

What's the answer? Write a question on the board, for example: "What language is spoken in Brazil?" Notice that the child knows what he is to listen for before the exercise begins, so he is listening for a specific purpose. Then, read a paragraph which contains the answer as well as other information. Ask the question again after reading the paragraph aloud. Compare the number of right answers. Discuss the reasons for any differences in the answers given.

Sound language List words that express sounds. LOUD SOUNDS are shouts, honking, crash, scream, clamor. SOFT SOUNDS are whispers,

[7] Sidney Tiedt and Iris Tiedt, *The Elementary Teacher's Complete Ideas Handbook* (Englewood Cliffs, N.J.: Prentice-Hall, 1965), p. 116.

singing, cooing, scraping, humming, buzzing. Have children listen for Sound Language as stories are read aloud.

Sound stories Tape a series of interesting sounds—a bell ringing, voices whispering, a motor running. Play this Sound Story as children tell the story they imagine fits around these sounds. The teacher can print the story that young children tell so that all can read it. Older children can write their stories which are combined in a Big Book of Sound Stories. Let children make Sound Stories, too, by taping various combinations of sounds.

I'm on the way to Zanzibar Play "I'm Going on a Trip to Zanzibar" in which the first child may say, "I'm going on a trip to Zanzibar, and I'm going to take along a toothbrush." The second child must say, "I'm going on a trip to Zanzibar, and I'm going to take along a toothbrush and a poodle." A third might say, "I'm going on a trip to Zanzibar, and I'm going to take along a toothbrush, a poodle, and a baseball bat." And so it goes, as children listen carefully and concentrate on remembering the sequence of the items listed. Younger children will help each other fill in the items as the list grows longer.

The listening center The Listening Post is a popular center in the classroom where a group of children can don earphones to share a story on records or tape. A good listing of educational records is available from the National Council of Teachers of English:

Schreiber, Morris, ed. *An Annotated List of Recordings in the Language Arts.* National Council of Teachers of English, 1111 Kenyon Rd., Urbana, Illinois.

For maximum effectiveness provide the printed story to accompany each recorded story so children can listen and read at the same time. Questions can be provided both before and after the recorded story is played to direct children's listening. Teachers can prepare tapes of many stories that are available as trade books in the classroom library.

Friendly listening Have children work in pairs as they listen to each other in turn. The task of the listener is to listen carefully, while his partner talks about what he likes to do most of all at home. When the talker's time is up (use a three-minute egg timer), the listener must repeat what he has heard as accurately as possible. Then the tasks are switched as the talker takes a turn listening. Notice that in this task the listener must listen "actively."

LEVELS OF LISTENING

"To listen is an effort, and just to hear is no merit. A duck also hears." Thus Igor Stravinsky expressed the importance of moving beyond the mere hearing of sounds. Listening is vital for the musician, but it is also a skill needed by every person every day.

Many sounds are in the air at any one time. Some of these sounds are heard. Others never reach the individual's level of awareness; he is "tuned out"; he is not listening. There are sounds which he may hear but does not listen to. Still other sounds will cause him to listen but with little attempt to understand or respond. The highest level of listening is reached when the individual listens with purpose and comprehension. The latter level of listening has been termed "auding" to distinguish the process described from mere hearing or listening without perception.

Levels of listening can be considered, therefore, as consisting of these degrees of advancement and effectiveness: (1) hearing, (2) listening without specific response, and (3) auding, or listening with intent and comprehension. It is auding that we are endeavoring to teach in the classroom as children learn to take notes from spoken recordings, to listen to the imagery of poetry, or to evaluate positions presented in a debate.

Listening is what a woman does when she's not supposed to hear.
WILL ROGERS

SENSORY AWARENESS

Help children become more aware of hearing or listening as one of the senses. As they compare this sense to seeing, feeling, smelling, and tasting, they may cease to take hearing so much for granted. Encourage children to experience all of these senses and to express them in their writing. Make class lists of Sound Words, Feeling Words, Seeing Words, Taste Words, and Smell Words.

Read together *Sound of Sunshine, Sound of Rain* by Florence P. Heide (New York: Parents' Magazine Press, 1970). Here is a blind child's expression of awareness as he says, "It must be morning, for I hear the morning voices." Children might consider what it would be like to be deprived of the sense of sight.

A number of other children's books help children to be aware of sounds around them. Have some of these available for children to read and talk about.

The Quiet Noisy Book by Margaret Wise Brown. Harper and Row, 1950.
Do You Hear What I Hear? by Helen Borton. Abelard-Schuman, 1960.
The Loudest Noise in the World by Benjamin Elkin. Viking Press, 1954.
What's That Sound? by Mary O'Neill. Doubleday, 1970.

PREPARING FOR EFFECTIVE LISTENING

What conditions will assist the teacher in promoting effective skills of listening? How can we overcome factors which impede listening efficiency? We can begin by checking the psysical conditions of the classroom and of the children themselves. We should also consider the content to be presented and the methods we use to present them.

First, check the physical conditions of the classroom. Little attentive listening will be done in a room that is poorly ventilated, poorly lighted, overheated, or unusually cold. Are some children overdressed for the type of work in which they are engaged? Have excess clothing—sweaters, sweatshirts, jackets—removed immediately on entering the classroom.

Recommend physical examinations for children who appear to have unusual difficulty hearing. Some children feign hearing difficulties as an excuse for inattentiveness or as a way of gaining the teacher's attention. A report from the doctor will clarify the child's ability so that the teacher is more certain in approaches to be used with each individual child.

Vary the routines of teaching so that children do not become overly fatigued or bored. The attention span or the listening attentiveness of the younger child in particular is relatively short. Long periods of uninterrupted listening are less efficient than are short experiences interspersed with more active learning activities.

Plan learning activities to include more speaking by children and less by the teacher. The observer in the typical elementary school classroom quickly notes that the majority of the speaking is by the teacher, with relatively infrequent opportunities for students to speak. Children who are involved in an activity listen more readily, more attentively, for there is a reason to listen.

Avoid distractions which prevent effective listening. Noises from the street or the activities of other children in the classroom may be so distracting as to make listening literally impossible. Listening Centers that provide earphones for each child have the advantage of closing out other sounds. Room dividers can prevent visual distraction of the child who is listening.

As a teacher, you should set the style in listening. How the teacher listens to children may influence their habits of listening. The teacher who obviously is not sufficiently interested in a child's presentation before the class to listen to it attentively cannot expect the class to listen.

If the teacher is busy grading papers or preparing art materials at the back of the room, what chance has the young speaker of holding the attention of the class?

Discuss the purpose of the listening experience. Are we listening to get the main idea of a story, or are we trying to compare two ways of presenting information? Are we listening especially to notice interesting ways of using words, or are we trying to gain information about a Greek myth?

CHARACTERISTICS OF GOOD LISTENING HABITS

The identification of desirable habits of listening should lend direction to classroom activities. Student-compiled lists of AIDS TO GOOD LISTENING have been found helpful in motivating individuals to work on specific skills. Nichols [8] published a list of "Eight Significant Listening Habits" which identifies the good listener as one who:

- I Maintains an awareness of his own motives in listening
  - A Develops speedily in each situation his own motives for effective listening
  - B Analyzes the speech and adjusts himself to his own motives
- II Shares with the conveyor responsibility for communication
  - A Applies himself to the different techniques of the speaker
  - B Assumes his half of the responsibility for communication
- III Arranges favorable conditions for listening
  - A Adjusts himself for any personal hearing disability or for poor room ventilation or temperature
  - B Ignores any outside or unnecessary distractions
- IV Exercises emotional control during listening
  - A Postpones personal worries
  - B Does not permit an immediate dislike for a speech or speaker
- V Structuralizes the presentation
  - A Recognizes conventional compositional techniques
  - B Adjusts his system of note taking to the organizational plan of the speech
- VI Strives always to grasp the central ideas in the presentation
  - A Focuses on central ideas and tends to recognize the characteristic language in which they are stated
  - B Has the ability to discriminate between fact and principle, idea and example, evidence and argument
- VII Exploits fully the rate differential between thought and speech
  - A Demands continuous attention—staying on the track with the speaker

[8] Ralph G. Nichols, "The Teaching of Listening," *Chicago Schools Journal*, Vol. XXX, pp. 273–78.

B Does these: mental anticipation of each of the speaker's points; identification of the techniques used in the development of each point; and mental recapitulation of points already developed

VIII Seeks frequent experience in listening to difficult expository material

A Is acquainted with such television programs as: "Face the Nation," "Issues and Answers," and "Meet the Press"

B Has experience in listening to difficult material

The listener must assume an active role in developing listening skills, for no other person can listen for him, and no one can force him to listen. The task of listening, therefore, must be approached with a positive attitude which assumes that the listener wants to hear, to find out something; he wants "to listen." We are all aware of the ease with which the mind can slip to thoughts of an unrelated subject as a well-meaning soul chats on and on about a movie he or she just saw. What's more, they will never be aware that we have ceased listening, for our outward appearance remains the same (with a little care about yawning).

The listener, too, must assume responsibility for the success of the speaking-listening encounter; he must be prepared to hear with an open mind what this speaker has to impart. The listener does everything he can to promote understanding. He keeps his eyes on the speaker, makes certain that he can both see and hear, and takes appropriate notes. Following the speaking-listening experience, the listener may ask questions, comment on the information discussed, and utilize the acquired information.

STUDYING LISTENING WITH STUDENTS

Present listening as an active process. The students can discuss their roles as listeners, for analysis of the responsibilities of the listener will lead to more active participation in the listening act. Training clearly directed toward increasing listening efficiency can be interesting to the group as they use themselves as guinea pigs in a scientific bit of research to determine whether their practicing will better their listening abilities.

Why is listening important? This question may lead to a study of time spent each day in listening as each child keeps a LISTENING DIARY. One fourth-grade boy recorded his daily listening activities, thus:

7:00 When I awoke, birds were singing.
7:15 I watched a TV show.
7:30 Mother called me for breakfast; we talked together.

7:45 My dog barked outside the door for his food.
8:00 Music was playing on the radio.
8:30 The telephone rang.
8:40 On the way to school I heard—
a horn blowing
children talking
cars moving
the traffic lady's whistle.
8:55 The school bell rang.
9:00 Miss Dell called the roll.
We talked about spring.
We read aloud in reading class.
10:10 We played "Flying Dutchman."
Miss Dell read a chapter of *Chitty-Chitty-Bang-Bang*.
She explained division and we did mental arithmetic.
12:00 At lunch we whispered; music was playing.
We played "Dodge Ball."
12:45 Joe read about the mission at Santa Barbara.
Then we answered questions about the missions.
We located missions on the map.
We saw a film about Father Serra.
Miss Dell asked if we would like to make dioramas.
1:30 We played ball.
We sang songs and played a new record.
Sandra reported on her science experiment.
We talked about a picture and wrote a story about it.
Some people read their stories.
3:00 Lots of noise on the way home.
A fire engine passed.
Mom told me she had two jobs for me.
Then Jim and I played astronauts.
6:30 We had dinner. Dad talked a lot, mostly to Mom.
7:15 I watched TV until Mom called me.
8:30 Dad talked to me after I was in bed.
Golly, there's listening in everything.

It is also helpful if students develop simple guides to good listening which are specific, thus:

LOOK at the speaker.
CONCENTRATE on what he or she is saying.
THINK about what has been said.
TALK about what has been said.
Ask questions.
Add information.

RELATIONSHIP OF LISTENING TO THINKING

Listening is a vital part of the complex thinking process. As the elementary school student participates in listening activities in the classroom, Jim hears words which symbolize meanings. Through practice he learns to abstract meaning from these words and the order in which they are arranged. Through listening he learns to:

Make generalizations
Sort ideas, reject or accept
Group into categories
Observe similarities and differences
Make comparisons
Develop or adapt concepts

Children should be exposed to varied types of thinking processes which will require careful listening and reaction. After hearing two poems about the same general topic, for example, "P's the Proud Policeman" by Phyllis McGinley and "Bobby Blue" by John Drinkwater, children can compare the treatment of the subject. In the second poem, for instance, the name *policeman* is never mentioned. How do we know that the poet is describing a policeman?

Phillip's listening vocabulary is the largest of all his vocabularies. He will understand many words which he would hesitate to use in speech or be unable to read or write. What factors account for the greater size of the listening vocabulary?

1 Meaning can be deduced from the general context provided by the speaker.
   The situation was so *ridiculous* that the whole family began laughing.
   (The word *ridiculous* obviously is associated with laughter.)
2 The exact meaning is not necessary to understanding.
   The *cheetah* is the fastest runner in the animal world.
   (The child may not know exactly what the cheetah looks like, but gathers enough meaning to permit discussion.)
3 The burden for introducing the new word lies with the speaker, not the listener; it is the speaker who must be more familiar with the meaning in order to use a word coherently.
4 The speaker's tone of voice implies certain connotations of approval or disapproval.
   The boys were just too *unruly*.

Because the listening vocabulary is so much more extensive than those of speaking, reading, and writing, we must be careful to provide stimulating discussion material for the primary-level classroom as well as for intermediate and upper grade levels. Discussion must not be limited to the content of controlled vocabulary readers, for instance, for these young minds are feasting on more exotic fare via television. We have a tendency to underestimate the abilities of children to understand broad concepts if couched in understandable terms, demonstrated visually, and presented in a stimulating context. This is one strong argument for the teacher's oral reading of books that are too difficult for children to read to themselves, for children can handle ideas orally and visually which may be too difficult for them to read about. First graders will enjoy listening to *Charlotte's Web* although few would be able to read it enjoyably.

Research indicates that there is a high correlation between reading and ability to listen with comprehension, and there is a corresponding increase in reading ability with increased ability to listen. A strong reading program therefore, should provide much listening experience, for the child requires time to develop aural-oral skills which in the long run will add to improved reading abilities. We will find this need recognized more clearly in working with the disadvantaged child and in the teaching of foreign languages which have long advocated the aural-oral approach to language before composition and reading are taught.

Kellogg and others have found that instruction in listening caused a significant difference in listening and reading achievement. He worked with first graders and taught listening skills as an integral part of the total language-arts program.[9] Here is an example of instruction that may serve to prevent reading failure as children strengthen their vocabulary, experiential background, and attentiveness to the task at hand.

Help students recognize the relationship between listening and reading which are both receptive skills. In both, the receiver has to decode a message and similar skills are used, for example, the use of context to comprehend an unknown word. Introduce reading activities through listening first. Read the following poem aloud to a group of students, or have it available on tape.

CLOUDS

White sheep, white sheep
On a blue hill,
When the wind stops,
You all stand still.

[9] Ralph E. Kellogg, *A Study of the Effect of a First Grade Listening Instructional Program upon Achievement in Listening and Reading.* Report No. BR–6–8469. San Diego, Calif.: San Diego County Dept. of Education, 1966.

When the wind blows,
You walk away slow.
White sheep, white sheep,
Where do you go?

Follow the reading of the poem by asking several questions about the meaning of the poem, thus:

What is this poem about?
What do the clouds looks like?
What makes the clouds move?
What is the blue hill the sheep walk on?

If you tape the poem and questions, allow time for the child to think about the answers to the question. Prepare a sheet for the students that duplicates the lesson in printed form so that they now read what they have heard and write answers that they previously thought or spoke aloud. (See below.) Here is an excellent way of integrating learnings in the language arts.

From: *The Elementary Teacher's Ideas and Materials Workshop,* November 1972, p. 15.

LISTENING TO WHAT?

Students need direct instruction in becoming aware of the listening act, for they are habituated to listening in an unstructured fashion. We as listeners can be likened to the television set with which they are so familiar. We receive sounds which are changed into thoughts, but if our listening mechanism is not properly tuned in, we fail to receive the proper message or we receive no message at all. Carrying the analogy further, the message may be severely distorted if the framing knob has been turned too far.

Listening is not an isolated skill to be practiced for fifteen minutes a day and then forgotten. We never know when a message will be directed toward us, for listening is an integral part of all of life. Because this skill, or complex of skills, permeates all areas of the curriculum, effective methods of listening will be better taught in the context of varied subject matters—social science, literature, science, language study, music, art.

Can we establish a sequence of listening abilities to be followed from primary grades through junior high school? It is only through sequential development of these abilities that true listening efficiency will be attained. Young children who have learned to identify similar sounds and to follow simple directions will attack progressively more difficult skills and eventually will learn to listen critically to recorded presentations of literary works or to the commentary of news analysts. Described briefly here are varied suggestions for teaching listening to elementary school students.

The sounds of silence Listen to Silence! Have everyone be as quiet as possible. Is it really silent? Are there still noises to be heard? Do you think it could ever be completely quiet?

Now hear this! Give a series of short directions with the children following them exactly. NOW HEAR THIS: Walk to the chalkboard; write your last name, and place the chalk on the reading table.

Children will enjoy being the Leader. The number of directions can be increased as listening ability develops.

The traveling tale Have one child start a story. Children take turns adding a line or two to the story as it travels around the group. Have a number of Traveling Tales going at one time in smaller groups for greater participation. Each child must listen to the developing story in order to make an appropriate addition when it is his turn.

A listening walk Take children for a walk. Have them list all the things they heard after they return. The items can be arranged in a poem in this manner.

LISTEN!

The sound of
    birds chirping,
    horns tooting,
    children talking.

The sound of
    leaves rustling
    a bell ringing,
    the teacher calling.

Repeat this technique after a week or two to see if the children's listening perception has improved. Are they aware of more sounds?

What's that sound? Hide several items under your desk. As you, or one of the children, make a sound with a specific item, let the class guess what the sound is. Use a hand mixer, a fork striking a glass, a pop-up toaster, a whistle. Let children plan a second listening experience as they bring items from home carefully concealed in paper bags.

Taking notes Practice taking notes from teacher-taped passages read from a textbook. Discuss the first set of talking notes taken. Project examples with the overhead projector to compare differences. Play the same material again as a new set of notes is produced. Repeat this procedure with other taped material.

What happened next? Develop skill in remembering sequence of events by playing a short taped story (fairy tale, myth) or a poem. List the events that happened in order. Then replay the selection to check accuracy. For variety provide a list of events in scrambled order with each child numbering the items in order of happening. Then compare results.

CRITICAL LISTENING

What is the function of the critic? Students must first develop concepts which lead to constructive criticism before serving as critics of fellow students' oral presentations. A discussion can lead to the following generalizations:

Criticism should help a student improve.
Criticism should assist the class in understanding the qualities of good speaking.
If criticism is totally negative, it is more discouraging than helpful.

Students can be given listening assignments in which they must make a Listening Report to evaluate what was heard. Listening assignments may be for speeches made on radio or television, taped talks available in the classroom Listening Center, or student speeches. A form for reporting might be something like this:

General Evaluation:
10 9 8 7 6 5 4 3 2 1 0
Excellent Could be better Not satisfactory
Report:
Who spoke? ______
What topic? ______
Where? ______
When? ______
Main idea? ______
______
Reactions: ______
______

Books to Investigate

Calder, Clarence R., and Antan, Eleanor M. *Techniques and Activities to Stimulate Verbal Learning*. New York: The Macmillan Co., 1970.

Denby, Robert V. "NCTE/ERIC Report on Research in Listening and Listening Skills." *Elementary English* (April, 1969), 511–17.

Devine, T. G. "Reading and Listening: New Research Findings." *Elementary English* (March, 1968), 346–48.

Educational Developmental Corporation. *The Listening Skills Program*. Palo Alto, Calif.: Science Research Associates, 1969.

Farrell, Muriel, and Flint, Shirley H. "Are They Listening?" *Childhood Education* (May, 1967), 528–29.

Kellogg, R. E. *A Study of the Effect of a First-Grade Listening Instructional Program upon Achievement in Listening and Reading*. San Diego, Calif.: San Diego County Department of Education, 1967.

Lundsteen, Sara W. *Listening. Its Impact on Reading and the Other Language Arts*. Urbana, Ill.: National Council of Teachers of English, 1971.

Russell, David H., and Russell, Elizabeth. *Listening Aids through the Grades*. New York: Teachers College, Columbia Uniiversity, 1959. An excellent collection of listening activities.

Taylor, Stanford E. *Listening*. No. 29. What Research Says to the Teacher, Dept. of Classroom Teachers, American Educational Research Assn. Washington, D.C.: National Education Association, 1964.

Tiedt, Sidney W., and Tiedt, Iris M. *The Elementary Teacher's Complete Ideas Handbook*. Englewood Cliffs, N.J.: Prentice-Hall, 1965. Chapter 4, "Listening to Learn," contains practical ideas for instruction.

Wagner, Guy et al. *Listening Games*. Darien, Conn.: Teachers Publishing Corporation, 1962. Activities to develop listening skills.

developing oral language

chapter 10

Conversation is the laboratory and workshop of the student.
Ralph Waldo Emerson

We cannot overemphasize the importance of speech as a means of communication in our verbal society, for we speak far more frequently than we write or read. Ability to speak effectively can mean the difference between success in life and the lack of success; indeed, verbal facility can actually mask an individual's deficiencies. Through the spoken word we transact business, express feelings, and communicate ideas; speech is a direct form of communication, a person-to-person relationship. Our purpose in this chapter is to explore the needs of the child in developing speech abilities and to examine strategies for providing varied experiences in speaking in the classroom.

Language Development

The child learns to speak language long before beginning to read or write it, and the process of learning to speak is a much more natural act. The child lives with the language, constantly experimenting in its use.

For the most part learning to speak is an enjoyable experience, for the child is encouraged through praise and attention. Throughout infancy efforts at imitating adult speech are positively reinforced by adult approval and assistance.

Before entering school the child has been practicing spoken language for four to five years and has usually developed an extensive speaking vocabulary before developing any reading or writing vocabulary at all. The extent to which this spoken vocabulary is developed determines success in beginning reading experiences, for the child must know words in order to read them with meaning or to use them in composing sentences. This preschool background in speaking not only provides the child with knowledge of words but also familiarizes children with the grammar of the English language. Thus, the child in kindergarten can tell a teacher which of these spoken groups of words is a sentence, which one "sounds right."

Mark goes to school.
Dog the street down runs the.

The child knows language "by ear," and as he or she begins to compose sentences we rely more on this intuitive sense of rightness than we do on rules. It is linguistically valid to ask the child, "Does that sound right to you?" Usually when children hear the sentence spoken aloud, they can hear that a word has been omitted or that words are out of order.

"The scraps of lore which children learn from each other are at once more real, more immediately serviceable, and more vastly entertaining to them than anything which they learn from grown-ups." [1] So begins the fascinating study, *The Lore and Language of Schoolchildren,* by Iona and Peter Opie, which explores the widely varied lore of children which has been transmitted orally. This extensive study reveals that the same rhymes and riddles appear in variant forms not only throughout Great Britain, the locale of the study, but also in the United States and even in non-English-speaking countries. At times it is noted also that a particular bit of lore has been discovered in early literature, indicating that children's lore transcends time as well as geographic boundaries.

The children's tales, it is observed also, are not intended for adult ears, for "part of their fun is the thought, usually correct, that adults

[1] Iona and Peter Opie, *The Lore and Language of Schoolchildren* (London: Oxford University Press, 1959), p. 1.

know nothing about them." Here is what the Opies term an "unself-conscious culture . . . unnoticed by the sophisticated world, and quite as little affected by it. . . ."[2]

Every day you speak 4800 words

OBJECTIVES OF ORAL LANGUAGE INSTRUCTION

What are our objectives in oral language instruction? We certainly would not list "preparation of each student to be a public speaker" as an aim of the elementary school oral language program. Recognizing the basic nature of oral language and the importance of effective speech, however, we direct instruction toward these ends:

1 Linguistic fluency
   - Ability to speak without hesitation
   - Information about which to talk (experiential background)
   - Vocabulary with which to speak
   - Gradual movement toward use of standard English
   - Familiarity with speech patterns

2 An extensive speaking vocabulary
   - Pronunciation
   - Meaning
   - Variety
   - Knowledge of usage levels

3 Effectiveness of speaking
   - Elements of successful speaking
     - Delivery
     - Voice
     - Content
     - Bearing
   - Specific parts of a speech
     - Introduction
     - Conclusion
     - Choice of topic
     - Use of words
   - Variety in style of presentation
     - Humor
     - Audience participation

The Contributions of Linguistics

Linguistics has pointed up the primacy of the spoken language and has gone directly to the oral language to observe the characteristics of

[2] *Ibid.*, p. 2.

language in action. It is noted that written language is actually a derived form of language, a kind of speech dialect.

As is discussed in a preceding chapter, the linguist clarifies certain concepts which are reflected in the teacher's attitude toward language in the classroom. Relevant to the growth of ability in speaking effectively are the following concepts:

1 The spoken language is the primary form of language.
2 Children learn language naturally through an aural-oral method.
3 The child knows the grammar of language before entering school.
4 Patterns of sentences typical to a language can be identified.
5 We gain meaning from word order.
6 Juncture, stress, and pitch (pauses, accents, tone) convey meaning.

We shall explore some of these concepts pertinent to spoken language as it is used in the elementary school classroom.

TECHNIQUES FOR PRACTICING ORAL PATTERNS

We can borrow techniques from instruction in foreign language to help children alleviate deficiencies in the easy use of patterns of oral English. Grammatical constructions can best be taught through aural-oral methods which include some of the following approaches.[3]

Repetition: Listen and repeat exactly as heard.

Teacher: I see a dog.
Child: I see a dog.

Analogy: Repeat exactly with one change.

Teacher: I am a man.
Anne: I am a woman.
Fred: I am a boy.
Sue: I am a person.

Begin a PROGRESSIVE CONVERSATION so that all members of the group participate in this type of analogical replacement, thus:

Teacher: I see a dog. What do you see, Jim?
Jim: I see a cat. What do you see, Janet?
Janet: I see a mouse. What do you see, Gerri?

---

[3] Nelson Brooks, *Language and Language Learning* (Harcourt, 1964), pp. 156–61.

Inflection: Change the form of a word.

Teacher: There is one girl.
Sue: There are two girls.
Teacher: There is one house.
Fred: There are two houses.

Completion: Finish the statement.

Teacher: Susan is tall, but . . .
Joan: Mary is taller.
Teacher: John is big, but . . .
Carol: Phil is bigger.

Expansion:

(See page 43 for more information on expanding sentences.)

Teacher: Steve is happy.
Chuck: Steve is happy because he finished his work.
Teacher: Milly is happy.
Ann: Milly is happy because she has a new dress.

Transformation: Change a given sentence to negative or interrogative form.

Teacher: Judy is here today.
Carol: Judy is not here today.
Teacher: Judy is here today.
Fred: Is Judy here today?

Restoration: Student makes sentences from a group of words.

Teacher: picture, wall, hanging
Chuck: The picture is hanging on the wall.
Phyllis: Is the picture hanging on that wall?

Response: Answer or make a rejoinder.

Teacher: It is chilly in this room.
Mary: It feels fine to me.
Jim: I think you are right.
Joan: Shall I close the door?

PITCH, STRESS, AND JUNCTURE

Linguists point out the varied shades of meaning possible through the spoken language which are not possible in written composition. Gestures and facial expression add meaning, as does the individual's use of intonation patterns, that is, stress, pitch, and juncture. What do we mean by these terms?

Stress: accent or loudness

Which word would you stress in the following sentences? Try stressing each word in turn.

What are you planning to do?

I'm not ready to go.

Who does he think he is!

Pitch: highness or lowness of tones

Which part of this sentence has the highest tone?

My name is Irene. (Can the pitch vary?)

Juncture: pauses (clues to punctuation in composition)

Can juncture change meaning? Explore the pauses in these sentences.

That lady is a queer bird.

Where did they find Joe's will?

Help somebody please.

Actually, to be more precise, the linguist notes four degrees of stress which can be marked in all speech, four degrees or levels of pitch, and four types of juncture according to the length of the pause. For our present purposes, however, it is sufficient to note the effect that each of these features of intonation has on meaning of the spoken language. We quickly notice the variation in meaning which is obtained by stressing different words in a sentence. There is truth in the statement: It isn't *what* you say, but *how* you say it, that matters. Students will enjoy experimenting with spoken language as they explore these concepts.

- **Tape several samples of student speech in the classroom. Analyze these samples sentence by sentence to note pitch which is recorded, thus:**

  2 1 1 4 3 3
  What are you doing here, Jim? (4 is high; 1 is low)

- **Work with several sentences on the board first so that disagreements can be discussed and the tape replayed to check points made. Then students can experiment with analyzing other sentences.**

- **Compare the different variations of pitch and stress possible in a simple interjection or phrase.**

  All right. (Say it with anger, annoyance, agreement, reluctance)
  Please.
  Go ahead and take it!
  Yes.
  No.

- **Compare the manner of speaking the same word in two different contexts. Is it exactly the same?**

What present did you give her?
Were you present when they arrived?

- Heteronyms provide provocative material for comparison of stress or accent as in these examples:

Did you present Mrs. Smithson with a present?
Should a rebel rebel?
Are you content with the content of his remark?
That magician standing in the entrance may entrance you.

- How does changing juncture change meaning? The results are often amusing. In what situation might the following have been appropriate?

"I will not hit any, Mother," she said sweetly.
"I will not hit any mother," she said sweetly.
"How will you help me?" he asked.
"How! Will you help me?" he asked.

Strategies for Speech Instruction

How can we teach students to speak effectively? Classroom instruction in oral language skills must be directed toward (1) providing many opportunities for speaking, (2) stimulating the child to want to speak, and (3) providing a supportive atmosphere. In this section we shall explore varied strategies to be used in the elementary school classroom to achieve these goals.

PROMISING PRACTICES IN ORAL LANGUAGE

As we observe in classrooms and talk to teachers throughout the nation, we note the use of specific techniques in promoting oral language, whether the person involved be a teacher working with primary or preschool boys and girls or an instructor of adults who are learning English as a foreign language. It is worthwhile to note a few of these general practices.

Small group work It is imperative that children work individually or in small groups (5–6) as they engage in activities designed specifically to develop speech abilities. This small group approach is especially well suited to a classroom with learning centers about the room. The advantages of the small group include:

1 A sense of security for children who are uncertain about language abilities
2 Greater opportunity for each individual to speak

3 A better diagnostic situation as the teacher strives to guide individual development

Unless a child is particularly aggressive (and the child who needs help with language is far from aggressive), he or she can be lost even in a group of twenty-five. It is interesting to analyze the amount of speaking that children actually do in the typical classroom. As noted in the preceding chapter, more than half of student time is spent in listening activities.[4] Speaking is more often done by the teacher than by class members.

Increased Focus on Oral Language Linguistics has pointed the way toward an emphasis on oral language in the elementary school. It has become evident that success in school depends on linguistic fluency and the development of an extensive vocabulary, and we note that speech development is related to later development in reading.

Why have teachers not stressed oral activities previously? A major deterrent is the unstructured nature of oral instruction and the fact that the teacher has had few materials to assist in developing oral abilities. There has been confusion about the aims of instruction in oral language with emphasis being placed largely on "correct usage." We have failed also, as in other aspects of elementary school English, to develop a sequential program for speech development.

Use of the tape recorder The tape recorder or cassette player is invaluable in speech development. Although all classrooms will not be equipped with language laboratory facilities, each can and should have a Listening and Speaking Center which is planned around a tape recorder fitted with earphones and microphones for listening and recording. In this way language development can be accomplished individually as children work with teacher-prepared tapes or those available commercially.

VARIETY IN CLASSROOM SPEAKING EXPERIENCES

Although children need many opportunities to engage in informal speaking situations, they also need a growing number of experiences in speaking with and before a group. There are various ways of providing speaking experiences in the classroom.

Discussion The most familiar form of speaking in the classroom is

[4] Miriam Wilt, "A Study of Teacher Awareness of Listening as a Factor in Elementary Education." *Journal of Educational Research* (April, 1950), pp. 626–36.

a discussion of a common topic which often arises from studies or activities undertaken by the class. These discussions may focus on:

- Answering questions to which there is no specific answer.
  Why did people move westward in the United States?
- Giving opinions about current issues.
  Should we continue spending money on space exploration?
- Solving a problem.
  How can our class raise enough money to go to Science Camp?
- Talking about ideas and feelings.
  What makes you happy?
  Would you like to live the life of Pippi Longstocking?
  What makes you feel uncomfortable?
- Talking about *What If.*
  What if pets could talk?
  What if I were invisible?
- Practicing an interview.
  How might you get a job babysitting or mowing lawns in your neighborhood?
  What questions might you ask a star baseball player or an expert rock hound?
- Practicing telephone conversations.
  How do you get information you need for a trip from the Auto Club?

Ability to participate successfully in discussions is a significant skill for an adult to acquire. Students can discuss what specific skills each should develop as a way of improving skill in discussion, for example:

- A feeling of responsibility for contributing to a group discussion.
- Ability to ask intelligent, pertinent questions.
- Willingness to listen to contributions of others.
- Ability to wait one's turn before speaking.

Assigned speaking Assigned speeches in the elementary school should never be long, and the topics assigned should allow for individual interests so that students are talking about topics which are interesting to them. Schedule delivery of speeches so there are never too many delivered at one time, for the whole class will lose enthusiasm if forced to listen to other students speaking for more than twenty minutes. Vary assigned speaking experiences, thus:

Explanation: How to do something.
How to make scrambled eggs
How to make money
How to make an impression
How to write a news story
Argument: Why I hold this opinion.
Girls are awful. (Boys are terrible.)
A woman should never be President of the United States.
We should reform our spelling system.
Everyone should know how to type.
No one should have to attend school unless he wants to.
No one should smoke cigarettes.
Humor: How these words came to be spoken.
"George, You are the cat's meow!"
"I got that story straight from the horse's mouth."
"Cross my heart and hope to die."

THE ART OF ASKING QUESTIONS

The inquiry method has drawn attention to the significance of question asking as a part of the thinking act. What kinds of questions are students asking? Are they sensible according to known information? Do they penetrate to the core of the problem? Students need experience in asking penetrating questions. They can be encouraged to compose more effective questions through some of the following methods:

Students write questions as they review a subject being studied. These questions can be asked during class to assist student review. From the questions submitted to the teacher, a number are selected to appear on the examination.

TWENTY QUESTIONS and ANIMAL, VEGETABLE, OR MINERAL? are games which encourage question asking. Students quickly learn the types of questions which best serve to narrow the field.

WHAT QUESTION WOULD YOU ASK? Given a specific situation, the student is requested to decide what question should be asked. Suggested questions are compared and discussed as to their merits, for example:

You are walking down the street when you notice a six-year-old boy you know on the roof of a house. WHAT QUESTION WOULD YOU ASK?
You are downtown alone when suddenly you find that you have lost your money. WHAT QUESTION WOULD YOU ASK?

Oral book reviews The oral book review provides a welcome relief from the overworked written book report form. Encourage students to explore novel ways of sharing books orally:

- Interview a character in the book. Two members of the class may share this review with one serving as the character to be interviewed.

- Give a first-person account of an event in the book read:

  Wilbur speaks, for example: "I tell you I was so lonesome I thought I'd die when suddenly I heard Charlotte's sweet voice . . ."

- Tape a portion of the story after having practiced reading that part of the book aloud in order to achieve the best interpretation.

- Present an award to the author of a prize-winning book (either for illustrations or for story content) explaining why this book was selected for the award.

- Prepare pictures of important incidents in a book. Then tell the story briefly as the pictures are shown. (This could be a scroll theater presentation prepared by several students who have read the same book.)

- Prepare a commercial to sell your book to your fellow students. This activity might involve several students and could be correlated with art.

Impromptu speaking The extemporaneous speech is presented without time for extensive planning and should be regarded as a "speech experiment." Certainly evaluation will take the form of praising any aspect of the experiment which turns out well. Sets of cards (3″ x 5″ file cards) can be developed with student assistance to provide stimulating topics for the short unrehearsed speech.

- *Quotations by famous people* [5]—Why I agree or disagree.

  You must look *into* people as well as at them.
  Lord Chesterfield

  Behavior is a mirror, in which everyone shows his image.
  Johann von Goethe

  No man is an Island, entire of itself.
  John Donne

  To be of use in the world is the only way to be happy.
  Hans Christian Andersen

[5] For additional quotations see *Quotes for Teaching* by Sidney W. Tiedt (San Jose, Calif.: Contemporary Press, 1964).

- *Small pictures*—how this illustration fits in a story.

- *Two words*—how these two words are related.

- *Questions*—answer the question.

  Have you ever been afraid?
  What is the funniest thing you have ever seen?
  What was the most exciting moment in your life?

- *Introductions*—Pretend you are asked to introduce a famous speaker. What would you say as you introduce:

  Mark Twain
  The President of the United States
  Theodore Geisel (Dr. Seuss)
  The Governor of your state

- *What do you do now?*—A card presents an improbable situation which the speaker reads aloud, concluding with his action. Motivate this speaking experience by reading from Sesyle Joslin's *What Do You Say, Dear?* (Harcourt). Cards can be written as a writing experiment after reading this book.

- *It's A Joke*—Read the joke on the card, and then tell it to the group without aid of the card.

- *Extra! Extra!*—Cut unusual headlines from old newspapers. Students may create "enchanting examples" by cutting out single words from the paper as needed. The speaker uses the headline as the topic for his speech.

LITERATURE MOTIVATES ORAL LANGUAGE EXPERIENCES

Literature serves as an excellent stimulus to oral language through expansion of ideas and vocabulary. Reading a title from children's literature provides a common body of knowledge about which the group can talk immediately without need to build up a background of information, for everyone can have an opinion about the book read. We can bring literature into the classroom as part of the oral language program, thus:

Sharing books Let's talk about books, use books, enjoy books together, for explorations in children's literature add to growth in reading, writing, general information, thinking, as well as speaking and listening. The following suggestions contribute to literature learning as well as oral language development.

READING TOGETHER. Small groups of students can form READING CIRCLES which meet at a specified time to read a book together. Each child takes a turn reading aloud, passing the book on when he is tired of reading. Emphasis is on enjoyment of the book in a group situation which brings readers together according to interests rather than abilities, for there is a need to learn to work with persons of mixed abilities. Time is spent on talking about points of interest as the story progresses.

WORDLESS BOOKS. In the Wordless Book the child creates literature himself, usually in an impromptu approach. A teacher can prepare a paperback booklet which may bear the title THE WORDLESS BOOK, or other titles may be used each of which suggests a story on a specific theme:

Tom's Adventures at the Beach
Camping in the Deep Woods

At a learning center several wordless books can be displayed with blank pages behind for writing down the story (of course, there can be more than one version) or tape cassettes for telling the story. Following is a selected list of commercially prepared wordless books:

Bobo's Dream by Martha Alexander. Dial Press, 1970.
Look What I Can Do by Jose Aruego. Charles Scribner's Sons, 1971.
What Whiskers Did by Ruth Carroll. Henry Z. Walck, 1965.
Shrewbettina's Birthday by John Goodall. Harcourt, Brace, 1971.
Look Again! by Tina Hoban. The Macmillan Co., 1971.
Making Friends by Eleanor Schick. The Macmillan Co., 1969.

Storytelling "Everyone is a potential storyteller," writes Ruth Sawyer, and she notes also that, whether conscious of it or not, "everyone has been telling stories since he learned to talk.[6] We all tell stories of things that have happened to us or our friends, often embroidering them a bit to add zest! We can encourage students to tell stories in the classroom with enthusiasm and effect by providing opportunities for telling stories and assisting students in finding good material for storytelling. Students will grow in self-esteem by finding ways to share their own experiences and use their own imaginations in telling stories.

RIDDLES AND JOKES: A first step in beginning storytelling might be the telling of riddles which have some story element. The joke contains a little more story content and requires much the same skill as the telling of a longer story. In each case practice is required, and close attention must be paid to the conclusion, the "punch line."

FAMILIAR STORIES: Young children will develop skill in following the sequence of a story as they tell stories cooperatively. "The Little Red Hen

[6] Ruth Sawyer, *"How To Tell a Story"* (New York: Compton's, n.d.), pp. 3–4. Reprint from *Compton's Pictured Encyclopedia.*

found a grain of wheat. What did she say then, Neil?" Each child contributes to the telling of this story, which may then be retold as the contributors stand in order before the class, each telling a line or two at the appropriate time. Legends, folktales, stories of mythology, fairy tales—all provide excellent storytelling material for the elementary school.

THE STORYTELLERS: A club can be formed of students who have special interest and ability in storytelling. This group can use varied approaches to storytelling, both individual and group, depending on the material. At times they can present samplings of their repertoire to an appreciative audience.

For students in the elementary school, storytelling is wisely directed toward short stories, verses, myths, folklore. Humor, surprise endings, and audience participation add to the effectiveness and the enjoyment of both performer and audience. The values of storytelling experiences include:

1 Attention to voice quality—pitch, tempo, enunciation.
2 Investigation of literature suiable for presentation, an interesting research project for able students.
3 A pleasurable combination of literature and language experiences, delight in words and their use.
4 Appreciation of literature—What makes a good story?

Almost all children's books can be used as storytelling material. Those which contain many illustrations can be used in storytelling before the child learns to read, for after hearing the story, he or she can retell it by following the illustrations. Bruno Munari's enchanting book, *Who's There? Open the Door* (World) is a favorite as is Albert Lamorisse's *The Red Balloon* (Doubleday). Children of all ages will enjoy retelling stories they have read and enjoyed. In addition we have listed here a selected few collections of short stories which provide excellent sources of storytelling material:

Anderson, Hans C., *Fairy Tales* (Walck).
Arbuthnot, May H., *The Arbuthnot Anthology* (Scott, Foresman).
Bacmeister, Rhoda, *Stories to Begin On* (Dutton).
De la Mare, Walter, *Tales Told Again* (Knopf).
Fenner, Phyllis, ed., *Giants and Witches and a Dragon or Two* (Knopf).
Hamilton, Edith, *Mythology* (Little, Brown).
Huber, Miriam B., *Story and Verse for Children* (Macmillan).
Kipling, Rudyard, *Just So Stories* (Doubleday).
Lang, Andrew, ed., *The Blue Fairy Book* (Longmans).
Leodhas, Sorchie, *Gaelic Ghosts* (Holt).
Sandburg, Carl, *Rootabaga Stories* (Harcourt).
Thorne-Thomsen, Gudren, ed., *East o' the Sun and West o' the Moon* (Harper).

Children can make up different endings to old favorites and tell them aloud; or, after hearing a good story read aloud, a group can do an add-on story. One student starts the story; then each participant in turn adds a few sentences.

Choric speaking Group recital of selections from literature, both poetry and prose, is an excellent technique for enriching the oral language program and for encouraging all children to speak. A wealth of material is appropriate for this purpose.

Poems are made for saying or reading aloud, for only through an oral approach to poetry do we truly get the full effect of the rhythm, the music of this phenomenon of language. Oral presentation of poems and verses, furthermore, permits a group to share the appreciation of the poet's work. In the chapter devoted to poetry we explore the use of a Voice Choir, but there is such a wide range of poetry available that we can add a few suggestions here without risk of duplicating our efforts.

- **Short humorous verse appeals to young children as well as to students in the intermediate grades. Stress clarity of enunciation, and a long questioning pause at the comma, when speaking this anonymous poem:**

A SLEEPER FROM THE AMAZON

A sleeper from the Amazon
Put nighties of his gra'mason—
  The reason, that
  He was too fat
To get his own pajamason.

- **An occasional Tongue Twister adds spice to speaking and adds to the child's awareness of wordplay:**

I saw Esau sawing wood [pause]
And Esau saw I saw him; [quickly]
Though Esau saw I saw him saw [pause]
Still Esau went on sawing.

A tutor who tooted the flute
Tried to tutor two tooters to toot.
Said the two to the tutor,
"Is it harder to toot, or
To tutor two tooters to toot?"

• Verses known to children, for example, rope-jumping songs, provide good rhythmical chants:

Not last night but the night before,
Twenty-four burglars at my door.
I went downstairs to let them in;
They hit me over the head
With a rolling pin!

• Combine actions with speaking a poem as in this selection from *Mother Goose:*

The noble Duke of York [majestically]
  He had ten thousand men.
He marched them up a very high hill; [last words quickly]
  Then he marched them down again.
And when he was up, he was up; [quickly]
  And when he was down, he was down; [quickly]
And when he was only halfway up
  He was neither *up nor down!* [distinctly]

• A poem that tells a story lends itself to clear enunciation and varied intonation:

THE SECRET

We have a secret, just we three,
The robin, and I, and the sweet cherry-tree;
The bird told the tree, and the tree told me,
And nobody knows it but just we three.

But of course the robin knows it best,
Because she built the—I shan't tell the rest;
And laid the four little—something in it
I'm afraid I shall tell it every minute.

But if the tree and the robin don't peep,
I'll try my best the secret to keep;
Though I know when the little birds fly about
Then the whole secret will be out.

UNKNOWN

• Repetition adds interest to a poem for younger children, and also makes it easier to learn.

SING OUT!

Sing, sing, sing;
Racing to the swing.

Hum, hum, hum;
Spring at last has come!

Call, call, call;
The grass is growing tall.

Shout, shout, shout;
School will soon be out!

IRIS M. TIEDT

- Older children will enjoy the humor and the actions of this delightful poem by William Makepeace Thackeray:

A TRAGIC STORY

There lived a sage in days of yore,
And he a handsome pigtail wore;
But wondered much and sorrowed more,
Because it hung behind him.

He mused upon this curious case,
And swore he'd change the pigtail's place,
And have it hanging at his face,
Not dangling there behind him.

Said he, "The mystery I've found—
I'll turn me round"—and he turned him round,
But still it hung behind him.

Then round and round, and out and in,
All day the puzzled sage did spin;
In vain—it mattered not a pin—
The pigtail hung behind him.

And right and left, and roundabout,
And up and down and in and out
He turned; but still the pigtail stout
Hung steadily behind him.

And though his efforts never slack,
And though he twist, and twirl, and tack,
Alas! still faithful to his back,
The pigtail hangs behind him.

Prose should not be ignored as a source of excellent material for speaking together. Explore the literature of the social sciences or combine storytelling techniques with choric speaking.

> Enrich a social studies experience by teaching children the Gettysburg Address, for there is no more beautiful piece of American literature than this famous speech:
>
>> Four score and seven years ago our fathers brought forth on this continent, a new nation, conceived in liberty, and dedicated to the proposition that all men are created equal.
>>
>> Now we are engaged in a great civil war, testing whether that nation, or any nation so conceived and so dedicated, can long endure. We are met on a great battlefield of that war. We have come to dedicate a portion of that field, as a final resting place for those who here gave their lives that that nation might live. It is altogether fitting and proper that we should do this.
>>
>> But, in a larger sense, we can not dedicate—we can not consecrate—we can not hallow—this ground. The brave men, living and dead, who struggled here have consecrated it, far above our poor power to add or detract. The world will little note, nor long remember, what we say here, but it can never forget what they did here. It is for us the living, rather, to be dedicated here to the unfinished work which they who fought here have thus far so nobly advanced. It is rather for us to be here dedicated to the great task remaining before us—that from these honored dead we take increased devotion to that cause for which they gave the last full measure of devotion—that we here highly resolve that these dead shall not have died in vain—that this nation, under God, shall have a new birth of freedom—and that government of the people, by the people, and for the people, shall not perish from the earth.
>
> Combine the arts of storytelling and choric speaking as several individual speakers, for example, tell the story of Wanda Cág's *Millions of Cats* with a chorus coming in on the repeated words which add so much to the story:
>
>> Hundreds of Cats, thousands of Cats, millions and billions and trillions of cats . . .

CREATIVE DRAMATIZATION

A way of stimulating speaking is through many forms of dramatization. The source of ideas for dramatization is endless, and variation in the form of dramatization is sufficiently wide to provide for all interests and abilities. As Winifred Ward explains:

> The term "creative dramatics" includes all forms of *improvised* drama—drama created by the children themselves and played with spontaneous

> dialogue and action. It begins with imaginative play of the young child, which mirrors life as the child sees and feels it, and is followed by simple story dramatizations. It also includes: creative plays based on ideas and on literature, dramatizations of incidents from the social studies, original dance, pantomimes, creative work in puppets and shadow plays, and integrated projects in which many of the subjects in the school program contribute to an adventurous play which the children create from a book or a story. . . .[7]

A major advantage of creative dramatics is that participants do not learn set parts or lines. For this reason they literally cannot "make a mistake." Varying from simple actions and dialogue to the dramatization of a lengthy story, this form of dramatics permits children to interpret roles freely. As Geraldine Siks observes:

> This freedom of imagination that characterizes child-thought is both the envy and terror of the adult. . . . Children in their own way are highly creative because of their innate freedom of imagination. . . . Creative dramatics utilizes and challenges the imagination of the child.[8]

Emphasis in creative dramatics is not on preparation of a drama to be presented before an audience, but on providing opportunity for the children to express themselves freely. All children will participate in the acting at one time when space and the type of dramatization permit, for there need be no audience at all. At other times one portion of the class, perhaps a third or a half, will participate while the others observe and await their own turns. An effective classroom arrangement for creative drama is the THEATER IN THE ROUND, with chairs forming a circle from which observers can readily view the action.

What are the advantages of dramatization as a way of developing language abilities? They include the following:

1 Pleasure is combined with learning.
2 Physical and social abilities are developed.
3 Freedom of action encourages the child's expression.
4 Preparatory discussion extends vocabulary and interests.

Specifically, we may choose to encourage language development through these enjoyable creative activities.

[7] Winifred Ward, *Creative Dramatics* (Washington, D.C.: Association for Childhood Education, 1961), p. 3.

[8] Geraldine B. Siks, *Children's Literature for Dramatization* (New York: Harper, 1964), pp. 1–3.

For an exciting collection of articles about drama in the classroom, see: *Elementary English*, January, 1974.

Pantomime A good dramatic activity to begin with; we include it here although the mime in performance uses no language.

Pantomime does include language, of course, as the children plan, talk about the mime's role, or try to guess what act is being mimed. Activities like these introduce children to creative dramatics.

GUESS WHAT I'M DOING: An interesting way to initiate experiments in pantomime is to ask students to mime an activity as others try to identify the activity depicted. Favorites are:

Peeling a banana and eating it
Unwrapping gum and chewing it, blowing bubbles
Opening an umbrella as it suddenly begins to rain
Person being bothered by a mosquito or fly
Petting a cat
Making a sandwich
Combing hair before a mirror

Variation: Bring a "magic bag" to class. Each student in turn reaches in and pulls out whatever he or she wishes—perhaps an ice cream cone, which they proceed to eat in pantomime, or a hair comb, or a tiny butterfly which they watch fly away. The first child to guess what is in the bag is the next to find another treasure in it.

INTERPRETING SITUATIONS: Briefly sketch a situation in pantomime. Have several groups try the same topic to see how the interpretation develops. Students enjoy suggesting *interesting* situations, for example:

Showing a bad report card to Mother and Dad
Teenage girls talking on the telephone
Father giving son first driving lesson
Two children watching puppies in a pet store window
Boy finds money, runs to store, buys candy
Child breaks vase, runs to hide

Finger play activities An oral activity that is particularly suitable for work with primary children is the finger play story which may aim at teaching some concept such as the difference between *left* and *right* or the order of the numerals in addition to encouraging young children to speak. "Ten Little Indians," usually sung, is an example of finger play that teaches children to count to ten while they are developing language abilities.

A favorite finger play is "Eency Weency Spider" which again is a song that has appeal for children. Children can also invent finger plays to accompany familiar songs, for example, "Three Blind Mice."

A wonderful story to motivate finger play activities after children have developed some familiarity with this technique is *A Handful of Surprises* by Anne Heather and Esteban Francés (Harcourt) which presents five puppets, named Mac, Marc, Tink, Tarc, and O'Tooley, who fight constantly but always stay together because each is a finger on the hand of Fleek, the clown. The story tells of their troubles and how they finally learn to get along together. (See illustration below.)

Puppetry. A form of dramatization which delights young people of all ages (up to ninety-five) is puppetry. Puppetry as a means of encouraging students to speak has many advantages, one of which is the hiding of the individual person who can then feel free to play a role with enthusiasm.

they are all hitched to the same hand!

Even the shyest third-grade boy can call out Maurice Sendak's wonderful line, "And now, let the wild rumpus start!" [9]

Puppets should be kept simple so that emphasis remains on the use rather than the construction, for our concern here is with language development. Simple, but effective, puppet heads can be made from:

Faces cut from magazines mounted on cardboard for stiffness
Styrofoam balls with features and hair pinned on
Toe of a sock stuffed with cotton or small rags
Layers of paper glued and dried over an orange or ball
Plasticine covered by white cloth
Papier mache strips glued around a small balloon

Encourage children to invent different kinds of original puppets. Clever puppets can be fashioned from almost any kind of scrap material:

Bottle caps (bugs with legs)
Walnut shells (wrinkled Indian faces)
Dixie cups stuck on popsicle sticks
Peanuts in shells (animals with tails, ears, legs added)
Potatoes and other vegetables (animals suggested by shapes)
Wooden spoons (faces painted on back of spoon)
Paper plates (glued to sticks; add hair, features)
Squares of cloth (tie knots for head and two hands) [10]

Dramatization of poetry Many poems have a great deal of narrative value which can be the basis for a skit, pantomime, or creative dramatization. For younger students the dramatic activity can take place after the teacher has read a poem to the class. "Jonathan Bing" is a good example which contains humor and a story which children can take turns portraying. Some teachers have several children be Jonathan at the same time while another group acts the part of the narrator who reminds Jonathan, "You can't go to court in pajamas, you know," sadly shaking their heads at the very thought.

Robert Louis Stevenson's "My Shadow" is another delightful poem when combined with dramatic play as a few children move according to the poem followed by "shadows" who imitate their behavior until the final verse when the shadow is left at home in bed.

[9] Maurice Sendak, *Where the Wild Things Are* (New York: Harper and Row, 1963).

[10] Sidney W. Tiedt and Iris M. Tiedt, *The Elementary Teacher's Complete Ideas Handbook* (Englewood Cliffs, N.J.: Prentice-Hall, 1965), p. 228.

MY SHADOW

I have a little shadow that goes in and out with me,
And what can be the use of him is more than I can see.
He is very, very like me from the heels up to the head;
And I see him jump before me, when I jump into my bed.

The funniest thing about him is the way he likes to grow—
Not at all like proper children, which is always very slow:
For he sometimes shoots up taller like an India-rubber ball,
And he sometimes gets so little that there's none of him at all.

He hasn't got a notion of how children ought to play,
And can only make a fool of me in every sort of way.
He stays so close beside me, he's a coward you can see;
I'd think shame to stick to nursie as that shadow sticks to me!

One morning, very early, before the sun was up,
I rose and found the shining dew on every buttercup;
But my lazy little shadow, like an arrant sleepyhead,
Had stayed at home behind me and was fast asleep in bed.

MULTIMEDIA TO MOTIVATE SPEECH

The use of multimedia is helpful in motivating children's speech. Records, tapes, films, filmstrips, slides, transparencies, the flannel board, pictures, bulletin board displays, and exhibits—all add variety and stimulus to the elementary school speech program. These media can be used in many ways as suggested in the following discussion.

Films Many fine films are being developed. Some present a title from children's literature visually, which extends the child's vocabulary and provides a source of discussion topics after the viewing. A variety of films of excellent books and stories are available from Weston Woods, Weston, Conn., among them *The Sorcerer's Apprentice, A Snowy Day,* and *The Doughnut Machine* (from *Homer Price*).

Another type of film which presents interesting possibilities to motivate both speech and writing is the "wordless" film. A beautiful example is *Rainshower* (Churchill Films, 662 N. Robertson Blvd., Los Angeles, Calif. 90069), a 15-minute film in color. The expert photography focuses on the effects of rain in the country compared to the effects in the city—the mother runs to get washing from the line, the geese move ponderously toward the poultry yard, the parched ground soaks up the first drops—and only natural sounds are heard.

A short filmed story without sound is *The Hunter in the Forest* (Encyclopaedia Britannica Film Company, Wilmette, Ill.) which portrays the story of a hunter. Again, fine photography depicts the hunter's experiences as he bags a game bird and finally sights a family of deer. Does he shoot? Some teachers find this moment an effective stopping place for writing or discussion, after which the remainder of the film is shown.

Flannel board An effective device for assisting language development is the flannel board, a device much used by primary teachers but less commonly employed in intermediate grades. It has distinct advantages for instruction at all levels, for the flannel board:

1 Provides the shy speaker with a "prop"
2 Guides students through a sequence
3 Motivates student interest
4 Combines visual and oral activities.

Figures prepared by students will guide the class in retelling stories, finger play activities, choric speaking of poetry, and singing songs which have many verses. These figures can be cut from flannel, felt, or construction paper backed with sandpaper, but perhaps most satisfactory is *pellon,* a synthetic innerlining material that is sold in any fabric store.

Children in the primary grades will benefit from a guided recitation of "This Is the House That Jack Built."

THE HOUSE THAT JACK BUILT

This is the house that Jack built.

This is the malt
That lay in the house that Jack built.

This is the rat,
That ate the malt
That lay in the house that Jack built.

This is the cat,
That killed the rat,
That ate the malt
That lay in the house that Jack built.

This is the dog,
That worried the cat,
That killed the rat,
That ate the malt
That lay in the house that Jack built.

Other songs and stories for this purpose are: "Old MacDonald Had a Farm," "The Farmer in the Dell," "The Mulberry Bush," *Goldilocks and the Three Bears, Three Little Pigs,* and *The Little Red Hen.*

Suitable for presentation via the flannel board in the intermediate grades are poems, for example, "Poor Old Woman," "Jonathan Bing," as well as songs, "I Gave My Love a Cherry," "The Frog Went A-Courtin'," and other folk songs. Students enjoy the repetitive song, "Green Grass Grows All Around," for which we have provided the words and music.

Tape a class-created poem or story with suitable musical background if desired. Using 16mm leader the students can create an art film to go with the tape for a multimedia experience. Each student draws with permanent inked felt pens small designs of his choice on a three-foot section of the film leader. If desired, the art film can be drawn first and the poem created orally by the class while viewing it, then typed on ditto, read aloud by the class as a choral poem, and recorded.

Records Again, recorded stories supply stimulating materials for discusion and for developing vocabulary. A fairy tale is featured, for example, in *Emperor's Nightingale* (Folkways/Scholastic Records, 906 Sylvan Ave., Englewood Cliffs, N.J. 07632).

We highly recommend the recording of *Ruth Sawyer, Storyteller,* who captures the listener from the moment she says, in the traditional Spanish manner, "Once there was and was not . . ." Two records by this author and storyteller are available from Weston Woods, Weston, Conn.

Tapes The use of the tape recorder has a fascination of its own whether individuals are recording or the teacher is recording the whole group. Once children become accustomed to the recorder through frequent use, they lose any fear of recording or being recorded. The flexibility of recording devices and the availability of inexpensive tape make this medium invaluable in working with speech development. The following uses of the tape recorder are recommended:

- Older children can tape stories for use in Listening Centers in primary grades. Primary teachers can request specific titles for which uppergrade students volunteer, for practice is required to produce a well-read recording.

- In the same way, record materials for blind students. This would be an excellent project for a student SPEAKER'S CLUB.

- Tape speeches made by students so each can hear his/her own speech for purposes of evaluation. Tape a discussion to determine ways of improving discussion techniques. Also a conversation or interview might be taped.

- Record poetry to accompany a group of illustrative slides from parent or teacher collections. Advanced students who have access to a camera might develop a series of slides specifically for use with certain titles which they enjoy.

- Use a teacher-prepared recording which assists the child in developing sentence patterns. The child repeats patterned sentences spoken first by the teacher, thus:

  Jimmy has a dog.
  Jimmy has ____________. (Child supplies "a dog.")
  Jimmy has a black dog.
  Jimmy has ____________.
  Jimmy has a big black dog.
  Jimmy has ____________.
  Jimmy has a big black dog. Can you say the whole sentence?
  ____

- Patterns can be developed to focus student learning on any aspect of language development—phonology, vocabulary development, sentence structure.

EVALUATING SPEAKING

As in all language experience, evaluation should be the responsibility of both student and teacher, and it should always be constructive in nature. Speaking should never become a traumatic experience. Evaluation should be directed toward helping the student improve, a goal which will most readily be achieved with the elementary school student through positive reinforcement rather than the shocked, "No, no" equivalent of the red pencil. Evaluation of speaking must take place immediately, for the effectiveness of the evaluation diminishes considerably with passage of time unless the speech is recorded. We shall explore techniques of evaluation which have been helpful in working with young students.

Note from teacher to speaker After hearing the student deliver a "speech" the teacher writes a short note to the individual who spoke, saying perhaps:

Dear Brian,
You spoke clearly, and the class enjoyed your story.
I liked your description of Onion John.
Mrs. K.

Taped replay The teacher (or a student) tapes the several speeches given at one time. Later Jerry has an opportunity to "hear himself as others hear him." He is asked to make *one* specific suggestion which will help him improve his next speech.

Student evaluation This technique must be used with care, for students can be brutal. The whole class should, therefore, be taught the purposes of "criticism," and they should be encouraged to use positive criticism when evaluating a fellow student's speaking. The following suggestions may serve to guide student evaluation in a more positive direction:

Have only three students (rotate positions) evaluate any speaker. These three serve as the critics, and the remainder of the class is observant not only of the speaker's abilities but also of the abilities of the critics.

Have one group of five students complete evaluation forms for the speech delivered. An evaluation form similar to that illustrated can be developed by the class.

Focus on one aspect of speech As in the evaluation of writing, speaking is more accurately evaluated if students are told in advance that they are to focus attention on the introduction, the use of gestures, the use of humor, or another specific component of the speech. All other aspects of the delivery except that specified are then ignored in evaluation.

ORAL PRESENTATION

	Possible	Achievement	Comments
Interest			
Enthusiasm of speaker	5		
Audience response	5		
Expression of voice	5		
Gesture, movement of hands	5		
Friendly attitude	5		
Total	25		
Voice			
Enunciation, clearness	5		
Pronouncing words	5		
Volume	5		
Use of words (meaning)	5		
Tempo	5		
Total	25		
Organization			
Introduction, effect	5		
Organized points	5		
Knowledge of material	5		
Conclusion	5		
Total	20		
Bearing			
Rising to speak	5		
Eye contact	5		
Posture	5		
Movement of body	5		
Total	20		

Test the results For specific types of speeches the effectiveness of the speaking can be tested by noting the results. In telling a joke, for example, the effectiveness can be judged by the audience response, laughter. When the student is assigned to explain how to do something, the success may be based on the ability of the group in general to follow the directions given.

Books to Investigate

Calder, Clarence R., Jr., and Antan, Eleanor M. *Techniques and Activities to Stimulate Verbal Learning*. New York: The Macmillan Co., 1970.

Chambers, Dewey W. *Storytelling and Creative Drama*. Dubuque, Ia.: Wm. C. Brown Co., 1970.

Cullum, Albert. *Shake Hands with Shakespeare*. New York: Citation Press, 1967.

Henry, Mabel Wright. *Creative Experiences in Oral Language*. Urbana, Ill.: National Council of Teachers of English, 1967.

McCaslin, Nellie. *Creative Dramatics in the Classroom*. New York: David McKay Co., 1968.

Moffett, James. *Drama: What Is Happening*. Urbana, Ill.: National Council of Teachers of English, 1967.

———. *Teaching the Universe of Discourse*. New York: Houghton Mifflin Co., 1968.

Phillips, Gerald M.; Dunhem, Robert E., et al. *The Development of Oral Communication in the Classroom*. Indianapolis: Bobbs-Merrill Co., 1970.

Possieu, Wilma M. *They All Need to Talk*. New York: Appleton-Century-Crofts, 1969.

Ross, Ramon R. *Storyteller*. Columbus, Ohio: Charles E. Merrill Publishing Co., 1972.

Sawyer, Ruth. *The Way of the Storyteller*. New York: Viking Press, 1955.

Shaftel, Fannie R., and Shaftel, George. *Role-Playing for Social Values*. Englewood Cliffs, N.J.: Prentice-Hall, 1967.

Siks, Geraldine Brain. *Creative Dramatics, An Art for Children*. New York: Harper and Row, 1958.

Wagner, Joseph A. *Children's Literature Through Storytelling*. Dubuque, Iowa: Wm. C. Brown Co., 1970.

Ward, Winifred. *Drama With and For Children*. Washington, D.C.: U.S. Government Printing Office, 1960.

communicating through writing

chapter 11

We are all apprentices in a craft where no one ever becomes a master.

Ernest Hemingway

Composition has the distinct advantage of representing a totally individualized approach to learning, for each child produces to the extent of his or her abilities. The teacher prepares the class to write through discussion, explanation, and suggestion; but after that it becomes an individual matter. Some children will require supportive encouragement as they move toward feeling secure about composing, whereas others will move ahead independently with confidence.

Problems of Composition Instruction

Instruction in composition has long been criticized by college instructors who decry the inability of college entrants to write coherently. Of course, the high school instructor is blamed. In the usual pecking order fashion, the high school blames the elementary school teacher.

Let us turn from this fruitless attempt to place blame and concentrate instead on studying the problems of teaching composition which may lead us toward more effective methods. Why have we been relatively unsuccessful in teaching writing? Might not some of the reasons be these?

1 The lack of a developmental sequence in writing so that children really do write at all levels.
2 Failure of all teachers to assume responsibility for the teaching of writing skills.
3 Teachers' lack of knowledge about English grammar and usage and their relationship to teaching writing.
4 No clearly defined aims for teaching composition.
5 Rigid approaches to evaluation which overwork the teacher and discourage the student.
6 The fact that writing is a difficult skill to learn.

SEQUENTIAL DEVELOPMENT IN WRITING

One of the problems in the English curriculum is the need for established sequences of learning based on both the needs and the abilities of children as well as on the nature of the content to be introduced. What experiences shall we include in a developmental sequence in composition?

PRIMARY (KG, 1-2)

Storytelling and dramatization
Dictation of stories—individually and as groups
Extension of vocabulary, experiential backgrounds
Writing of sentences and phrases, paragraph stories
Introduction to four basic sentence patterns and noun and verb classes
Experiments in expanding patterns through compounding and modification
Composing poetry—free verse, couplet, triplet, cinquain
Increased awareness of words through word play, discovery, experimenting
Skills of punctuation—period, question mark

INTERMEDIATE (3,4,5)

Many experiments in writing creatively
Poetry—free verse, haiku, limerick, quatrain
Review and extension of basic sentence patterns
Expanding through compounding, modification, and subordination
Identification of word classes—noun, verb, adjective, adverb
Introduction to the function words and their uses
Vocabulary development through analogical substitution in patterns, use of dictionary, exploration
Use of literary models in writing
Focus on writing the sentence and paragraph
Developing concepts of imagery—simile, metaphor

Word study—homonyms, synonyms, antonyms, heteronyms, affixes
Word play to extend interest in vocabulary development and in use of words
Writing skills emphasized in all subject areas
Beginning research techniques—outlining, note taking, library tools

ADVANCED (6,7,8)

Increased coordination of composition and literature study
Development of abilities of composing sentences and paragraphs
Writing the short story—beginning, setting, dialogue, characterization
Writing of nonfiction—articles, reviews, reports
Continued use of expansion techniques with basic sentence patterns—compounding, subordination, modification, apposition
Review of word classes and function words
Poetry appreciation and composition—free verse, quatrain, ballad, triplet, invented forms
Study of imagery in writing—simile, metaphor, symbolism
Use of irony, satire, personification, alliteration, onomatopoeia
Experiments with words—word play, use of thesaurus, discovery
Advanced research techniques—library tools, bibliography, conducting a research study

AIMS OF THE COMPOSITION PROGRAM

What are the aims of instruction in composition? According to Guth:

> A writing course cannot miraculously widen and enrich the student's experience but neither can it teach skill in a vacuum. What it can at least start to do is to teach disciplined self-expression, responsible interpretation of experience, articulate participation in the public dialogue.[1]

Writing is more than knowledge of sentence structure, parts of speech, punctuation, and spelling. It requires involvement of the author who expresses ideas; the author is revealed through writing. He or she must have something to say, a conviction, and be able to focus sentences toward that end. As LaBrant states:

> Writing, put down—word by word—selected ideas to a selected audience, is a labor, often painful, an ability to be improved by repetition, an act carrying both privilege and responsibility. It is neither learned nor taught without effort . . . But writing . . . is the culmination of language skills. There is great satisfaction in controlling writing and in producing a story, statement, poem, descriptive unit.[2]

[1] Hans Guth, "Rhetoric and the Quest of Certainty," *College English* (November, 1962), p. 136.
[2] Lou LaBrant, "Writing Is More Than Structure," *English Journal* (May, 1957), p. 256.

A writing program should aim to enable students:

To enjoy expressing ideas in a creative way
To write with clarity
To organize ideas for a coherent presentation of information
To use mechanical skills in composition to aid communication
To evaluate and edit individual work
To appreciate the writing abilities of others
To develop confidence in ability to write through many successful writing experiences

WRITING—A SHARED RESPONSIBILITY

Composition is not a skill, or composite of skills, to be strictly limited to a period designated as "English," for composition is an integral part of all areas of the elementary school curriculum. No teacher and no subject is unconcerned with composition, for we use written language in many contexts and in varied ways. For example, we use writing in:

diaries
announcements
directions
research reports
notes
answers to questions
book reviews
letters
news articles
speeches
evaluations
minutes of a meeting
results of experiments
words to music
reviews of films or television programs
jokes

Every teacher, therefore, should have some background in modern concepts of language, if for no other reason than to be familiar with the vocabulary of English. Teachers should also understand the aims of teaching composition to ensure that their "teaching of composition" is in keeping with the goals toward which other teachers are also directing their efforts.

PRIMARY-GRADE CHILDREN CAN WRITE

Often teachers of the primary grades, particularly the first grade, feel that writing has little to offer them. It is surprising, however, how much can be accomplished by these enthusiastic young students who are capable of doing almost anything.

During kindergarten and the beginning months of first grade, writing activities can be oral, for oral language leads directly to written language. The same activities described in this chapter for motivating writing can be adapted to oral approaches as children learn to think, and we develop *writing readiness*. A good atmosphere for writing is created naturally as the children learn language skills.

Dictation An activity which lends itself to this period of language development is the dictated sentence, story, or poem which can be handled in a number of different ways. One way to begin is to encourage students to share personal experiences. One morning, for instance, children may contribute ideas like these which the teacher prints directly on the chalkboard or on a large sheet of tagboard mounted on an easel:

Today is Tuesday, November 11 . . .
Julie has a new baby brother, David.
Steve lost a tooth this morning.
Jill is wearing her birthday dress today.

What are the advantages of this type of group dictation? The children are learning to use words to express ideas. They are learning to make simple sentences, and they are becoming oriented to words in print reading from left to right. As the teacher prints their sentences, they soon notice, too, the use of capital letters and marks of punctuation.

Later children learn to copy and to read this type of group dictation. After the class has taken a field trip to the fire station, the experience story dictated might read like this:

Yesterday we went to the fire station.
The fire station is close to our school.
We saw the hook and ladder wagon.
We saw the firemen's dog, Flame.
We heard the fire bell ring.

Another variety of group dictation is the short story or poem which the group composes orally. The teacher records this story as it develops sentence by sentence. You might begin by asking the class what animal they would like to write about, and someone might suggest a cat or dog, or sometimes there is a more adventurous suggestion of a tiger, an elephant, or a bear. The teacher's conversation with the class, as they prepare to "write," might proceed thus:

> All right, we will write a story about a dog. I'll need your help. Are you all ready to write with me? (They will nod enthusiastically or answer aloud.) Now what shall we name this dog? (Jock) Good, Jock's a fine name for a dog. Let's imagine what Jock looks like, so we all have a picture in our minds of the dog in our story. What color is Jock? (black) How big is he? (About two feet high and a yard long demonstrated by a volunteer.)
>
> Can you all picture Jock now—a black dog, about so big . . . ? What is Jock doing today? (Jock is playing with a little girl, Susan.) Fine, that's a good place to begin our story. Who would like to make the first sentence? (One day Jock was playing with Susan.) What might happen next?

So the story grows with the help and encouragement of the teacher who sees that each student gets a chance to participate in some way. The story is then typed for inclusion in the class Storybook, or it may be printed with a felt pen on a large sheet for use in reading activities.

A variation of group dictation is individual dictation, which is an excellent device but requires more teacher time or the assistance of a clerk, a parent, or an older child. Each student is given an opportunity to sit on the STORY CHAIR beside a primary typewriter. Ed tells his story while the typist records it. Individually dictated stories can be duplicated for use as reading material, or they may be stapled in book form with an attractive cover decorated by the author. Eddie is eager to read his story to his parents, and because he *wrote* the story himself, he reads it easily. This activity aids in developing orientation to the format of the book, left-to-right movement of reading and writing, and adds to the individual's feeling of personal potency. *He* can tell a story which is important enough to be typed, to be recorded, so that all can read it.

A modification of this idea is the use of the cassette tape recorder. The youngster can dictate his or her story into the recorder, and it can be transcribed at a later date.

Writing independently As soon as first-grade students learn the rudiments of printing, they are intrigued by printing words, many of which they soon learn to spell. Very quickly they can compose a sentence or two expressing the ideas which they have depicted in a painting. They can also compose several sentences based on a topic introduced on the chalkboard by the teacher such as these:

- **What do you do *on Sunday*?**

  Students are directed to begin the first sentence thus:

  On Sunday I . . .

  go to the park.
  visit my grandmother.
  go shopping.
  play ball.

- **What do you *like* best *to play*? (I like to play. . .)**

- **What *is your favorite food*? (My favorite food is . . .)**

Help can be given with spelling by printing requested words on the chalkboard or on the student's paper, although many teachers prefer to encourage spelling by sound so that writing is not inhibited by the need to make every word letter-perfect. There is little doubt that concern with spelling slows the child in recording ideas; spelling will improve as children add to their knowledge of words.

Once students have learned a simple writing vocabulary, they are ready to write creatively, for writing is an area that allows each child to progress and to produce at his or her own level of ability. The more able child may write six good sentences, while a slow child writes only one simple idea. Each is progressing, however, and can continue to progress through adulthood.

TEACHING GRAMMAR AND USAGE IN RELATIONSHIP TO COMPOSITION

As was noted in Chapter 2, Language Study, many educators have mistakenly conceived of the teaching of grammar as consisting of drill along these lines:

Choose the right word:
Gwen has (gone–went) to school.
Where have Billy and Brian (gone–went)?
They (gone–went) home already.

Work with sentences of this nature emphasizes specific points of usage (not grammar). There remains, however, much doubt about the transfer of the supposedly acquired knowledge to writing or to speaking. Children are just as likely to say, "The girls have went to the movie," after having completed the above exercise as they would if they had never been exposed to the drill.

How do we learn usage and grammar? We learn through our ears, and it may be that certain usage patterns which "sound right" to us may not "sound right" to others because of exposure to different language backgrounds. This is an example of levels of usage and the acceptability of specific usage in varied situations.

As outlined in Chapter 2, we also help children discover grammar, the structure of English sentences. They learn to recognize basic sentence patterns and to identify word classes. This information, however interesting, does little to increase the child's writing fluency, the ability to write freely. In fact, if the study of sentence structure is substituted for composing, that is, experience in writing, then the study of grammar will actually have a detrimental effect on composition, for the child is being denied valuable opportunities to write.

We must move beyond mere exercises in noting structure and classifying words, as in the case with usage, in order to develop ability to write. You learn to write by writing, by using words to communicate ideas. It is in the expansion of basic sentence patterns through (1) modification, (2) compounding, (3) subordination, and (4) apposition that the young writer may reach out toward more mature, varied ways of expressing ideas. The following basic sentence is an example representing the simplest of patterns containing only a noun and a verb:

Karen swam. (Pattern I, N-V)
Karen *swam and sunbathed.* (Compounding)
Karen swam and sunbathed *at the beach.* (Modification)
Karen, *the tall girl,* swam and sunbathed at the beach. (Apposition)
When she was on vacation, Karen, the tall girl, swam and sunbathed at the beach. (Subordination)

The development of ability in writing which can be assisted through practice of this nature has little to do with identification of word classes. It is not necessary, for instance, that children know that they are *compounding the predicate* when they use two verbs, "swam and sunbathed," instead of just "swam." We can just as effectively extend an idea being expressed by asking pertinent questions, thus:

What else did Karen do besides *swim?*
Where did she swim and sunbathe?
How can we describe Karen?
When did she swim?

This experiment in expansion of a very simple sentence would, of course, be followed by numerous other experiments each of which suggests variations. The student learns to extend ideas, not just add *a prepositional phrase, a clause,* or *an apposition,* for we are concerned with communicating ideas rather than with the terminology of these structural features. We might find Rudyard Kipling's short verse useful in extending ideas:

I keep six honest serving men
(They taught me all I know);
Their names are WHAT, and WHY, and WHEN
and HOW and WHERE and WHO.

We must be careful, therefore, that we do not become so involved with instruction in usage and grammar that we spend an undue amount of time on drill, a teaching technique that is familiar to us, but that has been proved to be less than effective. We must be jealous in our allocation of student time, for time is limited, and it must be used for the greatest good of the student. We must constantly question ourselves concerning the degree to which we are achieving the goals for English instruction.

I can't write five words but that I change seven.
Dorothy Parker

THE EVALUATION PROCESS

As a teacher, Dusel noted, "Teaching English composition is very much like giving a party: first there is the excitement of making all the preparations; next, the satisfaction of seeing the whole group busy expressing themselves; then the clock strikes and they leave you alone with a sink full of dirty dishes." [3] Unfortunately, this "sink full of dirty dishes" overwhelms many teachers and even leads them to the conclusion that composition is too much trouble, with the result that their students seldom write. It is important, therefore, that we tackle the problem of evaluation realistically.

What has been the typical approach to evaluation of student writing? In general, teachers have diligently read every paper the child wrote, marking spelling, punctuation, paragraphing, fragments of sentences. The red pencil has been wielded precisely, dogmatically, authoritatively. Is it possible that the teacher of today needs to rethink approaches to evaluation? Have we established too rigid a pattern of

[3] William Dusel, "How Should Student Writing Be Judged?" *English Journal* (May, 1957), p. 263.

evaluating composition, following the lead of teachers who evaluated our own composition?

Methods of guiding and evaluating writing must reflect the philosophy stated in our objectives of teaching children to write. To achieve these objectives we must avoid discouraging student writing endeavors by authoritarian approaches to evaluation. This is not to say that student writing is never to be reworked; we simply advocate a different emphasis in evaluation. The teacher cannot, for example, tear a story to shreds and still retain the student's sense of personal worth or an atmosphere conducive to free expression. Strickland[4] emphasizes the importance of security, interest, and constructive attitudes for the young writer. She terms the grading of papers and assigning of marks as inappropriate for beginning stages of language development. It is for these reasons that we recommend the following general rules for guiding student development in writing without discouraging the student:

Praise sincerely in public.
Make corrections and suggestions in private.

There are a number of methods for evaluating student work and making criticism which will assist the growth of writing ability without injuring an individual student's development as a person. Described here are examples of evaluation and guidance techniques which have been found successful in the elementary school classroom.

Individual conferences While students are writing independently, individuals are called to a table where the teacher reviews their writing with them. The work is examined together, and the teacher suggests areas for improvement verbally, simply underlining words which require a change. This method is effective for at least two reasons. First, it is much easier to explain orally the suggestions the teacher wishes to make about sentence structure or the development of a character than it is to write the comments on the paper. The teacher is able to determine whether the student understands the suggestions by questioning or having her or him make the changes orally before returning to work.

Another vital attribute of the individual conference bears on the personal relationship with the student, for the individual attention given the student is uplifting and rewarding to that student. Even Bill, a less verbal student, a student who receives less attention during regular class sessions, has a time for talking to the teacher about his work. For that brief period the teacher's attention is reserved for him. The

[4] Ruth Strickland, "The Language of Elementary School Children," *Bulletin of the School of Education,* Indiana University (July, 1962), pp. 1–131.

conference offers the teacher a way for getting better acquainted with more reticent students.

One or two conferences can be scheduled each day so that each student has about one individual conference per month. Since writing is such an individualized approach, students may be working on different projects as they complete specific writing experiments. Each student should be permitted to select the writing to discuss with the teacher during the conference. If, each week, the conference schedule for the coming week is announced, students will have time to complete or prepare a selection for examination.

Teacher correction Many teachers (and some school districts enforce this approach) feel that they must read everything that a student writes; they would not send home any written work without a grade on it. These teachers feel it is mandatory for them to mark every error in spelling, grammar, usage, and punctuation. If students write every day both in school and at home, it is literally impossible for the teacher to accomplish this enormous task. It is perhaps this task alone which has accounted for the failure to encourage students to write daily. What is the answer to this problem?

The answer is obvious although not always acceptable to teachers who resist changes in philosophy. The teacher should *make no attempt to read everything the students write*. Maize's study [5] of remedial students points up the validity of this approach. The control group in this study was taught punctuation, grammar, and spelling and wrote fourteen different compositions which were carefully corrected by the teacher. The experimental group, in contrast, wrote forty different compositions and did not receive formal instruction in punctuation, grammar, and spelling. Their writing was corrected and discussed during class time and was not personally read or graded by the instructor. The experimental group showed greater improvement in usage and writing ability.

Other approaches to evaluation of student writing need to be explored. Reading only representative selections each week has proved just as effective in guiding development. If all writing is placed in the student's writing folder, then one day each week can be designated for reviewing the writing that has been done and for the selection by each student of one piece of writing to be completed, proofread, and copied to turn in for evaluation.

There are varied ways to handle the task of making corrections on any piece of writing. Detailed corrections made with the formidable red

[5] Ray C. Maize, "A Study of Two Methods of Teaching English Composition to Retarded College Freshmen," Doctoral dissertation, Purdue University, 1952.

pencil in many cases serve only to discourage and to confuse. It is considered wiser, therefore, to focus the types of corrections made, thus:

The red pencil can be used to underline interesting imagery or the use of unusual words, in other words, to indicate teacher approval. When returning papers, the teacher must explain this novel approach or the students will immediately assume the underlined material is in error.

Marking for only one type of error on a set of papers is another way of focusing attention, and perhaps teaching more effectively. One set of papers, for example, can be examined for punctuation ability. Upon the return of these papers comments are made about common errors in punctuation.

The use of proofreading marks assists the teacher in noting common errors without undue effort and with less student confusion. Students will be interested in learning marks actually used by editors, or the class can develop a set of marks which have meaning for them:

¶ Begin a new paragraph here.
^ Insert comma (or other punctuation mark).
sp Spelling error.
U Usage.
S Not a sentence.
* Excellent choice of words!
ℓ Eliminate this word or phrase.

Types of assignments made The task of evaluation is facilitated if both teacher and student have a clear idea of the focus of the assignment. A short, focused assignment is more effective than a vague, lengthy project, for sheer length of effort seldom produces quality writing. It is far better that a student be able to write one or two polished sentences or a well-organized paragraph expounding one idea than that he or she be able to produce a theme of 500 words (counted to the last *a*). Try some of these ideas.

- Who is Michael Phant?

  Who might this man be? Where does he live?
  What is he doing? What does he look like?
  Compare the character sketches of this imaginary person.

- Create a mood.

  Imagine you are in a specific place. Is it hot or cold there?
  How do you like this place?
  Use words to convey the mood of the place.

- Write recipes.

  Use Marjorie Winslow's book, *Mud Pies and Other Recipes* (Macmillan) to motivate children to write humorous recipes like this:

Pencil Sharpener Pudding

Pour the contents of a pencil sharpener into a bowl. Add enough puddle water to soften and stir with a sharp pencil. Allow to set in the shade, either in the bowl or in individual dishes.

Publicizing student writing One of the most effective methods for guiding and evaluating student writing in a concrete fashion is through publicizing work that is well done. Of course, care must be taken that each student receives some measure of publicity for writing. Publicize writing in a variety of ways:

Displays on the classroom bulletin board can feature writing. A display might, for example, focus on a large picture mounted in the center of the board around which are pinned paragraphs written by each student based on this picture. Collections of writings can be made including something by each student. If you are writing tall tales, call the book WHOPPERS!

A student publication can be produced periodically bearing an appropriate title: REFLECTIONS, IMPRESSIONS, SHOWCASE, SPICE, VENTURE. Different types of writing can be featured, from interesting phrases to short stories so that all have a chance to write. The entire group can take part in "publishing."

Kids' Definitions

Nothing: Nothing is a balloon with its skin removed.

Comma: A comma is when you swallow your spit and go on.

Many teachers see composition as an easy subject to teach—just assign a topic and let the students write. To be truly effective, however, the teacher must assume responsibility for (1) motivating, (2) providing many opportunities for writing, (3) developing rapport with the group, (4) extending experiential backgrounds to supply content for writing, and, perhaps most important, (5) appreciating the results of student efforts.

The teacher can guide students to the development of a statement of aspects of writing which should be avoided and those toward which each should constantly be striving, thus:

What are we trying to achieve?
- Writing that indicates thought
- Use of exciting words which create effects
- Completeness, conciseness, and clarity
- Variety of content, words, sentence patterns

What are we trying to avoid?
- Passive, inactive verbs
- Overworked phrases, clichés
- Misplaced modifiers
- Wordiness, tautology
- Vague references
- Sweeping generalizations

Introduction of the terminology of composition assists the young writer in developing a vocabulary with which to discuss writing. Note, too, that the skills and concepts of composition discussed here represent ways of thinking as well as of writing, for writing reflects thought. It is a way of expressing thought. Students can be exposed to these concepts at their levels of ability.

PUNCTUATION

Punctuation, like spelling, has been overemphasized as an aspect of composition. Again, we stress the importance of placing primary emphasis in composition on the ideas expressed rather than on the mechanics of recording the ideas. On the other hand, knowledge and use of punctuation does facilitate communication as Charlton Laird illustrates:

> icertainlyshallnotkeepthisuplongitevenlooksrepulsive
>
> if you made anything of that you have the key to make something of this too but i shall not keep this one going very long either
>
> These samples represent an attempt/ to write modern english in ways that suggest writing in earlier days/ when there was no punctuation/ or when punctuation was not standardized as it is now/ this particular style is one used by the first english printer William Caxton/ who used a period to mark a paragraph.
>
> th's 's ' st'll "rl"r 'n' 's'd d'r'ng ' t'm' wh'n 'v'n v'w'ls w'r' 'nd'c't'd b' p'nct"t"n [6]

We can also observe humorous, and sometimes disastrous, effects of punctuation either misused or omitted as in these examples:

[6] Charlton Laird, *A Writer's Handbook* (Boston: Ginn, 1964), p. 358.

Don't! Stop!
Don't stop.

No help is coming.
No, help is coming.

Seventy-nine and thirty are the winning numbers.
Seventy, nine, and thirty are the winning numbers.

"Shift!" he cried.
"Shift?" he cried.

How might we punctuate these words?
What are you giving him dope
She bought a car coat and riding boots
Paula Marie Susan and Kathy were absent

Skill in using punctuation can be greatly assisted by knowledge of the intonation patterns of our speech. As we listen to a sentence, we can usually hear the pauses, the *juncture,* which may require punctuation to aid the reader in correctly interpreting what has been written. The falling pitch and full pause, for example, tell us clearly that a period is needed, whereas a slight pause may indicate a comma. Speak these sentences, noting the type of punctuation indicated by the juncture.

John will go with us
Is John going with us
My friend John Brownton will go with us
Although he doesn't like to ride John will go
John Brownton although he doesn't like to ride will go with us

Punctuation taught to students in the elementary school should be functional, that is, it should be punctuation needed by the student as he writes. It is easy to become so entangled in minute points of punctuation that we lose sight of the aims of teaching composition. Beginning from the first stages of writing, therefore, let us teach these skills as they are needed:

1 Period:
At the end of a declarative sentence. *He went home.*
After abbreviations. *Mr. Andrew R. Cooper*

2 Comma:
To separate parts of a series. *We ate corn, peas, and hot dogs.*
With an apposition. *Molly, my best friend, is here.*
After an introductory clause. *When I get there, I'll tell you.*
To separate a quotation from the speaker. *He said, "How are you?"*

After Yes or No. *Yes, I will be here.*
With direct address. *Jimmy, do you know?*

3 Question Mark:
At the end of an interrogative sentence. *Who is it?*

4 Quotation Marks:
Around quoted speech. *Mark called, "I can go!"*
Around a title of a short work–poem, article, short story. *We read "The Doughnut Machine."*

5 Exclamation Mark:
After a word or words showing excitement. *Help me!*

6 Apostrophe:
To show possession. *This is Sid's pencil.*
In contractions. *Don't you know better?*

The INTERABANG

This is the first innovation in punctuation since the seventeenth century. It is a combination of the exclamation point and the question mark. Examples of how it might be used are:

"How do you like that‽"
"What do you know‽

An occasional touch of humor helps the teaching of almost any content. Here are ways of providing practice in using punctuation.

Provide a paragraph or two which contains no punctuation at all. Have students compare their punctuation of the given paragraph with one you prepare on a transparency. Use a joke, thus:

> miserly Sam went to the dentist because he had a terrible toothache as dr fixem reached into sams mouth to pull out the aching tooth sam cried out doctor if it costs $4.00 to pull the tooth how much will it cost to loosen it a little

Cartoon figures can be used to assist students in learning to identify the portion of a sentence to be set off by quotation marks:

Jane said, "I'm delighted to see you."

SPELLING AND HANDWRITING

Although it is true that ideas expressed are more important than the mechanics of composition, frequent misspellings and illegible handwriting do prejudice the reader. The written words replace the winsome personality of the writer; there is nothing to plead for you except your writing, which stands exposed to the rude view of the critic. How far, for example, will the student advance who writes this sentence in sixth grade?

We hopt to Get Good grades on those importent examunoshuns.

There is admittedly a certain snobbery inherent in correct spelling, and those who spell English easily do "look down their noses" at those who never learned or were never taught the intricacies of English spelling. Spelling, in this case, becomes an outward sign of education or intelligence in the eyes of the public, although only low correlation has been found between spelling ability and the intelligence quotient.

In many cases, too, it becomes apparent that spelling and handwriting do directly affect the success of written communication. Compare these sentences as you note the possibilities for misunderstanding; it is not always possible to question the person who wrote the sentence to ascertain just what was meant.

1 He could not be *hear.* (Does the writer mean *here* or *heard,* perhaps?)
2 Mary Jane was hopping. (Was she? It could be that she was hoping.)
3 You owe me $54. (He may get cheated.)
4 They brought in the cot. (Does it meow?)

DEGREES OF SPECIFICITY

It is important that students be introduced to concepts of concreteness and abstraction, for as Hayakawa notes:

> The reason we must concern ourselves with the process of abstracting is that the study of language is all too often regarded as being a matter of examining such things as pronunciation, spelling, vocabulary, grammar, and sentence structure. . . . But as we know from everyday experience, learning language is not simply a matter of learning words; it is a matter of correctly relating our words to the things and happenings for which they stand.[7]

In presenting the concept of abstraction Hayakawa uses the illustration of Bessie, the cow, a familiar animal that can be touched and easily identified. As we move up the *Abstraction Ladder,* however, we find that *Bessie* can also be referred to as a member of the *cow* family and as part of the classification *livestock.* She is a "*farm asset*" and, therefore, a general "*asset,*" and still more abstractly, she is "*wealth.*"

Trips up and down the Abstraction Ladder will serve to acquaint young people with these degrees of specificity as they move from the concrete to the abstract or vice versa.

Make a ladder of construction paper or bamboo strips to serve as the Abstraction Ladder on which students can place cards bearing words which represent varied levels of abstraction, for example:

rose, climber, flower, plant, foliage, landscaping
turkey, poultry, meat, food, farm products
penny, coin, money, wages, income, wealth

In defining words we find that we must narrow the category to include only that which is defined, or the definition has little meaning. How can we define a "bed"?

bed = a piece of furniture (How about a chair?)
bed = furniture in a bedroom (How about a dresser?)

[7] S. I. Hayakawa, *Language and Thought in Action* (New York: Harcourt, 1972), p. 152.

bed = a large flat piece of furniture on which we usually sleep at night (Getting closer.)

In writing we stress the importance of dealing in specific cases rather than high levels of abstraction, for the skilled author holds our interest with the rich detail with which he enlivens his writing. We often are impressed by the effective use of detail as in this passage from *John Henry and His Hammer* by Howard W. Felton:

> "You're a fine, big boy, John Henry. Mos' a man now. You're as black as the night was that saw you come into this here world. You're as strong as the wind that blowed the trees down low. Your blood is as red as the moon that grew big an' red, an' stopped an' ran backwards. An' the eyes you got sparkle an' shine like the white of a angel's wing, an' your muscles is as powerful an' easy, an' moves strong an' quiet as the river that turned right 'round in its tracks an' ran uphill."[8]

As we move down the Abstraction Ladder, we come to the least abstract term, for instance, *rose, turkey or penny,* in the examples just cited. As we write, however, we find that we don't mean just any rose, but the red rose in Mrs. Kirk's garden, the one which always blooms in the month of May and perfumes the yards of all her neighbors. We want to become even more specific as we place characters in a setting and describe events. Experiments in language can lead children to become aware of degrees of specificity in this way:

Which of these terms is most specific?
_____a lady _____that lady _____Mrs. Wilma Jones
_____a Dolly Varden trout _____a gray fish _____a speckled trout
_____the dog _____the collie in the street _____the dog in the street
We can develop a chart of specificity something like this:

1	2	3	4
girl	a girl in my class	the girl who sits in front of me	Mary Jane Nelson
pet			
house			

[8] Howard W. Felton, *John Henry and His Hammer* (New York: Alfred Knopf, 1950), p. 11.

WAYS OF THINKING REVEALED IN WRITING

Writing is thought transferred to paper; our writing reveals us and discloses our ways of thinking. The student needs to become aware of fallacious thinking not only to avoid being influenced by the writing of others but also to avoid falling into dangerous ways of thinking.

A common error made by young people, and by far too many adults also, is the *sweeping generalization.* How often do you hear the unqualified generalization in ordinary conversation? "Oh, everyone knows how to dance!" "Teachers are mean!" "Those seniors are so conceited!" We often find ourselves falling into the habit of making unsubstantiated statements which, like those quoted, fail to allow for individual cases. True, some seniors are probably conceited; it is likely that some teachers are mean; and many people do know how to dance. But we know as we think more rationally that the statements made would not include the whole category described.

Display a variety of pictures on the bulletin board. With each picture supply a generalization which students can attack to demonstrate the fallacy of making unsubstantiated generalizations. The generalization, "Every boy should have a dog," for example, might elicit the following arguments:

My cousin, Tom, is allergic to fur, so a dog is not for him.
A family that lives in an apartment can't always have a dog.
I know a boy who is so mean to his dog that he shouldn't have one.

Search the newspaper for examples of generalizations which can be refuted in the same way. Students can also deliberately write generalizations, perhaps ones they have heard, which can be discussed in class. Advertising often supplies good examples of the "glittering generality" which strives to sway opinion or to sell a product.

Another type of thinking which merits attention is the *two-valued attitude* in which matters are decided as either "right" or "wrong" with no thought for the gradations of rightness or wrongness. Is a person *bad* or *good,* or is it possible that a person might have one vice mixed with some desirable traits? We have encouraged this type of thinking in students by concocting tests which demand "one right answer" and make no provision for variation. Research in creativity has led to encouragement of divergent thinking through the use of open-ended questions which stimulate thought. How can we assist students in developing more flexible modes of thinking, in breaking the rigid two-valued attitude toward life?

Analyze a character about whom the group is reading. What are the person's good traits? What traits are less desirable? Can we apply a simple adjective "good" or "bad" to a complex human being? Guide students to write character sketches which describe a person, real or imaginary, and show that people are both *good* and *bad* at the same time.

The study of antonyms emphasizes this "either-or" thinking. Examine sets of antonyms as you discuss the gradations which are involved in any pair of *opposite* words. Introduce students to the concept of a *continuum* as you draw a long line on the board with antonyms at each end, thus:

HOT warm cool **COLD**

What are the many gradations which lie between HOTNESS and COLDNESS? Fill in all the terms which can be thought of—cool, chilly, warm, sweltering, and so forth. Then try other opposite concepts which represent values—HAPPY-SAD, RIGHT-WRONG. Encourage students to discover examples of two-valued thinking which can be discussed in class.

Of particular importance in writing is the avoidance of *stereotyped thinking*, which is also an example of rigidity of thought. Is every woman over seventy a "sweet little old lady?" Does every Texan wear a ten-gallon hat and ride the range each day? Do all Eskimo families live in igloos? Do all women like to cook? An exciting study of language could focus class attention on ferreting out stereotypes.

Write a description which exemplifies a stereotype. Then rewrite the description eliminating the stereotyped thinking. Draw two pictures to illustrate the difference in thought.

An important distinction to be made in writing is that between *fact and opinion*. *Facts* are statements which can be proved, for example, the fact that a room is thirty feet long can be proved by measurement, and we would all have to agree that the statement is factual. We must recognize the changing quality of factual knowledge, however, for, as we are becoming increasingly aware, the facts of today are not always the facts of tomorrow. Facts, therefore, require constant verification.

Opinions or *judgments* are personal evaluations which reflect attitudes and values; they cannot be verified as facts can. We frequently hear opinions stated authoritatively as though they were facts, and therein lies the fallacy. Opinion has a place in thoughtful writing, but it should be identified as such by introductory words which qualify the statements as a personal judgment—"I think," "It seems to me," "According to the author," and so on. Opinion can be given a measure of validity through substantiation by quoting the opinions of others and by presenting cogent arguments which serve to support the personal judgment. We can provide many classroom experiences in working with fact and opinion.

Debates provide opportunity to support an opinion, with students taking both sides of an issue. It is particularly interesting for students to support the side with which they really do not agree, for they will need to think carefully to support their argument.

Even primary-level children can identify fact as distinguished from opinion. Let them decide which of these statements are fact and which are not by trying to prove each statement.

John's book is red. (We need to clarify our statement. Which boy named John? Which particular book?)

The reading table is in the northeast corner of the room. (This statement can be verified.)

Mr. Popper's Penguins is the best book Mr. Woods ever read to us. (Does everybody agree?)

Another important aspect of thought is the *drawing of inferences,* which we do continually without being conscious of the process. Again, however, we must be careful that the inferences we make are valid according to the facts known, for example:

May is often absent from school. Can we correctly infer that she dislikes school?

Chuck broke a window in the auditorium. Do we infer that he is an incorrigible troublemaker?

We see a little girl on the sidewalk. Can we infer that she is lost?

USE OF WORDS

The careful selection of words to be used in any writing experiment influences the clarity and effectiveness of the finished product. One aspect of using words which determines the effect of the author's writing is *wordiness*—verbosity, repetition, tautology—which is associated with boring writing. Wordiness is an indication that the writer has refused to accept responsibility to *select* the best wording. Once acquainted with this concept, the student will begin noticing writing which requires editing to weed out excessive words. Students should be encouraged to collect illustrative samples of this type of writing, for awareness of wordiness will lead to greater clarity in student writing as each strives to produce "tighter" writing.

Often sentences should be combined:

One day Jim was going home. He saw a tiny puppy.

One day on the way home Jim saw a tiny puppy.

Sometimes words are excessive and should be cut.

Larry said he would like to go along, too.
Larry would like to go along.

We also strive to call forth *varied words* to create effects. We endeavor to vary our vocabulary to maintain the reader's interest and to create exciting stories. One of the purposes of rewriting is to change words which are prosaic; why waste space on dull words when there are so many scintillating choices we might make? Experiments with rewriting sentences will aid students in making better selections of effective words, thus:

Mike called, "Wait for me!"
Mike shouted excitedly, "Wait for me!"

Louis walked out the door and walked down the street.
Louis ran out the door and hurried down the street.

Another method of adding variety to writing is to change the types of sentence patterns and word order used. The person who continually relies on the same sentence structure places a limit on the possibilities of writing. Experiments like these can increase student flexibility in constructing varied sentence patterns.

Madge is in third grade. She lives on Miller Street. She is eight.
Madge, who lives on Miller Street, is eight and is in third grade.

Brad was sick, but he was able to play the game.
Although Brad was sick, he was able to play the game.

Another aim of the student writer should be to avoid *triteness* of expression. As we have mentioned elsewhere, the cliché can be the subject of discussion, with experiments leading children to use more interesting comparisons of speed, heat, sound, and so on.

As hot as . . .
a pancake ready to flip
a rabbit in his fur coat in July

As quiet as . . .
a feather falling on snow
butterflies floating through the air

It is important also that students recognize the need for *clear references* in the sentences they write, for we often find ourselves puzzling over sentences which contain uncertain references or misplaced modifiers.

Usually the reference can be clarified by changing a word or two or by rearranging the phrases or clauses as in these examples:

Mrs. Muskopf told Mildred she might go. (Who is going?)
Hanging in the closet he found his coat. (Who or what was hanging?)
They are always saying things like that. (Who are *they?*)

Writing Nonfiction

When we think of writing, we often forget the importance of ability to write nonfiction—articles, research reports, letters. Writing of this nature, however, can prove as exciting as any imaginative tale, and it serves to stimulate the inquiring mind of the elementary school student. How can we encourage students to write nonfiction?

THE ARTICLE

Informative articles constitute some of the best writing which appears each year. The article may be on any topic—world affairs, preparing for college entrance, the enrollment of a six-year-old black girl in an all-white school, profile of a well-known person, review of a writer's work, and on and on. Introduce young people to the writers of nonfiction for elementary school students by examining several of the excellent magazines written for this age level.

American Girl, 830 Third Avenue, New York, N.Y. 10002
Boys' Life, Route 1, New Brunswick, N.J. 08902
National Geographic, 17th and M Streets, N.W., Washington, D.C. 20036
National Wildlife, 1412 16th Street, N.W., Washington, D.C. 20036
Popular Mechanics, 224 West 57th Street, New York, N.Y. 10019
Popular Science, 355 Lexington Avenue, New York, N.Y. 10017
Science Digest, 224 West 57th Street, New York, N.Y. 10019
Young Miss, 52 Vanderbilt Avenue, Nw York, N.Y. 10017

Students can also benefit from studying articles from general magazines: *Newsweek, Time, Reader's Digest,* and others which represent specialized interests. As they examine articles, students can be guided to observe:

- How the author began the article

    Telling an anecdote
    Flashback
    Dialogue
    Asking a question

- **The steps in developing the article's content**

- **Any devices the author used to add interest to this writing**

  Humor—joke, play on words
  Imagery—simile, metaphor
  Examples

- **The summary or conclusion**

An effective launching pad for the writing of nonfiction is provided by Holling C. Holling, author and illustrator of *Pagoo* (Houghton Mifflin, 1957), in a beautiful film entitled *Story of a Book.* This tall, genial man explains the way he and his wife, who did part of the illustrations for the book, became interested in writing about a hermit crab whose Latin name *pagurus* suggested the name of Pagoo. He describes their beginning study of the crab in the tidepool habitat, his research in the library, the writing of Pagoo's life, and the preparation of the illustrations. The finished product is not technically nonfiction, for the author has added interest to the reading of detailed factual information by imagining the adventures his main character might have growing up in Tide-Pool Town. The effect of the film is to give the elementary school student insight into the origin of an idea, the gathering of material, and the actual writing process.

Beginning with short experiments in writing nonfiction, the elementary school student can later progress to longer articles. Emphasis at this level should, however, remain on the ideas to be expressed and on the ability to communicate with clarity and effect; sheer length is never a valid criterion for success in writing. What kinds of writing experiments shall we explore?

EXPLANATION (HOW-TO-DO-IT):

After having completed a class project, each student can write an explanation of the process. Accuracy and clarity are stressed and can be checked by passing the "articles" around the room having each person read several and write a brief comment on the back. Comments are aimed at helping the student achieve the assignment.

HOLIDAY:

Short articles can explain how specific customs originated. In December, for instance, each student might tell about one symbol of Christmas—the tree, candles, bells, the star—explaining its origin, how it is associated with Christmas, and perhaps varied usages in different countries.

If a special celebration or program is held during the year, students can write about this event from any perspective they choose—as a participant in the program, as a teacher, as a member of the audience.

NEWS:

Cut out intriguing headlines from newspapers. Each student receives one about which to write. An interesting variation of this experiment is to provide the original newspaper article so the students can compare their versions with the original and realize the varied ways of thinking about any idea. Students can help collect short articles for this purpose.

LITERATURE:

Books can provide the stimulus for writing news articles. The class can prepare, for example, the CENTERBURG GAZETTE, which contains articles about the happenings in Centerburg based, of course, on McCloskey's *Homer Price* and *Centerburg Tales.*

EXPERIENCE:

After returning from a field trip each "reporter" can write about the trip as a way of summarizing the experience. Discussion will suggest various aspects of the trip to be reported; for instance, a visit to the library may elicit these headlines:

MR. YORK LIBRARIAN TEN YEARS
CARD CATALOG SHOWS THE WAY
WHO IS DR. SEUSS?
TRAVELING THROUGH THE STACKS

Personal experiences also provide excellent topics for articles. Here the student has an opportunity to tell about his feelings, his ideas, things he is doing outside of school. We must avoid some of the stereotyped topics that have been overworked through the years and provide a new slant to encourage students to look at familiar events and objects in new ways.

What were you doing between 4 and 8 o'clock on Friday, October 13th?

I turned the knob, flipped the channel button, and settled down to watch. It's my favorite show. Maybe it's yours, too.

REVIEWS:

TV programs can be reviewed by students as well as movies. The newspaper or *TV Guide* can be brought in and set up in a writing center where students can go to write their own reviews.

OPINION:

"What is your opinion?" (Substantiate it.)
Should sixth-grade girls wear lipstick?
Should we have an hour for lunch or only thirty-five minutes?

Should boys let girls get ahead of them in line?
What is the nicest time of day?
What is your favorite food?

RESEARCH

What is *research?* One dictionary definition of this term is "studious inquiry, usually critical, and exhaustive investigation or experimentation having for its aim the revision of accepted conclusions, in the light of newly discovered facts." Coming to English from the French word *recherche,* which means *search, quest, investigation,* just as in our English meaning, the term has the positive connotations associated with scientific study. The researcher may, however, be studying problems in widely varied fields; for example, in agriculture the researcher might study which seeds will produce the most corn per acre whereas the producer of sailboats might research the problem of which hull shape produces the greatest speed. Research takes place in all areas of endeavor, even in our schools.

For most teachers, *research* is synonymous with writing a report after reading several sources for information. Such library research is usually part of any research project, and involves special skills of taking notes, collecting information (data), developing a bibliography, and preparing a final report. Research is yet another aspect of English which is properly the concern of all teachers and is related to all subjects. The interest and the benefits of library research depend on several factors:

Library resources available
Nature of the topic under study
Guidance of the teacher
Involvement of the student

As Samuel Johnson wrote: "Knowledge is of two kinds. We know a subject ourselves, or we know where we can find information on it." It is important, therefore, that students know the tools of the library, and how to use them to gather needed information. We cannot overemphasize the necessity for having a well-equipped central library in every elementary school, with a librarian who is able to aid young researchers. Many authorities consider it more important to teach children the skills of discovering, searching, and drawing conclusions than to teach them specific facts, for the facts will change and become useless, whereas the skills prepare the student to continue inquiring and discovering throughout life. What library tools should the elementary school student know?

The card catalog is a basic tool which children can learn to use very early as they search for books by title or author. As they develop interests, they will want to look for Subject Entries, which will suggest titles on specific subjects—FRANCE, MYTHOLOGY, SOUTH AMERICA, TREES. We must move beyond the card catalog, however, to use more specialized indexes and reference books. Here are a number of titles which are useful in the elementary school.

Dictionaries of varied difficulty; foreign language dictionaries
Webster's unabridged dictionary
Roget's *Thesaurus*
Encyclopedias (several of varying difficulty)
Biographical dictionaries
  Who's Who
  Who's Who in America
  Current Biography
  Junior Book of Authors
Books of quotations
  Bartlett's *Familiar Quotations*
  Hoyt's *New Cyclopedia of Practical Quotations*
  Simpson's *Contemporary Quotations*
Statistical references
  World Almanac (available in paperback)
  Statesman's Yearbook
  Information Please Almanac, Atlas, and *Yearbook*
  Guinness' *Book of Records*
Geographic references
  Varied atlases
Specialized references
  Bullfinch's *Mythology*
Abridged Reader's Guide to Periodical Literature
  Many of the magazines indexed by this tool should be available or the index is worthless. Usually an elementary school library will hold these titles for a five-year period only.

Pascal stated: *"Connaître—c'est chercher"* ("To know is to search"). This is the attitude which we are trying to instill in students from their first learning experiences, for it is only when students feel the challenge, the excitement of discovering, that they will really begin to learn on their own initiative.

After students are acquainted with a number of the basic reference tools in the library, conduct a TREASURE HUNT. Prepare a list of reference questions to provide practice is using those tools available. The answer to the question is the reference book and page on which the answer is found. No one cares at this time to record the specific answer although students find themselves browsing as they search. Use questions like these (which can be constructed by the class itself):

What is the population of Kansas?
Who was the twelfth president of the United States?
Who said, "Give me Liberty or give me Death!"?

Let each student select one specific topic: George Washington Carver, The Vikings, Diamond Mining, Queen Elizabeth II. The object of this SEARCH is to discover *how many sources* of information can be found. Again, only the sources are listed, with no attempt being made at this time to record notes. Encourage students to investigate lesser-known references in other libraries.

To facilitate the collection of data it is important also that each student acquire skill in taking notes. According to the ability of the students involved, students can be taught to note information that will be needed in an efficient way. Certain guidelines can be established, thus:

Never copy long passages word for word.
Any sentences that are copied must be quoted. (Note the page number.)
Always refer to several sources; use sources other than encyclopedias.
Note information that fits the outline for your paper.

Few students develop expert skill in note taking without specific instruction. Instruction might be of this nature:

Provide each student with a copy of a duplicated article. After discussing the purpose for which notes are being taken, e.g., preparation of a hypothetical paper, each student takes notes. The notes can be compared (make transparencies of several for instructional purposes) and discussed as to the organization of the notes taken, the importance of items noted, any omissions, and so on.

Tape informational material—an article read by you, a radio or television presentation, a lecture—to provide practice in listening and taking notes. Again, all hear the same material so comparisons can be made to point out both valuable practices and those to be avoided. After working with the first attempts at note taking, the same tape can be replayed to permit students (particularly those who need additional aid) to take a better set of notes.

Frequently have students take notes as they search for information from varied sources. Have students use these notes in class discussion to substantiate arguments or to add information.

In conjunction with note taking, students should also learn to collect bibliographic information. There is nothing more frustrating than to try to locate a source after you've forgotten the author or someone else has taken the book. The development of the habit of noting all necessary bibliographic information before beginning to take notes is an invaluable practice which can be taught with the very first attempts at library research. Bibliographic forms used should be simple, but exact and sufficiently inclusive. Contrary to popular opinion, there is no *one* "right" bibliographic form; different publishers or universities often have their own stylebook or follow a specific guide. The chief aim of any guide is consistency, and it is for this reason that we establish a pattern which will be followed by the class in its work. The forms you select might be something like these:

BOOKS:

Provensen, Alice, and Martin Provensen. *Play on Words.* Random House, 1972.

The first author's name is inverted only to assist alphabetical arrangement. We choose to omit the location of the publisher as it is usually well known; any librarian will supply these addresses if they are needed and 90 percent of them are in New York.

ARTICLE:

Scott, Vance H. "Who Will Save Never-Never Land?" *National Wildlife.* August-September, 1973, pp. 40–47.

ENCYCLOPEDIA:

Encyclopaedia Britannica. "Cycling." Vol. 6, pp. 938–40.

Another type of research which should not be ignored by the elementary school teacher is *descriptive research,* which involves the gathering of data in a different way. Some of the same skills are involved as in library research, for the experimenter must explore the *literature* of the field to acquire sufficient background information to conduct the research. One distinction should be noted, however, for in this research the student will be producing original material and will be contributing to the store of information we have about any particular subject. As John Dewey observed, "Every great advance in science has issued from a new audacity of imagination." [9]

Research can be cooperative, that is, worked on by several people, or it can be an individual project, and the research problem may be derived from any field. Descriptive research is not limited to science but may explore aspects of the social sciences, language study, mathematics, art, music, and so on. The first step in conducting research is to identify a problem. What problems might be researched in English?

[9] John Dewey, *Art As Experience* (New York: Minton, Balch, 1934), p. 70.

Given a free choice, what subjects do students write about?
Do boys or girls score higher on a vocabulary test?
Which spelling words are most frequently missed on a review test? What kinds of errors are made? Do boys or girls miss more words?
What type of poetry do boys like? What kind do girls like?

Students who acquire the research frame of reference early will be better equipped to function in a society which is rapidly becoming research-oriented. Too often we fear research because it is unfamiliar to us; we don't feel at ease with its methodology.

We must constantly remember that we are teaching children who will live tomorrow. Research is sure to be a part of this tomorrow, and for this reason we have a responsibility for encouraging these "apprentice scholars" as they engage in bona fide research. We are not aiming at producing a roomful of research scientists but rather a class of alert, critical thinkers.

Students should be introduced to the terminology and the procedures followed by adult researchers. Most research consists, for example, of a sequence of systematic steps:

1 Selection of the problem
2 Formulation of a hypothesis
3 Choice of a method of procedure
4 Collection of data
5 Interpretation of the data
6 Report of the findings

The crucial task is the identification of the problem, which must be specific and researchable. Which of the following is a practicable research question? Which involves opinion only?

Should we use our school buildings all year long?
Do more girls study foreign languages than do boys?
Should the United States President be allowed to hold office for three terms?
Is the number of women earning doctorates increasing?

Students can suggest many problems in this fashion as they discuss the researchability of the suggested problems. Once a problem has been identified, we are ready to proceed with the study. Suppose, for instance, we select the following problem: To determine whether boys or girls score higher on a given vocabulary test. The next step is to formulate a hypothesis (an educated guess) which in this case might be: Girls will score higher on a given vocabulary test than will boys.

What method or procedure will assist us in proving or disproving the *hypothesis* (pl. *hypotheses*)? We shall construct a test of twenty items which will be administered to a group of boys and girls. We might decide to limit our *N* (the total group tested) to sixth-grade students; this limitation would then be added to the statement of the problem: To determine whether sixth-grade boys or sixth-grade girls will score higher on a given vocabulary test. After administering the test, the *data* (usually used in the plural; singular form is *datum*) are collected; that is, the tests are graded and the scores tallied. The results may be placed on a graph or compiled in a table. The findings are then summarized. This particular study might later be *replicated* (repeated to check the results) or might be extended to include other grades.

Another aspect of research which adds excitement to student learning is *experimental research,* which differs from descriptive research in the manner of collecting data. As the name indicates, experimental research involves the setting up of an experiment with an *X* group (the group on which the experiment is tried) and a Control group (a group on which the experiment is not tried). The two groups are tested before and after the experiment and the results are compared to note the effects of the experiment. Children will find experimental research particularly exciting as *a way of learning.*

Experiments can vary widely in topic, and they can be surprisingly simple in nature. Suggested here are a number of researchable questions which will result in challenging classroom studies:

> Does careful following of the Spelling Study Steps improve spelling grades? (Half the class uses these steps for a month; the other half studies without direction.)
>
> Does discussion of a film directly following viewing improve understanding and observation of details? (Half the class discusses the film while the others go outdoors; then comes the test!)
>
> Will practice in listening improve ability to note details? (The *X* group has several planned lessons in listening; Control has none. Both groups are given a listening test.)

Once students are introduced to research, they will generate many exciting ideas for study. Studies like those involving study skills will have more effect on student behavior than any words a teacher can speak, for the students are involved.

CORRESPONDING

"I have made this letter longer than usual because I lack the time to make it shorter," wrote Pascal. Relatively few people earn their living by writing, but everyone needs to be able to write letters. We write letters for many purposes—requesting information, keeping in touch with a friend, thanking someone for a gift. It is important that we learn forms for writing business letters as well as the art of writing interesting social letters.

An effective way to teach the writing of a friendly letter is through the stimulus of writing to someone in another city or in a foreign country. This activity can be carried out in lower grades as a group or individually by children in the upper grades.

The classroom can have a Letter Writing Center where paper, pencils, pens (fancy felt tipped ones), and a dictionary are provided. Along with these should be lists of people to write; for example, Congressmen, Senators, the local newspaper, writers of childrens' books (these writers can usually be reached through their publisher). If you can beg, borrow, or steal a typewriter, this will add a touch of class to the center. Finally, a phone book can come in handy for local addresses.

One excellent idea that correlates map study with letter writing is that of Adopting a Ship.[10] The basic description in brief is that the class or a group from the class corresponds with the captain of a merchant ship that is sailing from port to port. This correspondence with the captain provides an opportunity to plot his course on a map in the classroom and follow the ship's route as it moves to different ports of call.

In his letters the captain describes his position and gives short descriptions of the areas he is visiting. He also answers questions asked by the students in their letters to him. He may at times send maps and small realia appropriate to the locales.

The Adopt-A-Ship Plan can be utilized with the whole class participating, dividing the class into committees including one that will construct a map with a small ship to move as the course of the ship is plotted, another committee to supervise correspondence, another to do research about the areas reached by the ship and to prepare background information for the class.

This activity can also be conducted by a group of gifted students in the class. They might conduct the research, handle correspondence, and map the route of the ship, making periodic reports to the class which would benefit from the work done by these students.

This activity carries such interest that the route of the ship adopted by one class might be plotted in a central location in the school so that all students could note its progress. The school newspaper or the daily news report could carry informative items about the ship which the class is following.

[10] Sidney Tiedt and Iris Tiedt, *Imaginative Social Studies Activities* (New York: Atherton Press, 1963), pp. 50–51.

Letters of application and additional information may be obtained by a teacher from this address: Adopt-A-Ship Plan, Suite 2639, 17 Battery Place, New York 4, New York.

No individual person may adopt a ship; the project must be done by school class members under the supervision of a teacher. The teacher must file the application and supervise the class participation. The period of correspondence is from September through May, but the number of ships available each year is limited so it is wise to apply well in advance.

A book which we enjoy introducing to students to enliven instruction in letter writing is Sesyle Joslin's *Dear Dragon.* First an interesting situation is described which leads to the writing of a letter; for example, one illustration shows a smiling native queen welcoming the rider of an ostrich and the text reads:

> You are having a holiday traveling on ostrich-back up the Amazon and through the Rain Forest until finally you stop in a small village because there is a friendly native Queen who insists on having you for dinner.

On the next page appears the Social Letter which follows: [11]

Dear Friends:
I am having rather an exciting trip. This part of the world is beautiful and quite interesting as well.
I wish you were here.

Yours as ever,

The illustration opposite the letter shows the ostrich rider now thoroughly tied and in a stewpot over a blazing fire writing the letter while the friendly native Queen looks on. The letter forms are meticulously correct, and the understatement used by the author lends a delicious humor to what could be a dull study.

The business letter is a useful form which students can learn. As we have noted in other cases, there is no single correct form; the main object is to supply the needed information with clarity so that the purpose of the letter is achieved without misunderstanding. Collect a variety of examples which students can examine to determine a suitable form for the business letter. Here is an excellent opportunity for class research. What forms are currently being used for business letters? An attempt might also be made to collect old business letters to note any differences from modern style. How can differences be explained? One commonly used form of business letter is the following:

9100 Senter Ave.
Peoria, Illinois 61600
November 11, 19—

Elegant Eye Beauty Company
223 Washington Blvd.
Sacramento, California 95814

Dear Sirs:

I saw your newest product, Magical Miracle Eyelash Cream, advertised on television last night. I am writing to ask you to please send my free sample to the address above.
Thank you very much.

Yours truly,

Ms. Faye McPherson

A popular variation of this standard form is the following:

[11] From *Dear Dragon,* text © 1962, by Sesyle Joslin; illustration © 1962, by Irene Haas. Reproduced by permission of Harcourt Brace Jovanovich, Inc.

345 Oakwood Dr.
Vallejo, California 94590
March 18, 19—

Prentice-Hall, Inc.
Englewood Cliffs, New Jersey 07632

Dear Sirs:

Please send me one copy of *Contemporary English in the Elementary School* by Iris and Sidney Tiedt for examination.
You may bill me at the above address.
Thank you in advance.

Sincerely,

Dr. Glynn Douglas

It is wiser to write letters which have real purpose rather than those which are purely invented. Students can often assist the teacher in writing for free materials or in placing orders for materials, as in the samples. They can also write for information from real people or organizations—Congressmen, state legislators, state departments, travel bureaus, publishers, chambers of commerce, firms, and so on. After a field trip, letters of appreciation can be sent those who assisted the class. Other activities related to letter writing include the following.

- To provide practice in writing addresses, have each child cut several slips of paper the size of a postal card. Use tagboard if the cards are to be mailed. On one side of the card is a picture, perhaps associated with social studies or depicting your local area. On the other side is the address and a brief message.

- Each child may bring one stamped postal card to prepare to send to a friend or relative.

- Telegram techniques provide an interesting experiment in writing brief but complete information. The date, address, and signature are included without charge. No punctuation is used, and every word and figure (324 is three words) is counted. Supply fictitious information which is to be conveyed via telegram. At other times students can write the messages inventing a story to go with the message given them. Official telegram forms can be obtained from the local office.

- Write friendly greetings to patients in local hospitals or convalescent homes. Discuss the types of information which might be shared with an older person. An original poem or story might, for example, be much appreciated by these older men and women who enjoy the activities of children. Art work might also be shared.

Books to Investigate

Other books on writing can be found at the end of Chapter 7, Creative Writing.

Leavitt, Hart. *The Writer's Eye*. New York: Bantam Books, 1968.

Leavitt, Hart, and Sohn, David A. *Stop, Look and Write!* New York: Bantam Books, 1964.

Sohn, David A. *Pictures for Writing*. New York: Bantam Books, 1968.

Yates, Elizabeth. *Someday You'll Write*. New York: E. P. Dutton, 1962. Directed toward the young writer.

facilitating reading

chapter

When I am reading a book . . . it seems to me to be alive and talking to me.

Jonathan Swift

What is reading? How can we best help the child to read? These are essential questions to be considered today as new insights are being provided from the studies of psycholinguistics. "*Respond to what the child is trying to do,*" writes Frank Smith. The "motivation and the direction of learning to read can only come from the child, and he must look for the knowledge and skills that he needs only in the process of reading. Learning to read is a problem for the child to solve." [1]

Studies of the child's acquisition of language demonstrate the child's ability to derive the complex rules of English grammar from the speech heard. No one tells these rules to the child. No one tells the child how to learn language. Goodman and Smith believe that this is also the way children will learn to read.

[1] Frank Smith, "Twelve Easy Ways to Make Learning to Read Difficult," *Psycholinguistics and Reading*, ed. Frank Smith (New York: Holt, Rinehart, and Winston, 1973), p. 195.

> The child is already programmed to learn to read. He needs written language that is both interesting and comprehensible, and teachers who understand language-learning and who appreciate his competence as a language-learner.[2]

With these ideas in mind, we shall begin exploring the broad field of reading.

Teaching Reading

What is reading? We cannot return one glib definition, for reading is a many-faceted act viewed from many perspectives. It has been pointed out, for example, that reading involves skill development, a visual act, a type of perception, a reflection of cultural background, and an act of higher mental processes which has a continued relationship to a child's social and personal development.[3] Kress defines reading as "thinking that is stimulated by written symbols." [4] The definition of reading by the reader himself might focus on adventure, entertainment, and information, for the voracious reader knows that "Reading," as Charles de Montesquieu observed, "enables a man to exchange the wearisome hours of life which come to everyone for hours of delight."

However we define reading, one generalization which we can safely make is that reading is more than the physical visual act of recognizing words on a printed page, and it is a highly important aspect of learning about which there is yet much to be learned. As Heilman points out:

> Learning to read is probably one of the most important accomplishments that the child will achieve during his formal schooling. This is not to imply that learning to read will be his most difficult or dramatic academic achievement, for if he gets off to a good start the whole process may be so uneventful that he will not recall how this particular learning took place. On the other hand, if he fails in reading, the frustrations and defeats which can beset him in the future are so numerous and varied that they have never been tabulated in one source.[5]

Our schools have typically been reading-centered, and this tendency continues to be true of the elementary school. Reading is only one facet

[2] Op. cit., Kenneth Goodman and Frank Smith, p. 180.

[3] George D. Spache, *Reading in the Elementary School* (Boston: Allyn & Bacon, 1964), p. 26.

[4] Roy A. Kress, "That All May Learn to Read," First Annual Reading Conference at Syracuse University (June, 1959).

[5] Arthur Heilman, *Principles and Practices of Teaching Reading* (Columbus, Ohio: Merrill, 1961), p. 33.

of language development; like the skill of listening, reading is a perceptive skill and can be accomplished at a higher rate of speed than can speaking or composing, both of which require the human mechanism to "do something" physical. Although usually taught last, therefore, reading soon overtakes other language skills, particularly that of writing.

With the knowledge explosion comes an ever greater need to read, for the number of books and periodicals produced each year is overwhelming. Because it is literally impossible to read everything printed, emphasis must be placed on selection of that which is to be read. We become more aware, too, of our purposes in reading as we vary the type of reading to the purpose. The limited nature of time, that priceless commodity, also leads us to attempt to speed up the reading process. Concern for reading is universal as individual educational aspirations and social goals rise. As college attendance increases, a greater number of persons will require advanced skills of reading to accomplish the educational task.

HISTORY OF READING

Criticism there is, and critics there will always be, but when we survey the history of reading instruction in the United States, we cannot deny that reading has progressed. Analyzing trends in reading as they have appeared historically, we can develop the following outline: [6, 7]

Prior to 1900	Spelling and alphabet approach to reading
	Moralistic reading materials; the *Bible*
	The New England Primer, 1683
	The American Spelling Book, 1790
	McGuffey Readers, 1836
1900–1910	Reading-focused curriculum
	Emphasis on oral reading
1910–1920	Scientific analysis applied to reading achievement
	Standardized tests of reading
	Beginnings of silent reading
1920–1930	Many research studies
	Concept of individual differences
	Remediation in reading
1930–1940	Reading as part of the Activity Program
	Reading Readiness concept
1940–1950	Focus on adult literacy
	Mass media influence
	Interrelationships of language arts

[6] Nila B. Smith, "What Have We Accomplished in Reading?—A Review of the Past Fifty Years," *Elementary English* (March, 1961), pp. 141–50.

[7] Charles C. Fries, *Linguistics and Reading* (New York: Holt, Rinehart, and Winston, 1962), pp. 1–34.

1950–1960	Public criticism of reading instruction
	Influence of television
	Individualized instruction
1960–1970	Innovation in beginning reading instruction
	Concern for education of "disadvantaged" child
	Influence of linguistics on study of reading
	Technology in reading instruction
	Stress on literature in reading and English programs
1970–	Studies of child acquisition of language
	Psycholinguistic analysis of reading process
	Description of black English; writing of BE primers
	Concern for affective as well as cognitive learnings
	Studies of sexism in literature and textbooks
	Right to Read Effort at the national level
	Emphasis on reading in secondary schools

As you read through this developmental analysis of reading instruction, it is obvious that reading has changed in emphasis and methodology throughout the century. It would seem, however, that the developments of the present decade promise to offer the most exciting period of all for reading instructors. There are many fascinating concerns. Research is having a unique input at this time. There should be some really significant changes in our approaches to reading at all levels.

CONTEMPORARY OBJECTIVES OF TEACHING READING

What ends are we trying to achieve as we plan a reading program? Usually, lists of objectives are stated in terms of what we adults would have children do, but what are the aims of a reading program for the student himself? Might they not be stated somewhat like this?

A STUDENT'S READING AIMS

I want to read easily and with relative speed,
  To learn new words and to increase my vocabulary,
  To increase my rate of speed in reading,
  To reading interesting books for fun.

I want to explore all kinds of books,
  To browse freely in the library,
  To get help in choosing books sometimes,
  To hear about new books.

I want to find out things through reading,
  To learn about different lands,
  To discover new ideas,
  To find out how other people live.

I want to read good stories,
To compare different kinds of stories,
To admire an author's performance with words,
To enjoy the story he tells,
To try to write stories myself.

I want to tell others about the ideas I have,
To talk about ideas with other students,
To compare points of view about one book,
To be able to read aloud.

If we subscribe to these objectives for the reading program, we must seriously consider patterning the reading program to meet these needs. We shall explore the possibilities for incorporating these objectives in the reading curriculum as we describe an effective reading program for contemporary elementary school students.

INSTRUCTIONAL METHODS

It is impossible in one chapter to discuss all approaches to reading instruction with sufficient depth to be able to analyze their strengths and shortcomings. For that reason we will discuss only a few selected approaches which are both innovative in nature and appear to have unusual promise. New methods in reading include the Initial Teaching Alphabet, Programmed Instruction, Language-Experience Instruction, the Phonemic Approach, and Individualized Reading. Before studying innovative programs, we should briefly examine the reading program as it typically exists at present.

THE BASAL READER APPROACH

The method of instruction most widely used in reading is the "basal reader," or "controlled vocabulary," approach. Almost every textbook company has a series of reading books for grades one through eight, usually with two or more titles prepared for each grade level. This highly structured method of teaching reading is based on student texts, workbooks, and teacher's editions which provide detailed guidance for the teacher. Use of the basal reader series has the following attributes:

1 It represents an early attempt to provide for the sequential development of reading instruction.
2 It assists the beginning teacher who is uncertain about the teaching of reading.
3 It provides the poorly trained teacher with an approach to reading which is acceptable.

As new approaches to reading have been explored, the basal reader approach has received much critical attention. Slavish adherence to the "system" has sometimes resulted in attitudes like that of the principal who stated: "I don't care how well Ann reads. She is to go through the basic reader as any other fourth grader. And I don't want to find her in the library again doing special work." [8] The following questions have been raised:

1 Can any *one* system provide for individual needs of students?
2 Is the material read in this reading program of highest literary quality?
3 Is the basal reader program monopolizing the reading program to the exclusion of the teaching of literature in the elementary school?
4 Are teachers using the program to its fullest potential, or is it used as a "crutch"?
5 Are teachers, especially at upper grade levels, really *teaching* reading?
6 Are children motivated to read each story, or are reading experiences assigned routinely, with workbook pages used as *busy work*?
7 Has the basal reader program been successful in producing a citizenry that reads?

INITIAL TEACHING ALPHABET

Consisting of an augmented Roman alphabet of forty-letters, the Initial Teaching Alphabet, commonly known by the acronym ITA, represents an attempt to provide a one-to-one correspondence between the sounds of English and the letters which we use to signal each sound. To avoid confusion, no special upper case letters are used. This alphabet is reproduced on the following page.

The contribution of Sir James Pitman, ITA was introduced in England in 1959 and has been used in both England and the United States. The Early to Read Series consists of seven books using the Initial Teaching Alphabet; the last book of the series is aimed at assisting the transition to traditional orthography. Both the reading texts and titles from children's literature are available.

An experimental program in the Fremont Unified School District, California, found the following advantages in the use of ITA:

1 First-grade children learned to write creatively at the middle of the year.
2 Interest level of ITA materials was considered higher, with less repetition and with vocabulary similar to that used by the child.
3 With the sound symbols, the child could attack any word.
4 Parents were favorably impressed.

[8] Cynthia Parsons, Education Editor, *The Christian Science Monitor* (January 22, 1965).

face
bed
cat
dog
key
feet
leg
hat
fly
jug
key
letter
man
nest
over
pen
girl
red
spoon
tree
use
voice
window
yes
zebra
daisy
when
chair
three
the
shop
television
ring
father
ball
cap
egg
milk
box
up
book
spoon
out
oil

Disadvantages noted were:

1 Difficulties when children transferred to other schools.
2 Expense of the program (texts were not state-adopted).
3 Substitute teachers were unable to teach this alphabet.[9]

One creative teacher who teaches in the above school district produces materials like this to use with her class:

the beetls ar a swinging grωp,
thæ reelly ar the fad.
but when ie plæ thær records lωud,
it mæks mie pærents mad.

She has also found it relatively easy to adapt familiar songs for use with children who are reading with the Initial Teaching Alphabet as in this "translation" of the folksong, "Go Tell Aunt Rhody."

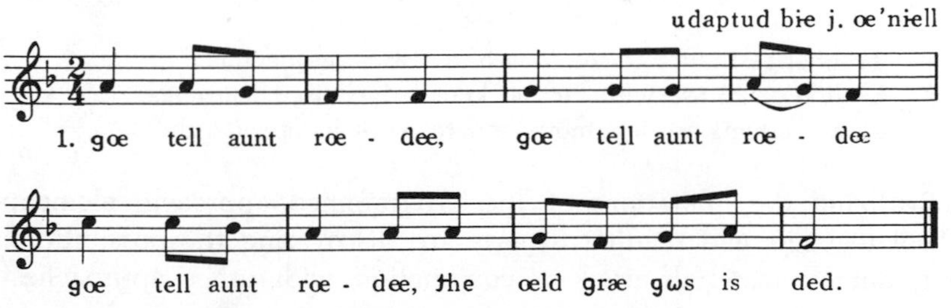

Words adapted by Janie O'Neill. Used by permission.

[9] James T. Howden, "Exploring the Initial Teaching Alphabet," *The First R* (Burlingame, Calif.: California Elementary School Administrators Assn., 1966), pp. 21–22.

Although modified alphabets seem to have promise and are still recommended by some researchers, ITA has not been adopted to any great extent. It may have some use as a remedial technique with students who have been "turned off" to reading.

PROGRAMMED INSTRUCTION

Books have been prepared by Sullivan Associates which guide the beginning reader step by step through the acquisition of reading skills. Programmed materials can be especially helpful at varied levels of reading development ranging from visual discrimination to the study of affixes to exploration of literature concepts. Programmed materials include not only books and workbooks but also "machines" which immediately indicate whether the student's answer is correct. An interesting study is being made of instruction in reading with a computer-assisted instructional system at Stanford University where first-grade children are being taught to read.[10]

The advantages of programmed instruction are several:

1 Programs can be used individually with little aid from the teacher, and each student works at his own rate of speed.
2 The response is immediately checked against the right answer; there is no waiting period for correction of papers.
3 A carefully designed sequence will cover all points in a developmental program.
4 Programs are planned in such small learning units that children are able to succeed.
5 The teacher is freed for *teaching;* drill type tasks, for example, spelling, identification of letters, can be programmed.

Disadvantages of the programmed approach lie in the following:

1 Teacher resistance to the idea of a "teaching machine."
2 Limitation to use with factual knowledge, fixed learnings.
3 Slow students are less motivated to work independently.

Realizing the limitations of the programmed approach, elementary school teachers and reading experts are discovering the possibilities of programmed materials used in conjunction with other approaches to reading.

[10] Richard C. Atkinson, Project Director, *Progress Report: A Reading Curriculum for a Computer-Assisted Instructional System: The Stanford Project* (Stanford, Calif.: Stanford University), 1966.

THE PHONEMIC APPROACH

Linguistic scholars, as we note in other chapters, have contributed much to our understanding of the English language and its functioning. Among their contributions have been the following concepts:

1 Language is constantly changing.
2 Change is normal.
3 English sentences follow specific patterns.
4 Word order conveys meaning.
5 There are specific phonemes and graphemes for the English language.
6 The grammar of a language is its structure.
7 Usage is not rigid but relative.

The application of these concepts of language has revolutionized the teaching of language and approaches to composition. It is not surprising that linguists have also attempted to apply linguistic concepts to reading instruction. Thus far, however, the results are disappointing, for the "linguistic" approach, almost solely a phonemic-graphemic presentation, has produced material like this:

had	can	cat	bag
lad	Dan	fat	nag
pad	man	hat	rag
sad	pan	rat	tag

Dan had a bat.
Has Ann a bag?
Ann had a bag.
Nat had a nag.
A fat cat had a rat.
A man had a hat.
Fat had a nap.[11]

The linguist's approach to reading is essentially based on the presentation of words by phonemic and graphemic groups. As in the linguistic approaches to spelling, the child is introduced to a family of words, for example, *look, book, cook, took, hook.* Those advocating this linguistic approach to beginning reading point out that children can learn groups of words rather than single words. While learning *eat,* the child might just as well learn *beat, heat, meat, neat, seat,* and so on. It is a simple step also to branch out to related phonograms as in this Linguistic Relationship Diagram.

[11] Leonard Bloomfield and Clarence L. Barnhart, *Let's Read, A Linguistic Approach* (Detroit: Wayne State University, 1961), p. 2.

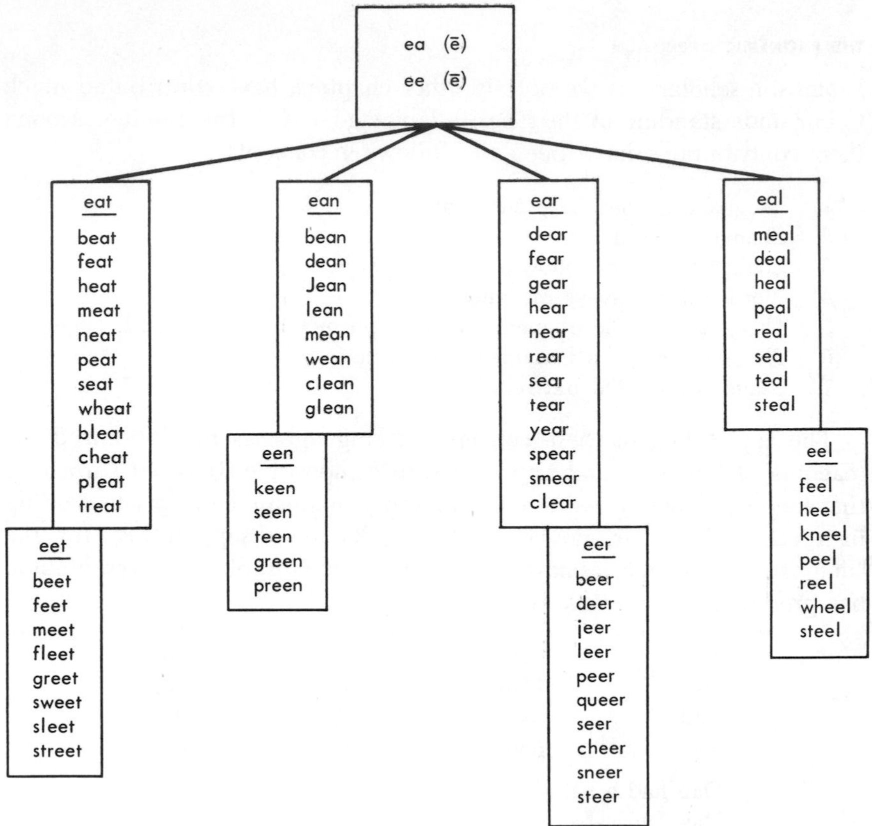

Although this approach has validity for the teaching of spelling, as an answer to beginning reading instruction, it leaves much to be desired. What is it that linguists are ignoring in approaching reading?—children's interests, their previously acquired large vocabulary, their knowledge of language patterns. Critics of the "basal reader" approach to reading instruction have long decried the "Dick and Jane" content of basal readers which relied on sight recognition of words which were repeated *ad nauseam* to enable the child to learn the words.

Are the linguists offering a more stimulating content when they suggest reading matter like that advocated by Fries //Pat a fat cat// //Pat a fat rat//.[12] It is audacious, perhaps, but enlightening, to compare this material with that produced by Theodore Geisel, hardly a linguistic scholar, in *The Cat in the Hat* (Random House).

[12] Charles C. Fries, *Linguistics and Reading* (New York: Holt, Rinehart, and Winston, 1962), p. 203.

As one critic of the linguistic approach notes:

> One danger of phonemic reading programs is that their scientific base will give them great respectability and they will gain wide use before they have been sufficiently tried. There are two other dangers. One is that fuller application of linguistics to reading will be delayed. The other is that educators will reject linguistics while rejecting phonemic reading programs.[13]

We must be cognizant of the "faddish" tendency to tack the magic "linguistic" label on all English and reading programs. It is important to probe further to determine how linguistic findings have been brought to bear on content presented, how linguistics has improved effectiveness of instruction. We must not hesitate to criticize because we are intimidated by the reputation of those who are, sometimes for the first time, delving into the field of reading instruction. Linguistics has made a tremendous contribution to the study of English, but much rethinking and study of applied linguistics must take place before its fullest potential is realized, particularly in the teaching of reading.

LANGUAGE-EXPERIENCE APPROACH

Associated with the work of teachers in San Diego County, California, the language-experience approach to reading considers reading as part of the total language development of the child. Beginning experiences in reading evolve from experiences with oral and written language. Child-dictated experiences, child-composed sentences and stories, furnish the material for reading as described by Allen and Lee.[14] The steps followed are these:

1 An experience common to the group—field trip, story read, an experiment, film, classroom incident, topic introduced by the teacher, a picture
2 Class discussion with sentences recorded by the teacher, aide, or students
3 Reading the composed story aloud, discussion of words
4 Duplicated copy of story used in individual and group reading experiences
5 Follow-up activities—varied reading opportunities, dictation of individual sentences according to ability, small group work to extend abilities, language study, listening to literature, extension of vocabularies

[13] Kenneth S. Goodman, "The Linguistics of Reading," *The Elementary School Journal* (April, 1964), pp. 357–58.
[14] R. Van Allen and Doris M. Lee, *Learning to Read through Experience* (New York: Appleton-Century-Crofts, 1963).

This approach to reading is distinctly different from others described, for it moves away from the prepared reading text. It appears to have the following advantages:

1 Reading material has high interest value; the child is able to read what he has composed. He knows the vocabulary.
2 The approach develops according to individual needs, interests, abilities; the child reads because he *wants* to read.
3 Repetition of skill instruction in separate areas of language study, for example, phonology, is eliminated through a total approach to language study.
4 Reading material reflects the child's knowledge of English grammar—sentence patterns, word order, intonation.

The chief disadvantage of the language-experience approach from the view of a teacher is that it is less highly structured. Each group of children, each child, having varied experiental backgrounds, will produce different reading material. The teacher is required to be more flexible, and for that reason, may feel less secure in working with this type of approach which develops spontaneously. This is the same difficulty the teacher encounters in any oral language program. Another disadvantage which is noted is that content is limited by the child's knowledge; there is no provision for vocabulary development. New concepts and vocabulary must be introduced through planned experiences, through wide reading of literature, and through incidental instruction.

Despite this demand on teacher ingenuity and skill in working with the group as it learns and develops its own materials (which makes for a more creative approach to teaching), this approach warrants careful consideration, for is it not a truly "linguistic" approach? Recognizing its limitations, it appears to the authors that the total language approach to language, composition, and reading (evolving quickly into literature) potentially incorporates all the concepts of linguistics with our knowledge of the needs of children and the best of learning theory. The language-experience approach, therefore, has much to commend it as a beginning approach to reading instruction.

INDIVIDUALIZED READING

The individualized approach to reading is scarcely a new concept, for it was an essential part of the Progressive Movement in the 1930s. The Winnetka Plan (Illinois) is one example of these earlier attempts to individualize learning. Children read silently at their individual rates of speed, answered prepared questions on the material read, and read aloud individually to the teacher.

Another plan for individualized learning was the Dalton Plan (Massachusetts) which used a laboratory approach to encourage students to achieve self-determined contracts for units of work to be accomplished. This plan granted the student much freedom and experience in planning and in budgeting time.

Both of these plans were rigid in content, however, and goals were in terms of adult needs rather than those of the child. Contemporary attempts at individualizing reading instruction stress not only quantity of reading but also the child's motivation to read more extensively. Great varieties of reading materials are needed for a successful individualized reading program.

The advantages of the individualized approach to reading include:

1 Wide use of library materials and free selection are possible.
2 Broader range of reading subjects is achieved.
3 Learning experiences are extended.
4 Reading skills are taught through small group approaches.
5 Evaluation includes personal conferences.
6 Stress is put on individual development to fullest potential.
7 The gifted student is stimulated.

There is no set prescription for the individualized program in reading. As Leland Jacobs observes:

> In the first place, "individualized reading" is not a single method with predetermined steps in procedures to be followed. It is not possible to say that every teacher who would individualize guidance in reading must do this or that. It is not feasible or desirable to present a simple, single methodological formulation of what is right in "individualized reading" which every teacher shall follow.[15]

The individualized approach to reading has had excellent results with average and superior readers. The one disadvantage noted is the inability of slow students to cope with the individualized method of working. Better readers enjoy the opportunity to read widely and to share their reading experiences with other students. They also respond to the stimulus of the individual conference.[16] We shall explore individualized reading as a means for bringing literature into the elementary school reading program in the next chapter.

[15] Leland Jacobs, "Individualized Reading Is Not a Thing," in *Individualizing Reading Practices,* Alice Miel, ed. (New York: Teachers College, 1958).

[16] Harry Sartain, "The Roseville Experiment with Individualized Reading," *The Reading Teacher* (April, 1960), p. 277.

A Forward-Looking Reading Program

Which of these reading programs shall we choose? None of them? All of them? Can we wait until the perfect program is developed? No single approach to reading appears to have all the answers. It is interesting to note that research findings are inconclusive. Studies of individualized instruction, for example, provide findings which favor group instruction as well as findings which show the individualized approach to be best.[17] This discrepancy in research findings points up the fact that the reader must beware of research which is not carefully structured. Also, one must note the nature of the specific programs being compared. At this stage we have no research evidence which conclusively recommends one approach to reading over another. There is a need for well-organized longitudinal studies in reading instruction.

Our only recourse, then, is to be eclectic, selecting those approaches which best serve the needs of a superior reading program, for we must assume the responsibility for providing students of the Space Age with a forward-looking reading program. Our students demand a program that:

1 Begins where the student is and permits progress at individual rates of speed
2 Guarantees success from the initial experiences
3 Stresses development of oral language skills and continues to be closely coordinated with the English program to avoid repetition, as in a well-planned phonological sequence
4 Teaches reading skills using reading material of interest to the child
5 Does not belabor the teaching of skills but moves quickly into a program of wide reading of literature with instruction in literary concepts
6 Uses multimedia to present information and to motivate reading
7 Extends abilities to think—analysis, comparison, criticism, comprehension
8 Experiments with varied approaches to meet individual needs incorporating the best of each approach to reading
9 Stimulates real interest in reading for pleasure and information; develops habits which will extent into adulthood
10 Develops research techniques and familiarity with library tools

As we turn our efforts toward development of an excellent reading program, we might note Stauffer's advice:

> . . . one must, first, drop the notion that a basic reader program in and of itself is final and sacred. It is not. Second, one must drop the notion that

[17] Nila B. Smith, *Reading Instruction for Today's Children* (Englewood Cliffs, N.J.: Prentice-Hall, 1963), pp. 154–59.

> time can be equated with equality. Not every group must be met every day for the same length of time. Third, the idea that a basic book recommended for a grade level must be "finished" by all pupils in a grade before they can be promoted must be discarded. Fourth, teaching reading as a *memoriter* process by presenting new words in advance of the reading and then having pupils tell back the story must be stopped. If reading is taught as a thinking process, even short basic-reader stories will be read with enthusiasm. . . . Sixth, effective skills of word attack must be taught. Basic reading books do not provide for such skill training; neither do trade books.[18]

How can we best meet the criteria we have established? Let us consider the various approaches to reading in terms of these criteria. It is our observation that the language-experience approach most nearly meets the first four requirements, for the students are highly motivated to read the stories which they have composed, and the stories can be successfully read because the vocabulary is known to the child. Included are interesting words as well as the commonly used vocabulary, the basic sight words which the child needs to know. This reading program is closely coordinated with the English program, for children develop skills of composition and reading as a direct result of spoken language, and children have repeated opportunities to use sentence patterns and varied classes of words before formal grammar study is initiated. Emphasis is placed on the development of listening skills as well as speaking skills as the teacher introduces literature through reading aloud and as many opportunities are provided for dramatization and sharing of experiences.

In order for the teacher to develop an exciting reading program that is firmly based in the whole language-arts curriculum, it is essential to know what materials are available. No single set of materials can provide everything that is most desirable. The teacher, however, has many kinds of materials and approaches to consider and to draw from. In addition to the series of English and reading textbooks published by most of the major publishing houses, explore these innovative ideas to see what you might derive from them:

The Aloha Project (based on the Hawaii English Project)
The Distar Program
Interaction (A Student-Centered Language-Arts and Reading Program for K–12 by James Moffett, published by Houghton Mifflin)

Greater understanding of the reading process is coming from psycholinguists who stress the fact that, although reading requires visual

[18] Russell G. Stauffer, "Individualized and Group Directed Reading Instruction," *Elementary English* (October, 1960), p. 381.

input, it also requires even greater input from the brain in terms of knowledge of language and of the world in general. Beginning readers, therefore, know much about reading before they even begin. In summary, psycholinguists state that:

1 Only a small part of the information necessary for reading comes from the printed page.
2 Comprehension must precede the identification of individual words (reading is not primarily visual).
3 Reading is not decoding to sound.[19]

These concepts may seem surprising to many teachers who have had earlier training in reading. It is often necessary to reconsider old methods in light of newer findings; it is important to keep our minds open to fresh input. Studies show us that the young reader requires feedback more than anything else during the beginning stages. The structured drill that we offer may serve no real purpose other than to stymie the child who wants to "get on with it." Essentially the child learns to read by reading, and our task as teachers is to assist the child in reading as freely, easily, and quickly as possible.

Individualized approaches to reading consider the child's needs first, whether children work in groups or alone. Teachers are gradually developing Learning Centers, first a small one in the corner, then two or three, and often the whole room becomes a Learning Center as shown in the illustration. As they work at self-selected tasks, children make discoveries and are excited about their work and their growth. Individual conferences between child and teacher provide a time to get acquainted, a time to talk together.

Discovery methods will encourage children to develop generalizations about phonology, syntax, and semantics. These discoveries will benefit the whole language program (including reading) and avoid the repetition of instruction. The coordination of spelling with reading and composition following the linguistics approach which presents linguistic families—*came, game, tame, lame, same, fame*—is a sound method which makes the spelling task more efficient. These aspects of language are taught in conjunction with the language-experience instruction in beginning reading rather than as three distinct "subjects"—reading, spelling, English.

As soon as the child develops a basic reading vocabulary—and this stage may be reached in first or second grade, depending on the background and ability of the child—he is able to begin reading selections

[19] Frank Smith, *Psycholinguistics and Reading* (New York: Holt, Rinehart, and Winston, 1973), p. 8.

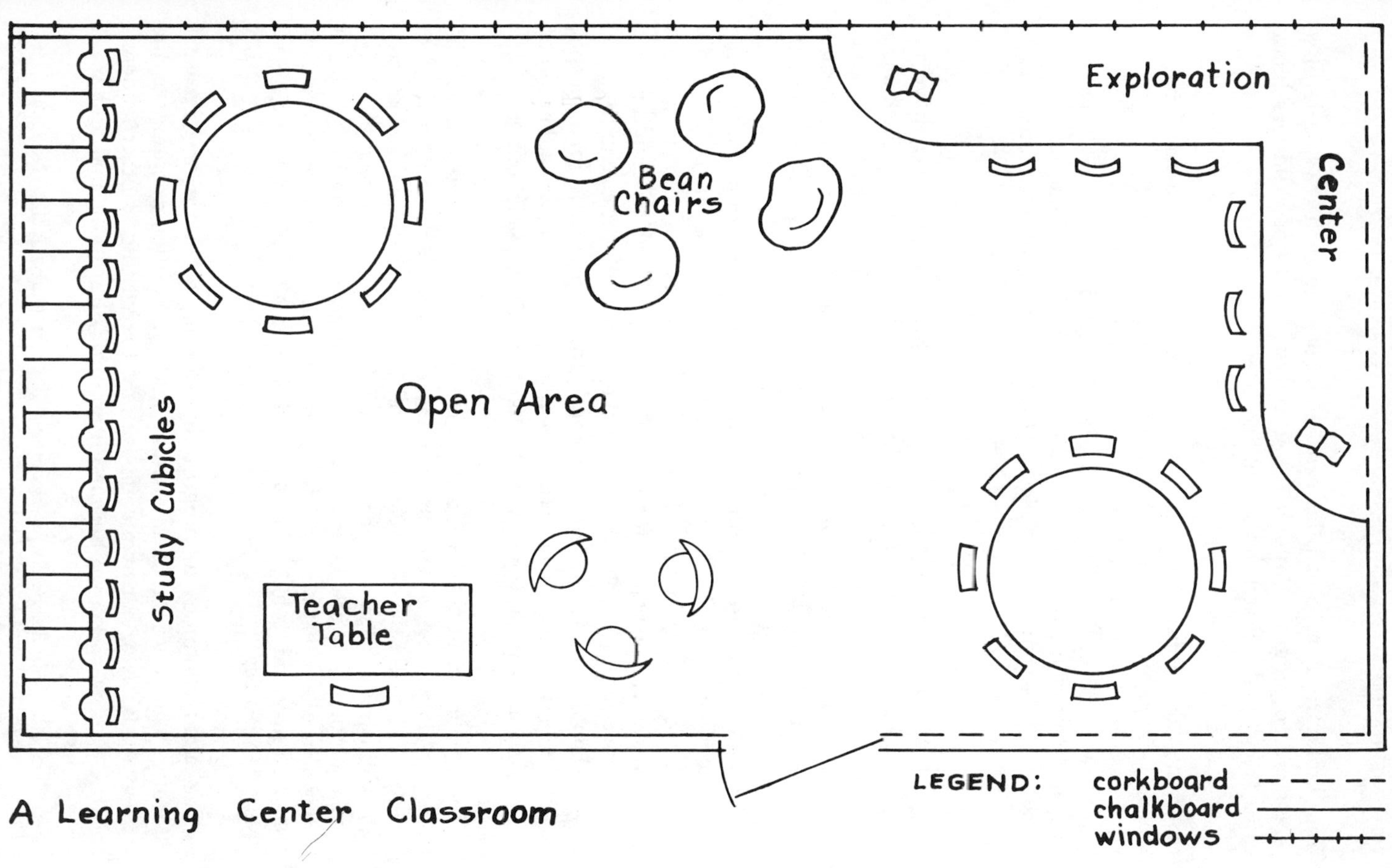

A Learning Center Classroom

from literature. A core of titles can be assigned to each reading level so that children progress through the wonderful world of children's literature. Titles at the first level might include: [20]

Maurice Sendak, *Where the Wild Things Are.* Monsters can be captivating.
Wanda Gág, *Millions of Cats.* The refrain has appeal.
Dr. Seuss, *The Cat in the Hat.* Simple vocabulary, but fun!
Else H. Minarik, *Little Bear.* Four stories, illustrated by Maurice Sendak.
Syd Hoff, *Danny and the Dinosaur.* Adventures with a museum dinosaur!
Mabel Watts, *When the Horses Galloped to London.* Imagine catching a highwayman!

What about vocabulary level? What about wordlists? We have too long been hampered by these scientific approaches to a child's vocabulary. The child who comes to school chattering about space flights and other adult information that he grasps with amazing enthusiasm and eagerness should not be hemmed in by that mythical 200 words which supposedly is all he can manage.

We must credit ideas and intriguing words with some motivating power in themselves. Children are fascinated by monsters, so the "wild things" portrayed by Maurice Sendak lead them to read the story which includes interesting words, for example, "rumpus," which children love. We are missing an opportunity to make *readers* of these children.

We should supply, furthermore, the "grown-up" words for concepts, objects, ideas for children hear them as in many cases they use them; they will delight in reading them, too. As Nancy Larrick points out:

> The practice of teaching children wrong names for things that have relatively simple names is certainly open to question. Indeed, if one purpose of reading is to help the child reach out and grow, why not use the exact word he will hear in school conversation and TV news reports instead of a baby-talk substitute? At first he may miss the more grown-up word in print, but the chances are that he knows it by ear. His pride in learning to read such a word may add to his self-respect and do a great deal to increase his interest in reading.[21]

The child continues to progress by reading literature of increasing difficulty. The coordination of reading and composition continues as the student reads his or her own compositions, the writing of other students, and the writing of known authors, literature. Both individual and small

[20] Elizabeth Guilfoile, *Books for Beginning Readers* (Urbana, Ill.: National Council of Teachers of English, 1962).

[21] Nancy Larrick, *A Teacher's Guide to Children's Books* (Columbus, Ohio: Charles E. Merrill, 1963), p. 26.

group approaches to the reading of literature are used, with students being encouraged to discuss literary concepts both as a composer and as one who appreciates the skill of others. This type of discussion is facilitated through individual conferences and student seminars. Varied reading skills are stressed as students work in other subject areas and engage in individual research.

Programmed materials can be drawn into the reading program for the teaching of word attack skills, development of vocabulary, and comprehension. The Initial Teaching Alphabet appears to offer excellent possibilities in reading remediation in that the "new alphabet" has appeal for the reader who has not been successful with other approaches.

We will discard "grade level" limitations which restrict progress and tend to routinize the teaching of reading in favor of an exploratory attitude toward reading which involves three stages: (1) preparation for reading, (2) introduction to reading, and (3) independent reading. Stage 1 occurs during preschool and kindergarten years; Stage 2 may begin in the kindergarten year and extend through first, second, and third grades; Stage 3 may begin in third grade and will continue throughout life.

PREPARATION FOR READING

Encourages positive attitudes toward learning
Develops oral abilities
Provides many listening experiences
Works toward linguistic fluency and sentence expansion
Develops vocabulary—speaking and listening
Orients the child to words and books
Develops auditory and visual perception
Provides experiential backgrounds
Enjoys literature through dramatization and listening

INTRODUCTION TO READING

Coordinates writing and reading activities
Develops a program in phonology for reading and spelling
Continues to extend vocabularies—oral, written, read
Introduces poetry appreciation and composition
Continues varied listening activities, increasing attention span
Encourages creativity in all language activities
Uses small group and individual approaches
Diagnoses individual needs through conferencing
Provides a broad background in literature

INDEPENDENT READING

Encourages wide reading of literature
Introduces literary concepts in poetry and prose

Uses individual and seminar approaches
Employs discovery techniques and individual research
Teaches library skills and basic library tools
Coordinates literature and language learnings
Stimulates the sharing of books and book reviewing
Extends learnings through reading
Assists the student in book selection
Develops the habit of reading for pleasure and information

Preparation for Reading

Perhaps the chief purpose for many parents in sending their child to school is to learn to read. It is with great expectancy on the parts of both parent and child that he or she enters first grade "ready to read." But is the child really "ready"?

WHAT IS READINESS?

Our first problem in determining readiness for reading is to clarify the meaning of this term. *Readiness* is no clearly defined time in a child's development, for we can talk about readiness to learn almost any new skill which may be taught at varied periods of a student's life. Readiness, we see, is not a term associated exclusively with reading. Readiness is a state of being prepared, sufficiently mature and mentally able, to undertake a task, and being interested in attacking the learning job. We are always ready to learn something.

When is a child ready to read? We cannot state with any certainty that Al will be ready, for example, to read at the age of six, if he has an IQ of 100, for readiness varies with each individual. The child is ready to read when he shows that he is ready, when he notices letters, asks what they are, and begins trying to read words. This state of readiness depends on a complex multiplicity of abilities which in many cases are acquired incidentally but which in other cases require formal instruction. We can develop readiness for reading as well as for other learning by stressing activities which develop (1) positive attitudes toward school, (2) oral language abilities, (3) experiential backgrounds, (4) visual and auditory discrimination, and (5) word and book orientation.

POSITIVE ATTITUDES TOWARD SCHOOL

An important aspect of preparing a child for learning is the development of a positive attitude toward learning, which for the child is usually concretely exemplified by the teacher and the school building. First experiences in the school situation must leave the child with a feeling of satisfaction, a sense of having succeeded in the adventure of moving out in the world. Al must also retain an assurance that the teacher likes him and respects him as a worthwhile individual. In order to produce positive feelings in the discerning child the teacher must project warmth and enthusiasm which is conveyed through many small acts during the day:

1 Eye contact with the students, as during a story hour
2 Physical contact—in a game, a friendly pat of encouragement, a hand on the shoulder while helping
3 Direct address by name when requesting assistance, greeting, saying good-bye, calling on students to respond
4 Smiling, a touch of humor, show of enthusiasm
5 PRAISE for the individual and the group to promote feelings of success

ORAL LANGUAGE

With the emphasis of linguistic studies on oral language has come renewed awareness of the importance of oral language development as a firm basis for beginning reading experiences. The interrelationship of oral language development and success in reading has been pointed out by the Task Force Report published by the National Council of Teachers of English, which recommends greater stress on oral language, for:

> Only as progress is made in the use of oral language will there be substantial improvement in reading and writing. The interdependence of these language skills has been demonstrated both in research and in practice.[22]

Walter Loban states: "Schools are beginning to be aware that research shows a powerful linkage between oral language and writing or reading—one much greater than has previously been realized."[23] The neglect of oral language instruction he attributes to the lack of clear-cut evaluation methods. It is obvious that teachers have shied away from oral instruction in favor of reading and writing possibly because oral activities are less structured.

The chapters on speaking and listening both supply numerous suggestions for developing oral language abilities, as does the chapter on language study. Let us note, however, the wide range of classroom activities that contribute directly to oral language abilities, which in turn contribute to reading success:

[22] NCTE Task Force on Teaching English to the Disadvantaged, *Language Programs for the Disadvantaged* (Urbana, Ill.: National Council of Teachers of English, 1965), pp. 272–73.

[23] Walter Loban, "Oral Language Proficiency Affects Reading and Writing," *Instructor* (March, 1966), p. 97.

LISTENING

Attention span
Auditory discrimination
Following directions
Understanding the other person
Listening for a purpose

INDIVIDUAL SPEAKING TO THE GROUP

"Sharing" or "Show and Tell"
Impromptu talks
Storytelling
Reporting
Telling a joke or riddle

SPEAKING SIMULTANEOUSLY

Choral approaches to poetry
Sentence pattern practice
Finger plays

DISCUSSIONS

Preparation of experience charts
Planned discussion about a picture, object, etc.
Exploring other subjects–science, social science, health
Planning together
Committee participation

SINGING

Repetitive songs
Familiar choruses
Folk music
Games and dances

CONVERSATION

Role playing
Dialogue in dramatizations
Telephone
Interview
Progressive pattern practice
Introductions

DRAMATIZATION

Puppetry
Creative play

Humorous skits by students
Pantomime
Retelling a story

How does the development of oral language prepare a child to read with greater success? One of the major contributions is in the enjoyment of language and the many ways we use language; the reading of language thus becomes a natural progression for the child who is prepared to be receptive to this new way of working with language. A second important aspect of oral language is the development of the child's vocabulary, for beginning readers will progress more surely if they are familiar with many words so that language to be read is understandable in meaning if not in form. The sounds of English are introduced orally, for aural discrimination between sounds is important to later identification of differences between words.

EXPERIENTIAL BACKGROUNDS

In the elementary school, experiential backgrounds typically vary widely in a single classroom. The horizons of some children may be very narrow compared to the broad horizons of those who have had many opportunities to explore. The experiential background of the child is the total product of his or her way of living, environment, family origins, and will be influenced by all of the following factors and more:

Education of parents
Encouragement of child's development
Socioeconomic status of the family
Number of books and periodicals in the home
Opportunities to travel, to explore the community
Encouragement of self-expression

The child who lacks the background which provides a wide variety of concepts must be assisted in developing a background of experiences to supplement meager knowledge, for experiences stimulate thinking. They provide referents for the reading of new words. The classroom teacher can expand horizons through:

Educational trips—zoo, post office, fire station, library, airport, parks, nearby cities, train and bus rides
Classroom adventures—a pet, interesting person, new games, unusual objects, different foods
Multimedia—films, records, filmstrips, pictures
Reading aloud—science information, stories, news items

VISUAL AND AUDITORY DISCRIMINATION

Before beginning the formal reading program, the child needs practice in making discriminations, in noting differences and likenesses. In this way he/she is prepared to make the more minute discriminations necessary when two similar words are encountered in reading. Experiences which help the child notice similarities and differences can be visual as in these examples:

Put an X on the two shapes which are the same. (Directions are oral.)

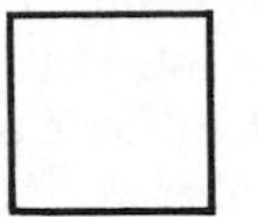  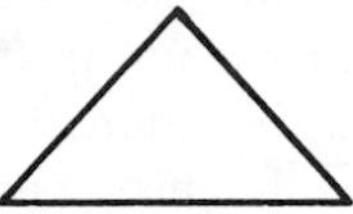

Draw a circle around the star which is biggest.

Which two letters are exactly alike?
B b T B

Underline the two words which look exactly alike.
book man go man

Auditory discrimination involves listening and the ability to hear differences and similarities of sound. A variety of activities will assist the child in making these discriminations:

Which word begins like FALL?
pan fence hello

Which two words begin alike?
happy bed horse

Which word does *not* begin like the others?
carrot help candy coffee

Can you name another word that begins like *chair?*

Many will be suggested; some will be wrong so the teacher will need to repeat CHAIR to help the child see the difference.

shell–The child is confusing the SH sound with CH.

mare–The child is rhyming the ending sound rather than comparing the beginning sound.

Which word begins like SHEEP? (Closer discrimination.)
slip shoe stay

WORD AND BOOK ORIENTATION

As a part of readiness for learning, the child is introduced to the word as a symbol which conveys meaning long before he is actually taught to read. Orientation to words is easily achieved by the use of words as identifying labels around the room: *chalkboard, Tom Turtle, Helpers, October, Mrs. Walton. . . .* These words are introduced casually with no effort to move into reading. Children will gradually show more interest, however, in knowing words, and certainly their questions along these lines should be answered, for there is little to be gained by saying, "Wait," to an eager child.

In this same way the child is introduced to books as something to read, and Al learns to hold a book right side up, to open the cover toward the left. He learns that the printed symbols are words which will tell him a story, that we read from left to right, and that we begin reading at the top of the page. (Later, students will be fascinated to learn that these habits are not the same for all countries or languages.) Book orientation is best achieved through the handling of books, and most children have already acquired much of this knowledge before entering school. The teacher can informally present these concepts as she reads aloud from a book. The left to right concept is reinforced as experience stories are printed on the chalkboard.

Introduction to Reading

We have already discussed in some detail various methods of teaching children to read. In this section, therefore, we shall concentrate on the development of a reading vocabulary. The recognition of words, the ability to associate the printed symbol with meaning, depends on a variety of skills as well as experiential background and the child's listening and speaking vocabularies. Clearly, reading is closely integrated with all language development and will be facilitated by development in other language skills.

The most important aspect of reading developed at this time is the child's attitude toward reading. The child approaches the learning of reading with great enthusiasm; it is essential that this enthusiasm not be diminished in any way. Do we make reading such a struggle for the beginner that many children become discouraged? The important thing is to make reading a successful experience, one that is highly enjoyable and desirable. We should make sure that reading never acquires the taste of bitter medicine that may be associated with excessive emphasis on drill. Let's reconsider several aspects of reading.

SIGHT WORDS

There are many small words that are used frequently and that do not usually lend themselves to analysis—*a, the, who, were* . . . These words are the ones which children must learn to recognize without hesitation if skill in reading is to be attained. Many lists have been compiled, for example, that by Edward Dolch [24] which consists of 220 words (no nouns).

There is some question whether a sight vocabulary need really be that large, however, for the newer trend of teaching words in linguistic groups would teach *all, call, fall, small* (included in the Dolch list) as part of the *all* family along with *ball, hall, tall,* and *wall.* In the same manner, *an, can,* and *ran* (from the Dolch list) would be taught with *Dan, fan, man, tan.* These words are regular in pronunciation and are readily learned on the basis of the phonogram represented.

Certainly there is a core of words which must be learned by sight, for they are not related to a linguistic family or are irregular in pronunciation—*are, been, does, from, of, one, said, very, was, what.* These words should be taught in context as much as possible rather than through drill on isolated words. Many words become "sight" words for the able reader who no longer needs to analyze every word he meets. We need chiefly to provide many opportunities for the child to read and to reinforce knowledge of words through use.

> Labels used around the room can develop into phrases and sentences which include words that trouble children.
>
> the chalkboard
> Many Helpers
> What does Tom Turtle eat?
> One fish is black. Two fish are gold.
>
> Introduce children to Reversals, which we sometimes call PUSH-ME-PULL-ME words because they can go either direction. Interest in this study of word oddities will assist children in identifying WAS and SAW which are just like other pairs they will discover:
>
> NOT—TON SPEED—DEEPS DRAW—WARD

Certainly we should not spend time in class reading lists of sight words or identifying isolated words on cards. The child will learn words that

[24] Edward W. Dolch, *Methods in Reading* (Champaign, Ill.: Garrard Publishing Co., 1955), pp. 373–74.

are used frequently through reading them in sentences. Have children dictate their own sentences as you print them on a sheet of paper or beneath a painted picture, thus:

This is my cat
under the table.

Since this is the child's sentence, all words are familiar. In this way the beginning reader becomes at ease in reading grammatical sentences that offer syntactic clues as well as the visual forms of letters and words. The prepositional phrase is far easier to read than these words would be individually for the young reader.

Group compositions that are printed on the board serve this same purpose as do Experience Charts. There are many opportunities for the child to see written language that has first been spoken aloud.

PHONICS

Phonics instruction has been under almost constant attack. First, it was attacked because we weren't teaching phonics during a period of emphasizing the learning of whole words; and, second, it was attacked because we were overdoing phonics instruction and many of the rules taught were not worth teaching.

What is the position on phonics instruction today? Studies show us that many of the rules taught by zealous teachers really are not sufficiently consistent to warrant teaching.[25] There is also a real question of the efficacy of teaching a rule for which the child has no expressed need. Suppose, for example, we discuss the phoneme /č/ which we associate with the spelling *ch*? We show the children a list of words in which this sound-spelling relationship appears and have them practice saying these isolated words aloud. What purpose have we really accomplished? The children may not encounter the need for this information for some time. When they see a sentence in which this relationship appears—for example, "The children were playing school"—it is likely that the word *children* will be identified through context or illustration clues. The *ch* combination in *school* doesn't fit the rule so would only prove confusing if the child noticed it. As Smith points out:

[25] Frank Smith, "The Efficiency of Phonics," in *Psycholinguistics and Reading* (New York: Holt, Rinehart, and Winston, 1973), pp. 84–90.

> The question that cannot yet be answered concerns the *effectiveness* of phonics: Is the limited degree of efficiency that might be attained worth acquiring? Other factors have to be taken into account related to the cost of trying to learn and use a phonic system. Our working memories do have an infinite capacity and reading is not a task that can be accomplished at too leisurely a pace. Other sources of information exist for finding out what a word in context might be, especially if the word is in the spoken vocabulary of the reader.[26]

Is there any phonic information that might be helpful to the child? In light of our concern for making reading as easy as possible at the beginning stages and moving toward some measure of fluency as fast as possible, it is best to begin reading with the child's own words. These words are both spoken and read, and they are set in the context orally and visually of sentences. The child may also begin writing at this time so that the relationship between speech and writing is developed implicitly.

Children quickly notice the obvious relationship between sounds and symbols, particularly those at the beginning of words. This can be reinforced by asking them to name some other words that begin with the same sound as the word just written, perhaps, *toot*. If they name words such as *tune, tick, tiny,* and *tough,* they have established this relationship firmly without drill at a time when the information was requested. This is the kind of feedback the beginning reader and writer needs. Only a more mature user of language can provide this kind of information. As noted elsewhere, we must provide these informants to work with beginning readers so children are not overburdened with rule learning and left to struggle with decoding.

WORD PLAY

Words, words, wonderful words! Students should be inspired with a positive attitude toward words as they learn to use them and to enjoy them. They should be introduced to "serendipity" and be prepared to make discoveries. Word play provides an excellent motivation toward learning more about words (See Chapter Five) as in these examples:

> CHAIN REACTION—An excellent way to practice knowledge of phonics is to begin a word chain. By changing only one letter to make a new word each time, see how long the chain can be made. A chain (or more than one) can be started with children adding to it in their free time, thus:

[26] *Ibid.*, p. 90.

TAME	FORT	SPOUT
tale	sort	sport
sale	port	short
pale	part	shirt
page	cart	shirk
wage	dart	shark
wade	dark	spark
wide	darn	spare
hide	dare	spire
side	care	spine

TREASURE HUNT—Begin a search for words of a specific nature as everyone adds to a list mounted on the bulletin board or the wordlist begun on the chalkboard. For example, begin a search for words which end in *tion, ong,* or *able* to provide practice with specific suffixes or phonograms. Lend interest to syllable practice by listing words of four, five, or six syllables. For younger children ask for words with three syllables or words with eight letters.

Independent Reading

"The more we read the better we read," is an excellent motto for the elementary school classroom. The child who develops skill with basic vocabulary begins reading independently with assistance from the teacher or a "buddy" only as needed. Good literature tends to provide its own motivation, but the wise teacher will continue to stimulate student reading and will also aid students in evaluating their own progress in reading. Some children may need individual or small group guidance to assist development in specific skills of word attack, extending vocabulary, and comprehension.

The teacher will plan classroom reading instructional activities, too, which will encourage interaction among students who are working independently. The following "guide to good reading" provides a humorous recipe for reading success which may be used to inspire students:

1 Read.
2 Read.
3 Read some more.
4 Read anything.
5 Read about everything.
6 Read enjoyable things.
7 Read things you yourself enjoy.
8 Read, and talk about it.

9 Read very carefully some things.
10 Read on the run, most things.
11 Don't think about reading, but
12 Just read.[27]

STIMULATING STUDENT READING

The best stimulus to wide reading is a large collection of varied titles in a well-organized central library. We can motivate student reading through a variety of strategies, thus:

- *Creative Art Techniques.* Students delight in creating favorite animal characters from newspaper glued in several layers (4–6) over a two-pound coffee can or a large bottle which has been rubbed with oil. After the paper shape has dried, legs, antennae, tails and other needed accouterments can be added as Charlotte, Wilbur, the goose, and other barnyard friends appear. The Musicians of Bremen provide other characters for this medium.

  Paper strips glued around an armature of rolled paper or wire permits the creation of upright figures. There's skinny, rollicking Ribsy, and coming along behind is Henry with a rolled newspaper in his hand. A group of students who like to work in miniature could produce the Borrowers—Pod, Homily, and Arrietty.

- *Bulletin Board Displays.* Let children take turns decorating a small bulletin board with the caption GUESS WHO? Displayed are pictures, drawings, small realia that suggest one book or one character. The creator then tells about his display explaining why he included various items.

- *Stimulating Innovation.* Encourage students to utilize innovative approaches to sharing their reading. After the teacher has demonstrated more exciting ways of presenting a book to the class, students will vie to produce the more unusual presentation. Suggestions might include:

  Mobile
  Diorama
  Peekbox
  Collage
  Puppetry
  Creative Dramatics
  Broadcasting
  Interviewing an author
  Poster
  Scroll Theater
  Book Jackets
  Bookmarks
  Mural
  Literature map
  Storytelling
  Displays
  Advertisement

- *Seminars.* Students will appreciate a mature approach to reading which permits them to gather to discuss a book which a number of the group have read. The

[27] Irving H. Anderson and Walter F. Dearborn, *The Psychology of Teaching Reading* (New York: The Ronald Press, 1952), pp. 165–66.

group can later unite their efforts to present the book to the class through dramatization or puppetry.

• *The Round Robin Book Club.* An interesting way of encouraging reading is the exchange of student-owned books through a Round Robin Book Club arrangement. On a specified day each child brings one book to school, and the exchange begins. To ensure each child's receiving every book, a list is made of the children's names, and each child passes his book to the person whose name follows his own name, that is, he always passes a book to the same child. The passing of books should be regularly scheduled, perhaps once a week, for instance, every Friday. If this proves too short a time, books can be exchanged every other Friday.

• *Teacher Aids.* Included here are a variety of books suggesting activities that assist the teacher in stimulating reading.

Darrow, Helen F., and Allen, R. Van. *Independent Activities for Creative Learning*. New York: Teachers College, 1961.

Games and Self-Testing Activities for the Classroom. Washington; D.C.: U.S. Government Printing Office, 1961.

Kingsley, Bernard. *Reading Skills.* San Francisco: Fearon Publishing Co., 1958.

Russell, David H., and Karp, Etta. *Reading Aids through the Grades.* New York: Teachers College, 1951.

Tiedt, Sidney W., and Tiedt, Iris M. *Exploring Words.* San Jose, Calif.: Contemporary Press, 1964. (Box 1524)

• *Periodicals for Young People.* There is an increasing interest in both magazines and newspapers for young people. These publications have the advantage of coming throughout the year, and for that reason tend to encourage the continuation of reading beyond the classroom. They also feature current information about interesting topics and can be used to stimulate both speaking and writing experiences. Magazines recommended for young people include:

American Forests. 1319-18th Street, N.W., Washington, D.C. 20036.

American Girl. 830 Third Ave., New York, N.Y. 10022.

Boy's Life. New Brunswick, N.J. 08902.

Child Life. 1100 Waterway Blvd, Indianapolis, Ind. 46202.

Children's Digest. 52 Vanderbilt Avenue, New York, N.Y. 10017.

Cricket. P.O. Box 100, LaSalle, Ill. 61301.

Highlights for Children. 2300 West 5th Avenue, Columbus, Ohio 43216.

Humpty Dumpty's Magazine. 52 Vanderbilt Avenue, New York, N.Y. 10017.

Jack and Jill. Box 528, Indianapolis, Ind. 46202.

My Weekly Reader. 245 Long Hill Rd., Middletown, Conn. 06457.

National Geographic and *National Geographic School Bulletin.* 17th and M Streets, N.W., Washington, D.C. 20036.

Scholastic Magazines. 50 West 44th Street, New York, N.Y. 10036.
Science Digest. 224 West 57th Street, New York, N.Y. 10019.

Commercial book clubs There are a number of commercial book clubs which are popular with children and serve to encourage reading and the exchange of books, as well as the acquisition of a personal library for the child. Several are offering inexpensive hardback editions while others specialize in paperback editions at very low prices. You can obtain information about these clubs to make available to children and parents.

Junior Literary Guild, 277 Park Avenue, New York, N.Y. 10017.
Parents' Magazine's Book Clubs, 52 Vanderbilt Avenue, New York, N.Y. 10017.
Scholastic Book Clubs, 50 West 44th Street, New York, N.Y. 10036.

For other suggestions about motivating children's interest in reading, review the following chapter on literature.

CONTINUING VOCABULARY GROWTH

The avid reader usually has no difficulty in acquiring an extensive vocabulary, but even he or she may require assistance with pronunciation and connotations, if not denotations, of words encountered. The study of words adds much to intellectual development at any stage, and it certainly is not limited to the reading period alone, for much effective learning about words takes place in other subject areas.

As noted frequently throughout this book, teacher interest and enthusiasm for words will be contagious. The teacher who leads the way in making discoveries and talking to children about words will produce students who are aware of words and their meanings and who often observe intriguing features of words. Through writing and speaking experiences they come to delight in using new, less common words, in searching for synonyms, and in "trying out" discoveries on classmates as well as the teacher. Our daughter, for example, referred to the rumblings of her stomach as "borborygmi" which mystified us all until she shared her discovery. And remember how delighted you were when you first heard of words like "expectorate" and "osculate"?

Use interesting words as you speak to children (not the above examples, perhaps); they will absorb them as their own. "You're an example of *sartorial* splendor, Mike! Do you know what that means?" Write it on the board, but let him do his own investigating. "I see Vicky has a new *coiffeur* today." "The king *abdicated* his throne." "Let's *specu-*

late about what might have happened if we had not entered the war." The only requirement for this approach to word study is knowledge on the part of the teacher; you may need to "grow a vocabulary" ahead of or with your students, and if you work with a group of able fifth or sixth graders, they may lead the way. Even in the primary grades we can eliminate "baby talk," avoid "talking down," and help them reach out to grasp new words to express new ideas. It's a pleasant, creative way of learning, and it's effective.

Walking Words—Introduce young children to varied ways of walking through creative dramatics. As they begin walking around a circle or "following the leader" in a line, ask them if they can *sneak* as if they didn't want anyone to see them. Suggest that they *march* like soldiers, *tramp* like noisy boys, *scamper* like puppies playing, *stride* like tall men, *waddle* like fat bears, *strut* like peacocks. Then discuss the words and ask if they can suggest different "ways of walking." Other synonym groups can be explored also.

Favorite Words—Share a group of your favorite words with the class—*scintillating, effervescent, exquisite, bombastic*—the choice is up to you! Write one of the words on the board as you say it. Ask them what they think it means. Use it in a sentence. Then invite them to share their favorite words they have discovered which they think are especially appealing. Display words which have been shared.

May I Sew You to a Sheet?—Here is an example of the Spoonerism, an inversion of beginning sounds attributed to Rev. William Spooner. Other examples of word play which can be researched by able students include Malapropisms and Wellerisms.

Books to Investigate

Chall, Jeanne. *Learning to Read: The Great Debate*. New York: McGraw-Hill Book Co., 1967.

Daniels, Steven. *How 2 Gerbils 20 Goldfish 200 Games 2,000 Books and I Taught Them to Read*. Philadelphia: Westminster Press, 1961.

Downing, John. *Experiments with an Augmented Alphabet for Beginning Readers*. New York: Educational Records Bureau, 1962.

Fries, Charles C. *Linguistics and Reading*. New York: Holt, Rinehart, and Winston, 1963.

Guilfoile, Elizabeth, ed. *Adventuring with Books*. Urbana, Ill.: National Council of Teachers of English, 1966.

Heilman, Arthur W., and Holmes, Elizabeth Ann. *Smuggling Language into the Teaching of Reading*. Columbus, Ohio: Charles E. Merrill, 1972.

Kohl, Herbert. *Reading—How to*. New York: E. P. Dutton, 1973.

Lee, Dorris M., and Allen, R. V. *Learning to Read through Experience*. New York: Appleton-Century-Crofts, 1963.

Lefevre, Carl A. *Linguistics and the Teaching of Reading*. New York: McGraw-Hill Book Co., 1964.

McCracken, Robert A., and McCracken, J., Marlene. *Reading Is Only the Tiger's Tail*. San Francisco: Leswing Press, 1972.

Smith, Frank. *Understanding Reading*. New York: Holt, Rinehart, and Winston, 1971.

Smith, James A. *Creative Teaching of Reading and Literature in the Elementary School*. Boston: Allyn and Bacon, 1967.

Spache, Evelyn B. *Reading Activities for Child Involvement*. Boston: Allyn and Bacon, 1967.

books and children

chapter 13

Except a living man there is nothing more wonderful than a book! a message to us from human souls we never saw.
Charles Kingsley

"Children need books to widen their horizons, deepen their understandings, and give them broader social insights," write May Hill Arbuthnot and Zena Sutherland. "They also need books that minister to their merriment and increase their appreciation of beauty."[1] By introducing children at a young age to challenging literature, we endeavor to ensure that each child has an opportunity to engage in conversation with many skilled authors. As children pore over an absorbing tale told by a master storyteller, they are also absorbing the wisdom of living. A storyteller like E. B. White, for instance, not only whispers the story of Charlotte and Wilbur but also conveys mature concepts of friendship, loneliness, and even death.

Literature communicates ideas, attitudes, values, and information. The elementary school must assume its share of the responsibility for bring-

[1] May Hill Arbuthnot and Zena Sutherland, *Children and Books* (Glenview, Ill.: Scott, Foresman and Co., 1972), p. 38.

ing children and books together, for the school is the only institution that reaches all children. The school alone is in a position to present an organized sequence of experiences, which will make certain that most children know the literature created for their age. From the slowest child to the brightest, each student will gain from having known Winnie-the-Pooh, Toad, and Peter Pan.

Teaching Literature

In the junior high school, in high school, and in college, literature has always been an integral part of the English program. Yet, literature appears in the elementary school only incidentally. Clearly, it is regarded as an "extra" to be included only after the important work is completed.

NEED FOR PLANNED PROGRAMS

A place must be made for literature in the elementary school curriculum so that it is no longer a "frill" but is drawn firmly into the essential content to be taught. Huck and Kuhn comment:

> The majority of elementary schools in the United States have no planned literature program; usually literature is subsumed under the "reading" or "English" program. . . . While the entire elementary school curriculum contributes to the apperciation of literature, a planned literature program should be a part of an integrated language arts curriculum.[2]

Questions regarding the development of a literature program that need to be discussed include:

1 Why should literature be included in the elementary school program?
2 Is there a need for a planned scope and sequence in literature?
3 Where does literature fit into the present elementary school curriculum?
4 How will literature be selected for this program?
5 How will teaching *literature* differ from teaching *reading*?

How can we best incorporate literature in the elementary school program? The obvious place for literature in the busy curriculum is in the language/reading program. There is a need for a carefully conceived developmental sequence for presenting various literature titles to avoid repetition and to ensure all children's knowing a major portion of this rich inheritance. Guidelines will assist articulation without unduly hampering the teacher's individual planning.

[2] Charlotte Huck and Doris Kuhn, *Children's Literature in the Elementary School* (New York: Holt, Rinehart, and Winston, 1968), pp. 649–50.

Will the study of literature, that is, analysis, destroy the child's enjoyment of a story as many purists fear? On the contrary, it has been our observation that exploring beyond the superficial story value of an author's work actually leads to greater interest in reading and aids in the development of critical thinking. Emphasis still remains on reading for enjoyment, but this enjoyment is enhanced through the addition of appreciation of the writer's skilled performance.

LITERATURE IN THE READING PROGRAM

Literature has seldom been part of the reading program in the elementary school, for reading has been dominated by the basal reader series. What are the advantages of a literature-reading program over the traditional controlled-vocabulary anthology? The use of literature in a reading program for elementary school students offers quality content to a course of study which has concentrated solely on the teaching of skills. It is time that we acknowledge the value of provocative material in exciting the student about reading. Until we have this excitement present in the reading lesson, we will not develop a nation of readers.

Many titles from children's literature can be, and are being, used as reading text material. The advantages of *Pippi Longstocking, A Wrinkle in Time,* and *Johnny Tremain* over the familiar basal reader are overwhelming:

1 Excellent writing—imagery, use of words, storytelling ability.
2 Continuity of a longer story—plot development, characterization.
3 Greater interest value—intrigue, atmosphere, entertainment.
4 Integration of literature, language, and composition studies.

The only advantage undeniably present in the basal reader is controlled vocabulary. In light of our singular lack of success in producing adults who read widely, however, one wonders if the controlled vocabulary may not literally drain the vitality from the fare served our enthusiastic beginning readers. As Phyllis McGinley observes in *Sixpence in Her Shoe:*

> Whose invention was this vocabulary restriction I cannot say. Librarians deplore the trend, publishers disclaim responsibility, authors declare themselves stifled by it, children detest it. But the fact remains that somebody has set up as gospel the rule that odd words, long words, interesting words, grown-up words must be as precisely sifted out from a book for, say, five-year-olds as chaff from wheat or profanity from a television program. . . .
>
> Are children never to climb? Must they be saved from all the healthy bumps

> and bruises of exploration? . . . The genuine reading child . . . wants, even at six or seven or eight, gourmet fare. . . .[3]

The study of literature offers infinite possibilities for a stimulating approach to the language arts, which coordinates the areas of language and composition with that of literature. Skills of reading, writing, speaking, and listening are utilized as the child attacks intellectually challenging material.

The Nebraska Curriculum Development Center has developed an elementary school English curriculum which focuses attention on core literature texts. The aims of this language, literature, and composition program are stated to be:

1 To teach students to comprehend the more frequent grammatical conventions
2 To teach students to comprehend the more frequent conventions of literature composed for young children—formal or generic conventions and simple rhetorical conventions
3 To teach students to control these linguistic and literary conventions in their own writing.[4]

Individualized reading programs The teaching of literature lends itself well to individualizing reading. Many teachers are experimenting with the use of trade titles, having each student read different books. The completely individualized approach to reading literature has the advantages of (1) individual selection of books, (2) progress at varied rates of speed, (3) usually greater quantity of reading, and (4) no child without something to do.

To operate with maximum effectiveness this approach requires that the teacher guide individual development through extensive student conferencing. Activities for extending learning must be planned (until they are commercially available) for each book so that students are doing more than just reading title after title. The standard book-report form hastily completed by the disinterested student is a waste of time and paper and may actually cause children to dislike reading. (See Chapter 12.)

Small group seminars Other teachers are finding that the purchase of multiple copies of several titles provides excellent material for small

[3] Phyllis McGinley, *Sixpence in Her Shoe* (New York: The Macmillan Company, 1964), pp. 213–14.

[4] Nebraska Curriculum Development Center, *A Curriculum for English; Introduction to the Elementary School Program: K–6,* Mimeographed report (Lincoln, Neb.: The University of Nebraska, 1965), p. 2.

group approaches to literature study. This approach to literature study limits student selection but offers certain advantages for the teaching of literature: (1) use of seminar techniques in discussing a common body of reading, (2) concentration of teacher and student efforts on fewer books to be examined in depth, (3) individualized responses to independent open-ended activities for extending learning, and (4) experiences in group dynamics.

Whether each child is reading a different title or a small group is reading the same title, the use of literature offers stimulating reading which should lead to greater enjoyment of reading and actually to *more reading*. Perhaps the best method of presentation will prove to be a combination of the individualized and the small group approaches described. Neither approach, we should add, actually teaches literature, however, for the success of these techniques of teaching lies essentially with the teacher. Teacher enthusiasm, knowledge of literature, ability to guide without domination, and wisdom in planning will, as in all of teaching, play a significant role.

PLANNING LITERATURE EXPERIENCES

What procedures shall we follow in presenting a title? The techniques used will vary according to the particular books under discussion, but each literature experience will be based on the reading of a sizeable portion of the book. Books that are divided into chapters are particularly adaptable for study with the chapter providing a natural division. A very short book might be treated as a whole. Steps in presenting the literature lesson will, however, usually follow a sequence like this:

1 *Reading a portion of the book.* Children may read silently, or they may take turns reading aloud. It is highly desirable that the teacher frequently read aloud to a group as this technique adds to the pleasure of the experience and prepares the group for immediate follow-up activities.

2 *Discussion or study of portion read.* Focus can be on any aspect of the literature being examined.

- a. vocabulary (talk about the words used, not just a list to study)
- b. theme (author's message, ideas behind the action)
- c. specific examples of imagery (similes, picturesque use of words)
- d. meaning of specific phrases or references (idioms, clichés)
- e. reaction to provocative statements
- f. discussion of action, characters, setting

3 *Extending Experiences.* A variety of ideas should be suggested with each student completing several; some may be group activities.

- a. Composition

  Write a reaction to points made by the author.

Write a story suggested by the content.
Write poetry based on an idea presented.

b. Language
Discuss unusual uses of words.
Observe description of sounds, colors, and so on.
Study a specific sentence structure.
Enact a portion of dialogue.

c. Art
Paint an imagined portrait of a character from the word picture.
Draw a pictorial map of the setting of the story.
Develop a mural depicting the action of the story.
Paint one vivid scene from the action.

d. Literature
Read another book similar in content and compare the two.
Read another title by the same author and compare.
Find out about the author who wrote the story.

e. Social Studies
Locate the setting of this story.
At what period of history does it take place?
Compare the life of the characters with your life—school, housing, family, clothing.

If students are reading individually, these experiences will usually be explored independently. Suggested activity sheets can be prepared so that the student can select several as he progresses with the book being read. Activities should be specific and should be directly related to the title read as in the sample Plans of Operation for three literature studies which are described subsequently.

We recommend the keeping of a Reading Log by each individual student in grades three through six as he reads any title. The Log is a highly individualized approach offering a challenge to the gifted student and permitting growth of the slower student. The term *log* is introduced through the explanation of its use by a ship's captain to record events during a trip. (This analogy can be extended.) Each student keeps a log in a small notebook in which he records:

1 Interesting new words
2 Colorful imagery
3 Written reactions to the story
4 Written answers to questions for Extending Learning
5 Special pages suggested—collections of synonyms, homonyms, other categories of words
6 Poetry and prose motivated by guided activities

These logs provide the teacher with a clear picture of what any student is doing (without routine book-report forms or test questions) and the progress the student is making. The logs can be used as the basis of individual conferences, or a few at a time can be read by the teacher.

PLAN OF OPERATION: GRADE 2

And To Think That I Saw It on Mulberry Street by Dr. Seuss (Vanguard, 1937)

This early work by Theodore Geisel tells the story of Marco, who usually diverts himself by imagining interesting things as he walks home from school. When he tells his father, however, his father does not appreciate the fanciful tales. The father's attitude forces Marco to face reality as he admits there was nothing but a "plain horse and wagon on Mulberry Street."

Extending learning activities This short book could be read aloud to the class if used at the beginning of the year. During the last half of the year, small groups of students could read the book together after which it could be discussed along the lines suggested.

1 Why did Marco enjoy imagining things?
2 Which of his imaginary things did you like most?
3 Do you ever imagine things? What is your favorite imagining?
4 What did Marco's father think about imagining? Did he perhaps think Marco was lying?
5 Is imagining things the same as lying? How are they different?
6 What words do you remember from the story? Why do you remember those particular words?

Follow-up and culminating activities can be a combination of individual and group activities. Many times these activities will be suggested by the questions and interests of the children involved.

- Name all the different things Marco imagined, printing them on the board for word orientation and for experience in reading. Plan a parade down Mulberry Street to be painted cooperatively as a mural. Encourage use of the imagination; the illustrations of the book should not confine production.

- Write sentence stories about individual imaginings. Give help as needed so that each child has a story about something he imagines. Crayon resist pictures of these imaginings can be produced (thin tempera wash over completed crayon picture). The picture is then shown as the story is read by each child.

- Write a group-composed letter to Marco to extend sympathy, to tell reasons for enjoying his ideas, and to share original ideas.

- Talk about color words used in the story. Have the class name other known color words. Add a few useful, but less common, examples to extend vocabularies—*scarlet, crimson, lime, olive.*

PLAN OF OPERATION: GRADE 4

The Children of Green Knowe by Lucy Boston (Harcourt, 1954)

This imaginative story of Tolly, a young boy who goes to live with his grandmother at Green Knowe, is set in Great Britain. It is rich in imagery and offers an opportunity to compare British English with American English. Although this book is not divided into chapters, it does fall easily into parts suitable for use as learning experiences. The following activities are based on the first section of the book (pp. 9-23).

1 Tolly thinks of the train as an Ark floating on flood waters, and he imagines all the noises of the animals.
What a noise there would be, with the lions roaring, elephants trumpeting, pigs squealing, donkeys braying, horses whinnying, bulls bellowing . . .
How many additions can you make to Tolly's list? Try to think of ideas no one else will include:

dogs *yapping*________________
cats ________________________
bears ________________________

(Each example in this exercise uses the present participle form of a verb. Explore the varied forms of verbs as: *go, went, going, gone.*)

2 This story is set in Great Britain. Although Britishers speak the same language we do, we find that they have different ways of saying some things. On page 14, for instance, the cab driver asks Tolly whether he has any "gum boots." What are "gum boots?"
Begin a list of examples like this one. Give an explanation in American English. Keep adding to this list:

p. 14. gum boots	rubber boots
p. 11. cheerio	goodby
p. 12. windscreen	____________

3 How do you know that Tolly is used to being lonely? After reading this much of the book, what do you know about Tolly? Write a description of this boy.

4 Heavy rains are falling on the flooded countryside. On the first page of this book the author describes the rain as it appears to Tolly, "splashing against the windows and blotching downward in an ugly, dirty way." On another page she talks of the women getting off the train "into the hissing rain."
What is your impression of rain? What does it sound like to you? Is it pleasant or unpleasant? How does it make you feel? Write your ideas about rain like this:

RAIN is . . .
the sprouter of bright umbrellas,
a cozy, snugged-in feeling,
a day for hiding games
RAIN is . . .
the fizzies ,
________________________,
________________________.

Write as many ideas about rain as you wish. Your ideas will form a poem. Paint a picture of one of your ideas to go with your poem.

PLAN OF OPERATION: GRADE 6

The Cat and Mrs. Cary by Doris Gates (Viking, 1962)

The story of twelve-year-old Brad's adventures as he visits his aunt, Mrs. Cary, has both a boy and a girl as leading characters. The chief character, however, is THE CAT, who condescends to live with Mrs. Cary and even to eat her food. An independent tomcat, he talks to Mrs. Cary although no one else ever hears his words. Mrs. Cary not only hears him, but replies aloud much to the amazement of those who just happen to be listening. Activities for extending learning are based on Chapter 1 of this book.

1 On page 12 notice the description of THE CAT. Describe an animal which you have observed. Can you make this animal seem real? Does your animal have personality?
2 Why does THE CAT say, "When it comes to catching fish, you've never seen anything to match my equal"? (p. 15.) How would you have said the same thing? Why do you think he said it in this unusual way?
3 Read the description of the Major on page 17. Can you draw a picture of this gentleman from the word picture painted by Doris Gates? Do you like the Major? Why or why not?
4 Usually when a person speaks, we use the word "said" followed by the speaker's name to make the identity of the speaker clear to the reader as in this sentence:

John said, "What are you doing?"

Notice the use of dialogue on page 14. Has the author always used the word "said" to identify the speaker? In your log begin a page listed SYNONYMS FOR SAID. On this page list the words used by Doris Gates and add others that you can think of.
What words might you substitute for "said" in these sentences? Can you suggest more than one each time?

1. Susan *said*, "I need help." shouted
2. Mother *said*, "I have a secret." whispered
3. "Who will help?" *said* Paul. questioned
4. "Wait for me," I *said*. called
5. "You will see," Mr. Day *said*. promised

Encouraging Reading Addiction

Most students who enroll in the first grade learn to read to a greater or lesser degree, yet it is surprising how many students in the sixth grade are not avid readers. It is obvious that the child needs more than the mere recognition of words to spark his own sense of involvement with reading. He has to acquire a real feeling for books, the knowledge that books have something which he *needs*, that they have something that he *wants*.

It has been pointed out that the mechanical, drill-focused approach to reading may kill interest in reading at a time when enthusiasm for learning is high, and even more significant, that this readiness for learning will not be easily achieved again. Discussing this problem in reading, an expert in child psychoanalysis observes:

> The long years spent by our children in mastery of the mechanics of reading rob them of pleasure and discoveries in literature, and also rob them of the possibility of *addiction*, which is one of the characteristics of the good reader. The addiction to reading is acquired at an early age—usually, I believe, under eight or nine.[5]

How do we ensure this addiction to reading? How do students acquire this sense of involvement with reading? How do we teachers motivate youngsters to read so widely that they will never lose the habit? There is no *one* answer, and there is no *right* answer; but there are many possibilities which are well worth exploring:

1 Use of exciting, quality literature in the reading program
2 Stress on stimulating coordinated reading and composition activities
3 Special attention to the reading interests of boys
4 Decrease in drill-type approaches to learning to read
5 Exposure to many, varied experiences with literature—storytelling, dramatization, discussions of books, choric speaking
6 Many opportunities to share the excitement of reading; new approaches to book reviewing
7 Teacher enthusiasm and knowledge of literature and ways of presenting literature in the classroom

FOCUSING ATTENTION ON BOOKS

Open books for students in varied ways, for few can resist the tempting illustrations, and the reading of a few intriguing words on a page is often

[5] Selma Fraiberg, "The American Reading Problem," *Commentary* (June, 1965).

enough to snag the interest of one who stops to look at a book propped open on the windowsill or a classroom table. Bookholders can be purchased or they can be made from two identical shapes cut from heavy cardboard taped together as illustrated.

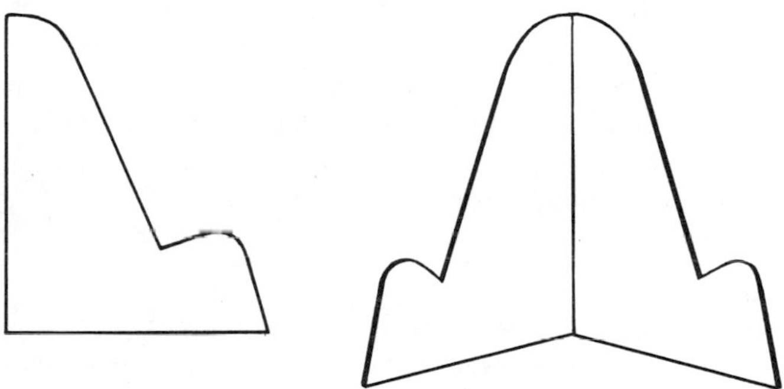

Another obvious way to open books is to *read aloud to a class.* After the last page of Mary Norton's *The Borrowers* (Harcourt) has just been completed, there will be many requests for that title and others by the same author. Showing the illustrations as the story is read is particularly important in the primary grades. The excellent illustrations by Maurice Sendak in Janice Udry's book, *Moon Jumpers* (Harper), for example, add much to the spell and deserve special attention.

Students can open books for each other by simply talking about a book that they have enjoyed and personally showing the book to the class or to an individual student. Writes the Director of the Junior Book Awards for Boys' Clubs of America:

> There is nothing like a child for word-of-mouth advertising among his peers. The librarian may recommend a book and the youngster will read it to please her because he likes her, but if he does not like the book, wild horses can not get him to recommend it to a Clubmate. But just let one of the boys say, "you ought to read such-and-such"—and the line can form on the right for those eager to read it.[6]

Displays of books also serve to whet the reading appetites of students. A display of colorful book jackets on a bulletin board is always eye-catching. Captions can be used, for example, THE BOOK BAG (with books spilling from a real bag) or IT'S BOOK TIME (a clock face with jackets at the number spaces). Another display might consist of scattered book jackets under the caption HAVE YOU READ? As children read these books,

[6] Iris Vinton, "What Children Like to Read," *Junior Libraries* (January, 1959), p. 5.

each one adds a name tag to the cover of that book. Comparisons of total books read should definitely be avoided, with stress remaining on individual development and enjoyment of books read.

Provocative methods of presenting stories to other members of a class can be explored as the children themselves strive to "sell" others on reading a book they have enjoyed. The *preparation of a collage* about a favorite title is an excellent way of interesting others in reading the book. Imagine, for instance, what a fascinating collage could be prepared featuring *The Twenty-One Balloons* by William Pène Du Bois (Viking), depicting the professor's misadventures on Krakatoa; the pictorial qualities of such a book are numerous.

SHARING BOOKS

The primary objective of reviewing or sharing books is not to "check on" student reading. Let's aim instead at multiple goals that really eliminate the need to check as we (1) stress the enjoyment of reading and sharing books, (2) encourage further reading of all kinds, and (3) stimulate critical thinking. If these goals are met, children will want to read because they find reading stimulating, entertaining, and informative. Our focus then is directly on the motivation of reading so that children will read, find it a pleasure, and wish to share their experiences with others. Sharing and book reviewing can more properly be regarded as means for motivation. In planning book review activities, we must bear these points in mind:

1 Not all reading needs to be reviewed; students should be encouraged to read widely without the penalty of reviewing the quantity they read.
2 Varied review techniques must be used to provide for stimulating experiences.

In what ways can we vary the sharing of books? Once we move away from the rigid concept of the book-report form, the possibilities for sharing books are numerous, provocative, and enriching. These approaches to book sharing can be oral or written. They can be related to other areas of the curriculum—history, geography, art, music, science, mathematics. They can take forms which branch out into more creative media. We can challenge our students to discover a different, more exciting way to share a book. Ideas will grow out of experimentation.

- The *diorama* is an excellent medium for depicting a scene from a story. Homer Price (cardboard or papier maché figure) could be shown with Aroma, his pet skunk, as they creep up on the robbers who are camping in the woods. The diorama also can be used to portray a scene from historical fiction or from the life of a figure in American history.

• A *mobile* can present a book by displaying the characters as well as objects or ideas essential to the story. *The 500 Hats of Bartholomew Cubbins* might, for instance, be interpreted through a mobile which features many unusual hats created in three dimensions.

• *Music* can be related to book sharing as a student or a small group of students composes a ballad about Charlotte, Wilbur, and their friends. Older students might write a calypso or a folk song about the adventures of Huckleberry Finn or a real person about whom they have read.

• A *collage* is an intriguing method of combining art with literature. *Chitty-Chitty-Bang Bang,* for example, might be depicted on a large poster which includes a cut-out drawing of this distinctive green car, the faces of Man-Mountain Fink, Joe, the Monster, and the twins. Portions of a map of England, the English Channel, and northern France might be worked into the background as would be other motifs taken from the story. Words can also be incorporated in the collage—*Paris, transmogrifications, Paragon Panther, Ian Fleming,* and so on.

INDIVIDUALIZED ACTIVITIES FOR THE LEARNING CENTER

Book-centered activities are an essential part of an individualized approach to learning, which includes work in a Language/Reading Learning Center. Develop a set of Task Cards which focus on Literature Learning and which, of course, develop reading skills as well as those of listening, speaking, and writing. Here are some sample ideas for developing Task Cards. Children will be able to select the cards individually and complete as directed or with modifications made by themselves and the teacher.

TASK CARD 1

Do you know what a *bibliography* is? How can you find out?

Make a bibliography for our library about one topic that especially interests you. Your bibliography might help other students discover good books they will enjoy about this subject.

Choose topics like this—anything that interests you:

Horses	Dogs	Cats
Space Travel	Mysteries	Science Fiction
Living in Africa	Ocean Life	Great American Women

Your list can include fiction and nonfiction. If you like, you can work with another person who is interested in the same subject.

TASK CARD 2

Who is your favorite author? Which books have you read by this writer? Do you know other books this author has written? Make a list of all the books written by your favorite writer.

Select two or three books by the author you have chosen. Compare them. How are they alike? How are they different? Think about:

the characters
the setting
the time in history
the length of the book
for whom is the book written

Prepare a BOOKTALK on tape about the author and the books you have reviewed. Others will enjoy listening to your comments.

These Task Cards would be suitable for students in the upper grades. Similar cards can be made for children in the primary grades also, as shown:

TASK CARD 3

Think of a story that you like very much. Who is the most important person in the story? Is it a boy, a girl, an animal?

Imagine that you are the character in the story.
Can you tell the story as if you were that character?

Begin with the words: I am ______________________. I have a story to tell.

Tell your story to the tape recorder. Play the story for some of your class friends.

TASK CARD 4

Choose a book that you would like to read. After you have finished reading the book, look again at the pictures.

Think about this story. What picture would you like to paint to show everyone what the story is about?

Paint a picture that shows everyone the most exciting thing that happened in the story. Show your picture to the class, and tell them about the story.

Many different kinds of Task Cards can be developed over a period of time to allow for developing interests. You might prepare cards on these topics featuring varied activities:

Dramatization of stories read by several students
Writing a letter to a favorite character
Advertising a book on a miniature billboard
Compiling a biography of a known author
Writing a nonfiction book about an interesting subject
Collecting poems on a specific topic
Writing another chapter to the book

Literature for all Children

One of the very real assets of children's literature is its infinite variety. Almost every subject matter is covered by titles prepared for both beginning and advanced readers.

YOUNG READERS

Perhaps some of the most intriguing, thought-provoking story material is appearing in books for the very youngest reader. Enhanced by artful, vivid illustrations, these books have instant appeal, first as books read to the child, and later as books to read independently.

The teacher will find a receptive audience, for the child who enters first grade today has usually had a wide background of experiences. His/her listening vocabulary is estimated at 20,000 words, and they can fully comprehend a surprising number of rather complex concepts. Through television, parental reading aloud, and talking with other children and adults, children today are exposed to varied topics which little concerned the child of a generation ago.

What do children of this age enjoy most in literature? Individual interests are varied, but in general they thrive on humor, repetition, action, and stories about real people. Young boys who follow the astronauts through space and back again will search for books about space. Favorite books for this age group are the Dr. Seuss stories—*McElligott's Pool, Horton Hatches the Egg;* Anderson's horse stories—*Blaze and the Gypsies, Billy and Blaze;* Jerrold Beim's stories of real children—*Andy and the School Bus, Twelve O'Clock Whistle;* Marjorie Flack's animal tales—*Story about Ping, New Pet;* Margaret Johnson's *Joey and Patches, Snowshoe Paws, Stablemates;* Lois Lenski's *Cowboy Small, Little Fire Engine, Surprise for Davy;* and Hans Rey's amusing tales of *Curious George.*

There are, of course, numerous other titles which could and should be named, but we shall leave that to your own exploration.

THE ABLE STUDENT

Grade-level categorization of books has little meaning for able readers, for they will almost certainly be reading several levels ahead of the school grade level. Many elementary school children may be reading adult literature—*Cheaper by the Dozen, Born Free, Incredible Journey, Tom Sawyer, The Hobbit,* and *The Lord of the Rings.* We need not fear that children will "run out of things" to read. It is impossible to read all of the world's literature in one lifetime, and the storehouse of books increases by thousands every year.

The growth of able readers can focus on creativity and activities that stimulate communication. The growth of these students might be encouraged, for example, through the formation of a BOOK CLUB organized by the students themselves. The group might choose to discuss one specific book each week with all members reading that selection and preparing questions, observations, and ideas to discuss. Each member of this small group could take the leadership in turn to conduct a discussion or to deliver a short prepared book review. The group might also decide to present a book to the class by preparing a display, dramatization, or a book talk.

Able students also learn much by serving as teacher aides in primary grade classes. Older children can prepare flannel board presentations of stories that appeal to first and second graders. Puppet shows of favorite stories are also popular. Able students might organize a school-wide campaign called EVERY CHILD A READER, which would reflect the National Right to Read Effort as the students themselves reach out to help other students learn to read.

ETHNIC MINORITIES

Many groups of students deserve special assistance in meeting their special needs. We can promote understanding of all children by providing more realistic pictures of minority groups and the beauty of the varied cultures that coexist within the larger culture of the nature.

Elementary school libraries need to provide numerous juvenile titles that depict characters who are black, Chinese, Japanese, Mexican-American, Puerto Rican, and so forth. Here is a portion of one list of books about American blacks, compiled by the Council on Interracial Books for Children, Inc. (9 East 40th Street, New York, N.Y. 10016).

KINDERGARTEN THROUGH SECOND GRADE

Beim, Lorraine, and Beim, Jerrold. *Two Is A Team.* illus. by Ernest Crichlow. New York: Harcourt, 1945. $2.75. 61 pp. A simple story of friendship and cooperation between two boys which can be read independently by younger children. Only the illustrations convey the fact that one of the boys is Negro.

Keats, Ezra Jack. *The Snowy Day.* illus. by author. New York: Viking, 1962. $3.00. 32 pp. Preschool and kindergarten age children will enjoy the adventures of a little Negro boy as he plays in the snow. Distinguished, colorful illustrations add to the beauty of this simple story. (Film available from Weston Woods, Weston, Conn.)

Keats, Ezra Jack. *Whistle for Willie.* illus. by author. New York: Viking, 1964. $3.50. 33 pp. Another book about the hero of *A Snowy Day.* A young child who has tried to whistle will thoroughly enjoy this beautifully illustrated picture book.

Showers, Paul. *Look at Your Eyes.* illus. by Paul Galdone. New York: Crowell, 1962. $2.75. Through easy text and attractive illustrations, chlidren discover, along with a young Negro boy, some of the basic facts about the function of the eyes. A beginning science book of general interest to young children.

THIRD THROUGH SIXTH GRADE

Bontemps, Arna. *Frederick Douglass: Slave, Fighter, Freeman;* illus. by Harper Johnson. New York: Knopf, 1959. $3.00. 177 pp. A vivid, dramatic account of the life of an ex-slave whose philosophy and actions continue to have great meaning in today's society.

Brooks, Gwendolyn. *Bronzeville Boys and Girls* (poems). illus. by Ronni Solbert. New York: Harper, 1956. $2.50. 40 pp. A delightful collection of poems about city children by a noted Negro poet and Pulitzer Prize winner. Delicate illustrations, especially of Negro children, capture the mood of the poetry.

Evans, Eva. *People Are Important.* illus. by Vana Earle. New York: Golden Press, 1951. $3.95. 86 pp. A factual appraisal of the world's peoples and their habits presented with a sparkling, often humorous approach.

Fritz, Jean. *Brady.* illus. by Lynd Ward. New York: Coward, 1960. $3.50. 223 pp. Excellent characterizations and a well-developed story of the underground railroad. Good supplementary reading for the study of the Civil War period.

Hughes, Langston, and Meltzer, Milton, eds. *Pictorial History of the Negro in America,* rev. ed. New York: Crown, 1963. $5.95. 337 pp. The broad panorama of the history of the American Negro, presented through excellent text and numerous photographs. Useful both for students, teachers, and many classroom libraries.

McGovern, Ann. *Runaway Slave.* illus. by R. M. Powers. New York: Scholastic Book Service, 1965. 212 pp. Simple, lyric prose and sensitive illustrations capture the dignity and strength of Harriet Tubman. Although primarily for third and fourth grades, it can also be handled comfortably by the "slow" or reluctant readers.

Shotwell, Louisa R. *Roosevelt Grady.* illus. by Peter Burchard. Cleveland, Ohio: World, 1963. $2.95. 151 pp. Although some events in the lives of this Negro migrant family may not be familiar, children in both urban and suburban communities will understand and sympathize with their hopes and dreams for a permanent home.

Sterling, Dorothy. *Mary Jane.* illus. by Ernest Crichlow. Garden City, N.J.: Doubleday, 1959. $2.95. 214 pp. A sensitive portrayal of a young girl's lonely experience as one of a small group of Negroes in a junior high school that provides token integration. A realistic yet optimistic presentation which will have significance for both white and Negro children today.

An interesting class project is the development of an annotated list like the one just presented. Here is the nucleus of a bibliography on Mexican-American children which could be prepared first on cards by each individual explorer and later compiled in a useful list:

Bailey, Bernadine. *Famous Latin American Liberators.* New York: Dodd, 1960. 158 pp.

———. *Picture Book of New Mexico.* New York: Albert Whitman, 1960. 26 pp.

Blecker, Sonia. *The Aztec: Indians of Mexico.* New York: Morrow, 1963. 160 pp.

———. *The Maya: Indians of Central America.* New York: Morrow, 1961. 160 pp.

Flack, Marjorie, and Larsson, Karl. *Pedro.* New York: Macmillan, 1940. 96 pp.

Goetz, Delia. *Neighbors to the South,* rev. ed. New York: Harcourt, 1959. 179 pp.

Good, Loren. *Panchito.* New York: Coward-McCann, 1955. 160 pp.

Hogner, Dorothy C. *Children of Mexico.* Boston: Heath, 1942. 64 pp.

Kidwell, Carl. *Arrow in the Sun.* New York: Viking, 1961. 254 pp.

Lay, Marion. *Wooden Saddles: The Adventures of a Mexican Boy in His Own Land.* New York: Morrow, 1939. 175 pp.

MacDonald, Etta B., and Dalrymple, Julia. *Manuel in Mexico.* Boston: Little, Brown, 1909. 118 pp.

Moon, Grace. *Tita of Mexico.* New York: Frederick A. Stokes, 1934. 213 pp.

Politi, Leo. *The Mission Bell.* New York: Scribners, 1953. 30 pp.

Rhoads, Dorothy. *The Story of Chan Yuc.* Garden City, N.J.: Doubleday, 1941. 43 pp.

Rose, Patricia. *Let's Read about Mexico.* Grand Rapids, Mich.: Fideler, 1955. 160 pp.

Sawyer, Ruth. *The Least One*. New York: Viking, 1941. 89 pp.
Schweitzer, Byrd B. *Amigo*. New York: Macmillan, 1963. 41 pp.
Thomas, Margaret L. *Carlos: Our Mexican Neighbor*. Indianapolis, Ind.: Bobbs-Merrill, 1938. 189 pp.
Wilson, Barbara K. *Fairy Tales of Mexico*. New York: Dutton, 1960. 39 pp.
Witton, Dorothy. *Crossroads for Chela*. New York: Messner, 1956. 192 pp.

Other good bibliographies about various ethnic groups include the following:

Jackson, Miles M. et al. *A Bibliography of Materials by and about Negro Americans for Young Readers*. Atlanta, Ga.. Atlanta University, 1967.
Negro History and Literature: A Selected Annotated Bibliography. New York: American Jewish Committee; Anti-Defamation League, B'Nai B'Rith; National Federation of Settlements and Neighborhood Centers, 1968. (232 Madison Ave., New York, N.Y. 10016. 35¢)
Torrance, E. Paul, and Meyers, R. E. "Instructional Materials Dealing with Creative Achievements of Major Disadvantaged and Minority Groups in the United States" in *Creative Learning and Teaching*. New York: Dodd, Mead and Co., 1970, pp. 297–305.
Baker, Augusta, ed. *The Black Experience in Children's Books*. New York: The New York Public Library, 1971.
Conwell, Mary K., and Belpre, Pura. *Libros en Español*. New York: The New York Public Library, 1971.

WOMEN AND GIRLS

Increasing criticism has been directed toward the image of women in children's tradebooks as well as in elementary school textbooks. This stereotyped image of women's roles and the socialization of young girls in our society places severe limitations on the young girl's expectations for her life.

Illustrations and content in children's literature help demonstrate the passive, unexciting roles that girls play, compared to the adventurous, active roles of boys. Mother is consistently depicted as a housewife in the kitchen wearing an apron. Publishers have leaned toward the production of books that would appeal to boys, stating that "girls will read books for boys, but boys won't touch books for girls." Few considered the insipid quality of "books for girls" or the fact that girls might be adversely affected by this consistent "put-down."

There is a growing movement to select books with more positive images of girls and women, books that would never include the line,

"Girls can't do that." Biographies of women are also appearing with titles on Rachel Carson, Lydia Maria Child, Margaret Sanger, Dr. Florence Sabin, Bessie Smith, and Margaret Chase Smith—women who have not followed a stereotyped existence. Here is a selected list of books you might explore:

Abramovitz, Anita. *Winifred.* Steck-Vaughn Co., 1971. (Pr.-Elem.)
Alexander, Anne. *Little Foreign Devil.* Atheneum, 1970. (Elem.-Jr.)
Babbitt, Natalie. *Phoebe's Revolt.* Farrar, Straus, and Giroux, 1968. (Elem.)
Buckley, Mary. *Six Brothers and a Witch.* Bobbs-Merrill, 1969. (Elem.)
Burnett, Frances Hodgson. *The Secret Garden.* Lippincott, 1911. (Elem.-Jr.)
Corcoran, Barbara. *The Long Journey.* Atheneum, 1970. (Elem.)
Corcoran, Barbara. *This Is a Recording.* Atheneum. (Jr.)
Crockett, Mary. *Rosanna the Goat.* Bobbs-Merill, 1970. (Elem.)
Gaeddert, LouAnn. *Noisy Nancy and Nick.* Doubleday, 1970. (Elem.)
Gauch, Patricia Lee. *Christina Katerina and THE BOX.* Coward-McCann, 1971. (Elem.)
Gill, Joan. *Sara's Granny and the Groodle.* Doubleday, 1969. (Elem.)
Goffstein, M. B. *Two Piano Tuners.* Farrar, Straus, and Giroux, 1970. (Elem.)
Hall, Elizabeth. *Stand Up, Lucy.* Houghton Mifflin, 1971. (Jr.)
Hunter, Kristin. *The Soul Brothers and Sister Lou.* Scribner's Sons, 1968. (Jr.)
Krasilovsky, Phyllis. *The Very Tall Little Girl.* Doubleday, 1969. (Pr.-Elem.)
Laurence. *Seymourina.* Bobbs-Merrill, 1970. (Elem.)
Lindgren, Astrid. *Pippi Longstocking.* Viking Press, 1950. (Elem.)
Malone, Mary. *Annie Sullivan.* G. P. Putnam's Sons, 1971. (Elem.)
Merriam, Eve. *Mommies at Work.* Viking Press, 1961. (Pr.-Elem.)
Renvoize, Jean. *A Wild Thing.* Little, Brown and Co., 1971. (Sr.)
Rich, Gibson. *Firegirl.* Feminist Press,[7] 1972. (Pr.-Elem.)
Rockwell, Anne and Harlow. *Molly's Woodland Garden.* Doubleday, 1971. (Elem.)
Sachs, Marily. *Peter and Veronica.* Doubleday, 1969. (Elem.)
Shulevitz, Uri. *Rain, Rain, Rivers.* Farrar, Straus, and Giroux, 1969. (Elem.)
Streatfield, Noel. *Thursday's Child.* Random House, 1970. (Jr.)
Swarthout, Glendon and Kathryn. *The Button Boat.* Doubleday, 1969. (Elem.-Jr.)
Swinburne, Laurence, *Detli.* Bobbs-Merrill, 1970. (Jr.)
Tallon, Robert. *The Thing in Dolores' Piano.* Bobbs-Merrill, 1970. (Elem.)
Wilson, Ellen. *American Painter in Paris: A Life of Mary Cassatt.* Farrar, Straus, and Giroux, 1971. (Jr.)

For more information about this topic, see the October, 1973 issue of *Elementary English,* which includes an excellent series of nineteen articles dealing with ways to break down stereotypes in elementary classrooms.

[7] The address of this company is: P. O. Box 694, Stuyvesant Station, N.Y. 10009.

The Teacher and Literature

As has been pointed out, the teacher's own enthusiasm for good stories and knowledge of children's literature will determine the success of any classroom literature program. Are books present in the classroom? Do children know authors? Are they developing a taste for good literature? Do they voluntarily share a book experience with the teacher?

In addition to establishing a classroom atmosphere that encourages the reading of literature the teacher also has other responsibilities. It is the teacher who (1) finds time for literature in the program, (2) provides for all levels of ability, (3) selects books to be presented to the class, and (4) selects those to be purchased for school libraries.

TIME FOR LITERATURE

Literature can appear in the elementary school classroom in many ways. Literature can, of course, be the material through which reading is taught. In this form literature becomes a text which is read, discussed, studied, as reading skills are practiced.

Literature is also an excellent starting point for many creative writing activities. Tall tales of Paul Bunyan, the adventures of Robin Hood, Aesop's fables serve to suggest short stories which children can write. The Moffat books by Eleanor Estes demonstrate the adventurous possibilities which are present in everyday happenings familiar to all children.

Literature is recreation as the teacher reads aloud. There are few children who do not hurry to their desks after recess as they notice the teacher seated with book in hand ready to read the third chapter of *The Lion, The Witch, and the Wardrobe* by C. S. Lewis (Macmillan). Other titles recommended for reading aloud include:

Mr. Popper's Penguins (Little, Brown, and Co.) by Richard and Florence Atwater.
Rabbit Hill (The Viking Press) by Robert Lawson.
The Children of Odin (The Macmillan Co.) by Padraic Colum.
Story of King Arthur and His Knights (C. Scribner's Sons) by Howard Pyle.
The Wind in the Willows (C. Scribner's Sons) by Kenneth Grahame.
Henry Huggins (Wm. Morrow and Co.) by Beverly Cleary.
The Long Winter (Harper and Row) by Laura I. Wilder.
The Witch of Blackbird Pond (Houghton Mifflin) by Elizabeth G. Speare.
Peterkin Papers (Harper and Row) by Lucretia P. Hale.
It's Perfectly True and Other Stories (Harcourt, Brace) by H. C. Andersen.

Although it is true that the teacher will often read a book aloud which a child could read himself (a technique that motivates reading), another purpose of reading aloud is to present material that stretches and makes the child's mind reach. The child can understand ideas and vocabulary far beyond his reading ability so that the first-grade child will chuckle delightedly over the antics of Pippi Longstocking although not able to read this book independently. Children will later enjoy reading the same book themselves as they rediscover Astrid Lindgren's humorous tale.

From *Pippi Longstocking* by Astrid Lindgren. Copyright 1950 by The Viking Press, Inc. Reprinted by permission of The Viking Press, Inc.

BOOK SELECTION

How do we choose books to read to a class? How do we select books for purchase by the school library? On what basis do we recommend books to students? It is obvious that the teacher needs to become acquainted with children's literature. A course in children's literature is a must for any elementary school teacher, but even that will not serve to keep the teacher's knowledge current. Frequent visits to the children's department of the library, reading of book reviews, noting publisher's advertisements, talking to others who enjoy children's books—these are some of the ways to inform yourself about news in the children's book world.

Personal examination of each title is fun and rewarding, but there is no denying that it is also time-consuming. The teacher must, therefore, often rely on the judgments of others in selecting books that cannot be personally examined. Following is a list of book selection aids which should be in the school's professional library or in the school library.

Arbuthnot, May H. et al., eds. *Children's Books Too Good to Miss.* 6th ed. Cleveland, Ohio: Western Reserve University Press, 1971.

The Booklist and Subscription Books Bulletin, A Guide to Current Books. American Library Assn., 60 East Huron Street, Chicago, Illinois.

Children's Catalog. New York: H. W. Wilson. The most complete annotated listing, with regular supplements.

Elementary English, The Official Journal of the Elementary Section of the National Council of Teachers of English. 1111 Kenyon Rd., Urbana, Ill. 61801. Especially helpful to classroom teachers (membership in NCTE).

The Horn Book Magazine. Write to 585 Boylston St., Boston, Mass. 02116. Boston, Mass.: The Horn Book.

Larrick, Nancy, ed. *A Parent's Guide to Children's Reading.* 3rd ed. Columbus, Ohio: C. E. Merrill, 1969.

Reid, Virginia, ed. *Reading Ladders for Human Relations.* Urbana Ill.: National Council of Teachers of English, 1972. 1111 Kenyon Rd., Urbana, Ill. 61801. An excellent annotated listing of books to further understandings among all peoples.

Root, Shelton, ed. *Adventuring with Books.* 2nd ed. Urbana, Ill.: The National Council of Teachers of English, 1973. An up-to-date list prepared by those who know the field. Write to 1111 Kenyon Rd., Urbana, Ill. 61801.

Let students take an active part in the selection of books whether it is the individual selection of a book to read or the purchase of a group of titles for the school library. As adults we sometimes have far different values than do the children we teach. Have a stock of 3 x 5 file cards on which students (and you, too) can throughout the year note books for purchase. If title, author, and publishing information are included, the compilation of a purchase list can then be done efficiently when the list is required.

One fifth-grade class studied books published in 1970 using a list published by the Library of Congress [8] as a basis for their exploration. Their task was to select one title to be purchased with PTA funds for each of twelve classroom libraries. Their teacher, as school library coordinator, wisely placed this selection job in the hands of three committees. The twelve books selected were:

GROUP 1:

Fuchs, Erich. *Journey to the Moon.* Delacorte. Striking, slightly surrealistic paintings give an artist's view of the sequence of events from rocket launch to the historic Apollo 11 moon landing.

Munari, Bruno. *The Circus in the Mist.* World Publishing Co. The reader moves through foggy city streets into the brilliant circus world and back through a mist-shrouded park.

Segal, Lore G. *Tell Me a Mitzi.* Illus. by Harriet Pincus. Farrar, Strauss, and Giroux. Three funny, imaginative stories about a little girl named Mitzi.

Wildsmith, Brian. *Brian Wildsmith's Circus.* Franklin Watts. "The circus is coming . . ." are the only words in this imaginative presentation of circus acts and the circus parade in brilliant colorful illustrations.

GROUP 2:

Goffstein, M. B. *Two Piano Tuners.* Farrar, Straus and Giroux. Humorous story of Debbie who wants to be a master piano tuner like her grandfather.

Link, Ruth. *A House Full of Mice.* Illus. by Marianne Dombret. Atheneum Publishers. Eight-year-old Jimmy spends his summer caring for forty-one mice.

Robertson, Keith. *Henry Reed's Big Show.* Illus. by Robert McCloskey. Viking Press. A sequel to other Henry Reed stories, this story tells of Galileo, an eccentric horse with a sense of humor.

White, Elwyn B. *The Trumpet of the Swan.* Illus. by Edward Frascino. Harper and Row. A fantastic story of how a mute young trumpeter swan finds a voice.

GROUP 3:

Berna, Paul. *They Didn't Come Back.* Trans. from the French by John Buchanan-Brown. Pantheon Books. A group of school children of today

[8] Virginia Haviland and Lois B. Watt, comps., *Children's Books: 1970; A List of Books for Preschool through Junior High School Age* (Washington, D.C.: Library of Congress, 1971). Available from the Supt. of Documents, U.S. Govt. Printing Office, Washington, D.C. 20402. Price 15¢. Up-dated annually.

solve the mystery of the one hundred French resistance fighters in World War II who sought safety in the forest and disappeared.

Ellis, Melvin R. *Flight to the White Wolf.* Holt, Rinehart, and Winston. Russ tries to save the big wolf he had raised from a puppy by taking him back to join his own kind.

Harris, Rosemary. *The Moon in the Cloud.* The Macmillan Co. A wild, unorthodox, and happy version of the gathering of the Ark's passengers.

O'Dell, Scott. *Sing Down the Moon.* Houghton Mifflin Co. A young Navaho girl quietly recounts the tragic story of her people's march into captivity at the hands of white men.

Book awards Each year selected titles in children's literature are awarded honors. Two of the most famous awards are the Newbery and Caldecott medals which were established by a publisher, Frederic G. Melcher.

The Newbery award was first given in 1922 to Hendrik Van Loon's *The Story of Mankind.* Named in honor of John Newbery, an early English publisher who is credited with "discovering" children's literature, this award is given for "distinguished literature." The award list includes many familiar titles:[9]

1922 Van Loon, Hendrik W. *The Story of Mankind.* Liveright. (7–9).
1923 Lofting, Hugh. *The Voyages of Dr. Doolittle.* Stokes. (4–6).
1924 Hawes, Charles B. *The Dark Frigate.* Little, Brown and Co. (7–9).
1925 Finger, Charles J. *Tales from Silver Lands.* Doubleday. (5–7).
1926 Chrisman, Arthur Bowie. *Shen of the Sea.* E. P. Dutton. (5–8).
1927 James, Will. *Smoky: The Cowhorse.* Scribner's Sons. (6–9).
1928 Mukerji, Dhan G. *Gay-Neck, The Story of a Pigeon.* E. P. Dutton. (5–9).
1929 Kelly, Eric. *The Trumpeter of Krakow.* The Macmillan Co. (7–8).
1930 Field, Rachel. *Hitty: Her First Hundred Years.* The Macmillan Co. (4–7).
1931 Coatsworth, Elizabeth. *The Cat Who Went to Heaven.* The Macmillan Co. (5–7).
1932 Armer, Laura. *Waterless Mountain.* Longmans. (5–8).
1933 Lewis, Elizabeth F. *Young Fu of the Upper Yangtze.* Winston. (7–9).
1934 Meigs, Cornelia. *Invincible Louisa.* Little, Brown and Co. (7–9).
1935 Shannon, Monica. *Dobry.* Viking Press. (5–8).
1936 Brink, Carol R. *Caddie Woodlawn.* The Macmillan Co. (6–8).
1937 Sawyer, Ruth. *Roller Skates.* Viking Press. (7–8).
1938 Seredy, Kate. *White Stag.* Viking Press. (6–9).
1939 Enright, Elizabeth. *Thimble Summer.* Farrar, Straus, and Giroux. (5–7).
1940 Daugherty, James. *Daniel Boone.* Viking Press. (5–9).

[9] Dates given are the years of the award. Each book was published in the year immediately preceding. Difficulty level is indicated by school grades.

1941 Sperry, Armstrong. *Call It Courage.* The Macmillan Co. (5–8).
1942 Edmonds, Walter. *The Matchlock Gun.* Dodd, Mead and Co. (4–6).
1943 Gray, Elizabeth J. *Adam of the Road.* Viking Press. (6–9).
1944 Forbes, Esther. *Johnny Tremain.* Houghton Mifflin. (7–9).
1945 Lawson, Robert. *Rabbit Hill.* Viking Press. (3–6).
1946 Lenski, Lois. *Strawberry Girl.* Lippincott. (4–6).
1947 Bailey, Carolyn S. *Miss Hickory.* Viking Press. (4–6).
1948 DuBois, William Pène. *The 21 Balloons.* Viking Press. (5–9).
1949 Henry, Marguerite. *King of the Wind.* Rand McNally and Co. (5–8).
1950 De Angeli, Marguerite. *Door in the Wall.* Doubleday. (4–6).
1951 Yates, Elizabeth. *Amos Fortune, Free Man.* Aladdin. (7–9).
1952 Estes, Eleanor. *Ginger Pye.* Harcourt, Brace. (4–7).
1953 Clark, Ann N. *Secret of the Andes.* Viking Press. (6–8).
1954 Krumgold, Joseph. *. . . And Now Miguel.* Thomas Crowell. (5–8).
1955 De Jong, Meindert. *Wheel on the School.* Harper and Row. (4–7).
1956 Latham, Jean L. *Carry On, Mr. Bowditch.* Houghton, Mifflin. (6–8).
1957 Sorenson, Virginia. *Miracles on Maple Hill.* Harcourt, Brace. (4–7).
1958 Keith, Harold. *Rifles for Watie.* Thomas Crowell. (6–9).
1959 Speare, Elizabeth. *Witch of Blackbird Pond.* Houghton, Mifflin. (6–9).
1960 Krumgold, Joseph. *Onion John.* Thomas Crowell. (5–8).
1961 O'Dell, Scott. *Island of the Blue Dolphins.* Houghton, Mifflin. (5–9).
1962 Speare, Elizabeth G. *The Bronze Bow.* Houghton, Mifflin. (5–9).
1963 L'Engle, Madeline. *A Wrinkle in Time.* Farrar, Straus, and Giroux. (5–8).
1964 Neville, Emily. *It's Like This, Cat.* Harper and Row. (4–7).
1965 Wojciechowska, Maia. *Shadow of a Bull.* Atheneum. (5–8).
1966 De Treviño, Elizabeth B. *I, Juan de Pareja.* Farrar, Straus, and Giroux. (5–9).
1967 Hunt, Irene. *Up a Road Slowly.* Follett Educational Corp. (6–9).
1968 Konigsberg, Elaine E. *From the Mixed-up Files of Mrs. Basil E. Frankweiler.* Atheneum. (5–7).
1969 Alexander, Lloyd. *The High King.* Holt, Rinehart, and Winston. (5–9).
1970 Armstrong, William Howard. *Sounder.* Harper and Row. (4–8).
1971 Byars, Betsy. *The Summer of the Swans.* Viking Press. (5–7).
1972 O'Brien, Robert C. *Mrs. Frisby and the Rats of Nimh.* Atheneum. (4–7).
1973 George, Jean Craighead. *Julie of the Wolves.* Harper. (4–7).
1974 Fox, Paula. *The Slave Dancer.* Bradbury Press. (5–8).

The Caldecott Medal is awarded to the best picture-book of the year. Named in honor of Randolph Caldecott (1846–1886), an English illustrator of children's books, the first Caldecott Medal was awarded in 1938 to Dorothy Lathrop for illustrating *Animals of the Bible.* Note in the following list that the first name given is that of the illustrator, who in some cases is also the author.

1938 Lathrop, Dorothy P. (illus.). *Animals of the Bible.* Text edited by Helen D. Dish. Stokes. (1–4).

1939 Handforth, Thomas (author-illus.). *Mei Li.* Doubleday. (1–3).
1940 Aulaire, Ingri and Edgar d' (author-illus.). *Abraham Lincoln.* Doubleday. (3–4).
1941 Lawson, Robert (author-illus.). *They Were Strong and Good.* Viking Press. (4–6).
1942 McCloskey, Robert (author-illus.). *Make Way for Ducklings.* Viking Press. (1–3).
1943 Burton, Virginia Lee (author-illus.). *The Little House.* Houghton Mifflin. (1–4).
1944 Slobodkin, Louis (illus.). *Many Moons.* Text by James Thurber. Harcourt, Brace. (4–5).
1945 Jones, Elizabeth Orton (illus.). *Prayer for a Child.* Text by Rachel Field. The Macmillan Co. (1–3).
1946 Petersham, Maud and Miska (author-illus.). *The Rooster Crows.* The Macmillan Co. (1–3).
1947 Weisgard, Leonard (illus.). *Little Island.* Text by Margaret W. Brown. Doubleday. (1–3).
1948 Duvoisin, Roger (illus.). *White Snow, Bright Snow.* Text by Alvin Tresselt. Lothrop, Lee and Shepard Co. (1–3).
1949 Hader, Berta and Elmer (author-illus.). *The Big Snow.* The Macmillan Co. (1–3).
1950 Politi, Leo (author-illus.). *Song of the Swallows.* Scribner's Sons. (1–3).
1951 Milhous, Katherine (author-illus.). *The Egg Tree.* Scribner's Sons. (1–3).
1952 Mordvinoff, Nicholas (illus.). *Finders Keepers.* Text by William Lipkind. Harcourt, Brace. (1–3).
1953 Ward, Lynd (author-illus.). *Biggest Bear.* Houghton, Mifflin. (2–3).
1954 Bemelmans, Ludwig (author-illus.). *Madeline's Rescue.* Viking Press. (1–3).
1955 Brown, Marcia J. (illus.). *Cinderella.* Text by Charles Perrault. Scribner's Sons. (1–5).
1956 Rojankovsky, Feodor (illus.). *Frog Went a-Courtin'.* Text by John Langstaff. (1–4).
1957 Simont, Marc (illus.). *A Tree Is Nice.* Text by Janice Udry. Harper and Row. (1–2).
1958 McCloskey, Robert (author-illus.). *Time of Wonder.* Viking Press. (2–4).
1959 Cooney, Barbara (illus.). *Chanticleer and the Fox.* Text by Chaucer. Thomas Crowell. (1–5).
1960 Ets, Marie Hall (co-author and illus.). *Nine Days to Christmas.* Co-author of text, Aurora Labastida. Viking Press. (2–4).
1961 Sidjakov, Nicholas (author-illus.). *Baboushka and the Three Kings.* Parnassus Press. (1–5).
1962 Brown, Marcia (author-illus.). *Once a Mouse.* Scribner's Sons. (1–3).
1963 Keats, Ezra J. (author-illus.). *The Snowy Day.* Viking Press. (1–2).
1964 Sendak, Maurice (author-illus.). *Where the Wild Things Are.* Harper and Row. (1–3).
1965 De Regniers, Bernice (author-illus.). *May I Bring a Friend?* Harcourt, Brace. (1–2).

1966 Hogrogian, Nonny (illus.). *Always Room for One More.* Text by Sorche Nic Leodhas. Holt, Rinehart, and Winston. (2–5).
1967 Ness, Evaline (author-illus.). *Sam, Bangs and Moonshine.* Holt, Rinehart, and Winston. (K–3).
1968 Emberly, Ed. *Drummer Hoff.* Prentice-Hall. (K–2).
1969 Ransome Arthur. *The Fool of the World and the Flying Ship.* Farrar, Strauss and Giroux. (1–4).
1970 Steig, William. *Sylvester and the Magic Pebble.* Windmill Books. (1–3).
1971 Haley, Gail E. *A Story, A Story; An African Tale.* Atheneum. (2–4).
1972 Hogrogian, Nonny. *One Fine Day.* The Macmillan Co. (1–3).
1973 Mosel, Arlene. *The Funny Little Woman.* Dutton. Ill. by Blair Lent. (1–3).
1974 Zemach, Harve. *Duffey and the Devil.* Farrar. Ill. by Margot Zemach. (1–4).

A more recently initiated award for children's literature is the National Book Award, the prize for which is contributed by the Children's Book Council. In March, 1969, the well-known National Book Award was, for the first time, extended to include an award for the most distinguished juvenile title written by an American citizen and published in the United States. Prizes awarded thus far include:

1969 DeJong, Meindert. *Journey from Peppermint Street.* Harper and Row. (6–8).
1970 Singer, Isaac Bashevis. *A Day of Pleasure: Stories of a Boy Growing Up in Warsaw.* Farrar, Straus, and Giroux. (6–9).
1971 Alexander, Lloyd. *The Marvelous Misadventures of Sebastian.* E. P. Dutton. (5–8).
1972 Barthelme, Donald. *The Slightly Irregular Fire Engine.* Farrrar. (6–8).
1973 Le Guin, Ursula K. *The Farthest Shore. Atheneum.* (5–8).
1974 Pynchon, Thomas. *Gravity's Rainbow.* Viking. (5–8) Singer, Isaac B. *A Crown of Feathers and Other Stories.* Farrar, Straus. (6–8)

Should these lists be used as purchase lists for a beginning library? A well-established elementary school library will contain all these titles, but one must remember that books are selected for varied reasons. In examining these lists, for example, one immediately notices that the Caldecott award list is composed of books for the primary grades judged on the value of their illustrations. The list of titles for the Newbery award focuses largely on books for grades four through nine with a heavy concentration of books for the junior high school level. Too, it must be remembered that much excellent nonfiction is required for the school library. These titles must be evaluated, therefore, in terms of the needs of the school library as a whole.

Remember, too, in examining award lists that many of these books were selected twenty, even thirty years ago. Some of these titles do not prove as tempting today as they may have been then, as new interests and tastes develop. One wonders also whether there is not a tinge of "what adults think children should like" about awards of this nature. An interesting study could be conducted by classes to determine which books are favorites with class members. Which titles from these lists are named as favorites? Which are not, and why? Here is an opportunity to develop critical thinking as children realize that a printed list proves nothing in itself.

Literature Enriches Learning

Literature pervades the curriculum. How much more exciting is the history lesson that talks of real people who live through their biographies, the science lesson that opens books that explain why, where, and how? The textbook can introduce, but beyond that introduction must come books, books, and more books to satisfy that "satiable curiosity," which is not typical of the elephant's child alone.

What do we require of the literature of learning? "Integrity, however achieved, is the quality we look for in children's books. This includes integrity with regard both to writing and to subject matter . . ." writes Alice Dalgliesh,[10] author of many fine titles for young people. In the classroom we are especially concerned with integrity, and we are concerned with accuracy of information provided and the qualifications of those who provide it.

SOCIAL STUDIES

There is a growing collection of excellent books for young people in the areas of history, geography, government, and citizenship. Both fiction and nonfiction offer many titles to augment understandings, to supply factual knowledge, and to extend interests.

Enlarge a United States (or world) map which can be mounted on a bulletin board. As students read books, have each pin a small pennant on the map bearing the title of the book with the location revealing the setting of the story. Figures of the main characters can also be used to mark the setting, with Tom Sawyer marching beside the Mississippi and Paul Bunyan in the North Woods.

Examine the names of children in the class. Are there Irish names, French, Italian? Were any children born abroad? How many are native to the state? Questions like these can lead to an interesting study of the origins

[10] Alice Dalgliesh, "A Matter of Integrity," *Saturday Review* (November 13, 1965), p. 51.

of the settlers of the United States. Biographies of Americans who came from other lands will add much to the understanding of these people; for example, *William Penn* by Hildegard Dolson (Holt, 1962). Many fine history books describe these pioneers and their lives in the new country.

Jamestown: First English Colony, by Marshall W. Fishwick. Harper and Row, 1965. Jamestown revisted; many photographs.

Gateway to America: Miss Liberty's First Hundred Years, by Hertha Pauli. McKay, 1965. Includes contributions of the immigrant.

America Is Born (1959), *America Grows Up* (1960), *America Moves Forward* (1960), by Gerald Johnson. Morrow. An excellent series for grades 5–8.

Understanding of the lives of people in different countries or regions of the United States can be gained through the reading of fiction. Kate Seredy's *The Good Master* is an excellent example of an exciting story which also describes, in this case, the Hungarian legends and holiday celebrations as well as the everyday life of the people. Other titles include:

Banner in the Sky, by James R. Ullman (Switzerland)
Call It Courage, by Armstrong Sperry (Polynesia)
Crow Boy, by Taro Yashima (Japan)
The Family Conspiracy, by Joan Phipson (Australia)
Lotte's Locket, by Virginia Sorensen (Denmark)
Spiro of the Sponge Fleet, by Henry Chapin (Greece)
The Wheel in the School, by Miendert DeJong (Holland)
Young Fu of the Upper Yangtze, by Elizabeth Lewis (China)

"*Where in the World?*" asks the title of Philip Egan's provocative, answer-filled book (Rand McNally, 1964), which is certain to appeal to children from grade four through six. "What was Columbus doing in Iceland?" "Where in the world are diamonds found?" "Where in the world can today become yesterday?" These questions arouse curiosity and immediately satisfy it.

Don't miss Miroslav Sasek's beautiful guidebooks which are for young and old a true delight. Titles of his books include *This Is San Francisco, This Is London,* and *This Is Paris.*

Folk tales are receiving well-deserved attention in titles such as *The Valiant Chattee-Maker; A Folk Tale of India Retold,* by Christine Price (Warne), and *The Sea of Gold and Other Tales from Japan,* adapted by Yohiko Uchida (Scribners). The folklore of a nation develops insight into the ways of its people.

Any topic or subject in the social studies can be enriched through the use of these stimulating titles. Use book selection aids; for example, the *Children's Catalog,* to suggest titles for units of study.

SCIENCE

Contemporary focus on science has led to the publication of many exciting books in the various fields of science. One of the leading writers in science for youth has been Isaac Asimov, who writes for the more advanced student. He is author of *Building Blocks of the Universe* (Abelard) and *The Clock We Live On* (Abelard), as well as *Words of Science* (Houghton Mifflin) and adult science fiction.

Another familiar name is Herbert Zim, whose small handbooks on mammals, insects, stars, trees, birds, and so on are inexpensive and reliable reference books. Now available in paperback editions, these books are popular purchases for the young scientist himself as he collects rocks, butterflies, or studies the stars.

Activities which relate science and literature might include the following:

Read the very fine description of the life of a hermit crab told by Holling C. Holling in *Pagoo* (Houghon Mifflin). This adventure story is accompanied by superb illustrations in both black and white and color. Follow the reading of this book by showing the unique film *The Story of a Book* (Churchill Films) which describes the work of Mr. and Mrs. Holling in developing this idea for a book—the origin of the idea, observation of the hermit crab, preparation of illustrations, writing of the text.

Use fishnet as an attractive background for a display of books about the sea. Include some of these titles:

Brindze, Ruth. *The Rise and Fall of the Seas; the Story of the Tides.* Harcourt, Brace.
Buck, Margaret W. *Along the Seashore.* Abingdon.
Clarke, Arthur C. *The Challenge of the Sea.* Holt, Rinehart, and Winston.
Kenyon, Ley. *Discovering the Under Sea World.* Sterling.

Books of experiments are intriguing as are books about space. Encourage the publicizing of new *finds* of this type which interest students.

Encourage students to read biographies of men and women of science. Gifted students will be especially interested in learning more about inventors, discoverers, scientists. Information gained can be shared by the preparation of a display which depicts the contributions of the individual.

Bigland, Eileen. *Madame Curie.* Criterion Books.
Dickinson, Alice. *Charles Darwin and Natural Selection.* Franklin Watts.
Freeman, Mae B. *The Story of Albert Einstein.* Random House.

Books to Investigate

Anderson, William, and Groff, Patrick. *A New Look at Children's Literature.* Belmont, Calif.: Wadsworth Publishing Co., 1972.

Arbuthnot, May Hill, and Sutherland, Zena. *Children and Books.* 4th ed. Glenview, Ill.: Scott, Foresman, 1972.

Elementary English. October, 1973. Focus on "Women and Girls."

Hopkins, Lee Bennett. *Books Are by People.* New York: Citation Press, 1969; and *More Books by More People.* New York: Citation Press, 1973.

Huck, Charlotte, and Young, Doris K. *Children's Literature in the Elementary School.* New York: Holt, Rinehart, and Winston, 1968.

Jacobs, Leland J., ed. *Using Literature with Young Children.* New York: Teachers College Press, 1965.

Ladley, Winifred C. *Source of Good Books and Magazines for Children.* Newark, Del.: International Reading Association, 1970.

Lonsdale, Bernard J., and Mackintosh, Helen K. *Children Experience Literature.* New York: Random House, 1973.

Montebello, Mary. *Children's Literature in the Curriculum.* Dubuque, Ia.: William C. Brown, 1970.

Reid, Virginia, ed. *Reading Ladders for Human Relations.* 5th ed. Urbana, Ill.: National Council of Teachers of English, 1972.

Tiedt, Iris M. *Sexism in Education.* Morristown, N.J.: General Learnings Corporation, 1974.

———. *Books/Literature/Children.* Boston: Houghton-Mifflin, 1975.

chapter 14 future imperfect

Education must shift into the future tense.

Alvin Toffler

One of the greatest challenges facing English education—all of education—at the present time is how to prepare students for the future. The six-year-old child who is entering the first grade, will be thirty by the end of the twentieth century. Will this youngster be ready to meet the demands of the twenty-first century? Will this child be able to cope with the century in which he or she will spend more than half of his or her life? As R. Buckminster Fuller writes in "The Prospect for Humanity":

> It is an easy matter to foresee the trend of physically dramatic events during the next 21-year generation. We will go to the moon and start communicating with humans in other parts of the universe and open up entirely unexpected new realizations of the significance of man in the universe. We will probably learn that Darwin was wrong and that man came to earth from another planet and monkeys are hybrids degenerated by over-long inbreeding of isolated humans.[1]

[1] Alvin Toffler, *Future Shock* (New York: Random House, 1970), p. 378.

How are we as teachers preparing students for even the immediate future? How do we as English teachers prepare students to live in a future we have never experienced? These are some of the questions we will probe in this concluding chapter.

Society of the Future

The society of the future will demand of its citizens the ability to absorb a tremendous flood of new ideas. Although we know little of the future, we can extrapolate from the past and from the present. All indications point to a period of rapid change as we move into this "post-industrial society," as Daniel Bell has termed it.

What will the future be?
Blacker, more feminine, more oriental, more emotional, more intuitive, more exuberant and maybe just better than yesterday's America. . . .

CHARACTERISTICS OF SOCIETY

Your children may live to be 100. And, in their lifetimes, they may take drugs to raise their intelligence, may have a "talking computer as a colleague, and may select the characteristics of their children before they are born—these developments were forecast by Theodore Gordon of the Douglas Space Systems Center. The characteristics of the society of the future will be technological, demographic, psychological, and socio-political.

Technological Technological factors will increase the amount of information available to us, thus increasing the demand for education and at the same time increasing the techniques available to us to disseminate the needed knowledge. For example, W. H. Ware predicts that by 1980 most homes will have a small computer just as they now have a television set or a washing machine. If you think that is too far out, look at the recent increased use of pocket calculators. Unless some unforeseen catastrophe envelops the world we will see tremendous growth in the use and sophistication of technology.

Advances in science and technology have rewritten the very terms and conditions of the human contract with no more warning than the morning's headlines.

Robert Heilbroner
The Future as History

Demographic Demographic factors include such data as the size of the population and specific characteristics of the population, for example, the average age of the population or the number of children. One of the factors that futurists have to deal with is the rapid growth of the world's population. The following chart from Don Fabun's *The Dynamics of Change* [2] indicates graphically what is meant by rapid growth.

IT TOOK FROM	FOR EARTH'S POPULATION TO REACH
the beginning of man to the Neolithic age	7,990,000 years to reach 10 million
Neolithic to the Birth of Christ	10,000 years to reach 300 million
Birth of Christ to the days of Columbus	1,500 years to reach 500 million
Columbus to 1850 A.D.	350 years to reach 1 BILLION
1850 to 1925 A.D.	75 years to reach 2 BILLION
1925 to 1962 A.D.	37 years to reach 3 BILLION
and will take to 1975	13 years to reach 4 BILLION
and from there to 1982	7 years to reach 5 BILLION

Demographers also indicate that we will soon become an aged society with few children as life expectancy increases. Thus education faces the challenge of providing some type of continuing education.

Psychological There are serious problems for the individual in maintaining identity in the face of massive changes. We are exploring the areas of parapsychology, meditation, bio-feedback, alpha waves, and right and left hemispheres of the brain as we begin to realize the potential in man. This realization will increase as we continue research into, for example, the use of drugs to expand awareness and learning.

[2] Don Fabun, *The Dynamics of Change,* Kaiser Aluminum & Chemical Corporation, © 1967.

Personally, I have a great faith in the resiliency and adaptability of man, and I tend to look to our tomorrows with a surge of excitement and hope. I feel that we're standing on the threshold of a liberating, and exhilarating world in which the human tribe can become truly one family and man's consciousness can be freed from the shackles of mechanical culture and enabled to roam the cosmos.

Marshall McLuhan [3]

Sociopolitical Factors such as the rise of the megalopolis and the resulting pressure of people into fewer and fewer population centers also characterize society of the future. There seems little doubt that large urban centers are developing and will continue to grow. At the present time the New York–New Jersey metropolitan area has a population of 16 million, making it the largest metropolitan area in the world according to the 1973 United Nations Demographic Yearbook.

The growth of cities is a recent phenomenon. During the Dark Ages most European cities were near extinction, for example, Rome's population was less than 20,000. Cities started growing following the Industrial Revolution. Since World War II, growth has been tremendous, for example, the population of Mexico City increased from 4½ million in 1960 to 8½ million in 1970.

ALTERNATIVE FUTURES

How do futurists arrive at their predictions? One of the devices they use is to extrapolate from what is happening now to what might possibly happen in the future. Another method that is commonly used is to generate a number of alternatives as an example of this type of prediction. The following three alternative futures for the U.S. were generated by Kahn and Bruce-Briggs in their book *Things to Come.*

THREE ALTERNATE U.S. FUTURES [4]

A Neutral Context

1 Vietnam has been settled. The domestic effects have largely vanished or been absorbed by 1975.

2 There is a further extension of the sensate technological and affluent society.

3 Vice, dissent, anarchism, and nihilism become very visible but are concentrated among relatively small groups.

[3] Marshall McLuhan. "Playboy Interview: Marshall McLuhan," *Playboy* (March, 1969), 16.3: 158.

[4] Herman Kahn and B. Bruce-Briggs, *Things to Come: Thinking about the 70's and 80's* (New York: The Macmillan Company, 1972). Reprinted by permission.

4 Life is extremely good for the overwhelming majority of American people by almost any of the classical materialistic, cultural or political standards, and to some degree even from the moral and morale points of view, but both the upper classes and the various types of dropouts prefer to emphasize the defects of American civilization.
5 Domestically, many of the "great society" problems are being alleviated, especially those susceptible to money and physical engineering.
6 Business has lost much of its prestige and charisma, and attempts to recoup its prestige by engaging in "social responsibility."
7 The gross national product (in 1967 dollars) reaches 1.1 trillion by 1975 and 1.6 trillion in 1985.
8 By the late 1970s, for the first time in history, a majority of married women are employed outside the household.
9 Some erosion of work effort is evident. Absenteeism and turn-over climb. Life is centered around weekends and vacations, but technological advance and steady substitution of capital for labor keeps productivity rising.
10 As it becomes clear that Negroes are not especially interested in social and residential integration, white liberals press less for it. The large numbers of prosperous Negroes relieve white guilt. Radicals—black and white—curse the "black bourgeoisie," which is more concerned with black crime than with white repression.
11 Despite myriad squabbles and prophecies of doom, pollution control begins to pay off.
12 U.S. productivity advantages over other industrial nations gradually erode and markets are lost to competitors, particularly Japanese. There is increasing agitation among affected industries, especially unions, for more protectionism.

A Modestly Optimistic Context

1 There is less erosion of the traditional U.S. work-oriented, achievement-oriented, advancement-oriented values than is envisaged in the neutral context, so that the American society and economy are more dynamic than might have been expected.
2 Poverty and student dissidence have been substantially overcome.
3 "Reverse discrimination policies" prove successful. Tens of thousands of Negroes are either at the top levels of U.S. society or clearly are on their way. Everywhere there is visible proof to the Negro that he can "make it." This reduces the tolerance both within and without the black community to illegal or unreasonable acts by destructive and extremist protest groups.
4 There is some return to religion, but it is motivated by a need for continuity and values, rather than a deep-felt religious faith.
5 Multi-channel cable television and cheap transmitting equipment permit a full spectrum of cultural, educational, political, and entertainment programs.
6 The most important single recreational activity is the cheerful hedonism of lying near-naked on a beach, but the overrunning of the shore by the lower classes drives the upper classes inland to more active leisure. Ski

resorts proliferate. American campers are increasingly found as far afield as Alaska and Central America.

A Modestly Pessimistic Context

1 There is a degree of stagnation in some sectors of intellectual life, and in general, diminishing satisfactions and élan in most elite occupations.

2 The prestige of physics, mathematics, engineering, and the life sciences has eroded more rapidly than was suggested in the neutral prognosis. Political activism by social scientists and psychologists has given them very low credibility among the public. There is widespread belief that science and reason have failed, and even educated people feel free to admit to being "unreasonable" and advocate moral nihilism and/or raw dogma.

3 The gross national product fails to reach 1.1 trillion (in 1967 dollars) by 1975 and falls short of 1.6 trillion by 1985. Unemployment is at least 5% on the average.

4 A striking feature of the society is the spread of *syndicalism,* a "gang" society wherein groups responsive to only their own self-interest compete for economic and political advantage.

5 Increasingly militant trade unions, particularly in government, take a "public-be-damned" attitude toward the common interest.

6 Labor indiscipline makes it advantageous for employers to retain older workers. "Old Power" slogans are heard.

7 Most Americans perceive that things are getting worse, and are discontented, even though by almost every historical measure of national well-being the U.S. remains the freest, most powerful, and most prosperous country in the world.

Education in the Future

What will education be like in the twenty-first century? As Margaret Mead says:

> We are now at the point where we must educate people in what nobody knew yesterday and prepare in our schools for what no one knows yet, but what some people must know tomorrow.[5]

CURRICULUM

Education in the twenty-first century will consist of many, many different elements, movements, and ideas. The following are some curriculum developments that we feel are important.

Curriculum explosion The curriculum is going to explode out of the classroom and the school. We will be using more outside resources. The

[5] Margaret Mead, "That Each Child May Learn What It Is to Be Completely Human." Address at 62nd Annual Convention of National Council of Teachers of English, Minneapolis, Minn., Nov. 23, 1972.

school will become a swinging door as we push the school outside and draw the outside inside.

Foxfire is one contemporary example of what can happen when we accept the fact that education can take place outside the four walls of the classroom. *Foxfire* is many things—a tiny organism that glows in the dark, a magazine, two books, so far—but basically it is an idea that has put Rabun Gap, Georgia on the map. The idea is Eliot Wigginton's attempt to get his students out of the classroom and in the community. We will describe this innovation in more detail as we consider the future of English.

Schools will lose their monopoly on knowledge. This is already happening but it will obviously increase. What education does about it may determine the story of whether schools are around in the twenty-first century or not. TV, specialized schools, skill schools, and Growth Institutions, such as Esalen, provide important information and knowledge that schools are not presently providing or are providing poorly.

There once was a lady named Bright
Who traveled much faster than light
She set out one day
In a relative way
And returned on the previous night.

Curriculum for the future Toffler states: "Nothing should be included in a required curriculum unless it can be strongly justified in terms of the future." [6] This is a strong statement but a useful one. Are the hours spent learning reading or spelling maximally useful or are we wasting students' time and effort? A lot of work is given youngsters merely to keep them busy, not necessarily because it is important for them to learn. Are we honestly looking at our objectives?

We need to take a real look at the elementary curriculum. Much of its content exists because no one has really questioned what we are doing in the classrooms of America. As the existentialist philosopher, Soren Kierkegaard, notes: "Life can only be understood backwards; but it must be lived forwards."

Common skills needed, or the new "three R's" of the future according to Toffler, will be LRG—Learning, Relating, and Choosing. Toffler states, furthermore, that future schools must teach not merely facts but ways to manipulate data—ways to discard old ideas, how and when to replace

[6] Alvin Toffler, *Future Shock* (New York: Random House, 1970), p. 363.

them. They must learn how to learn. Schools will need to teach youngsters not only how to learn but how to unlearn and relearn as well.

Education must teach us ways to relate to one another—to communicate, to learn how to make friends, to learn new ways of relating in lieu of the deep friendships that may not be available in the transient future.

Choosing or decision making will also become more intense as "overchoice" becomes even more common. Schools need to organize formal and informal activities that will help students define and test their values. Schools must not define a rigid set of values for the students of the future. It wouldn't be a bad idea for teachers to take a hard look at their values and attempt to make them explicit.

Can we employ such open activities as the following?

- Plan and design a city for the future. This might be in space or under water. Use your imagination. This could be an individualized activity or a group activity.

- Write a newspaper for the year 1999. Include all of what we think of in the normal newspaper. This too could be an individual project, or the newspaper could be divided up in various committees or task forces assigned to prepare each part of the newspaper.

- Invent a holiday for the future. As a further exploration of this activity, the students might specify how they would celebrate this holiday.

Word Brackets

F eatur E
U ndercove R
T ortuo US
U tmos T
R adi US
E vent F ul

Score: 29

Only the letters inside the brackets count. Can you get a better score?

TEACHING

Change should start in the classroom. The standard classroom with the teacher in the front of the room and the subordinated youngsters seated in rows has to go. Again, this traditional classroom is based on the industrial age. We need a new image of the classroom that is based on a post-industrial society.

New methods of teaching Students need experience in varied class arrangements—classes with several teachers and a group of students, classes with students organized on the basis of a task or project, classes that permit students to shift from group work to individual work. Students will need this experience as they prepare themselves to move about in the new world of the post-industrial society. The lecture method, still widely used, smacks of an older, more authoritarian time. This limited method must give way to a group of newer methods such as role playing, gaming, and stimulation, to the use of what might be called "contrived experiences" like the following example:

DECISION BY CONSENSUS

Prepared by NASA

1 Individual Decision.

Instructions:

You are a member of a space crew originally scheduled to rendezvous with a mother ship on the lighted surface of the moon. Because of mechanical difficulties, however, your ship was forced to land at a spot some two hundred miles from the rendezvous point. During the landing much of the ship and the equipment aboard were damaged, and since survival depends on reaching the mother ship, the most critical items still available must be chosen for the two-hundred-mile trip. Below are listed the 15 items left intact and undamaged after landing. Your task is to rank them in order of their importance in allowing your crew to reach the rendezvous point. Place the number 1 by the most important item, the number 2 by the second most important, and so on through number 15, the least important.

________Box of matches
________Food concentrate
________50 feet of nylon rope
________Parachute silk
________Portable heating unit
________Two .45-caliber pistols
________One case of dehydrated milk
________Two 100-pound tanks of oxygen
________Map of the stars as seen from the moon
________Life raft
________Magnetic compass
________5 gallons of water
________Signal flares
________First-aid kit containing injection needles
________Solar-powered FM receiver-transmitter

2 Group Consensus.

This is an exercise in group decision-making. Your group is to employ the method of group consensus in reaching its decision. This means that the prediction for each of the fifteen survival items *must* be agreed upon by each group member before it becomes a part of the group decision. Consensus is difficult to reach. Therefore, not every ranking will meet with everyone's complete approval. Try, as a group, to make each ranking one with which *all* group members can at least partially agree. Here are some guides to use in reaching consensus:

1. Avoid arguing for your own individual judgments. Approach the task on the basis of logic.
2. Avoid changing your mind only in order to reach agreement and eliminate conflict. Support only solutions with which you are able to agree to some extent, at least.
3. Avoid conflict-reducing techniques such as majority vote, averaging, or trading in reaching decisions.
4. View differences of opinion as helpful rather than as a hindrance in decision-making.

On the Group Summary Sheet place the individual rankings made earlier by each group member. Take as much time as you need in reaching your group decision.

Key Take the difference between your ranking and the ranking on the key. Add the differences. The lower the score the better. These answers are based on the best judgments that are now available to you. They are not absolute answers.

Rank	Item	Reason
15	Box of matches	Little or no use on moon.
4	Food concentrate	Supply daily food required.
6	50 feet of nylon rope	Useful in tying injured together; helpful in climbing.
8	Parachute silk	Shelter against sun's rays.
13	Portable heating unit	Useful only if party landed on dark side of moon.
11	Two .45-caliber pistols	Self-propulsion devices could be made from them.
12	One case of dehydrated milk	Food; mixed with water for drinking.
1	Two 100-pound tanks of oxygen	Fills respiration requirement.
3	Map of the stars as seen from the moon	One of the principal means of finding directions.
9	Life raft	CO_2 bottles for self-propulsion across chasms, etc.

14	Magnetic compass	Probably no magnetized poles, thus useless.
2	5 gallons of water	Replenishes loss by sweating, etc.
10	Signal flares	Distress call when line of sight possible.
7	First-aid kit containing injection needles	Oral pills of injection valuable.
5	Solar-powered FM receiver-transmitter	Distress-signal transmitter—possible communication with mother ship.

3 Critique.

Following the exercise, discuss the sources of the problem-solving techniques. How often did individuals use the affective domain in working out the problem? How often did the cognitive domain dominate? What kind of balance existed? How did their knowledge of the extensional world allow them to work with the unknowns? What did they learn about their own learning styles? Did they work better in groups or alone? Did they score higher as a group, or was the individual score better? How did the scores compare with the group average? Did they enjoy the individual work more than the group work?

Increased use of media Schools will use much more technology. The computer will be used in all areas of the curriculum. Students will use the computer language to communicate their problems. There will be more communication between machines than between people. Schools will be less book and reading oriented. At the same time they will be more efficient at receiving information and at finding new ways to learn. Schools are teaching speed listening, for example, to help students cope with the increase in information.

People will own tape libraries for cassette players as they now have encyclopedias. Libraries will check out whole learning systems. Most families will have a computer for information retrieval. Cable TV, along with satellite TV and Videotape, will revolutionize our concepts of disseminating information. Information will be readily available for the first time in history. This development has true revolutionary implications.

Research on learning The whole brain goes to school. Psychologists are reporting interesting research findings on the various functions of the right and left hemispheres of the brain. The left hemisphere seems to be involved with logical types of information, language, and digital types of learnings. This side of the brain is concerned with serial types of learning. The right hemisphere is involved with intuition, creativity and the forming of gestalts with holistic types of perception.

Expanded awareness Students, and education in general, will be attempting to tap unknown sources of potential psychic power and energy. Such techniques as self hypnosis will be used to aid learning. Biofeedback machines will check out learning. Even now in the 70s schools are using transcendental meditation and popular magazines are writing about it. Parapsychology will be accepted as an expanding area of knowledge.

English for the Year 2000

In some ways the above title is a classic contradiction in terms, for English has long been the caboose of the curriculum. While all other areas such as math, science, social sciences, and foreign languages have gone through many changes in materials and methodology, the English curriculum remains pretty much the same. Oh yes, we do have creative writing and the new grammar, but basically English has resisted change. In researching for this chapter on the future, therefore, we found very little future-oriented thinking expressed by members of the English profession.

What are the reasons for this lack of future orientation in English education? All of the components of English seem strongly hooked into the past. Acceptability in literature is often equated with age. Users of English have consistently refused to accept change in spelling. Only recently have we questioned "standard English" and admitted the existence of varied dialects. How many teachers today are really teaching the "new English"?

It is essential that English teachers, too, probe the future. We need to do our part in preparing students to think Future, not to limit them to the past. As Toffler states:

> It is no longer sufficient for Johnny to understand the past. It is not even enough for him to understand the present, for the here and now environment will soon vanish. Johnny must learn to anticipate the directions and rate of change. He must, to put it technically, learn to make repeated, probabilistic, increasingly long range assumptions about the future. And so must Johnny's teachers.[7]

[7] Alvin Toffler, *Future Shock* (New York: Random House, 1970), p. 351.

One serious problem for English education is accepting contemporary thinking and the whole concept of change. As Johann Wolfgang Von Goethe wrote some time ago: "Life belongs to the living, and he who lives must be prepared for changes." We who are teaching English need to begin by looking around us today to bring current ideas into the classroom. We need, furthermore, to permit English to move out of the classroom.

VARIED MEDIA

Computers are being used today to translate books, to compose music and art. They can also be used to compose poetry. Students need to master the computer as they do the typewriter. Students will either master the computer or be mastered by it. Whole new languages are being created for the computer such as COBAL and FORTRAN. A type of interaction is available between student and computer that is not available with other types of media.

Introduce students to the possibilities of the computer through these short films which combine music, color, and movement.

Binary Bit Patterns—3 minutes in length, Color, distributed by Pyramid Films (Box 1048, Santa Monica, Calif. 90406).

Catalog—10 minutes in length, Color, distributed by International Film Board.

A new form of composing is the use of cameras to compose, that is, to tell a story visually. The film is the paper, and the camera is the new "pen." We can also compose with sound and sound images. We can not only study films today, but we can also create films. Videotape offers a possibility for combining visual and sound images. New books are being published that help teachers develop films with young people, for example:

J. Bryne-Daniel, *Grafilm.* Studio Vista/Van Nostrand Reinhold, 1970.

John Lidstone and Don McIntosh, *Children as Film Makers.* Van Nostrand Reinhold Company, 1970.

Yvonne Andersen, *Teaching Film Animation to Children.* Van Nostrand Reinhold Company, 1970.

EXPLODING OUT OF THE CLASSROOM

English teacher Eliot Wigginton found that students were bored with his attempts to teach traditional English. He questioned whether his efforts were worth it and whether the kids were learning anything except that English was something they thoroughly disliked.

He and his students decided to throw away the textbooks and to create a quarterly magazine.[8] They planned to go out into the community, to ask questions, and to record results. They interviewed old timers in this Appalachian community on how, for example, they planted their crops. Wigginton's students go directly into the community to talk with the people who are doing the planting, building the log cabin, faith healing, wagon making, and other mountain crafts. Student interviewers record these ideas with tape recorders. Then the whole class produces the magazine *Foxfire*. They have written on such topics as:

Spring Wild Plant Foods
Boogers, Witches and Haints
From Raising Sheep to Weaving Cloth
"this is the way I was raised up"
Building a Log Cabin
A Quilt is Something Human
Snake Lore
Churning Your Own Butter

The important idea behind *Foxfire* is that the community can educate. Wigginton states:

> I believe that in most cases the most rewarding and significant things that happen to a kid happen outside the classroom: falling in love, climbing a mountain, rapping for hours with an adult who is loved or respected, building a house, seeing a part of the world never seen before, coming to some deep personal empathy with a kid from another background and culture, or genuinely understanding some serious community or national problem.[9]

Operation *Foxfire* has generated many other attempts on the part of schools to explore their communities and to use these communities to educate. Here are a number of titles and addresses:

Bittersweet: A quarterly published in the Ozarks of Missouri containing articles on Ozark johnboats, making and playing the mountain dulcimer, bluegrass music and photo essays on gates, fences, caves, barns, silos, and one-room school houses, and a lot more.
Subscription: $6.00/four issues.

Bittersweet
Lebanon High School
Lebanon, Mo. 65536

[8] *Foxfire,* Rabun Cap, Ga. 30568. Subscription: $6.00/four issues. Also available now in book form: *Foxfire 1* and *Foxfire 2* edited by Eliot Wigginton, Anchor, 1972, 1973.

[9] Eliot Wigginton, *Foxfire 2* (Garden City, N.Y.: Doubleday, 1973), p. 14.

Nanih Waiya: A quarterly published by Mississippi Choctaws containing articles on basket weaving, rabbit and kabucha sticks, hominy making, stickball, blow-gun construction, annual Coctaw Indian Fair, and much more.
Subscription: $8.00/four issues.

Nanih Waiya
Choctaw Central
Route 7, Box 72
Philadelphia, Miss. 39350

Kil-Káás-Git: A quarterly to be published by Alaskan native young people containing articles on the traditional culture of Pacific coastal tribes including halibut hook carving, smoking fish, canoe and totem carving, remedies, legends, et al.
Subscription: $6.00/four issues.

Kil-Káás-Git
Prince of Wales High School
Craig, Alaska 99921

Dovetail: A quarterly published by Indian and white students on the Flathead Reservation in Montana containing articles on stagecoaches, trading posts, hide tanning, Indian language and legends, handmade dolls, root cellars, et al.
Subscription: $12.00/four issues.

Dovetail
Ronan High School
Ronan, Mont. 59864

Skipjack: A quarterly from the Eastern Shore of Maryland containing articles on watermen and local folkways, including interviews with Skipjack captains and their wives, muskrat trapping, crab and eel pot construction, oyster recipes, decoy carving, and much more.
Subscription: $5.00/four issues.

Skipjack
South Dorchester High School
Church Creek, Md. 21622

Sea Chest: A quarterly from the Outer Banks of North Carolina containing articles on lighthouses and lighthouse keepers, storms and shipwrecks, smoking fish, making yaupon tea, Outer Banks dialect, tourists and other strange creatures.
Subscription: $5.50/three issues.

Sea Chest
Cape Hatteras
High School
Box 278
Buxton, N.C. 27920[10]

[10] Listed in *Media and Methods* (November, 1973), p. 18.

FOCUS ON THE INDIVIDUAL

As we look ahead to the future, it becomes increasingly important to focus on the individual. To begin with, we need to ask the question, "What type of education is it that strengthens the human spirit?" Emerson has said, "Society everywhere is in conspiracy against the mankind of every one of its members." If we substitute "education" for "society," we have a pretty good picture of what is going on in education at the present time.

"What is it to be human?" We learn to be human by accepting ourselves, by accepting who we are—our dark side and our bright side, that this is all a single aspect of what it means to be an individual, what it means to be human.

What kind of English curriculum would we have if we were really serious about focus on the individual? We would have a curriculum that deals with the emotions, with the affective as well as the cognitive, for man does not live by head alone.

We see children every day, but do we really "see" them? One attempt to help teachers see children as they really are is *I See a Child* by Cindy Herbert who tries to provide insight into the child's thinking.[11]

WALKING TO SCHOOL [12]

I'm late again.
I'm late.
And you don't care why.
"Tardiness is
unforgivable," you say.
I'm sick inside and
frightened of your eyes.
I'm late again
And you'll never
let me forget it.
I'm late.
I'm late.
I'm late.
I'm late.
I'm always late to school.

[11] Cindy Herbert, *I See a Child* (Garden City, N.Y.: Doubleday, Anchor Books, 1974).

[12] Reprinted by permission from: Herbert, Cindy. *I See a Child.* Doubleday, unpaged.

Then she considers the questions we as teachers might ask.

> How do I know what the child is really feeling?[13]
> How do I know when he's afraid? bored? tired? responsive?
> Do I look for reasons behind his actions?
> Do I look for reasons that may not be obvious?

Education too often has been a put-down of the human spirit. We have been taught what we can't do. We have been taught the many things that we are unable and not fit to do. Individuals do not come out of the present educational system with the feeling of any potency or of any importance.

If we were truly humanizing the educational system, individuals would constantly grow in their feelings for each other and for themselves and would grow in a realization of their own potential. Too many of our institutions are dehumanizing rather than humanizing at the present time. We can hope in the future that this can be turned around, and, indeed, it must be turned around. We need a transformation of the schools, a transformation that will raise the consciousness of everyone in terms of their potential. This is the true meaning of education.

FOCUS ON COMMUNICATION

One of the basic ideas behind English is to develop in students the ability to communicate and to receive communication. As Eliot Wigginton, the teacher behind *Foxfire* states:

> English, in its simplest definition, is communication—reaching out and touching people with words, sounds, and visual images. We are in the business of improving students' prowess in these areas. In their work with photography (which must tell the story with as much impact and clarity as the words), text (which must be grammatically correct except in the use of pure dialect from tapes that they transcribe), lay-out, make-up, correspondence, art and cover design, and selection of manuscripts from outside poets and writers—to say nothing of related skills such as fund raising, typing, retailing, advertising, and speaking at conferences and public meetings—they learn more about English than from any other curriculum I could devise. Moreover, this curriculum has built-in motivations and immediate and tangible rewards.[14]

[13] *Ibid.*

[14] Eliot Wigginton, "Introduction," *Foxfire 1* (Garden City, N.Y.: Doubleday, Anchor Books, 1973), p. 13.

We feel that this skill of communication will be even more important in the future. We will be exploring different types of communication with our bodies, for example, body language and eye language. As we begin to understand more about the body, we will undoubtedly find many types of communication.

In the future we will focus more on listening—not just hearing but what might be called active listening or, as Theodore Reik calls it, "listening with the third ear." We will also develop the ability to speed listen, a skill that will be vitally needed in a time of ever increasing knowledge.

We will also accept the intuitive part of the individual brain, the right hemisphere of the brain, as well as the left. Nonlinear types of learning, the type of learning that is found in creativity and in intuitive discoveries, will be promoted and valued.

ALTERNATIVES IN ENGLISH

We need different strokes for different folks. There must be many alternatives available to students and their parents, for it will always be impossible to predict the future with precise accuracy. As George Leonard states, "No one can guarantee a hard and fast picture of the future, for surprise is its very nature." [15]

What we need, therefore, is educational diversity, alternatives that allow us, as Toffler puts it, to "hedge our educational bets." The educational futurist movement must create a great diversity of offerings, including minicourses that might run from a day to two weeks. We need to give students more choices, a chance to determine their education—no sophomore English, but Body Language, Future Fiction, Videotape, Composition, and Computer Language.

We need to experiment with what might be called a "contingency curriculum" (Alvin Toffler's term). Why not, for example, develop a minicourse on solving the problem of communicating with other life in the universe. We need to be experimenting with living in space and living underwater at least at the theoretical level. English is communication; this study would be most appropriate for the communicative arts.

To paraphrase Adlai Stevenson, "We love English not, indeed, as it is but as it could be." The future of English must provide more alternatives that involve teacher and student choices. In a way, this is an expansion of the whole idea of individualization. However, it means a type of alternative that takes place outside of what would be considered the normal classroom. It might be that students, since they learn to write by writing,

[15] George Leonard, *The Transformation* (New York: Delacorte Press), p. 118.

would have the opportunity to go outside to sketch a tree in poetry form as well as doing it at their seats. It might be that they would have the opportunity of using their whole environment as part of the classroom; that there would be a lot of choices; that a school might focus on the future; that a school would focus on the arts; that even within a school the classrooms would involve real, viable choices for youngsters and teachers.

It is our opinion that there are learning styles as well as teaching styles, and the most effective learning takes place when students have a chance to match their learning styles with particular teaching styles. This, of course, involves teachers as facilitators of learning. It involves teachers as administrators of curriculum. It means that we have to keep asking ourselves, "Is this the best way for providing education?"

Teaching the Future

For educators, the Future is Now. The students in your class will live most of their lives in the twenty-first century. We have a responsibility, therefore, for helping them look forward, for preparing them for a future we cannot know with certitude. As Edwin Reischauer writes in *Toward the 21st Century for a Changing World,* "We need a profound reshaping of education if mankind is to survive in the sort of world that is fast evolving."[16]

FUTURE PROBES

Cervantes wrote long ago, "Fore-warned; fore-armed." Encourage students to explore the future, to try to predict future events, to perform as futurists. They can literally develop the future and make it theirs through activities such as these:

- Design and develop a utopian or ideal school. From our experience youngsters enjoy this activity. Sometimes we talk to everybody about schools except the pupils who attend.

- List ten predictions for the next ten years. Students can list things that might happen. Another variation would be to have them make their list in order of certainty.

Remember when you make predictions, students have as good a chance of being "right" as the teacher.

---

[16] Quoted in James Reston, "Where Are We Going?" New York *Times,* Sept. 22, 1973, p. 45.

- Play with time. Imagine a time machine which could be set for any time in the future. Students could then describe what life would be like for them in the year that they have selected. A variation would be a clock with a spinner. They could spin the year and then describe what it would be like. A further modification would be to have a space-type helmet which youngsters would put on. They could close their eyes and point to a year on a large chart.

- Develop a Crystal Ball Center. Here youngsters can have fun while predicting the future. Have students look into the crystal ball and make ten predictions for the next year.

- Divide the class into two groups or committees to study some topic or institution and how it might develop in the future such as:

clothing	food
transportation	government
schools	communities
families	housing

- Develop a Space Center that includes a rocket where students can go to write.

- Set up a phone conference with an expert on space.

- Bring in a scientist to talk about his or her work and how it relates to the future.

CREATIVE WRITING

Creative writing lends itself to this kind of exploratory activity. Be sure to include task cards in your individualized Writing Center that focus on the future, for example:

Write a science fiction story.
If you could have any type of future what would it be?
Write an autobiography of the *next* ten years of your life.

CONJECTURING

We need to develop in students the art of conjecture, to create ways that youngsters can surmise about the future. A center for conjecture might be set up. It could be called "In Search of Tomorrow" or, as Bertrand De Jouvenal calls it, a Surmising Forum. Let's surmise about the future. Develop task cards like these:

Let your imagination go. What is it like in the year 2000—What does your personal future look like? What are you doing?
What will be the future of schools, of automobiles, of homes, and of cities?

Acrostic

S atellite
P lanet
A steroid
C omet
E arth

RESOURCES ON THE FUTURE

In preparing to teach the future, we need first to prepare ourselves. One book that we recommend is Alvin Toffler's *Future Shock*. You could read portions of this book to your students. There is a section on education, for example, that might be useful. *Future Shock* is a very readable treatment of the topic, so if you read only one book, this is it.

An excellent magazine that has interesting, informative articles in it is *The Futurist*. Examine a sample copy, if possible. The address for this publication is Box 19285, Twentieth Station, Washington, D.C. 20036.

Films for the classroom Several worthwhile films are available for rental through your Learning Materials Center.

Toward the Year 2000 (30 min., color) Distributed in the U.S. by the Film Makers (628 E. Camino Real, Arcadia, Ca 91006).
The 21st Century (30 films, approximately 30 minutes each, color). Distributed in 16mm by McGraw-Hill Films (1221 Ave. of the Americas, New York, NY 10020).
Future Shock (42 min., color) Based on Alvin Toffler's book. Distributed by McGraw-Hill Films.

Books for students Following is a list of titles that include varied reading levels for young people exploring the future through fiction. Slobodkin's stories, for example, are easy to read while the collections of short stories edited by Damon Knight are for advanced readers. All are recommended for your school library.

A Wrinkle in Time	Madeline L'Engle
2001	Arthur C. Clark
The Promise of Space	Arthur C. Clark
S is for Space	Ray Bradbury
Toward Infinity	Damon Knight, ed.
Worlds to Come	Damon Knight, ed.
Round Trip Space Ship	Louis Slobodkin
Space Ship under the Apple Tree	Louis Slobodkin

The Endless Pavement	Jacqueline Jackson and William Perlmutter
Space Cat	Ruthven Todd
Spacetrack; Watchdog of the Skies	Charles Coombs
Cybernaut: A Space Poem	E. G. Valens
Space Child's Mother Goose	Frederick Winsor

DEVELOPING A MODULE ON FUTUROLOGY

Since there is little material available for teaching *The Future,* one way to approach this study is through preparation of a module. The module might be titled:

Futuring
Into the Unknown
Looking Ahead
Inventing Tomorrow

Exactly what is a module? We can best describe this type of text material by listing its characteristics:

1 It is a booklet of information and activities used by students.
2 It is short and focused—10 to 20 pages.
3 Objectives are stated; pre-tests and post-tests are given.
4 It speaks directly to the student.
5 It is self-contained: instructions for the teacher are provided.

The teacher's guide This guide, just a few pages long, contains suggested ways the module might be used, for example, with large groups or individualized instruction. It also indicates the approximate length of time required by the module. Suggested enrichment activities are also included. Resources are listed such as people from the community, films, and books (fiction and nonfiction) for both students and teachers. Field trips and other enriching experiences are suggested. Test answers or suggestions for evaluation for both pre-assessment and post-assessment are provided in the teacher's manual or guide.

The student module The module which the student actually uses is the exciting part. INVENTING TOMORROW—now that's a title to conjecture about. How would you extend an invitation to fifth grade students to begin inventing tomorrow? You need to develop the following elements:

1 First of all, what goals and objectives do you have in mind? You might list something like this as a goal.

Goal: To provide experience in exploring the future.

Under the goal you need to include several specific objectives in terms of what the student will be able to do, for example, the students will be able to:

a. Use terms associated with futurism.

b. Make predictions about what the future may be like.

c. Think about themselves in the future.

2 The second element to be prepared is the pre-assessment, just a few items to find out where the students are. Assessment items can be questions to which students respond, but they can also entail performance in terms of role playing, creative drama, or discussion.

3 The main portion of the module is composed of informational content interspersed with many activities for students to develop. You can use any content you like from books and articles about the future. Use some of the techniques described elsewhere in this chapter. You might begin like this.

INVENTING TOMORROW

How to Invent the Year 2000[17]

	2000 A.D.
Subtract this year	____ A.D.
Answer	____ Years until 2000 A.D.
Add your age	____
	____ your age in 2000 A.D.

In 2000 A.D. I will be living in

____

In 2000 A.D. I will be spending most of my time

____

____

In 2000 A.D. my most significant relationship will be with

____

____

In 2000 A.D. our planet's most troublesome problems will be

____

____

[17] From Tom McCollough, *Education in the Year 2000* (Morristown, N.J.: General Learning Press, 1974).

In 2000 A.D. the schools will be

_____ About the same as they are now.

_____ Totally different than they are now.

_____ I don't know; I just can't imagine.

Right away students are involved in an interesting activity. Additional information might include predicted changes in society, description of devices like the Delphi Technique used to predict the future or information about computer language.

Throughout the module introduce stimulating activities. You might include viewing the film *Future Shock*, discussing it, and then writing future-oriented poetry. Students can also play word games. They can invent new things for the future and write ads for them. Activities should require the use of all language skills—thinking, listening, speaking, reading, and writing, as in these examples.

- Have your class describe in as detailed a way as possible what a day will be like a week from now, for instance, next Thursday. They could focus on a local, national, or world scale. In other words they are predicting what will happen in one week. A modification of this would be to have students predict what will happen a month from today. These predictions can be written or they can be put on tape. Store them in a box to be opened on the specified date to see if the predictions were accurate.

- Ask your class what if:
  you are a rocketship
  you are an astronaut
  you are a comet
  you wake up and find yourself in the year 2001
  you are a member of the crew of the Enterprise

- Ask your class what would be mankind's greatest surprise. What do they think it would be? Herman Kahn has predicted that mankind's most profound surprise would be the discovery of extra terrestrial life. Each student could suggest the event they think would be the most profound, the most surprising. A modification of this would be to accept Mr. Kahn's surprise and have students speculate on how they would communicate with this extra terrestrial life.

- What if the South had won the war? What if Lincoln hadn't been shot? There are many of these "What if's." They offer the chance of showing the variety of possibilities in alternative futures. If the future *had* been changed, our present would be different.

- An activity that brings home the question of alternative futures is reading a story until you come to a crucial point. Then stop and have the students make their own ending. This can be viewed as a type of alternative to the story ending or a type of alternative future.

- Have your students list ten goals that they want to achieve in the next week. They can put this in a certain place and when the time comes take them out and see if they have reached their goals. This opens up all kinds of discussion questions, questions of values, questions of long and short term goals, and how to make goals come true.

- Another possibility is to have students list their life goals, their long term goals. In activities of this nature, we are not only probing what is known as the *shallow* future, the week or the month, but also the *deep future* as it is called, that of ten or twenty years.

- Remember that world shaping decisions in the year 2001 will be made by today's first graders. An activity suggested by Jerome Agel, is based on the old standby, the spelling bee, but with a switch. Before the start of the bee, the teacher identifies the winner and then distributes to each student cards that have on them the words that the teacher will ask. Included on each child's card are the mistakes the teacher predicts the child will make in the bee. In effect the teacher has determined how the bee will come out before playing the game. Discuss the implications of this experience for knowing how one's life will come out. How do you really feel about having such future knowledge? Do we really want a surprise free future? Would it spoil all the fun?

4 Each module should conclude with a Finale, a kind of culminating activity that encompasses the content and experience included in the whole presentation.

An example of a culminating activity for a class or group using this module would be a Futures Fair where students could display the results of their activities—poetry, inventions, ideas and thoughts. The Fair might also feature plays about the future as well as clothes, music, and much, much more—whatever students brainstorm as possibilities.

If the module is being completed individually at different times, the Finale should be something that one or just a few students can do, for example:

- Write a scenario for the future.

- Write a play about the future.

- Construct a diorama showing a scene from the future as you envision it.

5 At the very end of the module is the Post-Assessment, a means of evaluating growth or achievement. This can be exactly the same as the pre-assessment or a revised version of the same questions. It is appropriate

here to include assessment items that are broader and involve performance. You may, for instance, choose to view the Finale activity as an adequate means of assessing individual growth. The child who writes a scenario, for example, should demonstrate comprehension of the study which tells you what you need to know.

Books to Investigate

Asimov, Isaac. *Is Anyone There?* Garden City, N.Y.: Doubleday and Company, Inc., 1967.

Clark, Arthur C. *Profiles of the Future.* New York: Bantam Books, Inc., 1973.

———. *The Promise of Space.* New York: Pyramid Books, 1970.

Dunstan, Mary Jane, and Garlan, Patricia W. *Worlds in the Making.* Englewood Cliffs, N.J.: Prentice-Hall, Inc., 1970.

Fabun, Don. *The Dynamics of Change.* Kaiser Aluminum and Chemical Corporation, 1967.

Hirsch, Werner Z. et al. *Inventing Education for the Future.* San Francisco: Chandler Publishing Co., 1967.

Leonard, George B. *The Transformation.* New York: Delacorte Press, 1972.

Skinner, B. F. *Walden Two.* New York: The Macmillan Company, 1948.

Theobold, Robert, ed. *An Alternative Future for America II.* Chicago: Swallow Press, 1970.

Theobold, Robert, and Scott, J. M. *Teg's 1994: An Anticipation of the Near Future.* Chicago: Swallow Press, 1972.

Toffler, Alvin. *Future Shock.* New York: Random House, Inc., 1970.

———, ed. *Learning for Tomorrow.* New York: Vintage Books, 1974.

index

BIBLIOTHÈQUE CHAMPLAIN
3 9365 00144448 0